PROMOTING
PRESERVATION AWARENESS
IN LIBRARIES

**Recent Titles in
the Greenwood Library Management Collection**

Video Collection Development in Multi-type Libraries: A Handbook
Gary P. Handman, editor

A Library Manager's Guide to the Physical Processing of Nonprint Materials
Karen C. Driessen and Sheila A. Smyth

The Challenge and Practice of Academic Accreditation: A Sourcebook for Library
Administrators
Edward D. Garten, editor

Information Services for People with Developmental Disabilities
Linda Lucas Walling and Marilyn M. Irwin, editors

Public Library Planning: Case Studies for Management
Brett Sutton

Video Acquisitions and Cataloging: A Handbook
James C. Scholtz

Introducing and Managing Academic Library Automation Projects
John W. Head and Gerard B. McCabe, editors

The National Electronic Library: A Guide to the Future for Library Managers
Gary M. Pitkin, editor

Strategic Management for Public Libraries: A Handbook
Robert M. Hayes and Virginia A. Walter

Managing Business Collections in Libraries
Carolyn A. Sheehy, editor

Introduction to Health Sciences Librarianship: A Management Handbook
Frank R. Kellerman

Library Facility Siting and Location Handbook
Christine M. Koontz

Promoting Preservation Awareness in Libraries

A SOURCEBOOK FOR ACADEMIC, PUBLIC, SCHOOL, AND SPECIAL COLLECTIONS

Edited by
Jeanne M. Drewes
and Julie A. Page

THE GREENWOOD LIBRARY MANAGEMENT COLLECTION
Gerard B. McCabe, Series Adviser

GREENWOOD PRESS
Westport, Connecticut • London

Library of Congress Cataloging-in-Publication Data

Promoting preservation awareness in libraries : a sourcebook for academic, public,
    school, and special collections / edited by Jeanne M. Drewes and Julie
    A. Page.
        p.   cm.—(The Greenwood library management collection, ISSN
    0894–2986)
    Includes bibliographical references and index.
    ISBN 0–313–30206–5 (alk. paper)
    1. Library materials—Conservation and restoration—Study and
teaching—United States.   2. Library orientation—United States.
I. Drewes, Jeanne M.   II. Page, Julie A.   III. Series.
Z701.3.E38P75   1997
025.8'4—DC20   96–32981

British Library Cataloguing in Publication Data is available.

Library of Congress Catalog Card Number: 96–32981
ISBN: 0–313–30206–5
ISSN: 0894–2986

First published in 1997

Greenwood Press, 88 Post Road West, Westport, CT 06881
An imprint of Greenwood Publishing Group, Inc.

Printed in the United States of America

The paper used in this book complies with the
Permanent Paper Standard issued by the National
Information Standards Organization (Z39.48–1984).

10 9 8 7 6 5 4 3 2

Contents

Contents   vii

Figures and Tables

FIGURES

TABLES

Acknowledgments

The editors wish to acknowledge the support and contributions of the many individuals and institutions who made this book possible. Our special thanks go to the 40 contributors who shared their expertise and ideas for making effective preservation education a reality and to Gerard McCabe who saw the value in adding this title to a library management series.

We would like to thank the original 1992 Library Instruction Round Table (LIRT) speakers and the 1994 American Library Association/Association for Library Collections & Technical Services/Preservation and Reformatting Section (ALA/ALCTS/PARS) committee members and speakers, who joined the editors in presenting these programs: Thomas F. R. Clareson, Chuck Dintrone, Marcella Grendler, and Jill Rawnsley; Katharine Walter, as program member and speaker, along with Miriam Kahn and Carla Montori at the 1992 LIRT Forum; and Cheryl Holland, Lorraine Olley, Anne L. Reynolds, and Peggy Sullivan as 1994 program speakers.

We gratefully acknowledge Michigan State University at East Lansing and the University of California at San Diego for being supportive of our commitment to this publication. The Librarians Association of the University of California, San Diego Division, Research Grants for Librarians Program, provided funding for administrative support. We thank Marilyn Kwock for her diligent work in reviewing and inputting the text as well as David Jahn, William H. Allen, Merle Feldbaum, and Dwayne Petrey.

We thank LOEX Clearinghouse for Library Instruction at Eastern Michigan

University (Ypsilanti, Michigan) for housing and loaning a set of the preservation education exhibit materials from the 1994 ALA program, making them broadly available to libraries. And we gratefully acknowledge the American Library Association's ALCTS office for the transcription of the 1994 program and for encouragement during the early stages of development.

Finally, we wish to thank our families who have put up with a lot since the book first began as an embryo in 1992 to its final birth five years later—Mike Moore and Heather Allard; Tom, Allen, and Kaitlyn Page. We couldn't have made it without your support.

Introduction

This volume of the Greenwood Library Management Collection presents a comprehensive review of library user preservation education programs for personnel in school, public, academic, and special collections. As a professional reference sourcebook, it is designed especially for those staff members, librarians, and administrators who have no primary responsibility for preservation but who need information about preservation practices and issues. It emphasizes practical examples that can be used by libraries to educate and inform their community of customers.

Preservation education for library users is more than just posters and no-food-or-drink policies. It involves the commitment and involvement of all library staff and the active support of library administration to bring about a heightened awareness of preservation issues. The library's customers are referred to variously as *users, patrons, clientele*, or a similar term by the authors throughout this publication.

When educating your community of customers, some of the practices involved in the education process may take extra time and effort. However, you will be able to establish desirable preservation behaviors by the example you demonstrate, the attitude you portray, and the actions you take. For instance, the following actions send the message that the library staff appreciates the assistance of their customers:

- The library specialist asks schoolchildren to point out damaged material to staff rather than trying to mend the books themselves.

- The circulation desk staff in the public library thanks patrons for handing materials over the counter rather than stuffing them into the book return.

- The college library sponsors a Preservation Week and ties in exhibits and demonstrations that also relate to the proper care of the students' own books and nonprint materials.

- The special library prohibits the use of removable adhesive notes on its library materials and warns its users of the long-term damage that may result from the adhesive residue.

Promoting Preservation Awareness is organized to address both generally applicable preservation issues and the specialized needs of the four types of libraries. Most chapters lead off with a chapter introduction by a knowledgeable library professional and are followed by a collection of case studies giving practical examples of related preservation education programs. The publication's usefulness to you will be enhanced if you read the three general chapters (Chapters 1 through 3) before reading about your own specialty area. These three chapters focus on staff training issues as well as user education.

Chapter 1, "Preservation Issues and the Community of Customers," presents an overview with a cross section of preservation education issues and approaches for reaching the community of customers. It tackles the *why's* of preservation education and commonsense approaches for library application.

Chapter 2, "Creating Preservation Education Programs for Staff and Library Customers," includes a chapter introduction that presents the issues involved in creating education programs and their application to a statewide preservation training program. The chapter clarifies the need for staff training in preservation as a necessary first step for a successful user education program. Case studies from state and regional programs, as well as individual libraries, demonstrate a variety of both formal and informal approaches.

Chapter 3, "Evaluating Preservation Education Programs for Staff and Library Customers," presents the *who, what, when, where, why, and how* of evaluation. Evaluation is an important but infrequently used tool in preservation education programs, and the chapter introduction and case studies demonstrate practical approaches for integrating evaluation into the education process.

Chapters 4 through 7 address specific types of libraries—school, public, academic, and special—and are focused on user education almost exclusively. The reader is urged to keep in mind that overlap exists, especially between school and public libraries, where children and young adults are the audience, and between academic and special collections.

The book concludes with several useful appendixes. "Effective Graphics for Displays and Handouts" relates to all the previous chapters by presenting effective use of graphic design in library exhibits, publications, and visual messages. Examples of successful graphic presentations are included. Additional appendixes include a comprehensive annotated bibliography of book and journal sources on preservation education, video sources for instruction on care and handling of library materials, and books and kits for instructional sessions with children and young adults.

This book owes its genesis to the recognition by the American Library Association (ALA) that preservation is an area warranting attention by all types of libraries. In 1991, the ALA took a formal step toward a commitment to preservation education by adopting its *Preservation Policy*, which included a section called "Services and Responsibilities of Libraries." To ensure access to library materials through their preservation, the policy urges "all libraries and library professionals to initiate and support preservation efforts at all levels." As an endorsement for preservation education of staff and users, the policy states the importance of "educating current and future librarians, library users, and the public about preservation issues."

At the ALA 1992 Midwinter Conference in San Antonio, coeditor Jeanne M. Drewes organized a Library Instruction Round Table (LIRT) forum titled "Library Instruction and Preservation Education: Converging Concepts." Discussion leaders presented their methods for integrating preservation education into displays, handouts, library tours, informal teaching situations, and bibliographic instruction sessions.

Then, at the ALA 1994 Annual Conference in Miami, the coeditors chaired a program titled "Selling Preservation: What to Say to the Customer." This was the first national program to address specific school, public, and academic library approaches for preservation education of library users. Several of the speakers and program committee members for the 1994 program have contributed to this book.

Raising preservation awareness of staff and users takes the ongoing commitment of library personnel. The goal of this book is to help all levels of library staff in all types of libraries initiate the programs and training in preservation that will help them reach their goals for staff and user education.

1

Preservation Issues and the Community of Customers

Reaching Your Customers: The First Steps

Julie A. Page, University of California–San Diego, La Jolla, California, and Peggy Sullivan, Rosary College, River Forest, Illinois

Cultivating the public's awareness of the need to treat library materials with careful handling may be one of the most difficult tasks faced by library personnel. It is just this group—the people for whom the library exists—that unwittingly or carelessly does significant damage to the things they desire and need.

Most people do not cause this damage maliciously; malicious damage is almost impossible to control and may need to be dealt with legally. Rather, the damage is the result of thoughtless or careless behavior. Most citizens respect community property and do not destroy it willfully. But they are often unaware of the consequences of their actions. For instance, they may not even think about the damage caused by smashing the binding of a book when photocopying, or the nuisance to later users of underlining or highlighting passages in a book. To solve these types of problems, library personnel need to focus their preservation efforts when working with their community of customers.

The public takes for granted those community things (e.g., parks, sidewalks) we use every day and expect to continue to have available. For tax-supported institutions, we want our money spent wisely, for in a sense, they are ours. We take care of our individual possessions when their value is evident to us; and likewise, we care for community property when we see its value. The problem with library materials is that even those people who respect and value them as community property cause unthinking damage that leads to their gradual demise.

COMMUNITY PROBLEM

So how do we go about instilling in the library user's behavior pattern the awareness of how materials should be treated and then encouraging the application of this knowledge to his or her own materials-handling behavior? This is the great challenge. And meeting it requires that all library personnel become aware of the problem and address it with imaginative solutions.

What makes this problem so difficult to solve is that these unwelcome practices are largely out of the control of library personnel. Other aspects of materials preservation—such as disaster preparedness or pest control—can be addressed directly by the librarian with some expectation that solutions can be found. But the correction of destructive user practices depends on the recognition by the user of the destructive act and the willingness to change a behavior pattern.

We need to remember that everyone approaches the library with a personal need and usually behaves in a way that satisfies that need. So if that need is the photocopying of several pages, for example, that person is probably not concerned with possible damage that might be done to the binding. Similarly, if highlighting aids the student in reviewing or summarizing content, or if dog-earing takes less effort than using a bookmark, or if a patron finds it easier to tear a recipe out of the magazine than to copy it, that person will often follow the course that is easiest and most personally beneficial. So it is a tough problem for the librarian to solve because it is an attitudinal problem.

IMPORTANCE OF EARLY PRESERVATION EDUCATION

The habits of years of improper handling, theft, or mutilation of library materials are difficult to break, but the attitudes that form those habits are shaped early in life. Children learn sharing and respect for each other's property in their homes with family members and in school with their peers. This basic early training can carry over to their use of library materials.

Preservation education at the school-age level is focused on seeing that young library users start off in school and at their local public libraries understanding how to take care of both their own books and library books. These young school and public library users are the future customers of the college, university, and special collections. Everyone has a vested interest in their receiving preservation education programs at an early age.

The school librarian can work with teachers and administrators to ensure that specific attention is given to classroom and library instruction in proper book handling. Unfortunately, no amount of positive early training with respect to community property can compensate for the confusion children may feel when they observe their parents openly violate the norms of responsible library use. So the library must somehow both maintain the inherent desire of children to follow the rules and at the same time educate adults to meet those same standards.

RESPONSIBILITIES OF LIBRARY STAFF

Respect for community property needs to begin with library staff members who see the places where they work as public trusts, not as *my* library. They teach, both directly and by example, how to use and how to handle materials with respect. They know that simple, safe repairs of materials will cut down on major losses or repairs later. Wraps or plastic bags are provided during wet weather. Bookmarks are available to help prevent the use of damaging markers. Exhibits including library materials display the items without causing them damage.

When considering preservation education, we must think of the entire library environment, from its physical appearance and comfort level to its public services and collections. Control of a building's heating, ventilating, and air-conditioning systems not only impacts the comfort level of users but also affects the longevity and preservation of the collection. Explaining to users, from a preservation standpoint, why the temperature is set cooler, why the air circulation is strong, and why the blinds are pulled down on sunny windows shows in a visible way that the library staff and administration take action to care for the collections. Likewise, instructional graphics over photocopy machines can visually show the kindest and gentlest way to copy books. "No food/drink" posters can depict the damage done by spills on library materials and the lure of food in the building for insects and rodents. The community of customers can relate to all of these examples when they are presented positively and supported by further explanation by informed staff members.

Library administration and staff members are the key to successful preservation education for library staff and users. The administration must actively support the importance of preservation education for the staff, such as allowing release time for training, funding for proper book repair materials, and improved containers for interlibrary loan or branch-to-branch transport. Library staff must learn new ways of working and must be educated to the extent that they *buy into* the library's preservation effort and choose to participate. By utilizing programs and activities highlighted in this book, the broad community of customers can be drawn into the library's preservation education efforts.

The task of preservation education is never ending. The ways in which we educate the public are many and varied. Each of us may have different values or priorities, but the most important way that we teach preservation is by the way we treat library materials, the attitudes we convey, and the actions we take.

EDUCATION FOR BEHAVIOR CHANGE

To elicit a positive response to preservation education, it is more effective to use preservation-related messages in the library than to display a list of *do's* and *don'ts*. These might be termed the *why's* of preservation: *why* libraries do not allow food and drink; *why* users should not dog-ear, highlight, or use removable adhesive markers in library materials; *why* we do not want books smashed on the photocopy machine. Then, follow these *why's* with alternatives that will change their behavior. Decide what you want them to do instead, then tell them how to do it. Fit these little preservation bites of information into all sorts of library encounters, such as:

• Assistance at public service desks
• Bibliographic instruction sessions
• Story hours and library tours
• Point-of-use instructions for reference sources

The teachable moment is everywhere and should not be overlooked for its impact. And when you combine preservation bites of information with related posters, exhibits, handouts, and bookmarks, the preservation message will come across loud and clear.

PRESERVATION VERSUS ACCESS

The library is the purveyor and preserver of recorded knowledge. It is in the preserver function that the desires of current users for access to materials and the future needs of users may be perceived to come into conflict. Some people think that preservation of materials and access to them are conflicting ideas. They believe that materials might best be preserved by locking them away or restricting their use.

Preservation does not mean denial of access. Preservation of materials actually enhances access—access for present and future users, as long as those materials are needed. Preservation in the present means access in the future.

WHAT PRESERVATION EDUCATION MEANS

The goal of preservation education is to inform and educate the public in using library materials in the least damaging way. All use takes its toll, but there is use and there is misuse. It is this difference that librarians try to distinguish for their users. Access is the key, for it is not the intent of preservationists to stop use but rather to stop misuse. By keeping materials available and in good condition they are more inviting to use and to borrow. Furthermore, they will be available when future users need them.

Commonsense Solutions for Common Preservation Problems

Harlan Greene, North Carolina Preservation Consortium, Durham, North Carolina

Our memories are precious things. Over the years, we have evolved the ability to hand them down to those following. This happens not just in archives and libraries but in our homes and families. History, in fact, often begins at home, but it just may end there unless we do something.

Whether it is family histories, first editions, baseball cards, old photographs, or videos and clippings, all can benefit from our attention. Fortunately, it's not hard to learn how to extend their lives, for it is knowledge most of us have already. To take care of our belongings, we can follow the same general rules we use to keep ourselves healthy.

For just like us, our recorded memories *live* in physical bodies. They exist on materials prone to deterioration: paper, photographic emulsions, film stock, pigments. If we take care of these organic materials, their *spirits* can survive indefinitely.

Like us, it makes sense to keep these materials in good shape day to day and year to year rather than to ignore their conditions for extended periods, only to be faced with costly repair and reconstructive surgery. As in public health, our book and paper populations need a temperate environment, appropriate shelter, loving care, and *feeding*.

Based on a general public lecture given by the author and which appeared in a slightly different version in *Tar Heel Libraries* 18, no. 4 (July–August 1995): 4–5, published by the State Library of North Carolina.

The most crucial thing is to provide a good environment. And the rules are the same as in real estate: location, location, location. Bring your valuable papers, books, photographs, and films back from banishment in areas lacking temperature controls such as barns, basements, and attics. Keep them in the most comfortable part of your house. Perishable items keep better in cooler climates, and so do our documents. Most of us cannot afford to keep our papers in cold storage, but we can keep our houses around 70 degrees, which is a good compromise for humans and their documents.

A moderate humidity of around 40 to 50 percent is best. High humidity will encourage growth of mold and mildew, and the moisture absorbed out of humid air by paper will speed up chemical reactions. This moisture coming into contact with sulfur and nitrogen emissions can also create sulfuric and other acids in our documents. A very visible example of this damage is the higher incidence of embrittlement along the edges of pages of books. In conditions of high humidity, keep some lights on and the air flowing. Stagnant air and darkness support mold growth. But beware as well of too-low humidities; dry weather cracks our skin and will also dry out glues and emulsions.

Aim for storage conditions of about 70 degrees and about 45 percent relative humidity (RH). Try to avoid fluctuations; inside rooms and inside walls are the best areas for storage and display of materials. Rocks in the desert will crack over time in alternating heat and cold. Such constant change will also damage our documents. A constant temperature of 75 degrees and 40 percent RH is better than 70 degrees and 30 percent RH half the time and 80 degrees and 50 percent RH the other.

How do you achieve favorable storage conditions in the real world? For under $50, you can buy a good-quality digital hygrothermograph (see sources list on page 10) that gives fairly accurate readings on both temperature and humidity. Similar hygrothermographs can be purchased in stores such as Radio Shack. Use such a device to find the best area in your house and monitor conditions periodically.

Pay attention to light as well; sunlight will burn your skin and fade your clothing. Ultraviolet rays, also present in fluorescent light, are mostly responsible. That is why art museums keep their galleries dim and windowless. We can extend museum-level care to our collections by using blinds, curtains, and incandescent lighting only. If you display original items worth a lot to you, it might be best to replace glass in the frames with a special Plexiglas that will filter out much of the ultraviolet light.

After moving to the best place (location, location, location), find the best possible housing. We put our cars in garages, our money in safes, our silver in cloth bags, but we stick our paper and film treasures in cheap dime-store frames, old shoe boxes, and chemically coated albums.

It is a foolish thing to do. By choosing the wrong enclosures in which to seal our materials for years, we hasten their destruction. Most of us have seen pages in books stained with the acids from a newspaper clipping or a flower that has rested there for years. We may also have noticed how wood patterns on the back of picture frames transfer to the materials within. By shutting up our valuables next to substandard materials, we are condemning them to a similar state—poisoned *rooms* where they will *breathe* damaging fumes.

So unless you know better, consider all your folders, cardboard boxes, picture mats, photograph envelopes, and albums suspect. Have you ever bought a photograph album with sticky pages or that smelled of plastic? What you smell are chemicals being given off, chemicals that will break down your materials. The sticky glues and static electricity can turn your photograph albums into photograph cemeteries.

What do you do? Remove materials from bad enclosures and put them into good ones. If at all possible, determine what the contents of a product are before you use it and patronize only those sources you can trust. Remember to question all slogans and advertising. Often you will encounter such phrases as *archival, neutral pH, alkaline reserve, buffered*, or *chemically inert*.

Many of the catalogs from suppliers explain the meanings. Short definitions are also given here:

- *Archival* technically conveys no meaning other than pertaining to archives. Some may use it however, to signify quality materials safe to use in an archives. Read descriptions carefully.
- *Neutral pH* means that the material being described was neither acidic or alkaline at the time of its manufacture. It does not guarantee that the folder or paper or envelope or whatever will remain neutral over time.
- Materials with an *alkaline reserve* or described as *buffered* are items that not only are not acidic but have a slight measure of alkalinity in their composition. This means that they could help neutralize acids with which they come into contact. However, some archival materials, such as color photographs, should not be kept in alkaline enclosures. When in doubt, consult an expert.
- *Chemically inert* means that the plastic pouches or pages you have bought to house your photographs will emit no volatile chemicals to harm them. Look for storage materials that pass the PAT—the photographic activity test.

Buying the right materials may cost a little bit more, but you will get more than your money's worth. Good materials will buy you time, which, after all, is priceless.

There are other things you can do to extend the life of your materials:

- Separate photograph negatives and positives and store them apart. If one series is lost, you can always reproduce it from the other. Keeping them separated will also keep their damaging fumes from encouraging each other's destruction.
- Handle materials carefully. Use lint-free gloves for photographs. Make sure items are not curled or folded or need cleaning when you store them away.
- Avoid rubber bands that decompose and give off sulfur fumes.

- Avoid staples and paper clips that rust and damage paper.
- If using storage enclosures with seams and glues, turn the side with emulsion, decoration, and the like, away from the glued seam.

Avoid doing anything to valuables that you can't undo. Pressure-sensitive tape can permanently stain documents; rubber cement and many other adhesives will, too. Laminating a sheet seals it up forever in a toxic stew. Copy those materials that lend themselves to it; this will save the information in another version and limit damage from handling if you use the copies. Most important, look before you leap. If it takes a week to order a better photograph album, that is time well spent because it may now last a century.

The following vendors offer free catalogs of preservation-quality supplies, including Plexiglas and photograph albums. You can even buy a pH pen, like a felt marker, that will detect acid in paper. It is your money, and they are your treasures; so spend the former well to save the latter wisely. Remember, you can pre-serve the future if you preserve today.

- Gaylord Brothers, Box 4901, Syracuse, NY 13221-4901; 1-800-634-6307; Archival Help Line, 1-800-428-3631 (available limited hours). *Pathfinder* pamphlets are available free upon request.
- Light Impressions, 439 Monroe Avenue, P.O. Box 940, Rochester, NY 14603-0940; 1-800-828-9859.
- University Products, 517 Main Street, P.O. Box 101, Holyoke, MA 01041-0101; 1-800-762-1165 or 1-413-532-9431.

For a guide on all types of archival enclosures, see *Archival Enclosures: A Guide* by Edward Kulka, published by and available from the Canadian Council of Archives, 344 Wellington Street, Room 1009, Ottawa ON K1A ON3, Canada. It is also available from the Society of American Archivists, 600 South Federal, Suite 504, Chicago, IL 60605.

2

Creating Preservation Education Programs for Staff and Library Customers

Staff and User Education Programs for Local and Statewide Initiatives

Andrea Rolich, University of Wisconsin, Madison, Wisconsin, and Janice Mohlhenrich, Marquette University, Milwaukee, Wisconsin

INTRODUCTION

The need to educate library staff and library users to preservation concerns encompasses libraries of all sizes and descriptions. It involves all those who use them, work in them, and manage them, from customers, volunteers, and staff to administrators and trustees. Preservation is fundamentally about ensuring access to library collections and, when so stated, becomes a definable and desirable goal for all libraries.

The library community recognizes a need to educate itself in order to educate others. Continuing education for library personnel assumes a receptive audience that is anxious to learn and pass on information to colleagues and patrons of all ages. Adults are the primary audience for most formal preservation education programs. Younger patrons are also an important target audience whose good handling skills, when acquired early, become a natural part of their relationship with library materials.

In many cases, raising awareness of conditions and practices that damage library materials is sufficient to change the behavior of library staff and patrons and prevent damage. For this reason, effective instruction of those who will convey the message to others is particularly important.

The focus of this chapter is on staff training both within individual libraries and in larger-scale training programs. Many of the same principles apply to user education, but there is less opportunity to present formal training for library users. Therefore, well-trained staff members may be the best means of conveying preservation education to those with whom they interact on a daily basis.

ADULT EDUCATION

The opportunity to present preservation information to mature audiences requires that attention be paid to techniques proven successful with adult learners.[1] Adults draw on past experience and learn by connecting the new with the known. They possess a wealth of experience and may be approached as knowledgeable colleagues, untapped resources bringing talents and skills that can be used to solve the shared problem of preserving library collections. In this context, authoritarian lectures punctuated with do's and don'ts are far less effective than a presentation style that conveys a desire to work together to learn and to effect change. In fact, collaboration of instructor and students in defining objectives and shaping course content is a key element in meeting the needs of adult learners.

In any learning situation that relies on participants' input, exchange of knowledge and experience is facilitated when group members feel comfortable with each other. This feeling of comfort may be fostered early by a round of instructor and group introductions, which gives everyone a foundation for interaction and provides basic information (e.g., attendees' expectations, types and sizes of participants' libraries) that helps the instructor approach the group in a meaningful way. This may be followed later in the session by small group discussions, during which individuals can pool their experiences to arrive at solutions to preservation problems based either on real-life situations in their own institutions or on typical scenarios provided by the instructor. If there is time to alter the makeup of groups for additional problem solving, even more can be achieved as each person becomes better acquainted with a different set of fellow participants. A relaxed group is more receptive to the instructor's message and more willing to become involved in general discussions and interactions.

To further create an environment conducive to learning, the instructor must ensure that individuals feel comfortable with the material being discussed. Preservation, like any other field, has its own jargon and list of commonly used buzzwords and acronyms. Supplying a glossary to participants, defining terms when they are first used, and avoiding acronyms whenever possible facilitates communication and enhances understanding. This is especially important when members of the audience are not librarians. Trustees, volunteers, administrators, and others may be alienated by language that excludes them or puts them in the awkward position of asking for a definition they suspect everyone else knows. Effective presentations involve the audience in ways to which it can relate. Printed handouts distributed at the start of a workshop can reinforce essential concepts, clarify information, and ensure that correct information is retained.

Because preservation encompasses such broad territory, it is particularly important that instructors be well organized and thoroughly prepared. The content of preservation education sessions includes general preservation principles and commonsense reminders as well as situation-specific information. Therefore, it is incumbent on the instructor to impose structure on the learning experience. Adult learners are people with a purpose, and they have little time to waste. Strategies that lead to more successful outcomes include providing an agenda of the day's topics; following the well-established pattern of "tell them what you are going to teach, teach them, and tell them what you taught them"; and facilitating discussion and group work so that it stays focused on preservation issues.

When teaching adults, who come with a considerable store of knowledge and experience, instructor credibility is enhanced by a coherent, carefully structured presentation offered in a confident manner. This approach reinforces the importance of the subject matter and the value of the workshop. Team teaching is often quite effective in reaching diverse audiences. Overlapping experience gained from practice in different types and sizes of libraries assures the audience that instructors are sympathetic to their level of concern. This overcomes any perceptions that preservation is only for large academic libraries and reinforces the concept that all libraries—from the smallest public, special, or school setting to major research libraries—are involved in preservation.

DEVELOPMENT OF COURSE CONTENT AND FORMAT

The design of preservation education sessions is a significant element in their overall success. Content, teaching methods and tools, format, length, and scheduling of instruction periods must all be considered and adjusted to accommodate the audience and the aim of the training session. The variables are many: Will the focus be on a broad overview of preservation issues or on one topic to address a specific problem? Will there be an opportunity to meet with the target audience only once or several times? How much time will be allowed for the session(s)? What is the makeup of the audience—staff, volunteers, patrons, administrators? Do members of the audience all work in the same type and size of library, or is it a mixed group? What are their needs? What is their level of preservation awareness?

Preregistration information provides valuable insight for instructors in creating a program to meet the audiences' needs. Instructors should scrutinize the information available to them prior to the session and make a good-faith attempt to match curriculum to the expected audience. Including a question about what the participants hope to learn or questions they would like answered can prove useful for program planning. Preregistration for in-house training can help prepare instructors for gearing the session to public or technical services staff or special collections and archives. Staff will appreciate the extra effort taken to relate the training directly to their concerns and to what they have control over.

Flexibility is essential, and instructors must be capable of adjusting their plans to meet audience needs and ensure an effective training session.

Experienced instructors develop the ability to gauge audience response and take appropriate measures to maximize the learning experience. Changing tempo, alternating speakers in a team-teaching situation, and allowing for a five-minute break if concentration is wandering are useful techniques. It may also be necessary to elaborate on a topic that elicits great interest or to condense or delete material that is of little relevance or interest to the actual audience. Rote repetition of a canned presentation is deadly for both presenter and audience. A combination of knowledge and enthusiasm, tempered by a clear understanding of the goal of the instruction (by both presenter and audience), is a sure formula for success.

Setting maximum and minimum limits for attendance may also be necessary. A group exercise that is effective when an audience of 20 is split into four teams becomes unmanageable and ineffective when attempted with an audience of 50. On the other hand, lecture segments may be more readily received by large audiences than by small groups, when the opportunity for, and expectation of, participation is greater. The larger group can benefit from question and answer sessions and from the experiences of the audience.

Because library personnel who attend preservation education sessions are motivated by the need to gather information and skills that relate directly to preservation needs in their work environment, they arrive seeking practical, immediately applicable solutions. In fact, many preservation problems can be alleviated, if not solved entirely, in relatively inexpensive, uncomplicated ways.

Preservation information as presented in introductory workshops, for the most part, need not be technical. A great deal of it involves common sense and goodwill. This in itself poses a challenge to those who teach it, since a delicate balance must be found between stating the obvious—and boring the audience—and aggrandizing preservation problems and their solutions in the hope of building support. Balance can be achieved by encouraging participants to bring up concerns pertinent to their institutions, then expanding on these and placing them in the context of the larger preservation issues involved.

A wide range of topics fall under the umbrella of preservation education, including general book handling, book repair techniques, commercial binding, disaster preparedness, environmental control, preservation microfilming and photocopying, preservation of electronic formats, permanent paper, deacidification, and specialized staff training. Though many small libraries lack staff and funding to address some of these preservation issues, all libraries are able to address others.

In situations where all participants are from one type and size of library, a presentation may be greatly simplified by focusing on the special needs of that setting. When addressing a diverse audience, considerable attention must be paid to finding common ground, to covering the areas of preservation that are of concern to all, as well as the topics that may be of greater or lesser interest to individual libraries. Even when a participant's level of interest in a given topic is minimal, exposure to the nature and extent of preservation concerns of other libraries is a broadening experience that provides insight into the larger preservation picture and perhaps a new perspective for dealing with problems in one's own institution. From the instructor's viewpoint, presenting information in a way that is relevant to all audiences is challenging and may not always be totally successful, but it is possible to do this reasonably well without overloading some and boring others.

This may be done by pointing out that the basic problems and concerns of most libraries are similar but vary in degree in different library settings. It is often useful to describe the situation in a large library, with the broadest range of activities and specialized staff, and then include variations as they may manifest themselves in smaller libraries. As an example, academic libraries, which usually do very little weeding, generally have a significant problem with brittle books. In contrast the heavily weeded collections of smaller public libraries seldom include large numbers of brittle materials. However, many public libraries of all sizes have important, often unique local history collections in which embrittlement is a serious concern. Therefore, a discussion of how to deal with brittle items is a topic relevant to a broad range of library collections. In cases where individuals bring up specific topics that are of very little interest to the majority of participants, it is appropriate to limit discussion in the group setting. These issues are more effectively discussed on an individual basis during breaks and before or after the scheduled period. Follow-up mailings of pertinent information may also be useful in some cases.

Staff at all levels in the library have the responsibility of teaching library users, both directly and by example, practices that extend the usable life of library materials. Preventive preservation, based on the careful handling of materials to avoid unnecessary damage, should always be stressed, as should the concept of libraries as institutions charged with keeping community property accessible to all.

In making this point, it is often useful to draw analogies to other areas of life. For example, one would not invest in an expensive car and then never maintain it. While this may seem somewhat simplistic, such comparisons demystify preservation, stress the commonsense nature of most preservation principles, and foster the realization that preservation is squarely in the mainstream of daily library routines. This is important because preservation is often viewed in very narrow terms. Some may think of it as being synonymous with book repair. Others are convinced that it must involve highly technical chemical processes or sophisticated restoration work. Most consider it a separate activity, the exclusive responsibility of someone else, when it is in fact an element of every aspect of library work and within the domain of everyone who comes in contact with the collections.

To help define the range of issues and the roles and responsibilities of all the preservation players in any setting, one approach is to follow the path of materials through the library processes. The instructor should highlight factors that must be considered along the way—from the decision to acquire, through cataloging and processing, to shelving and storage, circulation, and return. Not to be overlooked is administrative oversight of collections and the physical environment of the building in which all these activities take place. This type of discussion reveals the broad-based nature of preservation, outlines the issues, and identifies the levels and responsibilities of staff typically involved. The concept that virtually every library decision has a preservation component is invariably a revelation to participants. Some of the activities that have preservation implications are mentioned below.

COLLECTION DEVELOPMENT

Collection development/acquisitions staff control a number of decisions with definite preservation implications.

- Should gifts be accepted because they are free, regardless of their conditions? If so, what can be reasonably spent repairing or reformatting them for use? Is the library in a position to properly store all formats, including films or photographs? What about mildewed books from someone's basement—how might these affect the rest of the collection?
- Out-of-print materials are often quite expensive and may be brittle—what should be the criteria for acquiring them?
- How are approval-plan materials constructed? And should book construction be a criterion for acquisition? What is the more economical purchase in the long run—hard- or softbound books? Will bindery prep time and rebinding fees cancel out any savings?
- What is the library's weeding policy? How is it coordinated with the responsibility to retain the last copy of a particular title? How is the rarity of the weeded item assessed?
- Are cartons of new acquisitions opened with knives, sometimes slashing book covers?

TECHNICAL SERVICES

Technical services/processing staff also have a significant preservation role to play in making sure that materials are not damaged during processing.

- Are items held together with tight rubber bands that bind and stain covers, or are they tied with gentler cotton tape?
- Are dust jackets taped to book covers, leaving brown stains or torn endpapers?
- Are books awaiting processing piled on floors, radiators, or window sills, exposing them to grit, heat, and damaging sunlight?
- How are property stamps, call numbers, magnetic security tags, and barcodes applied? Sloppily, so that materials are defaced or damaged, or carefully, so that patrons see that some care has gone into preparing them for use?

- How are uncut pages opened? With a thumb or with appropriately sharp tools to avoid rips and jagged edges?
- How are nonpaper materials handled? Are films and photographs handled by the edges to avoid fingerprints?

PUBLIC SERVICES

Public services/access services staff, in their interaction with customers, have an unparalleled opportunity to promote an awareness of preservation issues.

- Does the library distribute bookmarks and plastic rain bags? Have these been used for displaying preservation messages?
- Are signs about safe photocopying techniques posted near public machines?
- Are policies prohibiting food and drink enforced?
- Are stacks kept clean and neat? Are shelvers instructed in correct shelving techniques? Do they transport materials safely (e.g., without overturning book trucks)?
- Are circulating items, including interlibrary loans, evaluated for damage upon return? How are interlibrary loans packed for shipping; are contents protected from utility knives that may be used to open them at their destination?
- Are patrons encouraged to report damaged items to the circulation desk?

ADMINISTRATION

Administrators bearing budget responsibilities in institutions where funding is always a scarce resource are duty bound to protect the critical investment represented by a library's collection.

- Have they provided for appropriate climate control in the building in general? in special storage areas? in exhibit cases?
- Have they arranged for adequate building security—locks, alarms, door checks, patrol staff?
- Have they planned for sufficient expansion space; are materials cramped and piled in inappropriate places?
- Have they funded adequate staff levels and preservationally sound processing tools and repair supplies?
- Have they insured the collections and prepared disaster response plans?
- Have they supported attendance at training events so staff can develop the necessary expertise to implement preservationally sound practices (e.g., book repair)?

Reaching everyone who needs to know about preservation is not always a straightforward, easily accomplished task. Most are eager for information once they possess a minimal level of preservation awareness. However, potential audiences who are not yet acquainted with the nature of preservation or its relevance to all aspects of library work simply perceive no need to pursue education in this area. Therefore, preliminary efforts at consciousness raising must often precede plans to conduct more formal preservation education sessions. This may be done in a variety of ways—publishing preservation facts in a staff, community, or Friends newsletter ("25 percent of library collections are brittle and not repairable"); underscoring the preservation aspects of such common practices as opening a tightly bound book for the first time. Do not overlook raising the awareness of supervisors and other administrators since they are usually the ones in a position to effect change.

METHODOLOGY

Since most staff training is directed toward the adult learner, many of whom work in understaffed institutions, the length and format of presentation are important factors. Education sessions need to be long enough to allow adequate instruction but not so long as to disrupt the work environment of the participants.

In-house training for the staff of a single library may be more effectively conducted as short one-topic sessions offered on a continuing basis. This can be done within the context of an established general staff meeting in smaller libraries or, in larger libraries, at regularly scheduled meetings of smaller subgroups of staff, such as catalogers or shelvers, who may require more specific instruction. New staff and student orientation, bibliographic instruction, and library tours should also include a preservation component. Even though the time allotted to preservation may be brief in these situations, there is an opportunity to call attention to problems or distribute handouts that will help to raise awareness.

When preservation instruction is taken on the road, longer sessions are justified, in part because the time and expense of travel allow instructors to meet with participants only once. In addition, attendees frequently view education sessions held outside their building as special training events that are expected to last at least a half or full day. Since attendees are removed from their normal workplace, they are not distracted by close proximity to their normal duties. However, even in these circumstances, schedulers must consider that staff absences can create difficulties, particularly in smaller libraries with very limited staff. In general, one-day sessions create far fewer scheduling problems for attendees and their sponsoring institutions. One-day workshops are also less expensive to present if they are within a few hours' drive of the instructor's home base because of per diem expenses. More problematical may be the selection of conflict-free dates, especially when working with a broad target audience. When education is directed at all types of libraries, schedulers must consider everything from local and statewide library association and teachers' meetings to school and national holidays.

The very strict time constraints associated with most preservation education sessions are often a crucial determining factor in deciding what and how much to present. Even with a strong emphasis on practical tips and immediately useful techniques, carefully selected theoretical content should be included to provide the overall rationale for the recommended approach. In a full-day session geared to a broad audience, supplementary materials are essential. Citations for background readings or more detailed coverage of selected topics can be provided in take-home packets or a variety of printed materials that participants may choose according to their particular interests.

The methods of presentation will vary depending in part on the content of the education session. Straight (but engaging!) lectures may best convey the theoretical background information that is necessary to bring participants to the same level of understanding about the topic at hand. Judicious use of audiovisual aids and realia can change the pace of the presentation and clarify in a visual way issues and points that may be more difficult to describe orally. In smaller sessions, including in-house training, it is useful to pass around examples of what you are describing, such as pest-damaged books and before-and-after examples of repaired items. Another useful technique in a small group is to give attendees a piece of brittle paper with which to perform a brittleness test. These approaches can graphically demonstrate the points being discussed. If preservation education is to include skills such as minor book repair, demonstrations and hands-on components are essential. In most cases, a combination of such approaches for in-house and workshop training is quite effective.

The success of preservation education is heavily dependent on the methods and experience of the instructors and on their ability to build rapport with their audience and impart the necessary information and skills. They should be aware of both the broad preservation picture and preservation specifics as they might be applied in a variety of library situations. Classroom teaching experience and an employment history in several facets of library work are definite assets, as are consulting experience and familiarity with many types of materials and library environments. Above all, if instructors have only limited experience with the care of some types of collections (e.g., film or the newer media), they should provide supplementary materials and referrals to resource people at companies/ agencies/institutions that might be consulted for further information.

THE END RESULT

The objective of preservation training is to encourage participants to take the knowledge and skills gained, put them into practice or adapt them for use in their own work environment, and disseminate them to others in their library communities. Therefore, brief discussions relating to good training techniques are useful inclusions in any education session. These include tips for reaching the intended audiences on a number of levels.

The most basic level is perhaps the most elusive—raising enough awareness of the nature and scope of preservation so that patrons, volunteers, staff, administrators, and funders are convinced of its importance and committed to its support. This may be achieved via a variety of vehicles: preservation messages delivered in person to patrons at the library checkout desk, at special book discussion groups, or during children's story hours; library status reports for administrators, funding bodies, or service groups; feature articles in area newspapers, library Friends publications, or local historical society newsletters; eye-catching preservation posters, bookmarks, or rainy day plastic book bags; or any other ways open to the imagination.

After initial preservation awareness has been stimulated, it is time to move on to a different level of instruction with more focused training sessions for staff and volunteers. In whatever method preservation education is conveyed, it must be a continual effort, as turnover in all the target groups brings in individuals who have not yet been exposed to basic preservation principles.

Reaching the audience for preservation information—customers, staff, administrators, and funders—is a matter of taking and making the opportunity to engage everyone in a joint effort aimed at ensuring that community property remains accessible to all who might need it for as long as necessary. "Assets manager" is a lofty title that most librarians would be hesitant to assume. However, it is an accurate description of all who attempt to preserve the wealth that resides in our libraries.

The pages that follow describe how the ideas and approaches outlined in this chapter introduction have been applied to a series of preservation workshops for library-affiliated personnel, sponsored by the Wisconsin Preservation Program (WISPPR). The idea of selling preservation to staff and patrons was a major emphasis of all the workshops. A detailed description has been included for the workshop focused on staff and patron education. Background information on WISPPR and brief descriptions for the additional workshops are also included.[2]

WISPPR WORKSHOPS: BACKGROUND

In 1992, the Wisconsin Preservation Program, a joint program of the Council of Wisconsin Libraries (COWL) and the University of Wisconsin–Madison General Library System, began planning a series of 15 preservation workshops to be held throughout the state from September 1993 through June 1994. Funding was received through a Library Services and Construction Act (LSCA) grant. Instructors were identified for their areas of expertise, training experience, and interest in the grant project and WISPPR.[3]

Established in 1986, the primary aim of WISPPR has been to increase awareness of the scope of preservation and its importance for Wisconsin libraries and to support continuing education in the preservation of library materials. To this end, WISPPR resource staff provide preservation education and assistance to libraries, archives, and document repositories throughout the state. The organization also maintains a collection of books, videos, and environmental monitoring equipment that can be borrowed by Wisconsin libraries. WISPPR programs at library conferences, presentations to state planning and policy-making organizations, and workshops around the state focus on preservation basics.

The workshop format has traditionally been used in WISPPR education programs because it is an effective means of instruction in an interactive, participatory, problem-solving environment. A combination of brief lectures, small group collaboration, and hands-on directed learning is used. These are supported by multiple handouts that include bibliographies, glossaries, sources of supplies and assistance, written instructions, catalogs, and product samples. This workshop format is also effective for smaller-focused groups, as is the case with in-house training.

In the WISPPR workshops, course content is intended to be as practical as possible in terms of the everyday work of the participants. It is based on the perceived and stated needs of the COWL membership, as well as on comments from previous workshop evaluation forms, calls to WISPPR for assistance and advice, and instructors' personal observations from on-the-job experience. The workshops covered preservation education for staff and patrons; repair techniques; disaster preparedness planning; and the decision process leading to replacing, reformatting, repairing, or rebinding materials.

In presenting the series of LSCA-funded workshops, WISPPR hoped to reach library-affiliated personnel from all types of libraries in all areas of the state, with particular emphasis on small and medium-sized public, school, and college libraries. Actual participants included administrators, full- and part-time staff, and volunteers from libraries of many descriptions, including both large urban and small rural (one-person) public libraries, corporate/special libraries and record centers, and public and private school, college, and university libraries. Most attendees were from Wisconsin, with a few from Minnesota. Several attendees were library school students who might not have the opportunity to take preservation courses while in school.

WORKSHOP 1: PRESERVATION EDUCATION FOR STAFF AND PATRONS

Purpose

The workshop is based on the premise that all libraries have preservation concerns and that all libraries have constituents—staff, patrons, trustees, and volunteers—who can benefit from knowledge of preservation issues and practical tips on how best to care for collections.

Two instructors worked together to design the curriculum and to present the one-day workshop. One instructor is a preservation librarian at an academic library, the other, a humanities reference librarian at a large public library. Their perspectives on preservation challenges and the efficacy of means to meet the challenges complement each other and broaden the appeal for the audience by ensuring a firsthand knowledge of problems and concerns.

Workshop content includes a lecture component that covers both preservation fundamentals and a general discussion of the needs of adult learners and how to structure the delivery of preservation information to match recipients' needs. The instructors address these topics, and their talks are accompanied by an agenda and packets containing supplemental training and informational material.

Many preservation videos have been made, and their content, tone, and style suit them for different applications. To demonstrate appropriate use of this medium, one instructor presents a 30-minute book-handling program geared toward student workers in a university library. By so doing, workshop attendees (1) receive information about book handling, (2) are given the opportunity to evaluate the video *Murder in the Stacks* for its suitability for that target audience, and (3) are offered a model of a short, focused preservation outreach effort that they can adapt to suit their own needs.

Following the book-handling session and its discussion, snippets of other preservation videos are shown, including *Slow Fires* and *Disaster Response and Recovery*, and possible applications are discussed—staff training, volunteer education, administrator/trustee awareness enhancement, and Friends of the Library fund-raising potential.

Preservation Scenarios

A highly regarded portion of the "Preservation Education" workshop involves group reaction to preservation scenarios written by the instructors. The exercises, 11 in all, are devised as a means of demonstrating the practical daily use of preservation information in a wide range of libraries. Written in a light, humorous fashion, the scenarios draw upon real-life situations that occur in libraries. Finding appropriate and preservationally sound responses to the situations described affords workshop participants the opportunity to apply information presented to them during the workshop. They use resources made available by the instructors, reflect on practices currently in use in their institutions, contrast those practices with those of their peers, and recognize the practical applications of preservation for themselves.

In actual practice, the scenarios elicit so much reaction that the instructors must curtail discussion in order to preserve time to present all workshop information. A blackboard or flip chart is used to record participants' comments, solutions, and additional questions about these scenarios. Providing appropriate sourcebooks, catalogs, and handouts offers the opportunity to seek answers (about book drop features, for instance) from a preservation perspective and ensures responses based on more than just anecdotal evidence—although a great deal of that is offered. The realization that they "do" preservation in their libraries, and have been doing so all along, comes as a surprise to many of the attendees.

Texts of the scenarios appear below. The questions following each scenario are designed to prompt discussion.

1. *Helping patrons care for their books.* Many individuals in your town are members of the local historical society, and interest in genealogy runs high. On more than one occasion, you have been approached by someone lovingly cradling a huge old family Bible that contains priceless family records. They come to you seeking advice about how to repair torn pages and detached covers. What advice do you give them?

- How can reliable conservators be identified?
- Are there any mending techniques individuals can safely use on their own materials?
- Are there ways to identify materials that are beyond treatment?

2. *New building/addition: justifying air conditioning.* The new library building or major addition your community has been crying for has finally been funded after years of lobbying. At last, relief from your present cramped, musty building with the leaking roof is in sight. Tonight you will meet with the architects, the Library Board, and the budget manager to formulate plans.

- Why should a strong plea for air conditioning be on your agenda? After all, your library is in Wisconsin.
- The new building plans show numerous skylights and a wall of plate glass that will provide a stunning view of a local lake. You suspect the architect has spent a lot of time watching *This Old House* on TV and wants to "flood the library with light." What preservation concerns does this raise?
- You know the original plans will be scaled back, but the rendering of the atrium adjoining the local history room where you'll finally have room to display those neat old maps and plat books really appeals to you. Do you detect any inherent preservation problems?

3. *Pests and parties: a place in the library?* Your director wants to host a reception with cake and punch in the rare book room. The children's librarian wants a cage of gerbils. The staff are lobbying for a vending machine so they don't have to go across the street to the cafe at lunchtime. You want the library to be inviting, interesting, and a storehouse of information. You've noticed roaches and silverfish in the stacks, and judging by the scrabbling sounds you hear, you suspect you may have squirrels in the attic.

- What are the preservation implications of the items above, and what can be done about them?
- Does preservation awareness mean you can't have any fun in the library?
- What can be done about the bugs and vermin?

4. *Your gift is gratefully acknowledged.* Hilda Sternkrumpf, wife of the fire chief, sister of your alderman, and mover-and-shaker in her own right, appears

unexpectedly at the reference desk one morning. She happily announces that since she knows building the collection is a priority for the library, she has decided to help by donating six large cartons of books that have been stored in her basement. She has them with her, in the trunk and backseat of her car. The minute the car is opened, you smell mold and mildew. What do you do?

- What role does preservation play in devising a gifts policy?
- What precautions should be taken before bringing suspect material into the collection?
- What responsibility does the library have for preserving these books so that Hilda's grandchildren can use them?

5. *Exhibit planning.* Your library has a display window, which you change seasonally to highlight events, materials of community interest, and new acquisitions. For the holiday season, you will mount a display of children's books about holiday customs in many cultures. You draw on your library's wealth of turn-of-the-century children's literature and plan to use a montage of photographs showing past holiday decorations used in your town. The local bakery has offered to donate a beautiful gingerbread house for the window.

- What preservation considerations are presented by this task?
- What steps can you take to ensure that materials are secure and protected from environmental damage?
- You'd like to have some of the books open to reveal charming illustrations. What's the best way to do this without damaging the bindings?
- How should you mount the photographs?

6. *Staff training.* Your library is chronically understaffed, and as a result, you are terribly overworked. This year's budget miraculously allows you to hire a new librarian and two new support staff, one of whom will work at the circulation desk and the other whose duties will be mainly divided between shelving and mail room work. How can you include preservation awareness as part of their training?

- What preservation concepts are universal for all staff?
- What tasks require special preservation awareness?
- Your training time is limited. How can you be sure to cover the basics?
- The staff you hire expects to have coffee and a donut at their desk each morning. How can you change this habit without alienating new staff from the whole idea of preservation?

7. *Preservation: part of every job in the library.* Preservation workshops, preservation librarians, preservation awareness—what is all this ballyhoo anyway? You've been practicing preservation in your library from day one, only

no one gave it a name. Much of preservation is commonsense application of good handling and storage techniques. What does your staff do that helps preserve your collections?

- List the actions routinely carried out by the director, reference librarian, circulation clerk, and volunteer shelver that help preserve collections.

8. *The kids ripped this, but I fixed it for you.* Your collection receives quite a lot of use, and you and your staff pride yourselves on the care you take to see that your building, grounds, and the books themselves are kept in good order. Mess, carelessness, and clutter are frowned upon, especially by Mr. Green, your formidable circulation librarian.

Now Mr. Green stands in the doorway of your office, visibly displeased. He is flanked by an anxious young woman whose three young children are fidgeting restlessly. In his hands he grips two folio art volumes with lovely, expensive full-color reproductions of great art works. Before he can begin to speak, the young woman explains, "It really wasn't their fault. I had to dash to answer the phone, and by the time I got back, the youngest had ripped out a few pages from volume one and volume two, while the middle one, our artistic child, colored over some of the illustrations, but I'm sure he didn't mean it. I fixed the torn pages with clear tape, and I used an eraser to remove all that I could of the crayon. I noticed that the spine on one of the books was ripped too, so I used some duct tape to fix that."

- What do you do?
- What kind of preservation information can you provide for the children? for their mother? for Mr. Green?

9. *The book drop.* A new book drop has been added to next year's budget. In your travels, you have noted that there are various types. What kind of book drop will you recommend for purchase?

- What does preservation have to do with this decision?
- What features should you look for in a book drop?

10. *Preservation awareness.* The president of the library Friends group has asked you to give a speech. Since preservation is one of your responsibilities, you elect to speak about some facet of it.

- What facet would you choose? What are the possible choices? What information should you include in your talk?
- How would you explain preservation to the following audiences: your board of trustees? your city manager? a visiting class of sixth graders? an elderly library patron?

11. *Merit badges*. A Scout troop has asked for a project to help them in earning a merit badge. They are especially interested in community service and in the library.

• What preservation-related activities could you give them?

Many of these scenarios ring true to attendees who can identify strongly with the described situations and then move from ownership of the problem to recognition that preservation offers practical solutions with real-life applications in real libraries. The group work and subsequent general discussions are both fun and effective.

Another strength of the exercises is that library staff at all levels—directors, librarians, support staff, and volunteers—may contribute to the discussion and see the value of working together to address their needs. Working through these problems demonstrates the overlapping nature of preservation with every other library concern. If attendees take away only that realization, the cause of preservation education is advanced.

It is interesting to note that the "Preservation Education" workshops were the most difficult to sell of any offered by WISPPR. Although participants evaluated workshop content and presentation highly, the workshops were sparsely attended. Two of the four scheduled presentations were canceled for lack of sufficient registration. Why? WISPPR planners were confronted with contradictory indicators: positive evaluations, careful scheduling, and a minimal registration fee—offset by poor registration and lack of demonstrated interest expressed by the very institutions that hosted the workshops. Planners surmise that part of the problem is the general nature of this workshop and the lack of tangible rewards resulting from attendance.

The "Preservation Education" workshop failed to generate sufficient interest in the library community to warrant four presentations. This does not, however, negate its value. Those who did attend indicated that the workshop was valuable to them in a variety of ways. Some cited the book-handling tips and the information on adult education; others were happy to have had the interaction with their colleagues from other libraries and to realize how much they already knew about preservation.

Assessment of long-term benefits is difficult with this workshop. Unlike the others offered, where the completion of a disaster plan, implementation of repair techniques, or successful renegotiation of a binding contract can prove their worth, this workshop, with its general information and focus on raising awareness and changing long-term beliefs and behaviors, provides benefits that are of value that may not be obvious.

WORKSHOP 2: REPAIR TECHNIQUES

Practiced to some extent by virtually all libraries, repair of materials is a familiar activity executed in a variety of creative and unusual ways. The objective of the two-day "Repair Techniques" workshop is to encourage preservationally sound methods for repair as an integrated aspect of general library materials preservation. Nearly half of the session is devoted to discussion of the overall library environment and various practices and policies that have an impact on the condition of collections. Instructors include many anecdotes based on their own experience, and more are contributed by participants. This provides a nicely balanced view of typical situations in a number of library settings. Interspersed are demonstrations (e.g., encapsulation, mounting documents or damaged dust jackets onto Japanese paper) and hands-on practice in paper and spine repair, recasing a textblock, and box making.

Equally important are exercises in decision making, during which participants become familiar with book structure and mechanics, evaluate damaged materials, and weigh the merits of various treatment options for volumes provided by the instructors or problem materials brought in from the attendees' own libraries. Because past WISPPR workshops had revealed that many smaller libraries are unaware of the possibilities and advantages of commercial library binding, this treatment option is covered in some detail.

Throughout the workshop, instructors highlight the commonsense nature of preservation issues, stress the importance of preventive preservation (do no harm), and address what is practical in a variety of library situations. In dealing with a mixed audience, one piece of advice does not apply to all, and unnecessarily restrictive recommendations for treatment of materials are not useful. For example, participants appreciate knowing that while it is definitely inadvisable to use adhesive-backed plastic paperback stiffeners in the research library environment where materials are kept for the long term, these may be fine for materials in a public library collection that is frequently and heavily weeded. At the same time, public libraries need to be aware of the value of their special or unique local history collections and the need to treat such materials differently. Similarly, the sensible tip that it is more cost-effective to purchase durable hardbound books for heavily used collections may in fact not be so sensible in some situations. As many public librarians are aware, teenagers in particular prefer smaller, more portable paperbacks and will often refuse to check out books that are hardbound, thus undermining the wisdom of purchasing them, whether or not they are more durable.

In the discussion of solutions for preservation concerns, attendees are reassured that it is all right—even advisable—to start small, as time, staff, and money allow. For example, no harm is done by cleaning the stacks an area at a time, rather than embarking on a massive, disruptive effort all at once. Instructors also focus on solutions that employ familiar materials and do not require heavy investments of money, such as simple shades or drapes to shield collections from direct sunlight. Interlibrary cooperation is also stressed as a means for sharing information, skills, and financial resources, for example, in negotiating favorable prices with a commercial binder or with a provider of repair supplies and equipment.

Workshop participants also exchange ideas for expanding awareness of preservation issues among colleagues and customers. These range from preservation messages on posters, books, and rain bags to more formal instruction delivered wherever the opportunity arises. Such venues include regularly scheduled staff meetings to address a specific problem—in a general orientation for new staff and volunteers to call attention to issues and procedures or during children's story hours to begin the education process. "Why do you suppose this book is so sticky?" or, "What a shame! We can't see the puppy; someone scribbled on him."

Short evaluations submitted at the end of all repair workshops indicate that everyday needs are well addressed and that techniques are clear and immediately useful ("I may now be able to fix some books I shrugged my shoulders at"). Many participants are exposed to new information ("I learned a lot of interesting information that I was totally unaware of before this") and write that they are anxious to learn more.

WORKSHOP 3: DISASTER PREPAREDNESS PLANNING

Like hands-on book repair, disaster preparedness planning is practical, and workshop attendance provides both knowledge and tangible benefits such as written procedures, lists of suppliers, and sample disaster plans that can be implemented by libraries in solving a preservation problem. The one-day disaster workshops are well attended, and participants demonstrate a high level of interest.

The workshop presents information through lecture, handouts, videos, and group activities. The morning session brings participants to a realization of the range of situations that might be described as a disaster in the library context—not just fire or flood but incidents such as vandalism, insect infestation, or a patron suffering a heart attack—and emphasizes the need for planning at three levels: prevention, response, and recovery.

Often cited as "most useful" on evaluations are the group activities. In these, following a morning of lecture and discussion and the dissemination of much printed material, the instructor divides the class into small groups, usually of three people. One member of the three-person group volunteers his or her library as the site in which a disaster will be enacted. All three work together to list steps to be taken by that library in disaster prevention, response, and recovery. The resulting information is specific to a real library and becomes a real and useful component of their disaster plan.

Another component of the workshop that elicits a high level of interest and comment is the portion that deals with *selling* the completed plan to library administrators. Those who write the plan can become so caught up in the need for it that the political ramifications of this work are obscured. Through personal experience that has been borne out elsewhere, the instructor is able to explain to writers that in adopting a disaster preparedness plan an institution publicly acknowledges cognizance of potentially threatening conditions. This admission, if not swiftly acted upon, can cause administrators to appear negligent when and if a disaster does strike and the leaky roof remains unrepaired, or the faulty wiring has not been replaced. Workshop participants are urged to include administrators in the planning process to the greatest extent possible to avoid surprising them with the results of a building survey that reveals problems having enormous fiscal impact.

A goal of the workshop is to have all who attend go back to their libraries and write or improve disaster plans for their institutions. Many are inspired to do so. One participant commented, "My first thought when I heard about [library disasters] was that only a person with a degree in disaster preparedness could do this, but by the end of the day, my confidence was high and my degree was obtained." Another participant sent a copy of a newsletter article she had written to urge formation of a disaster preparedness committee following the workshop.

WORKSHOP 4: REPLACE, REFORMAT, REPAIR, REBIND

This one-day session focuses on the decision-making process in replacement, reformatting, repair, or rebinding of materials. A moderator and panel of four presenters give an overview of activities and organizational considerations relevant to a preservation program in larger libraries. Representative areas and topics are (1) bindery preparation, with a discussion of factors to be considered in contracting and dealing with commercial binderies; (2) book assessment, which deals with processes leading to reformatting and replacing deteriorated library materials with reprints, photocopies, or microforms; (3) microimaging, including in-house filming and digitizing as well as contracting for these services; and (4) conservation, with a discussion of options for in-house repair work.

Presentations include an emphasis on processes involved in each of the areas discussed, expertise and tools required, quality control issues, and the interrelationship of work flows and staff. Lecture and question and answer sessions are supplemented with handouts and with tours of preservation department work areas at the University of Wisconsin–Madison, where participants see examples of what has been discussed and engage in treatment decision-making exercises utilizing criteria put forward in the morning session.

The decision to hold this workshop at a large academic library, the home base of the instructors, was based on practical considerations. Since planners correctly assumed that this workshop would attract staff and administrators from larger libraries, they wanted participants to see firsthand the layout and interrelationship of an actual preservation department with several subunits. This approach appears to have been successful, based on evaluations, which included such comments as: "The workshop gave a good overall view of the different steps and processes involved in preservation. I feel I can now tackle problems in the collection that I have been avoiding." "Very useful—it's enlightening to see how other people actually do things. I learned several things that I will try to use."

WISPPR WORKSHOPS: CONCLUSION

"Preservation for Everyone" is the overarching title of the series of WISPPR workshops. Building on this basic premise, instructors point out the preservation role of each area of library activity, then give concrete means of reaching and educating the various groups, based in large part on methods that are actually employed in the instructors' institutions. For many participants, this stimulates a different way of thinking about the nature and scope of preservation, leads them to realize that they are already engaged in preservation activities, brings relief that they do not have to start from scratch, and encourages them to build on what they have already started. Such a foundation goes a long way toward meeting WISPPR's goal of spreading information about preservation throughout the state's libraries.

NOTES

1. Sources for further reading on adult education include: "Adult Learners, Learning and Public Libraries," *Library Trends* 31, no. 4 (Spring 1983) (the issue is edited by Elizabeth J. Burge); Stephen Brookfield, *Understanding and Facilitating Adult Learning* (San Francisco: Jossey-Bass, 1986); Rosemary S. Cafarella, *Planning Programs for Adult Learners: A Practical Guide for Educators, Trainers, and Staff Developers* (San Francisco: Jossey-Bass, 1994) (The Jossey-Bass Higher and Adult Education Series); Malcolm Shepherd Knowles, *The Modern Practice of Adult Education* (Chicago: Follett Publishing Co., 1980); Melvin L. Silberman, *Active Training: A Handbook of Techniques, Designs, Case Examples, and Tips* (Lexington, MA: Lexington Books, 1990).

2. For additional information on the Wisconsin Preservation Program (WISPPR) contact: Kathryn Schneider, director, WISPPR, 464 Memorial Library, 728 State Street, Madison, WI 53706.

3. The instructors for the 1993–1994 series of WISPPR workshops were the following: "Preservation Education for Staff and Patrons": Janice Mohlhenrich, preservation librarian, Marquette University; Virginia Schwartz, Humanities Reference Librarian, Milwaukee Public Library; "Repair Techniques": Andrea Rolich, preservation librarian, University of Wisconsin–Madison; Anne Tedeschi, preservation consultant; "Disaster Preparedness Planning": Janice Mohlhenrich; and "Replace, Reformat, Repair, Rebind": Anne Tedeschi; Andrea Rolich; James Dast, conservator, University of Wisconsin–Madison; Louise Coates, bindery supervisor, University of Wisconsin–Madison; Sandra Paske, Microimaging Lab supervisor, University of Wisconsin–Madison.

CASE STUDIES

Preservation Awareness Campaigns at the Indiana University Libraries– Bloomington

Richard Vaughan, Indiana University School of Law, Bloomington, Indiana

BACKGROUND

The clichés are endless: ''Reaching the top is one thing; staying on top is another.'' ''Winning one championship is easy; winning two consecutively is next to impossible.'' ''The toughest thing about success is that you've got to keep on being a success.'' When the Indiana University (Bloomington campus) Library Preservation Committee (LPC) was charged with producing a sequel to the university's 1992 Preservation Awareness Week, the question that was immediately on everyone's lips was, ''How do we top that?'' Not only was this 1992 campaign a success on the Bloomington campus, but it received national attention in several library journals[1] and international attention when it won an American Library Association (ALA) John Cotton Dana Special Award for Public Relations.

In April 1995, a five-person LPC subcommittee, the Preservation Awareness Group (PAG), began planning the sequel. At the PAG's first meeting, it was decided that the best way to answer the question was not to attempt to top the previous program but rather to build on it in 1995. Although none of the 1992 PAG members served in the 1995 group, the head of preservation, who is an ex officio member of both groups, served in the same capacity both years. Under her guidance, the 1995 PAG began by reviewing the successes and failures of the 1992 program.[2]

METHODOLOGY

The 1992 program had been a weeklong series of activities that featured tours, lectures, displays, and demonstrations. The most successful aspects of this campaign were preservation technique demonstrations offered by a preservation librarian and the distribution of free posters, bookmarks, and plastic bags adorned with preservation graphics and the preservation department's logo.

The elements of the 1992 campaign that proved to be the least successful were those activities that required the audience to attend an event, such as tours, films, and a lecture by an internationally known library preservation scholar. While the PAG never questioned the value of these events, the general feeling of the group was that 1995 activities should focus on the more successful aspects of the 1992 campaign.

As part of this decision, we developed the philosophy of "taking the campaign to the users" rather than "bringing the user to the campaign." We decided in our first two meetings that the 1995 campaign would feature some type of live demonstration in a visible area of the library, and new graphic arts materials would be displayed in both the library and throughout the campus.

As is often the case at a public institution, the plans made were largely influenced by our budget. The 1992 campaign cost approximately $9,000 and was funded through a National Endowment for the Humanities (NEH) grant. Anticipating that the same level of funding would not be available, the PAG determined that a small campaign featuring some type of live demonstration and one or two new graphic products could be produced for $5,000. The group then focused on three key questions: Who is the audience? When will the program be held? What will the theme be?

WHO IS THE AUDIENCE?

To answer the first question, the PAG again turned to the 1992 program, which had not been aimed at a specific audience other than library patrons. Lectures by international scholars, tours of the preservation department, and up-close demonstrations of preservation techniques were all designed to communicate preservation issues to a broad-based audience. In fact, one of the real successes of the 1992 campaign was that it reached so many segments of the library's patrons: undergraduate and graduate students, faculty, and library employees. With a reduced budget already set and our decision to "take the campaign to the user," the 1995 PAG decided to focus its efforts on the library's largest user group—the undergraduates.

WHEN WILL THE PROGRAM BE HELD?

This decision quickly led the group to determine that the best time for the program would be early in the fall semester, as soon after students arrived on campus as possible. As it turned out, however, many other library activities were scheduled for the early part of the semester. After consulting activity calendars, the earliest the program could be scheduled was the first week in November. While the 1992 activities had been known as Preservation Awareness Week, the 1995 committee decided to promote preservation awareness for an entire month, although limiting most of the activities to the first full week in November.

WHAT WILL THE THEME BE?

The final question to be answered was that of a theme. The committee decided that the idea they most wanted to communicate to users was that the preservation of library materials has a financial cost, and users can help to reduce that cost by helping to take care of materials. The committee came up with a slogan that would be used throughout the campaign: ''The life of a book. It's in your hands.''

In the course of answering these three questions, the PAG had investigated what other libraries had done in terms of preservation public relations (PR) programs. A literature search of several education databases revealed that while a few libraries had produced some small in-house preservation PR programs, few libraries were actively communicating preservation issues to their patrons (or at least few were communicating their successes and failures via the professional literature). A posting to a library preservation listserv asking for details of preservation education campaigns produced no replies.

With the general focus and theme of the campaign agreed upon within the first month of the PAG's formation, the group had approximately six months to plan and produce the specifics of the campaign. Throughout the months of planning, the workload of the PAG was divided up, with each member working on individual assignments and with group meetings approximately every three to five weeks to keep each other updated. As November approached, meetings were scheduled more frequently. Ideas, questions, and decisions that needed to be addressed before a meeting were communicated via e-mail.

IMPLEMENTING THE PRESERVATION CAMPAIGN: 1995

The idea of having a live demonstration in a highly visible area of the library grew out of a particularly successful aspect of the 1992 campaign—Dr. Book, a fictional name for a member of the preservation department. Twice during that campaign, Dr. Book set up shop in the main library's lobby to handle book repairs and provide diagnostic consultations for interested patrons. At first, the 1995 PAG suggested expanding this concept by physically transporting the library preservation department (or a large portion of it) from its location in the library's basement to the main lobby. The lobby was clearly the ideal location,

Figure 2.1
Preservation Program Logo

Preservation Program
Indiana University Libraries

as it is not only the main entrance to the library complex but also one of the most popular areas for undergraduates to gather at the library. This idea, however, proved to be logistically impractical. Instead, the group decided to expand the Dr. Book concept into a book clinic. The clinic featured preservation department personnel giving demonstrations and offering advice on book repair and other preservation issues. Clinics were held four times during the week, from 2:00 P.M. until 4:00 P.M. The timing of the clinics was based upon observations of when the lobby was most crowded. Also, films were shown as they had been in 1992, although they were shown on video loops at the clinics rather than being scheduled at specific times in remote locations.

Another element borrowed from 1992 activities was the use of graphic design preservation promotions. The 1992 program had featured several items (bookmarks, posters, plastic bags) that displayed the preservation department's "locking P/Infinity symbol" logo (see Figure 2.1). These items were handed out and displayed throughout the library. While some of these were still available, it was felt that new graphics and materials should focus on the 1995 theme and be geared toward undergraduates.

Again, via brainstorming sessions, the 1995 PAG settled on the design and production of two posters. The first poster was to be a still-life photograph depicting the costs that are associated with preserving library materials. The idea was to communicate the financial costs of preservation activities by showing preservation department ledger sheets and invoices. Once again, however, flexibility proved important when it was concluded that the concept was too complicated, and it really would not grab the attention of our intended audience—the undergraduates.

Keeping the idea of a still-life photograph, the final design featured a series of books that depicted common types of damage. A caption for each book provided common explanations for book damage and/or advice on how to prevent the damage. The captions, as well as the examples of damaged books, were created with humor and visual appeal in mind. At the same time, they were designed to communicate the idea that most damage is caused by careless or purposeful human behavior and, thus, can easily be prevented by those same humans. The use of fluorescent pink highlighting on the captions helped to make the posters stand out, giving them a 1990s feel that we hoped would connect with students. The Preservation Awareness Campaign slogan ran across the top

Figure 2.2
Preservation Awareness Campaign Poster

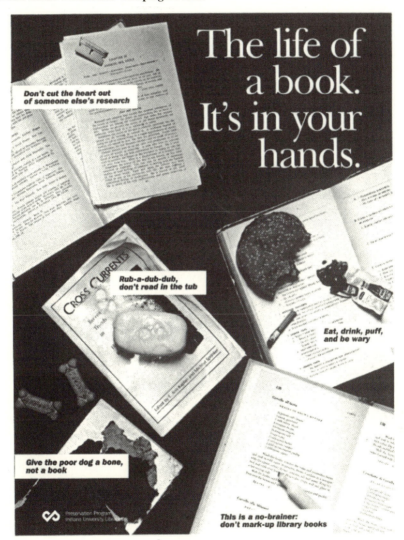

Designed by Inari Information Services, Bloomington, Indiana.

of the poster, while the Preservation Department logo appeared on the bottom (see Figure 2.2).

The second poster was to be a takeoff on the well-known ALA celebrity *Read* posters. This poster was to feature two local celebrities (graduates who have gone on to become nationally known icons of popular culture, e.g., coaches, politicians) holding a book of their choice. The hope was that the celebrities would be individuals that the students already admired, and the students would be receptive to their message "The life of a book. It's in your hands." Unfortunately, late in the planning process, the PAG learned that only $3,000 had been set aside for the entire campaign, rather than the anticipated $5,000. The miscommunication that the PAG experienced with the library budget office should have been avoided, but there was nothing the group could do other than stop the production of one of the posters.

The decision to drop the celebrity poster was largely due to the complexity of producing that particular poster, as well as some concern on the part of the library administration regarding the library's use of nationally known individuals for a local library campaign. Still, the idea is not dead. With the administration's blessing, the LPC is going to contact the Indiana University Foundation (a non-profit corporation that raises, manages, and administers funds and gifts for the university) and suggest the idea be pursued for future library fund-raising campaigns.

While the PAG came up with the concept of the posters, a professional graphic design company handled the actual production and printing. In addition to the technical aspects of the poster production, the company was helpful in advising us on how best to communicate in a visual medium. Several bids were solicited, along with examples of each company's work. The PAG decided that the posters would not mention the date of the activities so that they could be used for other promotional efforts. The posters were distributed to Indiana University system libraries (including the 12 libraries located in Bloomington dormitories), as well as to local patrons and libraries across the country.[3]

In addition to the posters, displays and bulletin boards were created for the library lobby and other high-traffic areas on the Bloomington campus. These displays depicted, via photographs and text, the different methods of preserving and restoring damaged materials (like the ones depicted in the poster). Not only did the displays show how the materials were restored, but the financial cost of each restoration was indicated. At the campaign's conclusion, a small portable display presented the campaign to other Indiana University campuses. (The portable display is a commercially manufactured display board similar to those seen at trade shows, upon which posters, pictures, and text are mounted.)

As the November 1995 date for the campaign approached, the PAG found itself working harder and harder. Coordinating press releases with the library administration offices, posting announcements, sending out flyers through the campus mail (using a hot pink colored paper), and generally just "getting the word out" took considerable time. In addition to posting announcements on traditional bulletin boards, electronic postings were placed on preservation-related listservs and on the Indiana University Preservation Department's World Wide Web home page.

EVALUATION

Just how successful was the 1995 Preservation Awareness campaign? The subjective nature of determining the success or failure of a public relations campaign left the PAG without a clear picture of the program's impact on library patrons. An evaluation questionnaire, to be distributed to individuals at the book clinic, failed to be developed as it fell through the cracks of committee member assignments. Thus, much of the short-term evaluation was based on observing people's reactions to the campaign. Did they read the display? Did they ask questions? Did they take our literature and posters? From this standpoint, the PAG was satisfied that the campaign successfully educated those who took the time to view the displays and book clinic.

Still, the long-term success/failure of the campaign has yet to be seen. The PAG's efforts placed the issue of library preservation in clear view of our patrons. In addition to the display and book clinic in the main library's lobby, the display was later assembled in one of the University's busiest classroom buildings, where it remained for more than two months. The portability of the display means it can continue to be used and be available for tours to other Indiana University campuses.

The success or failure of the campaign will ultimately be judged sometime in the future, when the individuals who viewed the displays think twice about how they treat library materials. Should they decide to treat the materials with the care they deserve, 1995's campaign can be counted every bit as successful as the 1992 campaign. In discussing the future of the campaign, the entire Preservation Committee felt that similar programs should be organized, perhaps on an every-other-year basis. The 1992 and 1995 campaigns were not ends in themselves but rather were steps in a long-term education effort—an effort that will continue as long as the staff and administration are supportive of preservation education.

NOTES

1. Lorraine Olley, "Indiana University Libraries Presents Preservation Awareness Week," *Conservation Administration News* no. 53 (April 1993): 10–11; Connie Vinita Dowell, "An Award Winner Brings Preservation Out of the Lab," *College & Research Libraries News* 54, no. 9 (October 1993): 524–526.

2. Members of the 1995 PAG committee were Phil Bantin, Andrea Morrison, Lorraine Olley (ex officio), Linda Rethmeyer, and Richard Vaughan.

3. For samples and ordering information, contact Preservation Department, Main Library E050, Indiana University, Bloomington, IN 47405. Examples of several posters and bookmarks may be viewed at the preservation department's home page (http://www.indiana.edu/~libpres).

Lite Preservation; Or How to Win Over Your Staff and Customers Without Being a *Heavy*

Harlan Greene, North Carolina Preservation Consortium, Durham, North Carolina

In trying to reach audiences and make preservation relevant, preservationists, like physicians, have often searched for a *magic bullet*—an effective metaphoric way to get the medicine or message across. In presentations of the North Carolina Preservation Consortium, we have appropriated concepts from medicine itself to help us. Since these medical concepts are basic and common, the approach can be used for any audience—staff and customers of high school, public, community college, and academic libraries as well as the general public.

Most of the North Carolina Preservation Consortium sessions have been conducted in public libraries. They are effective for in-house training or public meetings as they are lively and take a different tact from many other types of training or lectures. They can readily adapt to 15 or 50, and the audience makeup can be from a variety of types and sizes of libraries or from the general public. The trick is to keep the topic relevant and *lite* so that you don't lose audience interest or become mired in the do's and don'ts of preservation.

Since the information we convey is useful to staff in their private lives—and not just their lives on the job—they appear more willing to learn it and incorporate it. And library users see the connection between care of library materials and how they want their personal collections respected. If they learn how to keep their home videos in better condition, they may keep the library's in better shape, too. Indeed, the more parallels one can make with the real world, and with commonsense approaches, the more likely listeners are to agree with what you are saying. By linking preservation with generally accepted truths and axioms, preservation itself comes across as commonsensical and logical. Thus, the audience does not have to master entirely new concepts. And staff do not jump to the conclusion that you are merely a management tool trying to boost their productiveness! The audience can go off in new directions, applying constructs they already know.

It may be a gimmick, but it works.

In teaching care and handling of materials, for instance, we immediately make comparisons to medical school. If you were studying anything in the health field, the first thing you would learn would be human anatomy. You would have to know how a human body works and how to manipulate it before you could touch a patient. The same holds true for a car mechanic, an appliance repairman, or a chemist. Why should libraries be different? So a lesson in book or film or compact disc (CD) anatomy is needed.

Comparisons of human and book anatomies are appropriate. We all have spines, heads, and tails. Yes, there really are names for the parts of a book. And not only names but rules. Just as the way we treat a human body derives from the body itself, so the rules on how to treat a book derive from the book. We are not saying do this and that because we say so but do this and that because the book itself demands it.

From that point, it is easy to proceed in almost any direction. Books are organic; people are organic. Some people have genetic predispositions to be healthy or unhealthy. Some library materials are inherently unstable due to their chemical composition; others are more hardy. This provides a natural segue to the nature of materials and the manner in which books are manufactured.

Along the way, we tap into greater societal themes of how greed and paying attention to the bottom line is wrecking society and how it is also wrecking library books. We show how poorly books are made, how manufacturers use cheap glues and papers, and so on. And we demonstrate how our slavish dedication to technology has gotten us into trouble. Not only has this resulted in smart bombs, and other possibilities of total human destruction, but "better living through chemistry" has also resulted in acidic papers with short lives, beta videos, and key punch cards no one can read anymore. The Food and Drug Administration demands we study drugs before we put them into our bodies, while technologies are launched into the world for anyone to buy and use.

No concept is explained without tying it to physical objects. Acidic brittle paper is crumbled. Poorly made books are compared to better-made books. To show the poor adhesion in some perfect bound books, we pull pages out as if from a memo pad. We then hold up a heavy double fan adhesive bound textblock by a single page, attesting to the superiority of this kind of binding. We do not expect our audiences to take our word for it. We advise a similar practice in ordering supplies—don't believe everything you read; test them; it is your money. The more you can reveal about the across-the-board nature of preservation, the more people can learn. Continually stress the commonsense, good business nature of preservation.

Eventually, the dilemma is posed: What are libraries and archives to do now that products are worse, money is scarce, and less support is provided? Libraries should, we answer, do the same things we do in the real world. We have come to realize that we have to recycle to conserve trees and minerals and other limited natural resources. In the same manner, we have to change our behavior and our basic assumptions in order to preserve our limited library resources.

How can we change behavior? By comparing preservation to public health, we suggest an answer. In the latter field, we know it is cheaper and better on our systems to exercise a little every day to avoid major injury and heart attacks. We should do the same commonsense things to keep our library populations healthy. And intuitively, we know this. We know "an ounce of prevention is worth a pound of cure," just as we know "a stitch in time saves nine." So, if we do little things to keep books in shape from day to day, we can minimize our use of expensive conservators, book *surgeons*, and time away from the shelves in a library bindery. We can handle books better, repair them when damage first becomes evident, and take precautions including disaster preparedness planning.

Another way of linking preservation and public health is to make comparisons between the contents of books and the contents of our psyches. We know we don't do human beings justice if we just tend to their spirits while ignoring their bodies. So if we pay attention only to such issues as access, censorship, and ideas, we are ignoring the basic fact that library materials are anchored in physical bodies. If we do not pay attention to that, there will soon be left no spirit or information. Taking commonsense precautions to keep the body healthy makes sense.

The theme of linking book health and people health can be continued in a number of ways. For the importance of maintaining a proper environment, we mention how stressed we get in the hot, humid South, as we go in and out of air conditioning. By the end of the day, we have perspired, dried off, and perspired again; we feel pretty wrung out. Well, books also get stressed by the constant fluctuations. Just as we are happy in stable and temperate climates, so too are library materials. You can use analogies of hair frizzing in high humidities to show how books also try to reach equilibrium with the ambient conditions.

Pollution affects us; pollution affects books. Imagine, the analogy goes, if you visited a friend's house that had radon. Maybe you would not be upset spending an afternoon there, but imagine if you lived there for 10 years. Sitting on an off-gassing shelf or in a substandard photography album or in a polluted room for an hour or a day may not be so bad, but imagine what happens to an object over time.

Other knowledge we have can be used to help us mend our ways in treating library materials. Sunlight burns our skin so that it breaks down. Fortunately, we can regenerate, but books cannot. And in trying to explain the conditions that foster the growth of mold and mildew, it is easy in the South to remind the audience where they are likely to see it first—perhaps in their closets in the summer where it is hot, humid, and dark and the air is stagnant.

As every public speaker knows, it boosts your effectiveness to tie your subject to developments in the news. The prehistoric man found frozen in the Alps was useful a few years ago to show the benefits of cold storage. Any new Egyptian discovery, or mention of the Dead Sea Scrolls, shows the advantage of less humid environments. In the summer of 1994, the twenty-fifth anniversary of the first lunar landing gave us ample opportunity to bewail the loss of National Aeronautics and Space Administration (NASA) computer data. And unfortunately, there are always horror stories in the news to help preach the virtues of disaster preparedness.

In speaking to library audiences, after making many of these points, we take the book through its life cycle in the library. Unpacking a box, we pull out a new, unprocessed book and let the audience listen to it *crack* as it is opened for the first time, demonstrating how vulnerable books are and how mistreatment from their very introduction into the system leads to their destruction. Big, expensive books, we show, can *limber up* and be opened bit by bit, just as you would before you attempted to do a split. We show how sticking pencils or card packs inside the inner hinge, between the textblock and the board, stresses the book's Achilles heel. We quote insurance statistics to show that most people are injured not in faraway exotic locales but in their own cars and homes. Similarly, we acknowledge that although some books are damaged when they visit patrons' houses, many are also damaged in library book truck accidents and on their own home ranges.

To prove this, we show head cap *wounds* caused by prying fingers removing books from shelves incorrectly, and pages torn and bent in the middle of the textblock that are knife wounds from metal bookends. It is a diagnostic clinic, like hospital rounds, in which we show the damage and ask the audience to guess how it was done. Cloth-covered books showing insect nibbles are passed around, and everyone has to guess what caused it. You always get squeals when they realize the truth and graphically see a reason why food and drinks are not allowed in a library.

In book repair clinics, we practice triage skills—which wound to fix first? In general lectures, we combine home-test kits and "Mr. Wizard." Instead of pregnancy, it is acidity. We make marks with pH pens to show how they can test their own supplies. We show how acid-detecting strips for cellulose acetate negatives and microfilm do indeed turn colors in the presence of acetic acid. All of these demonstrations and devices are aimed at showing off the theoretical concepts we have presented.

Before it is over, we set preservation in a realistic context. Do not ignore book health, we say, but don't be a hypochondriac. Not every book needs life support. If the cheap paperback has to last only a year, go ahead and use tape for repair. But your important reference books that cost a lot and need to last should not be treated that way. We do not want the law of the jungle in our libraries. If preservation is survival of the fittest, we need to make sure the best, the most worthy of survival, become the fittest. With these and other examples, we link common sense and preservation principles and relate the importance of the actions taken by staff and users to the healthy lives of our library materials.

Taming the Chimera: Preservation in a Public Library

*Pat Ryckman, Public Library of Charlotte &
Mecklenburg County, Charlotte, North Carolina*

The fire-breathing chimera, a beast with the head of a lion, the body of a goat, and the tail of a serpent, terrorized the Lycian countryside. It took a goddess, a hero, and another fantastic beast, Pegasus, to subdue it. Today, many public libraries face another chimera when dealing with preservation issues—a tripartite monster made up of lack of time, money, and expertise. At the Public Library of Charlotte and Mecklenburg County (PLCMC), we have no budget for preservation, no trained archivist, and with the main library open to serve the public 74 hours a week, very little time to devote to preservation activities. Yet with an arsenal of affordable programs and activities, we have begun to tame the chimera and address our preservation concerns.

Why are public libraries concerned about preservation? Even the tiniest public library holds unique materials, usually relating to its community's local history. The 1992–1993 edition of the *American Library Directory* includes entries for 183 public libraries in North Carolina. Of these, 107 claim special collections ranging from local history and genealogy to oral history, pottery, and even spiders. All of these materials (even the spiders, we suppose) need to be protected from the environment, our patrons, and ourselves to assure their survival for the long term.

At PLCMC, special collections including genealogy, local history, photographs, maps, sound recordings, and manuscripts are housed in the Robinson-

First published in *North Carolina Libraries* 52, no. 1 (Spring 1994): 8–9.

Spangler Carolina Room. By segregating these materials, we can provide them a little more protection and control. It is clear, though, that preservation is not just the concern of the special collections staff. Most Carolina Room materials first must pass through the library's technical services department for processing and cataloging. It is desirable that library materials in the general collections be handled in such a way as to maximize their useful life.

Our first step in addressing the concerns about preservation at PLCMC was to develop a plan for preservation; to do that we needed to understand our collection, its environment, and use. A preservation committee, formed in 1988, was charged to (1) survey the collections, evaluate the needs in each area, set system priorities, and develop a proposed budget to meet the needs; (2) examine and train/retrain staff on current handling, processing, and in-house mending practices and make recommendations to bring these practices into conformity with accepted conservation principles; (3) develop staff training/workshop opportunities that provide staff with professional conservation and bindery expertise; (4) examine the library's physical environments and make recommendations for their enhancement, if necessary; and (5) prepare a disaster plan for the library system. The work by this committee, made up of a cross section of public service and technical service staff, did much to raise collective awareness of preservation issues at PLCMC. Today, preservation is not an isolated activity performed by one department but a philosophy that permeates our policies, procedures, and services.

Education can provide the highest returns for the lowest cost of any preservation activity a library might initiate. Like Pogo, "We have met the enemy, and it is us." The PLCMC collection abounds in examples of mistreatment by both staff and the public. Over the years, we librarians have stamped, taped, labeled, bound, and rebound materials with good intentions but sad results. Our patrons have dog-eared, torn, inked, and mistreated the collection in even more creative ways, but they are often unaware of the harm they have done.

Education is the answer. Each new Carolina Room staffer receives orientation and training that emphasize our preservation goals. Each new staff member views a videotape, *Use or Abuse: The Role of Staff and Patrons in Maintaining General Library Collections*, a 24-minute introduction to good housekeeping practices, including shelf maintenance, loading book trucks, and safe handling of materials. As part of the initial training packet each newcomer also receives a checklist, "Reminders for Shelvers," that encourages safe handling.

In fall 1992, all 300 employees of the library system attended one of six mandatory sessions of "Don't Drop That Book," a half-day training program that emphasized the idea that everyone, no matter what his or her job title, handles library materials and is responsible for their safety. The presenters, Sharon Bennett, archivist for the Charleston Museum, and Harlan Greene, director of the North Carolina Preservation Consortium, provided practical tips and hands-on demonstrations of proper care and handling for a wide range of library materials.

SOLINET's preservation field service provides excellent workshops on a variety of preservation topics, but they can be expensive for some smaller libraries. There is sometimes a way around that cost. As host for their May 1993 Book Repair Workshop, the library was allowed to send one staff member free of charge, and the registration fee was waived in consideration of our sweat equity in preparing for the workshop and providing refreshments. This staff member is now prepared to do a variety of simple repairs—recasing, tipping in pages, tightening hinges, mending tears—at a work area that has been established on an available countertop. By handling these most frequently needed treatments in-house, we not only save money but also are able to return items to the collection more quickly.

Educating the public to the preservation cause is a more delicate matter. We obviously can't require them to attend a workshop or view a video. Instead, we try to develop their appreciation of the issues in more subtle ways. Every tour is an opportunity to mention preservation concerns; for example, when pointing out the photocopier to a tour group, we mention its "book edge" feature, which can help prevent spine damage if used correctly. A quick peek into our vault and a few words about humidity, temperature, and acid impress on the group our own concern for preservation and encourage them to begin to treat materials more carefully. Staff members approach pen-wielding patrons and offer pencils in a nonjudgmental but informative way. A library-produced brochure "Caring for Your Photo Memories" gives tips on safeguarding family photographs. We hope this information will also influence patrons' use of library photographs. Patrons value the materials and want them to be safe, just as we do, but may not realize the destructiveness of some of their own actions.

It is easy to see that preventative preservation measures can save both money and time by helping to avoid costly corrective procedures in the future. Pamphlets coming into the collection are routinely placed in archival enclosures when judged to have lasting value. A book with a paper, spiral, or other less-than-satisfactory binding is sent to a commercial bindery for recasing before being added to the collection. Archival donations arriving in shoe boxes and milk crates are transferred to Hollinger boxes to await processing.

The Carolina Room is responsible for a large image collection—approximately 7,000 historic photographs and close to 10 million negatives. Our subject index to the photograph collection includes oversized contact prints for researchers to peruse to help reduce wear and tear on the originals. As we develop computer databases for access to portions of this collection, we have been experimenting with storing images on Photo CD.

The bulk of the negative collection (comprising the *Charlotte Observer* negative files, 1956–1989) is currently accessible only by date. A project to provide a subject index is also addressing the preservation needs of the collection. As negatives are identified, they are placed in individual mylar sleeves and acid-free envelopes and boxes. To date, 15,000 negatives have been identified and transferred to safe storage. The negatives project is undertaken entirely by volunteers. With Carolina Room staff almost always tied to the reference desk, it would be impossible to accomplish this labor-intensive task without our volunteers. Each month, they contribute an average of 70 hours to the Carolina Room, and many of these hours involve preservation activities.

Donations of large collections of papers can mean many weeks of work for library staff to prepare the materials for addition to the collection. Universities and museums sometimes request an additional monetary gift to support this work. At PLCMC we have been successful in involving the donors as volunteers. In 1989, the Theatre Charlotte/Martha Akers collection arrived in the Carolina Room ready for use. Theatre volunteers, trained by library staff, had already completed organization of the collection, including transferring the entire collection to archival folders, files, and boxes provided by the library. Volunteers from the League of Women Voters, Charlotte Chapter, are currently working on their own organizational papers, which have recently been donated.

Another strategy that can be successful is to take advantage of the library school practicum programs. This year, a University of North Carolina at Greensboro library science student completed processing the Mary Howell Papers, including attending to their physical needs.

Funding preservation activities may seem daunting to public libraries with so many other pressing needs. But if preservation is considered an integral part of the library program rather than a separate concern, the funding can be more readily available. At PLCMC, archival boxes, folders, and photograph sleeves are all purchased through the regular supply budget. Training materials and preservation workshop fees are covered under staff development/continuing education funds. These monies are less susceptible to the budget ax than a separate preservation line item might be. The gift fund has proved a good source for special conservation work on prized items in the collection. Donors are often as happy to have their monetary gift used to preserve a valuable item of local importance as they would be with a purchase of new materials.

PLCMC has begun to address preservation needs through education, through creative use of limited funds and human resources, and by learning to "think preservation" every day. Once preservation thinking became embedded in the library's overall operation, the chimera was tamed.

Preservation Orientation for Library Staff: The University of California at San Diego Approach

Julie A. Page, University of California–San Diego, La Jolla, California, and George J. Soete, Organizational Library Consultant, San Diego, California

In 1990 the library of the University of California at San Diego (UCSD) developed a comprehensive five-year Preservation Program Plan. The plan covered disaster planning, selection and treatment decision making, organization and administration, and staff and user education for preservation and environmental control. The library established detailed action plans for two-year and five-year target periods. A top priority was preservation education, and one of the first projects carried out was development of a required preservation orientation session for library staff.

Three years later, virtually all library staff have gone through the orientation, as well as selected student library employees. Contract custodial staff, campus police, and physical plant managers have also completed the session. In all, 325 individuals have gone through the orientation program in 15 sessions.

Though we have not formally evaluated the impact of the sessions, it is the perception of the authors that attendees now demonstrate a much better understanding of both preservation problems and the importance of their role in the preservation program. The purpose of this case study is to provide an outline for other libraries as they develop a similar staff education program.

THE IMPORTANCE OF STAFF EDUCATION

Staff education was chosen as a high priority for several reasons:

First published in *College & Research Libraries News* 55, no. 6 (June 1994): 358–360. Revised, with addendum, for this book.

- All staff have a serious responsibility in the preservation program. Even those who rarely touch library materials need to understand the integral purpose of materials preservation in the life of their organization.

- As a group, library staff probably handle library materials more than all other groups combined.

- Staff can play an important role in engaging users in advancing the cause of library preservation.

DESIGNING THE SESSION

Having decided that staff orientation was a high priority, we then developed the following criteria for the design of a session for all staff:

- The session had to be brief—no more than an hour and a quarter—since it was to be required of all staff.

- The level of presentation had to be suitable for all staff, from students to administrators, and it had to be portable to other audiences—custodians, campus police, and so on.

- Participants had to be engaged and interested from the beginning. We wanted them to say to themselves within the first five minutes, "This is important," or at any rate, "This is more interesting than I thought it would be!" To this end, we included hands-on experiences. Moreover, we decided to be shameless in declaring the monetary worth of collections and the cost of our preservation strategies as we went through the session.

- Though we wanted to introduce some basic ideas and techniques, the session could not be a mini–library school course. Technical content was kept to a minimum.

- The session had to focus on the individual's scope and responsibility. We would not, therefore, spend time talking about preservation of specialized materials, such as audiotapes, that only trained staff are allowed to handle.

- The key points had to focus on the practical. What few messages would make a difference?

- It had to be clear that the "lessons" of the session had the backing of library administrators.

- The session had to have a high impact but be low in cost.

THE BASIC POINTS

We next developed a conceptual outline—the basic messages we wanted all participants to hear:

- Library collections represent a resource of great monetary and incalculable cultural worth. Their preservation is an important trust that the library has committed to fulfilling.

- Individual library staff already have a great deal of basic knowledge about preservation.

The purpose of the session is to build on it, to suggest key responsibilities, and to promote a consistent view of the importance of preservation.

- Library materials are subject to damage from both *natural* and *human* enemies.
- The library's preservation program, though functioning largely behind the scenes, is extensive and expensive.
- There are simple things that everyone can do to improve the chances of library materials having a long life.
- Furthermore, there are some additional strategies that staff can engage in voluntarily to help in the preservation effort.

PRACTICAL OBJECTIVES

The practical training objectives were:

- To train staff in specific handling techniques for printed materials.
- To engage them in assisting with preventive measures.
- To provide a basic level of information about threats to the collections and about the library's preservation program.
- To suggest clearly the library's expectations for individual performance.

THE SESSION ITSELF

Preservation orientation sessions are team taught by the authors—the associate university librarian (AUL) for collections and the preservation librarian. Tools are simple and portable: a prepared flip chart, several flip chart sheets for recording participant ideas, colored markers, examples of damaged materials, and other realia—for example, a hygrothermograph, good/bad bookends.

Following is a more detailed outline of the session, with the presenter indicated.

I. *AUL/Collections.* The purpose of this segment is to get the group engaged, to establish their present knowledge of preservation information. After a very few words about the importance of the topic, some "gee-whiz" facts are presented: the size of the collections (specifying formats—maps, slides, bound volumes, documents, pamphlets, etc.); growth of collections over the past 40 years; key Association of Research Libraries (ARL) rankings; insured value of the collections (millions and millions of dollars); and the importance of the collections in the regional, national, and international settings. Then a question is posed: "What are the physical dangers that printed materials are subject to? What contributes to shortening their life?" Participants come up with answers such as heat, food, moisture, book drops, and inappropriate repairs.

II. *Preservation Librarian.* This prepared presentation is the centerpiece of the session. The content is divided into *natural* enemies and *human* enemies. Throughout, the trainers make references back to the ideas the participants suggested earlier, and points are consistently related to the practical strategies that the staff themselves can use. The natural enemies are first displayed on a flip chart sheet:

Heat/fire	Water
Moisture	Mold/mildew
Light	Embrittlement
Pollutants	Pests

Real objects are used throughout this segment: Examples of water-damaged and insect-damaged books are passed around, as are brittle pages on which the participants perform a simple fold test. Participants are encouraged to take an active role in the preservation program. For example, if a library user complains about excessive cold in the stacks, the employee can explain about the adverse effect of heat on the collection. Staff are encouraged to report all instances of water leaks, excessive light, and other harmful environmental conditions.

The human enemies flip chart is then displayed:

Routine handling	Mutilation
Shelving methods	Stick-on notes
Food and drink	Clips/bands
Incorrect repairs	Book drops
Highlighting	Marginalia
Photocopy machines	

Here the emphasis is on everyday handling of materials: how to take volumes off the shelf, how to put them on copy machines, which bookends are safe and which ones damage the volumes. Again, examples of mishandled materials are passed around. And staff are encouraged to take an active role—for example, to suggest to a user about to dump volumes in a book return that it would be much less damaging to take them inside the library.

Throughout the session, participants are encouraged to ask questions and make comments. Since most know each other, the sessions are quite informal.

III. *AUL/Collections*. The session here shifts to the library's preservation program—the strategies we use and the money we spend to preserve materials. Again, a prepared flip chart sheet guides the discussion. Brief comments are made about each of the following:

Controlling environment	Binding

Special conservation measures	Repair
Restrictions on use	Reformatting
Disaster preparedness	Training

Realia for this segment include acid-free containers, encapsulation supplies, a hygrothermograph (for measuring temperature and humidity), and examples of materials damaged by water, heat, and other natural and human enemies.

IV. *Preservation Librarians.* The session closes with a review of staff responsibilities, as well as ways in which staff can provide assistance beyond what is required in their job descriptions. Here are the actual flip chart texts:

Your Job

- Use proper shelving/handling techniques
- Handle materials properly during photocopying
- No eating/drinking when working with library materials
- Refer damaged materials for proper repair
- Do not use stick-on notes, clips, bands improperly

Your Further Help

- Help enforce no food/no drink rules
- Learn to identify library materials in need of help
- Report all potential disaster situations
- Help educate users
- Be aware of environmental conditions that might be harmful to collections

A more complete two-page guideline, "Care of Library Collections," has been distributed to all staff and is given to all new staff and student employees as they are processed through the library personnel office. As a means of reinforcing the importance of preservation, we have included two statements in all staff job descriptions indicating their responsibility for preservation:

1. "Handles all library materials according to accepted library preservation practices as presented in library training sessions."
2. "General knowledge of library preservation principles."

Library staff in all departments have indicated an enjoyment of and appreciation for the preservation training sessions. From grudging ("I hate to admit it, but I got a lot out of the session") to effusive ("Best ever general library training session"), staff comments indicate that the preservation orientation program has very effectively met its training objectives.

REFERENCES

Boomgaarden, Wesley L. *Staff Training and User Awareness in Preservation Management*. Washington, DC: Association of Research Libraries, 1993.

The most up-to-date compilation of training-related issues. Includes examples of training practices and policies, as well as a brief bibliography.

Preservation Education in ARL Libraries: SPEC Kit 113. Washington DC: Association of Research Libraries, Office of Management Studies, 1985.

Sample materials from ARL member libraries, including training materials for staff preservation orientation.

ADDENDUM

The preservation orientation sessions continue to be presented annually by the preservation librarian and the head of the library's Acquisitions Department. The subject content and presentation remain the same. To date, over 400 staff members have attended the sessions. The importance given to preservation issues and training remains high with library staff and administration.

A user education campaign was launched in fall 1994, with a three-month display in the library lobby. Titled "Handle with Care," several flat cases displayed evidence of the damage caused by human and natural enemies. One case presented information about the library's preservation program and efforts made by library staff to deal with potential damage and deterioration to the collection.

A second part of the exhibit, titled "New Preservation Technologies," addressed the pros and cons of digitization versus micrographics. This part of the exhibit drew heavily from the Commission on Preservation and Access publications for its graphics and technical information.

No formal evaluation was conducted to determine response to the exhibit. The circulation staff reported that many staff and users stopped to look at the information over the course of its three-month display.

In conjunction with the exhibit, an afternoon demonstration event was planned. Called "When Bad Things Happen to Good Books," the program included ongoing demonstrations of circulating book repair. An announcement of this event was placed in the campus newspaper, as well as in a newsletter for UCSD staff, faculty, and Friends of the Library (see Figure 2.3). A Preservation Department member answered questions as she repaired books from the collection. In addition, preservation housing and fine book repair of special collections materials were displayed. A local conservator took part in the demonstration, along with special collections staff. Two televisions with videocassette recorders showed a selection of preservation videos. Several short videos were repeated and could be viewed while standing in the demonstration area. A longer video, *Slow Fires*, was in a nearby room with seating available.

Attendance at the afternoon event was light. Better attendance would likely

Figure 2.3
Preservation Exhibit Advertisement

have resulted if the displays and videos had been directly inside the library's front door near the preservation exhibit, where traffic flow was higher.

The intention is to stage exhibits and demonstration events every two to three years. In between these events, posters, handouts, smaller displays, and group presentations can be utilized to raise the preservation awareness of staff and users.

On the Road: Preservation Education Outreach in Colorado

Karen Jones, Jefferson County Public Library,
Lakewood, Colorado

The Colorado Preservation Alliance (CPA) is a nonprofit consortium of libraries, archives, museums, historical and genealogical societies, governmental agencies, and other interested organizations and individuals committed to preserving the cultural and historical documentary heritage of Colorado. The CPA board consists of four officers, three committee chairs (education, membership, fiscal), three at-large members, and five area representatives. The state is divided into five geographical regions to maximize local representation.

The Colorado Preservation Alliance was formed in 1990 as Colorado's response to a national mandate for cooperative preservation activities. In 1992–1993 the CPA received Library Services and Construction Act (LSCA) funding to develop and publish *On the Road: A Statewide Plan for Preservation in Colorado*.[1] In 1994 the CPA began implementing the goals specified in the plan:

- To improve housing and care of identified collections through education
- To build public support for preservation
- To coordinate preservation activities statewide

As an organization totally dependent on its volunteer board and with no permanent institutional base, the CPA tailors its efforts accordingly. For instance, the CPA works by building alliances with like-minded organizations to coordinate preservation activities. Formal liaisons and active collaborative efforts are ongoing with several organizations, including the Colorado Wyoming Association of Museums; Society of Rocky Mountain Archivists; Colorado Library Association; Colorado Council of Academic Libraries; Colorado Library Resource Sharing and Information Access Board; and the Colorado Historical Records Administration Board. The strategies for implementing the statewide preservation plan are structured in terms of ongoing activity that can be undertaken by volunteers.

Most CPA projects and activities focus on preservation education. These include:

• Maintaining the Myra Jo Moon Memorial Preservation Reference Collection, which is the most extensive collection of preservation information in the state. The collection is housed at the Jefferson County Public Library in Lakewood. Items can be borrowed through interlibrary loan. The catalog is available on the Internet through ACLIN (Access Colorado Library Information Network) and CARL (Colorado Alliance of Research Libraries). An annotated bibliography of the collection has been published.[2] An endowment allows the CPA to purchase current reference material.

• Providing current preservation information through the quarterly *CPAlert* newsletter.

• Responding to individual and institutional requests for preservation information by mail and phone and through periodic workshops.

• Producing three preservation self-study kits. The CPA was awarded monies through the Colorado Historical Society State Historic Fund to develop these kits for environmental monitoring, paper deterioration, and photograph/negative care and identification.

Consistent publication of preservation articles has proven to be a very effective vehicle for the CPA, both in getting the preservation word out and in making one product serve a variety of uses. The CPA has been publishing articles since its inception in 1990. More than 20 articles are now available. Titles range from ''Drying Wet Books and Records'' to ''Book Bugs in Colorado.'' The articles are chosen from a variety of sources. Many are reprints of articles written by other organizations, such as the Northeast Document Conservation Center and the National Park Service. Some are reprints of articles published in preservation journals such as *Abbey Newsletter* or *Conservation Administration News*. Several were written by preservation professionals in Colorado. There are also preservation bibliographies and videographies available. The articles are reviewed and updated as needed by members of the CPA Education Committee.

The CPA board has found that while articles like these may be old news to preservation professionals, there is a great demand for this type of information from staff of small libraries and historical societies, individuals who want to care for their family records, and staff of institutions that are far from the Denver metro area and its training opportunities. Colorado is a big and mountainous state. Many of these people do not read the professional journals but are interested in finding answers to their specific problems. Selected articles answer their questions and raise their preservation awareness as well. These articles help fulfill two of the CPA goals: to improve housing and care of identified collections through education and to build public support for preservation.

The articles themselves are used in a variety of venues:

- The articles are published as inserts in the quarterly *CPAlert* newsletter.
- The articles are sent to targeted journals around the state for possible reprinting.
- An updated list of available articles makes up a part of each CPA information packet.
- Organizations are given permission to reprint selected articles for their own clientele. For example, packets containing several articles pertaining to caring for home library collections were compiled for the Colorado Antiquarian Booksellers Association (CABA). This association sponsors an annual antiquarian book fair. The CPA developed packets for CABA to be included as part of the registration materials distributed to dealers at the fair, who in turn made the information available to their customers. The packets contained an introductory letter about the CPA, with permission to reprint contents; a CPA membership brochure; and several previously published articles on basic preservation, such as caring for the home library, care of photographs and scrapbooks, and encapsulation. The masters for the packet materials were redesigned when necessary to allow space for dealer identification.

A major outreach project of the CPA has been the creation of the previously mentioned preservation study kits. The purpose of these kits is twofold: to assist in educating those responsible for the housing and care of historical resources and to gather data on environmental conditions, paper longevity, and the condition of photographic collections in a wide range of repositories. The topics addressed cover basic preservation concerns and were chosen based on a survey of the membership: monitoring the environment; paper treatment/deacidification; and care of photographic materials. Each kit contains both reference and instructional materials; equipment for testing and/or accomplishing a specific preservation task; and an evaluation questionnaire.

All the kit manuals follow the same basic format: table of contents; borrowing information; explanatory material; instructions for use of equipment; resource materials; bibliography; and an evaluation. Because it is anticipated that the manuals will need periodic updating, they are in loose-leaf format. Kit materials are packed in a heavy-duty case with custom foam cutouts to hold components securely. The cases were designed to carry professional audiovisual equipment and can take a lot of abuse. The kits are rented on a cost-recovery basis. A rental fee of $35 covers shipping, handling, and item replacement costs. Borrowers keep some of the low-cost supplies. They may also purchase selected supplies by remitting payment when returning the kit.

The kits were presented at the CPA/SRMA (Society of Rocky Mountain Archivists) annual meeting held in 1995 in Colorado Springs. Response was enthusiastic, especially for the environmental monitoring kit, which immediately resulted in a large borrowers' waiting list. In the fall of 1995, all kits were made available for rental. Throughout the summer and fall, CPA area representatives organized local presentations with demonstrations (funded by the grant) to advertise the usefulness and availability of the kits. All kits were made available for rental after completion of the presentations.

The kits were designed to address the educational needs of a diverse group of individuals and institutions, realizing the need is most pressing in small libraries, archives, and historical societies. To be considered a success, the project had to demonstrate a collaborative statewide effort, and the lists had to function as a self-educational tool. To meet these goals, the CPA board area representatives serve as the technical advisers and informational resource people in their respective parts of the state. Kit users in their area can call for advice if needed. Each kit has a home base (site sponsor) in a different part of the state. Expertise and support have come from all over the state through the kit design and modification process. Each kit was sent to a minimum of two test sites for critique and evaluation before final modifications. The test sites were chosen to represent the diverse range of institutions in the state.

Project workers were astounded at the myriad of detail necessary to make these kits absolutely self-explanatory to any interested user so they would meet the goal of being self-educational. In addition to simplifying topic descriptions and instructional materials, procedures for borrowing, packing, and return shipping had to be considered. Feedback from users of other kits, as well as from the test site users, was invaluable in helping accomplish this task. In addition, Nancy Carlson Schrock, author of the Gaylord *Pathfinder* series, reviewed each manual and made many useful suggestions. A short description of each kit follows.

ENVIRONMENTAL MONITORING

The maintenance of a stable environment is the single most cost-effective method to reduce deterioration of all types of collections. The environmental monitoring kit manual begins with information about the elements that constitute the environment and how these elements interact and relate to collection preservation. Instructions on the use of the monitoring instruments and supplies in the kit follow. Finally, a selection of reference handouts (the user may make one photocopy of each), a bibliography, and evaluation questionnaire complete the manual.

The monitoring instruments chosen run the gamut from low to high tech:

- Electronic data logger with remote sensors for measuring temperature and relative humidity
- Digital humidity/temperature meter
- Humidity indicator paper
- Humidity indicator cards
- Digital illuminometer

- Blue wool cards
- Light damage slide rule
- Insect traps—beetle (two), sticky (one), cockroach (five)

Instruments that needed frequent calibration or complicated instructions for use were avoided. The data logger, in particular, was chosen for that reason. This instrument also provides both the user and CPA with valuable information about the user's repository. The user returns the kit, and the data logger is plugged into the kit sponsor's computer. A printout is returned to the user, and one copy is kept for a CPA environmental survey compilation.

The evaluation is short and designed specifically for this kit. Data requested include:

- Information about the borrowing facility (type, annual budget, number of staff, staff training, existing environmental controls)
- Usability of kit equipment and reference material
- Borrower's intent to purchase specified monitoring equipment or to borrow the kit in the future

Information about the borrowing institution is integrated with the data logger readings to document the need for possible future environmental improvement projects. This kit is based in southwestern Colorado at Fort Lewis College in Durango.

PAPER TREATMENT/DEACIDIFICATION

The problems caused by acidic paper have been documented for many years. The paper treatment/deacidification kit enables the user to address this problem. The kit manual contains information explaining paper deterioration, its consequences, and options for paper treatment. A pH testing pen and pH strips are included to test collection materials for acidity, as well as to test acid-free purchases and so become a more informed consumer of archival supplies. Materials are included to demonstrate polyester encapsulation and deacidification; resource handouts offer information on various paper treatment options, condition surveys, and reformatting. This kit is based in northeast Colorado in Fort Collins at Colorado State University.

CARE AND IDENTIFICATION OF PHOTOGRAPHIC MATERIALS

Photographs and negatives sometimes demand care that differs from that of general paper-based collections. In order to store and care for them optimally, the type of photograph (emulsion, process, support) should be known. The kit, a compilation of information, walks the user through the process of identifying, handling, housing, and displaying a variety of photographic materials. This kit contains photographic samples, a 30X light scope, reference materials (book on photographic terminology, process identification chart, acetate deterioration guide), extensive resource handouts, and cotton gloves. As with the other kits, the user may keep selected items (gloves, handouts), purchase some items, and make one photocopy of the resource materials. Although the information on different processes is fairly extensive, with identified samples, the main focus of the kit is optimal care and housing of photographs and negatives. This kit is based near the Denver metropolitan area in Boulder at the University of Colorado.

The CPA is optimistic that the kits will prove to be a success. They have the benefit of being self-educational and requiring a minimum of administrative effort. It is hoped that they will be a prototype for future kits and the genesis for future projects as additional needs are identified in Colorado repositories. It is hoped that these educational outreach efforts will take us further down the road to meeting Colorado's preservation goals.

NOTES

1. For more information about the Colorado Preservation Alliance, write care of the Colorado State Archives, 1313 Sherman Street, Denver, CO 80203.

2. *Myra Jo Moon Memorial Preservation Reference Collection*, Sharon Partridge and Karen Jones for the Colorado Preservation Alliance, 1994.

South Carolina Preservation Education Project

Sharon Bennett, Charleston Museum, Charleston,
South Carolina

INTRODUCTION

From 1992 to 1995, the South Carolina State Library funded a Preservation Education Project (PEP) with two consecutive Library Services and Construction Act (LSCA) grants. The project was designed to raise the awareness of administrators, librarians, and the public about the importance of preserving library and local history materials. As preservation education coordinator, I was able to work closely with many library staffs throughout the state to assist them in and audiotapestheir understanding of the role of preservation in a public library. I was also able to offer suggestions to help prolong the life of important local history collections and served as a preservation consultant to other types of libraries.

BACKGROUND

The goals for the PEP were twofold. The project provided knowledgeable preservation information for the librarians and library staffs, as well as increased awareness on the part of the public. To meet these goals, the project involved not only site surveys and workshops on basic care and handling programs for staff, volunteers, and student workers but also preservation programming aimed at Friends' groups and the general public, both children and adults.

SITE SURVEYS

A total of eight public library site surveys were conducted around the state. Even in those libraries with new buildings, problems due to light damage and improper temperature and humidity control were evident. In most cases, modifying routine tasks and monitoring the situation were all that was needed to help prolong the useful life of collections. Suggestions were made to change the daily routine and technical processing tasks. For example, the discontinuing of the use of rubber bands, removable adhesive notes, and paper clips was suggested. Also, the proper placement of date-due slips and security strips was demonstrated along with the suggestion to move photocopy machines to be in clear view of the staff as a deterrent to abuse by patrons.

Site visits also included a one-hour slide/lecture followed by a tour of the facility. The presentation covered all aspects of library operations from removing books from cartons and inspection upon arrival to preservation issues in the processing, shelving, and circulation of the materials. Suggestions were made for improvement of book returns and special consideration for rare book or local history rooms. The tour through the library provided an opportunity to point out both the positive and negative aspects of the current situation. Most staff members expressed a genuine concern and enthusiasm for handling the collections properly.

STAFF EDUCATION

Sixteen workshops on the care and handling of book collections were presented to educate public librarians, staff, and volunteers—no matter what their particular job—about the importance each person plays in the longevity of library materials. It was stressed that much of the damage that library materials sustain is the result of actions by staff as books move through the library operations. Few of the workshop participants had received previous training in proper care and handling of materials or other aspects of preservation. The workshops served as in-service training for the staff and volunteers, including information on shelving; circulation and technical services operations; monitoring of temperature, humidity, and light levels; and proper transport of books and library materials.

Two-day book repair workshops were held in six different geographic regions of the state. Staff were taught to recognize early signs of damage and to make simple, quick repairs to books before bindings started to fail, necessitating rebinding. The hands-on workshops were both fun and educational and were directed toward minimizing the amount of time books were out of circulation.

Recognizing that libraries face a growing demand for audio and video materials, each of which requires special preservation considerations, eight magnetic media workshops were presented. Issues included acquisition, use, care and handling, proper storage, and cataloging of various types of media. Participants were given hands-on experience with tape splicing and repair or replacement of cassette containers. Preservation problems and possible solutions for CD-ROMs, compact discs, and microfilm were also discussed.

During all the staff training sessions, suggestions were made for preservation exhibits that would display the types of damage that library materials sustain. The approach was taken that the majority of damage done by library users is the result of innocent acts on their part. Increasing user awareness via displays and exhibits is a very visual way to present preservation education, for example, the effect of food, mold, and rough photocopying on book materials and the effect of heat on video- and audiotapes. The exhibits could ask the question, "Can you guess what happened to this book?" and include the time and cost of repairs. Exhibits provide an excellent first step in user education.

USER EDUCATION: ADULT WORKSHOPS

Eighteen workshops on the care and handling of family papers and photographs were presented across the state. These workshops were especially important in helping the public understand the significance of preservation and the difficulties libraries face in caring for collections. They offered insight into how people might better store and handle their own materials, and attendees were encouraged to bring in their own family documents, photographs, and memorabilia for help in identifying possible preservation problems. Participants were from a range of interest groups: churches, genealogists, local historians, retired employees, and Friends of the Library.

A wide assortment of items was brought to these lectures—everything from newspaper clippings to family Bibles and historically significant and valuable items, most of which needed improved storage and handling conditions. Participants were able to examine proper archival storage materials and to get tips on organizing papers and photographs, and they were given catalogs for acquiring proper storage enclosures.

Once the participants understood what was involved in the care and handling of photographs and family papers, they were able to see the difficult task faced by libraries in caring for thousands of such items. The need for preservation monies in library budgets to properly preserve these items as well as the book and audiovisual collections was emphasized. The workshops provided the opportunity to reach out to the public. It was hoped that a result would be increased local and legislative support for library and preservation funding.

USER EDUCATION: WORKSHOPS FOR CHILDREN

As part of the Charleston County Library System's summer reading program, workshops were conducted in an effort to teach children how to care for books and how easily books are damaged. The children pretended that they were the books. We would remove and replace them on the shelves, the way that most patrons do—by grabbing the head or foot of the book and jerking it forward! In order to get across the negative effects of eating and drinking while reading books, one child would pretend to be a book and would be covered in rain gear, usually a cheap poncho and plastic hat. Another child pretended to eat something over their head, usually something very gooey or runny, so that it invariably ended up on the child below. The children had a great deal of fun with this activity.

With the permission of the parents, we would let children have a piece of candy, then asked them what would happen if they then licked their fingers to turn the page, or what would happen if they were to put on lotion or bug spray. The instruction included the importance of washing hands before reading. We also stressed that it was not a way to make just library books last but their own books as well. The children loved the workshops because they were interactive and hands-on. They also came up with some great solutions for identified problems, such as recycling grocery bags at the library. That way, patrons could cover the books when it rained, rather than holding them over their heads to use as an umbrella, a situation they had seen many times!

CONCLUSION

We accomplished our goals for the four-year project. We taught public library staff across the state the preservation information they needed to improve collections care and handling and to continue the staff and user training in their libraries. In addition, we focused on good preservation behaviors with children and raised the awareness of the general public to library preservation issues and funding realities.

Preservation Awareness for Student Workers: Adding a Quiz to the Agenda

*Anthony J. Amodeo, Loyola Marymount
University, Los Angeles, California*

With binding costs up and budgets down, and with many titles going out of print permanently, the shelf life of books in academic libraries is a real concern. Since circulation staff handle materials more than anyone, poor handling and shelving habits on the part of desk attendants and reshelvers can cause damage in even a short time.

As stated in a current library science textbook, people are not born knowing how to use a library.[1] A corollary is that most student workers are not hired knowing how to shelve a book. Specific attention has to be paid to handling practice and preservation awareness in training student workers.

BACKGROUND

Over the last several years, preservation awareness has gradually been brought into the training of circulation student workers at Loyola Marymount University. It began with the inclusion of a short talk by a librarian at the fall general orientation. Allotted only 10 minutes because of the multiplicity of subjects to be covered at the meeting, the librarian gave a brief introduction to book structure, discussed the importance of good book-handling habits, showed examples of warped and knifed bindings, and demonstrated the correct way to use book-ends and shelve oversized books. The librarian closed by emphasizing the importance of the work the students would perform to both their own and future generations of students.

In the years following, the short video *Murder in the Stacks*[2] was introduced as a follow-up to be viewed by the student workers sometime during their work schedule within the week. The video was also used by circulation staff as a substitute for the preservation talk for new hires during the course of the year. Progress was made as each year more of the student supervisors who trained new workers had themselves been exposed to the preservation training. With fewer and fewer exceptions, oversized books were shelved on their spines instead of fore-edges and were not wedged in where they did not fit. Eventually, most large books were identified by students and reclassified to the newly constituted shelf ranges for flat and oversize books.

However, in some years, no general circulation orientation took place. Personal observation showed a decline in the quality of book shelving without these sessions. Also, due to the closure of the periodicals service desk, circulation had to assume a new responsibility. Students were given much more territory to cover and reshelve, and the library had to absorb cutbacks in student hours. The neat geography of assigned responsibility for set ranges of shelving to specific students, which had worked very well to improve morale and efficiency, began to break down. More students were making mistakes, not straightening shelves, not replacing bookends, and so on. There was more cramped shelving as the shortage of labor resulted in inadequate stack shifting.

METHODOLOGY

With staffing cuts a permanent reality, something had to be done to improve the attention given to the condition of the stacks. A quiz was designed for newly hired circulation students to reinforce the information in the video showings of *Murder in the Stacks* and the 10-minute preservation talk when it could be given (see Figure 2.4). The quiz was created to be a learning tool and to improve awareness of the good work done by student workers for the library and its clientele. The quiz was tested on experienced and inexperienced student workers, as well as being given out at a meeting of the student supervisors before the general orientation for new hires.

At the fall 1992 general orientation, the preservation talk covered the usual territory:

- Basic book structure, including the weakness of the hinge in modern bindings.
- The correct way to remove books from the shelf without tugging on the headcap.
- The damage done to books by leaning or being stood on their fore-edges.
- The correct way to insert and weigh down a bookend, and the danger of *knifing* with either wire or thin bookends.
- How to support book structures when charging out or stamping due dates in both hardcover and softcover books.
- The expense and difficulty of replacing scholarly books.

- Why eating and drinking are forbidden in the building.
- The fact that student workers handle materials more than anyone else and the importance of their good shelving and checkout habits.
- The importance of the example set by library staff in general, and circulation desk workers in particular, in forming patron attitudes toward handling of library materials.

During the next week, the new hires took the mostly multiple-choice quiz during their work shifts. After completing the questions, they were given the answer sheet by their supervisor and told to go over the quiz. The answer sheet was designed to reinforce their learning by explaining the correct answers, to correct invalid assumptions, and to ensure that they understood the importance of the material presented.

The quiz was intended for student workers before they shelved for the first time; bad habits are harder to correct than good habits are to learn. It is also used for new hires who see *Murder in the Stacks*, although some information on the quiz is not covered there. It can also be used, along with the video, as a review for those students found to be performing below handling standards.

With a few changes, the quiz could be adapted for other student workers, whether in public or technical services. Attention to behavior such as excessive inking of identification stamps, high piling of books, stuffing thick sheaves of paper into bindings, careless handling of sound discs, and the like, could be added or substituted appropriately.

CONCLUSION

The quiz is hardly the most comprehensive presentation of preservation awareness and student training. As the years without training demonstrated, the success of any such endeavor had less to do with the instructor than with the attitude of both the permanent staff and student supervisors. Preservation awareness has to be a part of day-to-day supervision. Even if the introductory talk were extended in length and the quiz given more often, it would do little good without the acceptance of training goals by the staff and their reinforcement by the example set in their own handling of books and interaction with the public.

Here are some additional points to consider for your local situation:

- The size of the student worker population may work against the effectiveness of a large group orientation session; a small group or team approach may be better.
- Information on handling should be given at the very outset of training and be reinforced during the first few weeks of work. Bad shelving habits are harder to change.
- It is best to have experienced staff with a good attitude work closely with new student workers and to continue to monitor them from time to time. Modeling works!
- If students have had prior library experience, there may need to be some retraining and monitoring, since not all libraries embrace preservation as a conscious goal.

Figure 2.4
Preservation Awareness Quiz for Student Workers

Name: _____

A QUICK QUIZ TO TEST YOUR KNOWLEDGE OF BOOK HANDLING

Please CIRCLE THE LETTER(S) representing the correct response(s).
NOTE: There may be more than one correct response for any question.

1. In the following illustration, which books are shelved correctly?

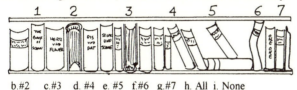

a.#1   b.#2   c.#3   d. #4   e. #5   f.#6   g.#7   h. All   i. None

2. Which of the following are **potentially** harmful to books?
a. Abrasion (harsh rubbing against another surface)
b. Pressure from sides (tight shelving) or from above (books or shelving on top)
c. Leaning (tilted) books/ very loose shelving
d. Spine-up shelving (hanging text block)
e. Bookends, if not used correctly
f. Piling books up too high
g. Rubber bands (cutting or sticky deterioration)
h. Inserts (paper clips, pens, pencils, thick or acidic bookmarks, stuffed-in paper, etc.)
i. Food, food wrappers, crumbs
j. Water or liquid refreshments
k. Circulation workers at checkout
l. Patrons, including students and faculty
m. All of the above

3. Who teaches library patrons how to handle books?
a. Librarians
b. Library Assistants
c. Student workers

4. Where is a book especially vulnerable to damage?
a. At the headcap (top of the spine)
b. At the hinges
c. When it is open, face up
d. When it is open, face down
e. All of the above

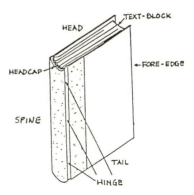

5. Who handles library books the most?
a. Librarians
b. Patrons
c. Shelvers and circulation desk attendants

- OVER, please -

Figure 2.4 Continued

6. How many books can you safely carry without using a booktruck?
   a. About 10
   b. About 8
   c. About 4

7. What kinds of loaded booktrucks are the most likely to turn over and spill?
   a. Bottom-heavy
   b. Middle-heavy
   c. Top-heavy
   d. One that is pushed too fast, especially on turns
   e. One that is pushed into an elevator improperly

8. A patron presents 8 books to be checked out. How should books be readied for stamping and/or scanning?
   a. Open one at a time, with the cover or text block to be stamped laid flat on the counter
   b. With all the books piled up open and face up, one on top of the other, like they do in public libraries
   c. With all the books neatly stacked up. You can do one book and just push it over onto the counter
   d. However the book lies when it is open

9. The price on an LMU paperback book is $7.95. How much did it cost the Library?
   a. Between $6 -$10
   b. Between $10-$15
   c. Between $35-55

10. What is the best way to stamp a date when the date due slip is on a book's inside cover -- especially a paperback?
   a. Hold the cover up with your hand and stamp it sideways
   b. Just stretch it down until it lays on the counter and stamp it
   c. Hold the text block vertically (up & down), with the cover at 90 degrees (flat on the counter) and stamp it

11. If a book won't fit where it belongs, you should
   a. Squeeze or force it in
   b. Lay it flat on top of the books on that shelf
   c. Lay it gently on the floor directly in front of the exact vertical position where it belongs
   d. Look for out-of-place books on that shelf and remove them to make room
   e. Shift the books up or down to make room, keeping the exact order
   f. Inform your supervisor or library assistant about the location of the needed shift

12. If you see a patron damaging library materials, you should
   a. Go up and holler at him/her
   b. Immediately inform your supervisor or the library assistant
   c. Politely inform them that what they are doing may be destructive to the materials, and show them the right way to treat materials

Charles Von der Ahe Library • Loyola Marymount University • Los Angeles, CA

Figure 2.4 Continued

BOOK HANDLING QUIZ ANSWERS:

1. **a.#1, c.#3, and g.#7.** #1 sits vertically on the shelf. #2 (spine up) hangs the whole weight of the text block from the hinges, which will eventually tear off. #3 (spine down) is the proper way to shelve a non-Oversize book that won't fit vertically; the text block isn't being torn out by gravity. #4 is leaning, which means the hinges are being stretched and the spine warped. #5 is obviously wrong. Book #6 has been jammed in where it doesn't fit; no book should be forced, ever, and no books should be touching the shelf above. #7 are vertical and square with and in contact with the vertical part of the bookend. This insures that the weight of the book will keep the bookend from sliding.

2. **n. All of the above** have the potential to cause harm. Some things, like bookends, can be good or bad, depending on how they're used. Other things, like rough treatment or harmful inserts, are always bad.

3. All are correct. However, librarians and library assistants have few opportunities to teach handling. **c. Student workers**, in the way they handle materials and in the shape they leave the book stacks, have far and away the most influence in setting a good example -- observation is the most common teacher, and patrons do observe.

4. **e. All of the above.** Pulling a book off the shelf by the headcap instead of the "waist" produces the most common kind of tearing of the cover. Book hinges are weak, so lifting a book by one cover is very destructive. An open book, face up or especially face down, is vulnerable to anything that might happen. When open face down on a flat surface, a book is undergoing continuous weakening of the binding. That's why careful photocopying is so important.

5. **c. Student workers**, including shelvers, circulation and cataloging clerks, handle library materials more than anyone else, so a little habitual carelessness adds up to a lot of damage.

6. **c. About 4.** It is almost always better to use a booktruck.

7. **c. Top-heavy, d. Pushed too fast & e. Pushed into an elevator improperly.** Always center a single row of books; if you have only two rows of books, don't double-shelf: put the second row on the middle shelf to avoid top-heaviness. Single rows of oversize books are best. When pushing a cart into an elevator, line up the wheels perpendicular to an elevator door, then go around and pull the cart safely into the elevator.

8. **a. One at a time, with the surface to be stamped flat on the counter.** Any other way can damage hinges or loosen the text block. If you've worked in a public library, you know that they get rid of most books within a few years, so there is less attention paid to preservation. Most academic library books are selected for their continuing research value over a period of many years, and have to be treated with a lot more care. *(see also #10)*

- OVER, please -

Figure 2.4 Continued

9. **c. Between $35-55.** The costs of acquiring, cataloging, marking and keeping track of a book in the Library catalog (*LINUS*) is quite high. The average purchase price of new academic titles is now close to $50, so an academic hardback book averages close to $100 to put on the shelf.

10. **c. Hold the text block vertically, with the cover at 90 degrees** -- like the letter L (cover flat on the counter).

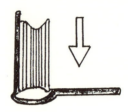

11. If easy to do, **e. Shift a few books up or down to make room.**
    If it will involve a lot of shifting, **f. Inform your supervisor or library assistant about the location of the needed shift.**
    If a quick scan of the shelf shows misshelved books, then **d. remove them to a sorting or pickup shelf, or put them on the cart for later shelving.**

12. If what the patron is doing is a <u>minor</u> problem, such as putting books on the floor, piling books dangerously, or reshelving books, you can **c. politely inform them** that the library prefers that they do it another way.
    But if the action is actually <u>destructive</u>, such as page-tearing, underlining/highlighting, or other mutilation, it is best to **b. Immediately inform a librarian, the library assistant or your supervisor.** Remember, book vandals are stealing YOUR potential knowledge -- and maybe stealing a better term paper grade from you or your fellow student.

Remember: if you develop good handling <u>habits</u>, and a good attitude, you won't even have to think about handling problems after a while; you'll just do it right the first time.
And, if you run in to a situation you're not sure about, just ASK! It's the best way to learn, and no one will think the less of you for it. In fact, asking is the sign of a good employee -- and a good student.

Charles Von der Ahe Library • Loyola Marymount University • Los Angeles, CA
- TAmodeo rv 5/95

Given a little information, both instruction librarians and those who train and supervise student workers have shown sincere interest in improving staff training and preservation awareness in the library. Postings to nonpreservation listservs such as BI-L and CIRCPLUS[3] are indicative of the need for broader dissemination of this information.

Preservation awareness saves money, increases longevity of materials, and even makes the stacks look neat. Experienced library staff realize the importance of modeling for preservation awareness. The example set by those who work with and in view of the public, whether student worker, support staff, or professional librarian, does more to teach patrons good (or bad) habits and attitudes than all the signs, bookmarks, and corrective measures we can devise.

NOTES

1. "Library Instruction," in G. Edward Evans, Anthony J. Amodeo, and Thomas L. Carter, *Introduction to Library Public Services*, 5th ed. (Englewood, CO: Libraries Unlimited, 1992), p. 133.

2. Columbia University Libraries Preservation Committee, *Murder in the Stacks* (New York: Center for Biomedical Communications, College of Physicians & Surgeons, Columbia University, [1987]), 1 videocassette (15 min.): sd., col.; ½" VHS.

3. BI-L is a moderated listserv devoted to library instruction and draws membership from all types of institutions in several countries. The list is run from the State University of New York at Binghamton and is moderated by Martin Raish. Subscribe by sending the E-mail message: SUBSCRIBE BI-L *your name*. Address to: LISTSERV@bingvmb.cc.binghamton.edu.

CIRCPLUS is an electronic discussion group devoted to library circulation and access services such as collection maintenance. Subscribe by E-mail to: LISTSERV@idbsu.idbsu.edu.

Awareness, Communication, and Action: The Shelving and Handling Workshop Series at the New York Public Library

Cynthia Frame, Union Theological Seminary,
New York, New York

It is ironic that the very act of handling a book contributes to its degradation. Yet handling is inevitable in a library with over 6 million volumes and 31 million nonbook materials, used by over 1 million people a year. While it is hardly possible to train such a large number of patrons, it is possible to improve handling practices among the library staff who regularly service the collection.

At the Research Libraries of the New York Public Library (NYPL), we solved the quandary of shelving and handling training for 155 staff from 30 diverse and specialized collections by focusing on individualized meetings. Instead of asking staff to come to us, we went to them. We presented workshops within the collection areas in which staff shelved and retrieved materials. We discussed preservation issues specifically relevant to both the collections and the people who serviced them.

As Mellon Intern for Preservation Administration, I chaired the committee that developed the Shelving and Handling Workshop series in 1993. Within the five-member task force, there was a good understanding of the individuals who service the collection, the institution and its history, and preservation.[1] These are the steps we took to develop the workshop series:

1. The Shelving and Handling Workshop Committee met for initial planning meetings.
2. The library's assistant directors sent out letters of support to divisions.
3. Members of the committee conducted two sessions with division supervisors in which the supervisors described the preservation issues as they saw them.

4. Members of the committee met individually with division representatives to review what the workshop would entail for their divisions and to find out what they specifically wanted covered.

5. The Shelving and Handling Workshop series was conducted over a six-month period.

With so many people involved, the library was immersed in preservation discussions and awareness.

PLANNING AND ADMINISTRATIVE SUPPORT

The initial planning meetings shaped the workshop series. Three committee members had many years of experience at NYPL and talked about preservation problems they had witnessed over the years. We then brainstormed about how preservation training might be most effective as we considered the practical issues that were raised. The method for the workshop series was developed, and the ''Care and Handling of Library Material Guidelines'' handout was designed.

To gain administrative backing the committee wrote to two assistant directors, explaining the project and asking for their support by writing a memo to division heads. We provided language they could adopt. In the memo, one assistant director wrote, ''These workshops are critical to the preservation program at NYPL. I strongly encourage you to support this effort.'' The letters of support were sent to the 30 divisions, which spread over four building locations: the annex, Lincoln Center, Schomburg Center, and the central Research Library. Some of the major divisions are General Research, Science and Technology, Periodicals, Economics and Public Affairs, and Slavonic/Baltic. Special collections are those such as the Dance Collection, Berg Collection of English and American Literature, and U.S. Local History and Genealogy. Other divisions are Copy Services, Cooperative Services, and Stack Maintenance and Delivery.

SUPERVISOR AND DIVISION INVOLVEMENT

The first meetings that introduced the Shelving and Handling Workshops to the supervisory staff were held in a conference room. Here the committee introduced the idea of the workshop series. We wanted feedback from supervisors about any and all preservation issues with which they were concerned. The meetings opened up a dialogue in which several issues were raised. The supervisors had challenging questions, pointed out issues we may have overlooked, and made numerous suggestions. They talked about the restraints on their divisions primarily in relation to staffing problems, specifically that they do not always have enough staff and that staff often work at low wages.

By soliciting supervisors' opinions, we gained their support and understanding of the goals of the workshop series. Some of the questions could have been the basis for longer discussions, such as: When is a book too deteriorated for public use? How do they tell readers not to deface books? What should they do with books too brittle to microfilm? Phase boxes add to the space problem because of their width—how should this be handled? Other questions allowed more definite responses, such as: How should book trucks be loaded? How does one recognize a storage problem? Still other questions made us aware that the Conservation Division had more work to do, such as improving the quality of the book trucks and continuing preservation training. Several suggestions were made for raising awareness among staff: Keep hands off printed plates; use proper methods for reaching items on high shelves; and have a good attitude!

The supervisor meetings gave us a strong base of information. We then went to division curators and representatives and explained how the workshops would be conducted and the outline we would follow. We asked what they wanted emphasized and what examples they felt we should use. Since we would be responding to questions from staff during the workshop, we wanted a clear understanding about the topics discussed.

Thanks to the sessions with the supervisors and the individual interviews with division heads, we were able to tailor each workshop both to the individual collections and to the individuals. Within the collection areas of each division, we specifically addressed points that had been suggested.

THE WORKSHOP SERIES

The Shelving and Handling Workshops were tailored to each division's needs because the duties of staff vary dramatically from one division to another. The staff in the Copy Services Division must know how to gingerly handle brittle books when photocopying. Map Division staff must regularly shelve and retrieve unwieldy oversize volumes. The staff from the Print Division must remove large and fragile prints from flat files. Other divisions regularly handle other types of media, such as photographs, record albums, videos, microforms, and archives.

The workshops were conducted by one or two committee members. With a committee of five people, this allowed us to share the responsibility and to ease potential scheduling conflicts. The workshops were held in the stacks and divisions to increase their relevance. In an article describing the workshop series, Robert DeCandido describes how our attitudes in conducting the workshops had to shift from one of teaching and training to one of learning and appreciating the excellent work of the staff. Many of the staff understand and seek out preservation techniques; the workshops brought together ideas, awareness, and methods for action.[2]

All the workshops began with a reflection of the value of the collections. I say *reflection* because everybody knows, in one way or another, how valuable the collections are. Articulating their value reminds us why the details of proper shelving and handling are so important. The staff's contributions were illuminating and inspiring and set the stage as to why we were taking their time to talk about preservation.

Next we discussed shelving and handling practices. While the discussion was based on a handout titled "Care and Handling of Library Material Guidelines," information provided by division representatives to emphasize or add certain issues or points was the focus. Examples of books, shelves, files, or whatever the staff regularly faced were used for demonstrating the problems, issues, and possible solutions.

The "Care and Handling of Library Material Guidelines" is a one-page handout with guidelines on the subjects of: Value of Material, Environment, Housekeeping, Shelving, Handling, Book Trucks, Damaged Books, and Disasters. The information included was gleaned from the practical experience of both the committee and the supervisors, so some of the comments are specific to NYPL. Here are a few of the more general guidelines:

- When reshelving, be sure that books are properly supported so that they stand upright.
- Do not leave books on the floor or edges of tables or hanging on a shelf where they may fall.
- Carefully replace books on the shelf; make room, loosening up the space first.
- Do not undertake any mending yourself.
- Do not speed, sit, or ride on the book truck.

The handout states, "When considering preservation, remember: Awareness, Communication, Action." The concepts of awareness, communication, and action provided the vehicle for making the guidelines work.

Awareness. Most of the library staff understand the value of the collections and the need to preserve them. By talking about preservation and reminding ourselves of the responsibility we have as caretakers of information, we can be more careful and thoughtful about how we handle material. Also, we sometimes become used to seeing the same things day after day and overlook or forget that they are preservation problems. By talking about basic preservation concerns, our awareness is raised so that we can once again recognize shelving and handling problems.

Communication. The next step after noticing a preservation problem is to talk to someone who can help solve it. For example, if a staff member notices that books are slumping on the shelves and in need of bookends, that person then needs to communicate with the person who can provide more bookends. Sometimes solving a problem not only involves immediate action; often it leads to larger issues or policy changes. For example, a preservation-aware person would realize that a candy wrapper lying on a book could attract bugs or damage the book and would dispose of it properly. A supervisor notified of this might realize it indicated sloppy housekeeping and could take action to remind staff not to eat in the stacks (which are closed at NYPL) and about related preservation issues.

Action. This is the important follow-through step: doing something about the situation. The activities that follow up the original point of concern have the potential of greatly improving the care and handling of the collections. In the bookend example, it is placing the bookends properly next to the books. Sometimes the action is as simple as discarding a piece of trash. The actions may make shelving and retrieving items easier through providing step stools, bookends, or adequate book trucks or may involve demonstrating for staff how to improve their shelving and handling techniques.

The Shelving and Handling Workshop series involved the substantial activity of the committee, the commitment of administrators, the support and input of supervisors, and the willingness of staff to participate. The series increased awareness and enthusiasm for dealing with the often complex and challenging preservation issues required of a collection as vast as that of the Research Libraries of the New York Public Library.

NOTES

1. The committee consisted of Robert DeCandido, Shelf and Binding Preparation Unit, Conservation Division; Leacy Pryor, Science and Technology Division; Stephan Saks, Stacks Maintenance and Delivery Division; Jackie Gold, Economics and Public Affairs Division; and Cynthia Frame, Mellon Intern, Conservation Division.

2. Robert DeCandido, "Out of the Question: R-E-S-P-E-C-T," *Conservation Administration News* no. 57 (April 1994): 13–14.

The World Wide Web as a Preservation Resource

*Michael G. Moore, University of Michigan
Health System, Ann Arbor, Michigan, and
Jeanne M. Drewes, Michigan State University,
East Lansing, Michigan*

Many people still think of preservation as dealing only with old books, a quaint but increasingly erroneous notion. Digital technology has been an integral part of preservation strategies at many institutions for some time, and the issue of digital archiving and retention of records has been a major topic of discussion in preservation circles for years. Preservation librarians continue to push for new and improved technologies in the areas of reformatting, electronic record keeping, and communications to improve the effectiveness of their efforts to preserve and provide access to library resources.

One of the most interesting uses of digital technology is the popularization of the Internet and, in particular, the World Wide Web, most often designated as "the Web." The explosion of interest in the Web is an amazing phenomenon in its own right, but of particular interest to preservation librarians is that the Web enables them to, in effect, become publishers of electronic information to an audience of their choosing. This opens up exciting possibilities for preservation education and outreach initiatives, preservation information dissemination, and professional collaboration, which were much more difficult a few short years ago.

The purpose of this case study is to focus on the qualities of a Web site that make it a dynamic and useful preservation resource for all who visit it. It will not include how you actually create Web-based information, or HTML (HyperText Markup Language). That subject goes well beyond the scope of this case study and since the Web is very fluid and undergoing constant change, any attempt to do so would certainly have a limited life span. There are many books available covering every Web topic which will help you learn how to create and publish information. Many publishers have adopted a system of targeting their books to different skill levels, with a chart printed in the lower left corner of the back cover, that may be helpful in finding the right book for you.

AUDIENCE

Implementing a Web site will be most successful if you devote time to planning before you actually begin the creative task. Careful planning and execution will result in a site that is more appealing and useful to users, and it is a critical factor in whether the site will be a success or failure.

To be effective, the information you provide should be directed specifically at an audience and often at several distinct audiences. Some examples of targeted content include:

- Information directed specifically at the patrons of your library. This may include preservation education and outreach materials, links to information provided by other libraries that enhance local information, and event calendars.
- Information for the preservation community at large. This might include general preservation information such as disaster plans, procedural documentation, and equipment evaluations.
- Information that is intended for use by other staff within your library. This might include organizational charts, telephone and contact information, procedural documentation, disaster plan, and internal databases.

Separating your Web information into distinct sites with specific audiences will also make it easier to manage the security of your information. If you plan to publish information that you don't want accessible to everyone, you will have to implement access restrictions. For example, if you plan to publish an internal database of library staff for disaster contacts, you would want to restrict access to library staff only. At the same time that you are determining which audiences you will be targeting and what content you will be providing, you should be considering what security restrictions will be required.

Another aspect of Web security has to do with the type of Web site you will be running. Currently, there are two types, Internet Web sites and Intranet Web sites. Internet Web sites are connected directly to the Internet and are usually visible to anyone who chooses to look, although they can be restricted in a number of ways. Depending on your target audience and the kind of information you are publishing, you may need to implement access restrictions for all or part of your Web site.

Intranets, on the other hand, are self-contained Web sites that are not accessible from the Internet, usually running over a local area network. Lack of access via the Internet does not mean you won't need to add security features, especially if you publish personnel information.

You should give special consideration to the content of your Web pages. There is a large amount of information available on preservation issues, so you can simply provide links to that information. Your own content should be specific to your particular library and your audience. Perhaps the best way to decide what should be on your Web pages is to think about what information you want to disseminate to what audience. Will patrons be interested in the organizational chart? Would care and handling tips for personal CD collections have appeal?

Patron information should be carefully written and organized so that it is easy to find from the institution's home page or from a search using one of the many Web spiders or Web robots. From the institution's home page create a preservation link; use wording that will attract attention. Perhaps "disaster help" would lead to another page with general information such as was done at the University of Oregon (http://libweb.uoregon.edu/uo/preservnhomepage.html). Another idea is to include preservation information in a FAQ, or frequently asked questions, section. There is a long-held idea that educating patrons to care for their own collections will improve their care of the library collections. The Web offers easy access to such information for the patron. Links can provide information without taking space on your computer system. For example, Kodak has a useful page on the care and handling of CDs (http://www.kodak.com:80/daiHome/techInfo/permanence7.shtml).

The same information you provide on bookmarks and flyers can also be available on the Web. An example of this is Indiana University's award-winning designs of bookmarks and posters that are mounted (http://www.indiana.edu/~libpres/materials.html). You should also consider placing your Web's URL (Universal Resource Locator) on printed materials such as bookmarks and handouts.

While care and handling information may be targeted at patrons, it will also be easily accessible to staff. Additional information targeted for staff might be procedures for sending materials to the commercial binding prep area, personnel and their responsibilities, and E-mail addresses and information on what to do in a disaster. If there is a new staff tutorial on the Web, that is a logical place for preservation care and handling tips as well. Perhaps you can add information to other division Web pages such as handling tips for shelvers and packaging tips for interlibrary loan. Often this information is already available in paper format, so it is easily transferable to Web pages. Information that might be injudicious to make available to the "world," such as disaster plans that have home phone numbers, can be mounted on an Intranet as mentioned. Information about the value of, and ordering procedures for, preservation supplies such as dust cloths, pink ties, nonacidic boxes, and folders might be incorporated into a general stock room page, or included on the preservation pages.

Another audience for Web preservation information is library colleagues. The sharing of information between librarians on a multitude of topics is part of library culture. Using the Web to mount information such as evaluation of equipment, procedures, and organizational charts means easier access. Walter Henry, the moderator for CoOL (http://palimpsest.stanford.edu/), a full-text database for conservators, provides links to a large variety of information including publications of the Commission on Preservation and Access, the Guild of Book Workers, and the International Council of Museums, to name a few. The preservation community embraces a large number of relevant subject areas, and the use of the Web can provide networking that makes that transfer of information easier and more readily available. Links from your home page to useful sites is helpful not only to patrons and staff but to others in the field as well. Yale University (http://www.library.yale.edu/pres/presyale.html) and Columbia University (http://www.columbia.edu/dlc/nysmbl) both have digital imaging projects— Yale digitizing microfilm and Columbia digitizing large maps. Both have mounted images and information about their projects on the Web. Many preservation departments already have Web pages; only a few have been included here. The list of possible information uses for the Web is nearly endless. Targeting your audience and trying to appeal to their interests will help keep your content relevant and interesting. After you have selected the topics and wording for your page, the next step is to consider your design.

DESIGN

Once you have compiled all of the information you plan to publish and have decided on the audience or audiences you are trying to reach, you must settle on a design for your Web site. One approach to Web page design, and there are many, is to use the magazine layout paradigm. When you read a magazine, there is a carefully constructed and consistent graphic design, an index, page numbers, sections, and so on. You quickly become accustomed to the magazine's layout and find it easy to navigate and find the articles that interest you. Books and magazines are one of the most efficient ways to distribute information, and everyone knows how to use them. Using a similar structural approach for your Web pages will have a big payoff in usability. Regardless of which approach you take, there are some general guidelines that you may want to keep in mind:

- *Create a consistent look for your pages* and apply that look to every page or at least to all pages that are related to one another or linked together. The design should be appealing to the eye but not overly busy. Judicious use of color and graphics is important, as people tend not to revisit visually boring pages.
- *Create a home page that is an index for the rest of the documents.* This page should be the ''home base'' for your Web users from which they can access all of the information. The weblike linking structure of the Web makes it possible to embed information in places that make it virtually impossible to find again if you can't remember how you got there in the first place. A home page that organizes the site and informs the user is extremely important.
- *Place a link to the home page on every page in your site.* Doing so will make it much easier for the user to return to a known starting point and branch to other locations. If the pages are meant to be viewed in a particular sequence, you should also consider

placing Next and Previous navigation buttons that permit the user to move through the page sequence.

- *Organize your pages in a logical fashion that makes sense to the targeted audience.* One mistake to avoid is to use structures that are known to you but may be completely lost on someone else. For example, using your library's organizational chart to structure a series of departmental Web pages for patrons would probably be very confusing for the user who didn't know that section X was a division of department Y, and so forth.

- *Create a searchable keyword index for your Web documents.* If your site is a large one, it can be very difficult to find a particular piece of information. Indexing your site is a convenience that your users will truly appreciate, especially if you place a link to the search dialogue on the index page of your site where it is easy to find. The downside to indexing is that it will probably require the assistance of your system administrator to implement and possibly some additional software. If you implement searching, be sure to have it set up to automatically reindex at regular intervals to keep the indexes current.

- *Include graphics in your pages.* Graphics lend a look of polish and quality to Web pages when used appropriately. One of the most beneficial uses of graphics is the clickable image map. Image maps allow you to create graphics that have links to other pages embedded in them. Instead of looking at line after line of text indexes, you can use an image map to show the choices in a colorful and visually pleasing manner. Here are a few rules of thumb to consider when using graphics in a Web page:

  1. *Graphics take much more time to load and view than text.* This is particularly important if your users have slow links to the network such as over a modem.

  2. *Don't overuse graphics.* Although graphics look nice, they usually add little value beyond aesthetics to the information. A good approach is to use graphics as headers to pages or image maps for navigational purposes and forego the temptation to include graphics as pure decoration.

  3. *Use transparent GIF images in your pages.* Transparent Graphics Interchange Formats allow the background to "pass through" a selected color of the image, usually the background color. The effect makes the graphic seem much more a part of the page and eliminates the colored border around the image.

  4. *Avoid combinations that are difficult to read.* In particular, you should avoid using textured backgrounds that contain large light to dark color variations, as the overlaid text will appear to fade in and out with the colors. If you use solid color backgrounds, you should choose a font color that has sufficient contrast to be readable, including the link colors.

- *Include links to relevant resources from other libraries and institutions.* Many of us keep hotlists of Web sites that we find valuable and visit on a regular basis. Adding those sites of general interest to your user audience can be a welcome convenience. If you are adding a large number of links, it's a good idea to group them in some logical fashion. It's also a good idea to only list those links that have some obvious value to the user. Since Web sites come and go at an alarming rate, you should occasionally check the links to make sure they still function.

- *Keep the focus on what you are trying to provide.* Avoid adding inappropriate or irrelevant information just because it is available. If you can't think of a good Web-oriented use for information, it's probably something you should not supply.

WEB TOOLS

The last aspect of design that you must consider is what tools you will use to create your Web documents. Choosing a publishing tool or tools may depend on what kind of information you are publishing and from what source it originated. If you are creating most of your information from scratch and not using a lot of preexisting documents, then you will probably want to use an HTML editor. Some of the newest HTML editors have limited WYSIWYG (what you see is what you get) capabilities and make it fairly easy to create basic Web documents. If you are converting preexisting paper documentation to Web documents, you will want to look at systems that translate word processing documents directly into HTML such as Microsoft FrontPage or HTML Transit. This is particularly important if these documents are long or updated frequently. If you are publishing information that originated in a database or spreadsheet and wish to keep it current, you should look into interfacing the database directly into your Web site, which will always provide the most up-to-date information. There are many other approaches to creating and maintaining Web-based information, so you should consider your alternatives before making a choice.

Using the Web for preservation is one way to help dispel the notion that preservation is only dealing with old books. It is also a new avenue to teach care and handling techniques, instruct other members of the staff about preservation procedures and policy, and share information with colleagues. The Web is a convenient solution for users, but it is not an easy solution to create; work is required to develop and craft a useful vehicle for the information you wish to display. The end result can be a new view of preservation to a much wider audience.

3

Evaluating Preservation Education Programs for Staff and Library Customers

The *Why* and *How* of Evaluating Education Initiatives

Merrily Smith, Library of Congress,
Washington, D.C.

Child! do not throw this book about;
Refrain from the unholy pleasure
Of cutting all the pictures out!
Preserve it as your chiefest treasure.

> —Hillaire Belloc (1870–1953),
> *A Bad Child's Book of Beasts* [1896], dedication

"I need your help!" she said urgently, an undertone of panic coming through the phone. It was a librarian calling from a university library in Georgia. "Somebody dumped a pound of bait crickets in our book return, and now they're all over the library. What should I do?" This was a challenging problem. What if the crickets, now running up and down the four stories of the library, were to start eating the glue in the books? What if they left frass all over the pages? What if they got comfortably reproductive and started to multiply into a major infestation?

It wasn't a pretty picture. If the crickets won, preservation would lose. Countless books might be damaged and become unusable and no longer accessible to the staff and users. As librarians, preservation professionals, and book lovers we are committed to keeping our collections available for as long as they may be needed. Although this might not mean "for the life of the Republic," as an archivist of the United States once said, it still means as long as possible.

This commitment to access is what Julie A. Page has coined "The Big Why" of preservation education. "Once we make it clear that access is the issue, then we can teach the users the 'hows' of caring for library materials."[1] Other chapters in this text provide useful information about how preservation education can be integrated into exhibits, bibliographic instruction, awareness-raising publications (bookmarks, posters, fact sheets), and other educational initiatives. In this chapter, the role of evaluation in staff and user education programs will be discussed.

Evaluation is a process we all practice, both consciously and unconsciously, in virtually every aspect of our daily lives. It is so familiar and ongoing we scarcely realize that most of our decisions and actions are based on a series of evaluative thought processes. Think of the children's story of Goldilocks and the three bears, for example. One bowl of porridge was too hot, another too cold, and only the third was just right. Papa Bear's bed was too hard, Mama Bear's was too soft, and Baby Bear's was just right. Education programs are evaluated in much the same way Goldilocks handled the porridge and the beds. She had specific and defined goals (she wanted to eat and nap), she systematically gathered valid data (she tasted each bowl of porridge and tried each bed), she analyzed and evaluated the data (too hot, too cold, just right; too hard, too soft, just right), and she took action based on her conclusions (she ate, she slept).

Evaluating staff and user education programs is more complex because it involves assessing other people. Nevertheless, your efforts can be just as successful as Goldilocks's evaluative escapade. All you need to do is answer five simple questions: *Who* are you evaluating? *What* are you evaluating? *When* do you design the evaluation process and actually evaluate? *Why* do you evaluate? and *How* do you evaluate?

WHO ARE YOU EVALUATING?

Madeleine Hunter, professor of education at UCLA and longtime teacher of teachers, once commented, "You can't say that you've taught until somebody has learned." Most of the time, the "somebody" she is talking about—the *who* in evaluation—is the intended audience of our educational efforts. We want to know whether or not the audience has learned from the instruction or information they have received. This audience is both large and diverse including, usually, the users of the library (children, high school or college students, researchers, recreational readers, street people), the library staff (catalogers, student workers, reference librarians, book repairers), and library supporters (school board, Friends group, library management team, general public).

The who in evaluation of staff and user education programs may not be limited to the intended audience, however. The who could also be *you*—the administrator of the program; the teacher of bibliographic instruction; or the designer and purveyor of posters, bookmarks, exhibits, conferences, and other public information.

Whatever the case, who you are evaluating must be considered and defined for every educational initiative, regardless of whether that initiative is presented as an information bite in "the teachable moment," as a series of instructional classes, or as a bookmark and poster campaign. If you know "Who's on first," as the famous comedians Abbott and Costello's baseball routine goes, it will be much easier to figure out "What's on second."

WHAT ARE YOU EVALUATING?

The purpose of this chapter is to provide the reader with information that can be used to improve the effectiveness of preservation education activities and programs for library staff and users. It is written in a style intended to be understandable, interesting, and easy to read. How will I or the editors of this book know whether the chapter has succeeded in meeting these goals? What could be evaluated that would provide the information needed to answer this question?

At a minimum, we could assess your reactions to the chapter. We could measure what you learned from it. We could also evaluate whether, having read the chapter, you made changes in the way you evaluate your staff and user education and training programs. These three elements—reaction, learning, and change in behavior—represent the first three levels of a four-level model for evaluation that was first proposed by Donald L. Kirkpatrick. The Kirkpatrick model is probably most frequently used in the education and training profession because it is comprehensive, simple, and widely applicable.

Kirkpatrick's fourth level of evaluation is *results*. Long-term results that might be hoped for from preservation education and training programs could be tangible, intangible, or both. For example, desired intangible results might include increased preservation awareness or increased respect for library materials. Tangible results could include such things as reduction in number of books mutilated or stolen, increased dollar support for preservation from nonprofit community sources, or reduced binding costs. Strictly from the standpoint of evaluation, it would be best to evaluate all training programs in terms of desired results. But numerous complicating factors make it nearly impossible to evaluate results for certain kinds of programs. For this reason, in the field of training as a whole, training directors tend to limit their evaluations to the first three elements in the Kirkpatrick model. I would also recommend this approach with staff and user education programs.

Reaction

The first level of evaluation, reaction, evaluates whether the participants were satisfied with the program—their happiness level. Did they like it? Did they think they learned something from it? How quickly were the preservation book-marks scooped up by library patrons? Did the demonstration of how to open a book hold the attention of the grade school children in the public library reading group? Did library staff members in the ''Care and Handling of Books'' seminar participate in the discussions? Were any compliments received about the instruc-tor or the presentation? Although useful information can be obtained from re-action evaluations, an important thing to remember is that they provide no information at all about whether any learning has taken place.

Learning

The second level of evaluation measures what participants actually learned as a result of the education or training initiative. Learning can be separated into two major components: knowledge and skills. Knowledge is what goes on in a person's head, what he or she understands intellectually. Skills, on the other hand, are what a person can actually do. For example, a library patron may never have seen a brittle book and may not know the proper way to handle it during use. With instruction, this person may learn to recognize the signs of brittleness in a book and develop an understanding of how pages should be turned or supported in the course of use. In that case, we can say he has acquired knowledge. He now knows how to identify and appropriately handle brittle paper. However, though understanding the matter in principle, he may not ac-tually be able to support and turn the pages properly. Thus, we say that he lacks the needed skills—that is, he can't do it. On the other hand, if he demonstrates at the end of the training session that he can support and turn brittle pages properly, one can say that he has learned a new skill.

Change in Behavior

The third level of Kirkpatrick's framework involves determining whether, and how, people actually apply the knowledge and skills they have learned. How much of what was learned in training will be transferred to the job? One hundred percent? 95 percent? 90 percent? After a consciousness-raising campaign, will more library patrons take the time to return their books to the circulation desk, or will they continue tossing them into the book return?

In education research, evaluation of training is generally equated with mea-suring degree of change, such as that described in the examples above. However, in applied situations characteristic of the business world, some believe evalua-tion should be used primarily to determine whether some targeted level of per-formance (attained skill level) had been achieved. For example, can the trained person now shelve a predetermined number of books per hour?

In the case of preservation, there are situations in which both change and attained level of skill might be evaluated, especially when the education and training programs are created to raise the knowledge and skill of staff who routinely handle library materials. For example, consider the case of an improvement project for a vast collection of manuscripts. The project requires that the manuscripts be removed from old enclosures (usually acidic boxes and folders) and placed in new ones (preservation-quality folders and boxes). In the process of this transfer, old fasteners are removed, surface dirt may be cleaned off, and bent corners or folded pages are opened. The work is carried out by technicians, under the general supervision of a conservator. In preparation to perform at an acceptable level, the technicians attend education and training sessions prior to starting the job.

Because this hypothetical collection is so large, the process of rehousing has to be both efficient and safe. The curators want to see the largest possible number of folders and boxes replaced every day. They also want the materials, many of which are brittle, to be handled in a manner that does not damage them. If the goal in training were only to increase efficiency, that is, rehouse materials more rapidly, posttraining evaluation of behavior would focus on measuring how much change in performance occurred as a result of the training. One could say, for example, as a measurement of this change this technician was able to rehouse three boxes per hour at the beginning of training and five boxes per hour by the end of training. The next goal would be to increase the number of boxes rehoused per given time period even more, and managers might provide incentive by awarding the technicians per-box bonuses.

In preservation, increasing the efficiency of an operation is only part of the goal. The quality of performance is also important. In our example, the safety of the materials as they are rehoused must also be part of the evaluation process. In large-scale preservation projects where the relationship between production quantity and time is very important to managers, it is tempting to focus training goals and evaluations entirely on that criterion. If training for a certain level and evaluation of quality (at a certain level) of performance is neglected, the quality of the work will not be there. Then, manuscripts may be damaged in handling, may wind up on the floor, or may protrude from folders when they are replaced in the new housing. Thus, the benefits of rehousing can be lost entirely if quality is sacrificed for quantity.

Evaluation of preservation education and training programs can provide a lot of useful information, regardless of the audience—staff, researchers, public library patrons, Friends. The best information, however, is produced when one approaches the evaluation process knowing exactly what is to be evaluated.

WHEN IS EVALUATION BENEFICIAL?

Evaluations are based on assessments of data that have been gathered from numerous sources. They are beneficial whenever some measure of the quality, content, effectiveness, or impact of education and training programs is needed. If done well, evaluation provides valid and reliable information on which to base future plans, decisions, or actions. The important point to consider is whether or not they will provide valid and reliable information.

Validity in this context refers to the accuracy or truth of the data. For example, suppose that a dozen people are looking at an exhibit on preservation. They are all given a piece of paper and asked to record their reactions to the display on a scale of 1 to 5, where 1 is "I disliked it intensely" and 5 is "I thought it was fabulous." They all give it a 5. The next day, the slips are given out again to the same number of people, and again every reaction is 5. The same thing happens on the third day with the same result. Thirty-six pieces of paper have now been collected. All of them have been filled out to say "I thought it was fabulous." As the designer and chief instigator of the exhibit, you are elated. But then, quite by accident, you learn that two members of your staff were at the exhibit on all three days, observing people's reactions to it, and every day, each had filled out an evaluation slip. And, oh yes, your mother-in-law, aunt, uncle, and four cousins had been among the individuals polled on the second day.

Conclusions based on these 36 evaluations could not be considered valid. Why not? The staff, having helped mount the exhibit, were probably biased and had also "stuffed the ballot box" by voting more than once. They had unfairly weighted their views in the results. Your family, in their close relationship to you, were also most likely biased, too; so without additional, unbiased, corroborating data, the results of these evaluations have to be considered invalid. In short, your evaluation was inadvertently useless.

Reliability refers to the consistency of measurement—the extent to which results would be the same if the evaluation were repeated. It's a good guess that everybody who filled out the original evaluation sheets for this exhibit would give the same response if asked to do so again. Even if the question were phrased a little differently, or the scale were changed, the end result would probably be the same, given the makeup of the group. Getting the same response again and again would make this evaluation effort highly reliable. Thus, in terms of reliability, your ballot was well planned, but it would still not be valid.

WHEN DO YOU DESIGN THE EVALUATION PROCESS?

When the idea was first suggested to have a preservation exhibit like the one just mentioned, many questions were probably raised before you actually decided to do it. For example, would people be interested in an exhibit? Do we have a place in the library to put it? Do we have the resources—time, money, and so forth—to support such a project?

This would be the appropriate time, right at the beginning, to ask yourself whether it would be a good idea to do some evaluations in connection with the exhibit. If the answer is yes, the design of a systematic evaluation plan should be incorporated into the overall planning process for the exhibit. Why? Because thinking about evaluation from the beginning makes it easier to get the most benefit from it. An evaluation plan should do the following:

1. *Define the purpose of the evaluation.* An evaluation plan should define the purposes of the evaluation, because if you haven't decided how the results will be used, the right questions will not be asked. For example, if the purpose of evaluating the exhibit is to determine viewer reaction to it, the questions and approach of the evaluation would be very different from that taken if the purpose is to determine whether the viewer's level of knowledge about preservation had been raised. An evaluation of viewer reaction would help you decide whether it would be a good idea to mount another preservation exhibit in the future. An evaluation of increased level of knowledge would provide you with information about how effectively the exhibit portrayed the information you wanted viewers to know.

2. *Identify audience for evaluation data.* The plan should also state the ultimate audience for the evaluation data—who's going to see the results. Most of the time, *you* will be the ultimate audience, that is, the exhibit designer, trainer, or person making decisions about the program content. However, the audience could also be a funding agency or upper management in the library.

3. *Identify issues to be addressed.* The specific issues to be addressed in the evaluation should be identified so appropriate questions can be formulated. For example, two issues that might be addressed in a bibliographic instruction session on the care and handling of books might be proper photocopying and appropriate handling during shelving or reading. Usually, more issues are identified than can be dealt with feasibly in a single evaluation, so priorities must be set. Presumably, these priorities will correspond to the priority you give the issues in the training session.

4. *Define criteria that limit the questions.* Once the issues to be evaluated have been identified, criteria must be defined that shape or limit the questions. For example, criteria for questions involving the appropriate handling when shelving might include: arrangement of books (in an upright position), packing of books (not too loosely or too tightly on the shelf), use of bookends (appropriate size and correctly placed at the end of a book row). Standards must also be set. For example, a standard that states what constitutes acceptable tightness/looseness of shelf packing would have to be defined. To evaluate whether a person is doing something correctly, you must be able to state precisely what is considered to be correct.

5. *Assess availability of resources.* One of the most important matters to address in the evaluation plan is the availability of the resources needed to carry out the evaluation. The greater the resources, the more complex an evaluation can be. It takes time to design an appropriate evaluation form. Depending on how the evaluation is to be carried out, more than one person may be required to administer the evaluation, tabulate the data, or both. If people, time, and money are limited, it will be necessary to design an evaluation in which the

methods of data collection are simple, and analysis is neither complicated nor time-consuming.

6. Decide what information will be gathered. When the key issues and questions have been defined, make decisions about exactly what information will be gathered to answer them. A common error in evaluation is to collect information that, while interesting, has no direct bearing on the questions to be answered. For example, if you are evaluating for reaction to a bibliographic instruction session, don't ask the participants questions like, "What did you learn today that you didn't expect to learn?" Although such a question yields information—maybe even interesting information—it doesn't focus directly on the issues that had previously been defined as most important (see number 3 above). Obtaining such "Gee-whiz!" information is wasteful of time and energy and also dilutes the focus of the evaluation. Be sure, too, that appropriate data collection procedures are used. For example, don't collect information about whether an individual has passive knowledge about how books should be shelved when what you really want to measure is whether he or she has the skill—as you have defined it (see number 4 above)—to shelve the books properly.

7. Outline how data will be analyzed and findings reported. The evaluation plan should also outline how the data are to be analyzed and the findings reported. For example, if your intention is to gather in-depth quantitative data, computer analysis might be better than hand collation. If no prior plan for computer analysis has been developed for such a circumstance, the evaluators may be inundated with data that are very difficult to analyze either efficiently or quickly.

In the same way that the method of analysis should be appropriate to the data, the reporting of the findings should be appropriate to the issues and audience defined at the outset. For example, if you are gathering reaction information about your exhibit strictly for your own in-house use, you may wish to present the results to your staff or colleagues informally, maybe orally reporting some percentages of like/dislike but not issuing a long, written report. If you're evaluating a program for the purpose of using the data in support of an effort to obtain a major grant, a written report well documented with information obtained through analysis of quantitative data might be most appropriate. If you are gathering data to support a report to upper management, the best approach would probably be to present your information either orally or written in brief to-the-point bullets. The details of how data analysis and reporting are handled will be governed by decisions you have made previously (see numbers 1, 2, and 5 above).

WHEN DO YOU EVALUATE?

The simple answer to this question is: All the time. The best time to evaluate is throughout the whole process of developing, conducting, and completing an education or training event. In the developmental stages of the program, your evaluation would consist of a preprogram assessment. Evaluation in the course of an event can be thought of as feedback. And when the event is over, evaluation provides information about how well the whole thing went.

Preprogram Assessment

A preprogram assessment of your intended audience can contribute considerably to the quality of the event you are planning. First, it helps you determine the *content* of the program. Second, it enables you to gather *case study* information that can be used in the training. Less tangible, but equally important, it allows you to begin developing a *relationship* with the participants. Following are some examples that illustrate the usefulness of information gathered in a preprogram assessment.

A seminar on the care and handling of books in general collections is in preparation. The first proposed group to attend the seminar is composed of library staff who are responsible for moving books from shelf to shelf, room to room, and floor to floor. Because this group handles and transports the books without opening them, the seminar *content* can be tailored to eliminate portions that discuss topics such as appropriate handling during photocopying, how to support the covers of a book when reading it, or how to turn pages in a brittle book.

Since a seminar of this kind generally doesn't have many participants (perhaps 12 to 15), it's a good idea to get in touch with those who will be attending. Talk to as many as you can—in person or over the telephone—before they come to the seminar. Ask about their jobs. Find out if they already have some knowledge of preservation. Ask what they are expecting from the seminar. You may be surprised at how much you can learn that will help you shape the seminar's final content and presentation.

In response to your inquiry about expectations, a person might say, "I have no expectations whatsoever. I'm only going because my supervisor said I had to." A knot begins to form in the pit of your stomach. "This person sounds like a problem," you think to yourself. "She doesn't really want to come." Perhaps so. See if you can find out why. Maybe she can't see any relationship between your seminar and what she's doing on the job. Maybe she's been shifting books around for 15 years. She may think that she already knows everything you're going to tell her and that she could probably teach the seminar herself—as well as you can, if not better.

Concern about relevance is typical in adult learners because their motivation to learn depends a lot on whether the anticipated content of a learning experience is something they think they need to know. Your task is to show them why they want to participate in the event you are planning. Do a little marketing for preservation. In the case of the 15-year veteran, you could talk to her about the purpose of the seminar, about your concern for the preservation of the books, and about why you are trying to encourage staff and users to handle them properly. Win converts by explaining the mission of preservation as a lifeline to the future. Win supporters by emphasizing the important role that all staff and users play in the library's preservation program. Win advocates by co-opting them into the cause. Let the veteran book handler know—with sincerity, because it's true—that her participation in the seminar will make it a better learning event. Everyone there, including you, will benefit from the knowledge she has gained from her years of experience handling the books.

As the above example implies, interaction with prospective "customers" will affect the content and focus of your seminar. By obtaining information from a number of individuals, you can formulate a general picture of what they know and what they don't know about preservation, about book-handling techniques, and even about the library. If it turns out that most of your prospective attendees already know some of the material you had intended to teach, you can adjust the seminar's content by making it more technical, by expanding the skill-based elements, by adding a topic or exercise that you had previously omitted for lack of time, and so forth. If some of them know the material already and some of them don't, discussion and exercises can be designed in a way that allows the experienced ones to mentor the novices.

Why is this kind of customizing important? Because every person with whom an instructor, librarian, or docent interacts will be starting from a different place on the learning curve, both in terms of knowledge and in terms of motivation to learn. To be effective, an educational effort—be it formal or informal—must take these individual differences into account. The idea is to engage the learner at a level where he or she is most challenged, most involved, and most interested. If the material is too easy, they lose interest; if it's too hard, they lose interest.

The task for the designer or teacher is to start at a level that participants can understand, then to challenge them so they will become engaged. It's sort of like fishing. You ask around and find out if the fish are on the bottom, under the rocks, or close to the surface. You know from your own experience (or because an old salt told you so), which bait or lure is most likely to draw the attention of the fish you want. You throw out your line, you wait for a strike, and then you set the hook.

Preassessments, regardless of how they are conducted, can also generate case study material (real issues that participants face) that can be discussed in the seminar. For example, proposed participants could be asked to make a short list of conditions in the library stacks that make their jobs easier or more difficult. These might include books jammed too tightly on the shelf, which makes them hard to remove; books lying on the floor, which causes people to trip over them and blocks the path for book trucks; or sprinkler system heads hanging down over the top shelves, which makes it almost impossible to retrieve the books safely. These examples of recognizable situations engage participants' interest and stimulate discussions that sometimes reveal useful information that would not otherwise have surfaced.

The third benefit of interacting with participants in a preassessment is that it initiates a relationship between the instructor and the participant. They are introduced to one another. They learn a little bit about each other through the give and take of conversation. Even this brief interaction reduces initial awkwardness and begins a positive feeling that carries over into the classroom, bringing benefits to both the participant and the instructor.

The use of a preassessment to gather information needn't be confined to personal contact. Surveys, polls, focus sessions, or other information-gathering methods are also used. In addition, preassessments need not be limited to formal instructional events. Depending on the event, you might gather your information from such diverse sources as the kids in the children's center in the public library, the students in the basement snack bar of the university library, or the person on the street. With a creative approach to preassessment, you can get your exhibits, public tours, and bibliographic instruction sessions off to the best possible start.

Feedback

Evaluation during training is conducted primarily as a feedback mechanism, both for instructors and trainees. Feedback during a learning event lets you know if the event is getting off track or going badly. Are immediate goals and objectives being met—children paying attention, people stopping to look at the exhibit, exercises being completed correctly? Is the pace and approach to teaching appropriate—talking too fast, lecturing too much, addressing the right level of learning? Are factors at work that impede learning—chairs too small for large adults, sun shining in somebody's eyes, room temperature too cold? By obtaining feedback in the midst of your program, you also have the opportunity to fix whatever might need fixing. Feedback is invaluable in this regard, particularly because it can be solicited at any point—5 minutes into a 10-minute talk, halfway through a one-day seminar, or once a week for a six-week exhibition. One word of caution, however: Don't seek feedback during an event if you aren't prepared to deal effectively with negative reactions.

How It Went

Evaluation is most commonly conducted immediately following the learning event. In fact, some instructors require the completion of evaluation forms before attendees ever leave the room. Almost all postevent evaluations of this type are designed to measure participant reaction to what went on (level 1 on the Kirkpatrick scale of evaluations). Reaction evaluations, as mentioned earlier, only provide information about how satisfied the participants are with the event. When the responses are tallied and analyzed, the event and its evaluation are finished until next time. If you want to evaluate what participants learned (level 2 on Kirkpatrick's scale) from having participated in your seminar or visited your exhibition, evaluation results will have more validity if an evaluation is conducted both before and after the event, then at intervals thereafter. The section on how to evaluate will deal with this kind of evaluation in a little more detail.

WHY DO YOU EVALUATE?

Evaluations of education and training activities are conducted for four basic reasons. Three of them pertain to the interests of instructors, program organizers, or researchers; and one pertains to the interests of the participants. Instructors, organizers, and researchers use evaluations to *obtain information*—Did the project reach the intended audience? Was information presented at the right level for participants? Were goals and objectives met? The answers to such questions will reveal the successes and failures, the merit of the effort.

The second reason evaluations are used in education and research is to *assist with decision making*—Would it be useful to repeat the class, or shall we simply leave it as a onetime program? If we keep it, should we expand it? Were the positive benefits sufficiently high to justify continuing the program? Does program content need modification? Should we get a different instructor next time? Should we initiate a preservation awareness campaign?

The third reason for conducting evaluations is to *increase understanding* of something or to rally support or opposition to a program. For example, Why don't more students attend bibliographic instruction classes? Why are staff and student workers shelving books improperly? What percentage of the library staff consider preservation an important component of the library's programs? What is the staff view about eating and drinking in the library? Does anybody but you understand why bait crickets in the book return are a preservation problem, not just another cute prank?

The fourth reason for conducting evaluations pertains to those who participate in educational events. For this group, evaluations are used by instructors and planners to *assist with learning*. Testing is the form such evaluations most commonly take. Although usually thought of as a method by which instructors can evaluate learning, testing also benefits the student by solidifying new learning. The tests don't have to be the "keep-your-eyes-on-your-own-paper" variety. They can take the form of a drill, or even a game. For example, Name the part of the book that I'm pointing to. Show me the gutter, the endcap, the fore-edge. Explain to the rest of the group what's wrong with the way these books are shelved. Show your neighbor the correct way to remove a book from a shelf. Of course, written tests can also be used. The point is to create an environment that helps drive the information home.

HOW DO YOU EVALUATE?

Many methods of evaluation are described at length in the measurement and evaluation literature. The three that I believe will be most helpful in evaluating preservation education programs for library staff and users are surveying, testing, and performance observation. *Surveying* is a method of measuring participant reaction to programs (the first level of Kirkpatrick's evaluation scale). *Testing* is the most common method for measuring learning (level 2), and *performance observation* is most frequently used to determine whether and how people actually apply to the job the knowledge and skills they learned in the classroom (level 3).

Surveying

If surveys are designed and conducted appropriately, they can be valid, reliable, and effective evaluation tools. Public opinion polls, product satisfaction assessments, and television-watching habits are types of surveys familiar to us all. Their purpose is to assess the current status of opinions, beliefs, and attitudes of a particular group. Written surveys of the type we would use in staff and user education programs serve the same function. They are most commonly used for preprogram assessments and postprogram reaction evaluations. A survey can also be used during a program as a method of obtaining feedback.

Because surveys measure how people think and feel, having the cooperation of the respondents is necessary to help ensure good results. Thus, before administering a survey, it's important to explain its purpose and what you intend to do with the information you gather. As part of these introductory remarks, encourage people to be honest in their responses; discuss the impact of inaccurate information on the usefulness of the survey (its validity).

Some people are nervous about committing their thoughts to paper because they worry that, somehow, what they say will come back to haunt them. Reassure them that the information they provide will be kept completely confidential—and make sure you make it so. Confidentiality can be achieved easily by not requiring a name on the questionnaire. It can also be achieved by assigning a number to each person's name, then identifying questionnaires only by the assigned number. You, as the instructor, would keep the key.

For best results when measuring attitudes and perceived knowledge, conduct your survey both before and after the event. By comparing preprogram results with reaction results, you will be able to draw conclusions about changes in these variables that resulted from the event. Without the two sets of data, the validity of your conclusions will be considerably reduced.

If the primary goal in conducting the survey is to gather information about participants' reactions to the program and its content, your needs will be met sufficiently if the questionnaire is administered only once, at the end of the event. If, on the other hand, your goal is to determine whether midcourse corrections are needed, surveying can take place at any time during an event.

Testing

As stated previously, testing is the most common method for measuring learning (level 2 on the Kirkpatrick scale). In staff and user education programs, we usually use tests to measure either what a person knows (this is achievement) or what he or she is able to do (skills). In an evaluative setting, these measurements are being taken to determine whether learning objectives have been met.

The most important thing to remember about tests is that they only measure current knowledge and performance. For example, suppose I conduct a two-hour seminar on the care and handling of bound materials and include some instruction on the parts of a book. At the end of the seminar, I give you a written test that asks you to identify the parts of a book. You identify them all without making a single mistake. Obviously, one of my learning objectives has been met—you now know the parts of a book like the alphabet. Thus, I conclude that you are a fabulous student and I am a wonderful teacher, not only because of your splendid performance but also because I infer that you will carry this important knowledge with you forever. Right? *Wrong!*

Wrong for two reasons. First, I didn't give you a test on the parts of a book at the beginning of the class, so I can't conclude that you learned them from me. You may have already known them when you walked through the door. The test, therefore, evaluates only what you know at that moment in time. It reveals nothing about your ability to learn or my ability to teach. Second, I can't infer that just because you demonstrate knowledge of the parts of the book at the end of my seminar, you will still be able to do so an hour later.

To draw such conclusions requires that a pretest be taken to establish a baseline knowledge level. If you didn't know the parts of the book at the beginning of my seminar, but did know them at the end, I could conclude that you had learned them in the class. Similarly, the only way to determine whether your knowledge is retained is to test you again later, and again later, and maybe even again still later.

Most knowledge, skills, and attitude testing in an educational environment is done with paper-and-pencil tests. However, as we become more enmeshed in the electronic environment, the ability to construct computer-based tests (with video displays and sound) will rapidly become part of the library community as well as the education community. Regardless of the medium, preparing a good question for a test is harder than it might seem at first glance. All you need to remember, though, is that the most important element of any test—one that is stressed repeatedly in the educational measurement and evaluation literature—is the preparation of questions that truly reflect whether your previously designed learning objectives have been met.

Another method of skill testing is performance testing. Although the skill could be verbal, analytical, or manual, our primary concern in staff and user education generally revolves around appropriate care and handling of materials. An example of a performance test that could be conducted at the conclusion of such a seminar would be to ask each participant to demonstrate how to remove a book from the shelf properly. School library users might be asked to demonstrate that they know how to open a book properly and support its covers adequately. Public library users might be asked to demonstrate their understanding by selecting books that can be photocopied safely, then to demonstrate their ability to handle them correctly while photocopying.

If library staff are being trained in collections maintenance procedures, they might be asked at the end of training to demonstrate their ability to rehouse manuscript materials correctly and efficiently. Any of these skills could be demonstrated either to the teacher or to another student while the teacher observes. Keep in mind, however, that, as before, such demonstrations show only what an individual is capable of doing at that moment in time and space. He or she is not providing information about prior knowledge, in-class learning, or skills that will be exported to the job.

A well-designed performance test has several characteristics of design and administration. For example, it should allow the participant to demonstrate as many skills as possible. Since the care and handling class would typically include methods for taking books off shelves, putting them back on, placing them onto or into transport carriers, straightening, shelf and bookend adjustment, and so forth, these should all be included in the test to the degree possible. This inclusiveness increases test validity and makes the exercise more meaningful for the participants.

As with all aspects of evaluation, a performance test must be well planned— the length of time required to carry it out, the materials that are needed (bookends, book trucks, books), and preparation of the participant. Make sure that your instructions for participants are complete, clear, and concise; and be sure to demonstrate exactly how you expect the skill you are observing to be practiced. Make the scene as real as possible by bringing to the test area any furniture or other items normally at the workplace.

All your effort will be wasted without clear guidelines by which you will judge the quality of each person's performance. Also, you must determine the distance between perfect, acceptable, and unacceptable. If the participant makes some mistakes, does he still pass? Which mistakes—either commissions or omissions—are great enough to be considered failure? How many little mistakes does it take to add up to a big mistake that causes a person to fail? Also, and perhaps most important, keep in mind that your goal is for people to pass the test. Therefore, unlike some written exams that may be testing knowledge, alertness, or attitude, it would be inappropriate and counterproductive to create trick situations or throw in distractions that are anomalous to the workplace.

Performance Observation

When it comes to preservation education for staff and users, the goal is that people will make some kind of connection between what they hear or see during the instruction class and what they will experience in the library. The purpose of performance observation, then, is to see if this connection has occurred. Not to be confused with performance testing, performance observation is specifically concerned with determining the degree to which training is transferred from the instructional setting into the workplace (level 3 on the Kirkpatrick scale).

The only way to know for sure whether behavior has changed is to measure it after training, when people are functioning again in their usual environment—as students, staff, or patrons. Evaluating change in behavior is considerably more difficult than evaluating either reaction or learning. First, one does not necessarily know how the person behaved before the training; and second, the evaluator may not have the opportunity to determine how they behave after the training. Just because students in a bibliographic instruction class come through performance testing with flying colors does not mean that they will continue to use correct procedures after leaving the instructional environment.

The trick to assessing accurately whether an education or training experience has resulted in behavior change requires two things: first, analysis of performance objectives prior to designing the training experience; second, access to trainees when they are functioning in their normal environment. To assess through observation, however, is very different from assessing through interviews, questionnaires, or tests. Gathering information through observation requires that the observer be able to see, hear, and record observations accurately. As an observer, he or she must be completely detached from the subject of observation, not participating in any way, simply recording information. Depending on the situation, the observer's role may vary from recording specific behaviors only (low inference observation) to recording observed behavior and making judgments about it (high inference observation). An in-between role is also possible in which the observer makes judgments, then records specific behaviors and the context that led to his or her conclusion.

The first step in undertaking behavior observation is to define precisely what is to be observed. To help yourself along with this, start out with a question. For example, are books being removed from shelves properly? This question would be broken into little components, such as, Are books being removed from the shelves by hooking a finger over the endcap and pulling? This approach is necessary because the observer cannot really observe everything that is happening. By deciding on specific behavior that will be observed, information can be recorded objectively and accurately.

The biggest limitation of behavioral observation lies with the person who is observing. Objective, unbiased, and accurate information can be hard to obtain because the observers always run the risk that they will influence the subjects, or will themselves introduce some bias into the data. Although bias is almost impossible to eliminate altogether, it can be limited. One way to do that is to choose observers very carefully. Also, avoid individuals who have personal involvement with the people under observation or who have opinions that might color what they observe. For example, don't ask a preservation professional to observe care and handling behavior. Bias can also be reduced if carefully trained observers compare observations with each other in similar and different situations. A third way to minimize bias is to use two observers in each setting.

Opinions in the literature differ about whether individuals under observation should be notified that they are going to be observed, and why. Some say that advance notification will ensure that observations aren't made at a time of crisis, when, for example, information obtained would not reflect normal working conditions. On the other hand, if participants realize they are being questioned or watched, argue other researchers, their behavior may be affected, which would skew the results. I usually just do my best in selecting an observer, then make every effort to help her "blend into the woodwork" so performance behavior doesn't change because of her presence.

Regardless of the decisions made about who will be chosen as an observer, several steps can be taken to ensure that your behavioral observation will be as successful as possible. Jack Phillips lists them succinctly in his book *Handbook of Training Evaluation and Measurement Methods*. The first step, as with observation testing, is to determine what behavior will be observed. Next, prepare the forms that the observers will use and select the observers. Then put together a schedule of observations. Work with the observers to train them in what to observe and what not to observe. Inform the participants of the upcoming observations if you have decided to do so. Last, conduct the observations and summarize the data.

If you are committed to measuring behavior change as accurately as possible, various unobtrusive measures can be taken without the subjects knowing that they were participating in a study. One of these measures is known as *physical traces*. Physical traces are data that are gathered by noticing physical changes that occur in something over time. Librarians collect such data constantly by examining circulation records to determine reading patterns of patrons. In the context of preservation, physical traces might be a long-term record of the number of rebinds sent to the library binder.

Another unobtrusive measure is *simple observation*. Simple unobtrusive observation occurs when the observer is not seen and the situation under observation is unaffected by his or her presence. For example, a simple observer could observe how books were being handled in a reading room by sitting in the reading room with his own stack of books and watching those around him. This method of observation is typical of police investigations when persistent theft or mutilation to collections has occurred.

Figure 3.1
Open-Ended Questions

1. Why did you read this chapter on evaluation? _____

_____

2. What was your overall reaction to the chapter? _____

_____

3. In this chapter, how could the section on "How to Evaluate" be improved? _____

_____

TYPES OF QUESTIONS

Open-Ended Questions

We are all familiar with open-ended questions because they can almost always be found on evaluation questionnaires. They are called open-ended because the respondent can write in any answer he or she wants (see Figure 3.1). Examples of open-ended questions include, "What is your reaction to this exhibit?" "How do you think this program could be improved?" and "What was your overall reaction to the program?" The answers generated by open-ended questions could vary in length from one or two cryptic words to paragraphs of cramped handwriting that spills over into the margins and onto the back of the sheet.

One benefit of the open-ended question is that it can yield a lot of useful information that one might never have thought to request. The information is also provided in a genuine way, which is why one can learn a lot from it, both directly and from reading between the lines. For example, note the order in which comments are made; the strongest emotion is most likely to appear first. Thus, if several people's first response to my question about their reaction to the exhibit is, "It was cold in the exhibit hall," I have learned two things. First, I have learned that the hall really was too cool—it wasn't just that this respondent was coming down with the flu. Second, I can further speculate that the temperature was uncomfortable enough that it may have affected people's other reactions to the exhibit.

Open-ended questions are also good sources for quotable quotes that can be incorporated into subsequent reports for exhibit sponsors, library administrators, or other interested parties. For example, "Overall, a very worthwhile and high-quality exhibit. I intend to bring my Boy Scout troop over to see it because we've been talking lately about civic responsibility and the exhibit will give me a good jumping off place for further discussion of values."

If you are evaluating viewer reaction for your own information, you might want to ask open-ended questions that address specific details. These might include questions such as: "How could accessibility to the exhibit be improved?'' ''What other locations would you recommend for exhibits of this kind?'' The responses to questions of this nature will help you determine whether to make logistic, technical, or presentation adjustments in your next exhibit.

If a funding agency or upper management will be getting results from the evaluation, you will also want to be sure to throw in a couple of questions that bring out those ''quotable quotes.'' Give people a chance to say, ''The exhibit was fabulous. It should have been done years ago. It ought to travel to every public library in the state.''

Open-ended questions also have some drawbacks. The most obvious is that compilation and analysis of the answers can be enormously time-consuming, especially if the number of responses is large. Another drawback is that responses to open-ended questions are highly subjective. Keep in mind the old adage, One man's trash is another man's treasure. A third drawback is that the answers to open-ended questions may not be very informative. For example, a response to the question, ''What is your reaction to this exhibit?'' could be something like, ''Really boring; the labels were bad, and I don't think we should have any more exhibits like this.''

At first glance, this answer seems to yield a lot of information. But a closer look reveals a different picture. No clue is given about what exactly was wrong with the exhibit. What made it so boring? Were the labels bad because the print was too small, the light too dim, the text confusing? Does ''any more exhibits like this'' mean exhibits on preservation, exhibits on preservation of library materials, exhibits mounted in cases instead of on walls? Anything is possible. The only clear message from the response is that the person answering the question liked neither the exhibit labels nor the exhibit as a whole.

Scaled Questions

Another type of question often found in survey and reaction questionnaires is the scaled question (see Figure 3.2). *Scale* in this context is used to mean a series of levels, values, or gradations that describe degrees of something. Scales are used extensively in questionnaires because they enable fairly accurate assessments of opinion or reaction. They are effective because they fit well with the way most of us categorize our strong beliefs or reactions: Are you mildly irritated, a little angry, very angry, or totally furious?

Of the scaled approaches that might be used in a questionnaire, the Likert scale or Likert-like scale is probably chosen most frequently. In its pure form, a Likert scale would present a statement that demonstrated a particular value or direction. For example, ''Preservation of library materials is very important.'' The respondent then agrees or disagrees according to one of five options: strongly agree, agree, neither agree nor disagree, disagree, strongly disagree. Likert-type scales use different responses, which gives them great flexibility because the scaled response can be customized to fit the nature of the question

Figure 3.2
Scaled Questions

Evaluating preservation education initiatives is	Critical	Very Important	Important	Somewhat Important	Very Unimportant
	_____	_____	_____	_____	_____
The chapter met my expectations	[1] Strongly Agree	[2] Agree	[3] Undecided	[4] Disagree	[5] Strongly Disagree
The writing style was <u>Engaging</u>	1 2	3 4	5 6	7	The writing style was <u>Boring</u>
The chapter held my interest.	Always _____	Mostly _____	Sometimes _____	Rarely _____	Never _____

Please check face that shows how you feel now that you've read this chapter.	☺	😐	☹

or statement. For example, if you are dealing with kids, you can make a reaction scale that ranges from Yuk! to Awesome!

Fixed Response Questions

Of the question types that could be chosen to test knowledge, the most useful for staff and user education programs are the so-called fixed-response items.

Figure 3.3
Multiple-Choice Questions

1. The first step in designing an evaluation process is to

    [   ] Identify the audience for evaluation data.

    [   ] Identify issues to be addressed.

    [   ] Define the purpose of the evaluation.

    [   ] Define criteria that limit questions.

2. The best time to evaluate preservation education programs for staff and users is

    A. All the time.

    B. Mid-way through the event.

    C. At the end of the event.

    D. None of the above.

These are questions for which only a limited number of response options are offered. They include multiple-choice, true-false, and matching questions. The advantages of fixed-response items are that they are applicable to just about any subject matter, they can be scored easily and accurately, and they are very efficient.

The most common type of fixed-response item is the multiple-choice question (see Figure 3.3). It consists of a *stem* followed by several options (usually four). Only one option completes the stem correctly. The others are written in a way that makes them look plausible and attractive to people who don't know the right answer. That's why they are known as *distracters*. Specialists in test design say that the single most important skill in constructing good multiple-choice questions is the ability to devise these delectable distracters. The task of the individual being tested is to discriminate among the alternatives and select the correct answer. Multiple-choice questions can be presented in numerous ways, two of which are illustrated in Figure 3.3.

The true-false question is another fixed-response item that can be used effectively in knowledge testing (see Figure 3.4). Its prime advantage is that many more questions can be answered in a given time period than the multiple-choice item allows. But to be effective, true-false questions must be carefully worded. It's all to easy to give clues to the answer, on the one hand, and to be very

Figure 3.4
True-False Questions

1. An evaluation question that asks whether a person learned a lot from an educational event is measuring learning, as defined by Kirkpatrick's second level of evaluation.

   ____ True   ____ False

2. An important goal in preprogram assessment is to develop a relationship with participants.

   ____ Yes   ____ No

unclear, on the other. To write these questions well, avoid using a disproportionate number of either true statements or false statements, avoid trick statements, avoid excessive use of negative words and phrases, and avoid complicated sentences filled with difficult words. Also, be sure to construct the test so the method for giving a response is as simple as possible.

Matching items are a good test of knowledge, because they require the association of two things in the learner's mind. They are very good for "who, what, when, where" situations and particularly good for linking words with images. They are most useful for testing memory, not understanding. Two particular drawbacks are that it's easy to include clues to the correct answer and completing the question is relatively time-consuming. I like to use matching exercises to test knowledge of parts of the book. To ensure the best construction for these items, be sure to arrange items and options systematically, keep all items and options for one question on the same page, and don't ask that more than 10 to 15 items be matched.

As has been suggested, if you want to get good answers, you have to write good questions—regardless of their type or purpose. Lest you feel discouraged, let me assure you that writing good questions is not easy. To do so requires knowledge of the subject matter, sufficient time, and a good bit of creativity. Some people have a knack for it; others achieve proficiency only with considerable practice and feedback. However, anyone can learn to write good questions, and that ability can be developed by following a few simple guidelines.

Good Questions

A good question has a number of characteristics. First, the question is clear; every person reading it will interpret it exactly the same way. For example, "What was your reaction to the bibliographic instruction session?" could leave the responder wondering whether you are asking about reaction to the content, the instruction, or the teaching environment of the session. Clarity is also lost when jargon and vague or ambiguous words are used. For some people, it would still be confusing to hear a question like, "What URL would bring up the preservation education home page?" or "What browser gives the best image of the page?" *Best* is a vague term that leaves a lot to individual taste. Some of our other favorite vague terms include *usually* and *sometimes*.

A second characteristic of a good question is that it focuses on a single idea. If two concepts are combined in one question, the respondent might be in a position where he would answer each part differently. For example, consider the statement, "The preservation exhibit contained too much on vandalism and not enough on brittle paper." Your respondents could agree with the first part (too much about vandalism) and disagree with the second part (more on brittle paper). The problem can be avoided by splitting the question into two.

Good questions also elicit accurate responses. Sometimes questions are inadvertently written that call upon the respondent to provide information that may very well be inaccurate. For example, "During the past two months, how many grade school students asked preservation-related questions in the 'Young Reader' sessions you conducted?" A reliable answer to this question can't be counted on because a person can't always remember what happened several weeks ago. If a question of this sort is important to your information gathering, be sure to provide a "don't know" or "not sure" option for an answer.

A good question is also relevant. As stated previously, don't complicate your life and confuse your respondents by asking questions whose answers you don't really need. For example, if you have just spent an hour conducting a staff seminar on care and handling of bound volumes, don't ask participants whether they think the information you presented would be useful in the care and handling of magnetic media. They won't have thought about it, and they won't understand why you asked. Consequently, their answers are likely to be thoughtless and misleading.

Keep your questions simple. Like any kind of writing, the longer and more convoluted a question(s) (or sentence) is (are), the harder it is (they are) to understand, and the less willing respondents are to make an effort to understand it (them), which is logical, considering that people are usually eager, especially the younger ones, to get on with other things when they have finished a training event (or program), regardless of whether they enjoyed it or not. (*Phew!*) By writing simply stated questions, you provide an evaluation that is easy to understand and easy to answer. (*See what I mean?*)

In general, it's a good idea to avoid negative phraseology in evaluations. An example would be, "The practice session on handling books was not useful." People tend to read evaluation questions rapidly. The negative ("not") part of this sentence would be easy to overlook. If that were the case, the respondent could unintentionally give an answer that is the exact opposite of what she actually thought. On the other hand, some evaluators like to use negative phraseology occasionally. They throw negative statements of this kind into an evaluation to determine whether the respondents are really reading the questions or whether they are just selecting the same response for each question.

Finally, a good question is unbiased. It's easy to write questions whose wording encourages certain responses over others. For example, suppose I am in charge of the preservation program for a public library. I present a lecture to the staff on the causes of deterioration and suggest that the lights in all stack areas should be turned off when no one is in the area. An evaluation of that lecture might contain the question, "Do you agree or disagree with Merrily Smith's proposal that the lights should always be turned off when leaving the stacks?" Some responses may be based unconsciously on the respondent's reaction to me, rather than to my proposal about the lights. If they don't like me, they won't like the proposal either.

It's also easy to get biased data in an evaluation if the respondent thinks the answer he gives will make him look good. For example, if I am conducting a preseminar survey of library employees, one question I might ask is, "Do you ever drop books on the floor when you are retrieving materials for patrons?" Would you say yes to a questions like that? Being fully aware that dropping books on the floor is not looked upon with favor, most people would probably answer no regardless of the facts. It takes a lot of trust for a person to be honest in such a situation.

CONCLUSION

Evaluation is a process we all practice in virtually every aspect of our personal and professional lives. It is an important component of effective preservation education and training programs because it provides important information to both instructors and planners. Good evaluations show whether learning objectives were met, yield information about future program content, and provide data that can be used to garner support for further programs. They can be designed to measure participant reaction, learning (both knowledge and skills), and behavior change. Well-designed evaluations are easy to prepare if one always remains focused on who, what, when, how, and why to evaluate. If you can do that, then Goldilocks has nothing on you!

NOTE

1. Julie Page, "Selling Preservation: What to Say to the Customer" (presentation to the ALCTS/LIRT Program, ALA Annual Conference, Miami, FL, June 27, 1994). Audiotapes of the program are available from the American Library Association (ALA) (Tape no. 454).

REFERENCES

"Adult Learners, Learning and Public Libraries." *Library Trends* 31, no. 4 (Spring 1983): 513–686.
Anderson, S. B., and S. Ball. *The Profession and Practice of Program Evaluation*. San Francisco: Jossey-Bass, 1978.

Baldwin, T., and K. Ford. "Transfer of Training: A Review and Directions for Future Research." *Personnel Psychology* 41 (1988): 63–105.

Blank, E. W. *Handbook for Developing Competency-Based Training Programs.* Englewood Cliffs, NJ: Regents/Prentice-Hall, 1982.

Broad, M. L., and J. W. Newstrom. *Transfer of Training.* Reading, MA: Addison-Wesley, 1992.

Brookfield, S. D. *Understanding and Facilitating Adult Learning.* San Francisco: Jossey-Bass, 1986.

Burnbauer, H. "Evaluation Techniques That Work." In *More Evaluating Training Programs: A Collection of Articles From Training and Development Journal,* comp. D. L. Kirkpatrick. Alexandria, VA: American Society for Training and Development, 1987, pp. 190–192.

Dopyera, J. and L. Pitone. "Decision Points in Planning the Evaluation of Training." In *More Evaluating Training Programs: A Collection of Articles from Training and Development Journal,* comp. D. L. Kirkpatrick. Alexandria, VA: American Society for Training and Development, 1987, pp. 174–177.

Gaines, D., and J. Robinson. *Training for Impact.* San Francisco: Jossey-Bass, 1989.

Green, J. S., S. R. Grosswald, E. Suter, and D. B. Walthall III, eds. *Continuing Education for the Health Professions.* San Francisco: Jossey-Bass, 1984.

Hopkins, K. D., J. C. Stanley, and B. R. Hopkins. *Educational and Psychological Measurement and Evaluation.* 7th ed. Boston: Allyn and Bacon, 1990.

Joyce, B., and M. Weil. *Models of Teaching.* 4th ed. Boston: Allyn and Bacon, 1992.

Kirkpatrick, D. L. "Evaluating In-house Training Programs." In *More Evaluating Training Programs: A Collection of Articles from Training and Development Journal,* comp. D. L. Kirkpatrick. Alexandria, VA: American Society for Training and Development, 1987, pp. 17–19.

Kirkpatrick, D. L. "Four Steps to Measuring Training Effectiveness." *Personnel Administrator* (November 1983): 19–25.

Kirkpatrick, D. L. "Techniques for Evaluating Training Programs." In *More Evaluating Training Programs: A Collection of Articles from Training and Development Journal,* comp. D. L. Kirkpatrick. Alexandria, VA: American Society for Training and Development, 1987, pp. 4–16.

Kirkpatrick, D. L., comp. *Evaluating Training Programs: A Collection of Articles from the Journal of the American Society for Training and Development.* Madison, WI: American Society for Training and Development, 1975.

Kirkpatrick, D. L., comp. *More Evaluating Training Programs: A Collection of Articles from Training and Development Journal.* Alexandria, VA: American Society for Training and Development, 1987.

Knowles, M. *The Modern Practice of Adult Education.* rev. and updated. Englewood Cliffs, NJ: Prentice-Hall, 1980.

Levine, H. G., D. E. Moore, Jr., and F. C. Pennington. "Evaluating Continuing Education Activities and Outcomes." In *Continuing Education for the Health Professions,* ed. J. S. Green, S. J. Grosswald, E. Suter, and D. B. Walthall III. San Francisco: Jossey-Bass, 1984.

McMillan, J. H., and S. Schumacher. *Research in Education: A Conceptual Introduction.* 3rd ed. New York: HarperCollins, 1993.

Phillips, J. J. *Handbook of Training Evaluation and Measurement Methods.* 2nd ed. Houston, TX: Gulf Publishing Company, 1991.

Sackett, P. R., and E. J. Mullen. "Beyond Formal Experimental Design: Towards an Expanded View of the Training Evaluation Process." *Personnel Psychology* 46, no. 3 (Autumn 1993): 613–627.

Salinger, R. D., and B. S. Deming. "Practical Strategies for Evaluating Training." In *More Evaluating Training Programs: A Collection of Articles from Training and Development Journal*, comp. D. L. Kirkpatrick. Alexandria, VA: American Society for Training and Development, 1987, pp. 157–165.

Silberman, M. *Active Training: A Handbook of Techniques, Designs, Case Examples, and Tips*. New York, Toronto, and San Diego, CA: Lexington Books, D.C. Heath, and University Associates, 1990.

CASE STUDIES

Library Exhibits: Evaluation via Observation

Jeanne M. Drewes, Michigan State University,
East Lansing, Michigan

The educating of patrons in the proper use and handling of library materials has a long history. In reading Barbra Higginbotham's *Our Past Preserved: A History of American Library Preservation 1876–1910*, I was struck by the sameness of the past approaches to education with those in use today. While perhaps somewhat more admonishing in tone, the 1890s methods use similar vehicles: bookmarks with information on handling procedures, as well as staff speaking directly to patrons with cautionary comments.[1] The continuing efforts to educate patrons in the proper care and handling of materials seem to follow certain tracks. Passive outreach in the form of printed instructions on handouts and display cases or bulletin boards with graphic and printed messages are standard tracks. Designating a Preservation Awareness Week has become another method of drawing attention to the issue.

While there has been a history of educating the public in care of library materials, there have not been many instances of evaluation to determine the usefulness of such campaigns. Do libraries survey patrons to learn their impressions of displays? Do libraries assign student workers to observe patrons as they walk past displays to see whether or not anyone pauses to look, or to count how many patrons actually stop and read the displayed information? A query in 1994 on a heavily used preservation/conservation listserv regarding evaluation resulted in few replies with no responses from anyone actually conducting evaluation of current programs. In searching the library literature, there was nothing on evaluation of exhibits and displays, but a broader search of a wider variety of literature was more successful. Museums, whose heart and blood are exhibitions of one sort or another, provide interesting and useful information on the hows and whys of evaluating visual displays.[2]

However, a library's primary function is not one of display of information, as it is in a museum. In most cases the overseeing of the management, scheduling, and design of exhibits and displays is not the primary job for anyone; rather, it is an added task—perhaps for someone interested in visual art or someone whose close proximity to the display cases earns them the job. As one librarian commented when asked about evaluating displays, "Displays are such a small part of my job that I can hardly think about anything more than just getting them up on time." It is not practical for libraries to attempt to attain the same level of expertise as museums in evaluating such passive outreach methods. Large-scale sample surveys and pencil-and-paper tests of knowledge would be hard to do and quite possibly not worth the time, given that most library exhibits do not remain mounted for long periods of time. Knowing the number of viewers can give information that can be useful in evaluating exhibition space and the exhibit itself. Behavioral observation, while not yielding the highest information return, does provide a useful base of data for evaluation. It is simple to devise, requires limited amounts of time, and without disturbing patrons can provide data to assess the interest in an exhibit. From these data other conclusions may be drawn, such as the best location for displays and patterns of traffic. The following study was conducted to provide data from observations that could be used to assess both the value of a Preservation Awareness Week exhibit and the usefulness of the display cases.

OBSERVATIONS

Observations are an effective way to gather data on the behavior of your targeted group, in this case the people who have the opportunity to view an exhibit or display. The observer should choose a location where all people entering and exiting the targeted area can be viewed. The observer should refrain from speaking to anyone. The object is to remain as unobtrusive as possible so as not to influence the behavior of the targeted people. A clipboard with a sheet divided by time and by categories you wish to record will make tallying much easier. Leave plenty of space for tallying and have extra space to note any behavior you hadn't anticipated but that appears relevant. A watch with a large face is useful for accurate timing. Fifteen-minute segments provide enough time while segmenting enough that the numbers counted don't get unwieldy.

If observations are done for any length of time, a chair or place to sit is helpful. Make sure that you are not obstructing any of the cases that people may be inclined to view. Do not fix your gaze on any one display case, as that may influence the reaction of others. Make sure that others in the library know about the observation study so that they do not feel the need to question the observer. Think about what you want to know before you start and decide what behavior fits your criteria for tallying. For example, if you want to count the people who stop and look at a display separately from the people who only slow their walk but don't stop, make sure you have that clearly in your mind. If more than one person is doing the observation, be certain that everyone is tallying the same behaviors under the same categories in order to get an accurate count. Observations have potential as a student project for a number of courses such as psychology, library science, and sociology.

BACKGROUND

At the University of Michigan Libraries, there is a committee that schedules and mounts the exhibits in the main lobby. Interested staff serve and assist with displays when necessary. The preservation awareness exhibit is designed and mounted by the Preservation Department. In November 1994 the University of Michigan Libraries did their yearly Preservation Awareness Week with a host of activities and an exhibition in the display cases in the main lobby of Harlan Hatcher Graduate Library. In 1994 a variety of activities were planned. These included an open house at the Conservation Lab and a guest speaker, Lorraine Olley from Indiana University. In addition, a poster was designed and premiered during the week. While only a week was designated for the activities, the exhibition remained in the lobby area for a month. No evaluation of exhibitions in this space had been done before, according to the chair of the exhibits committee, so there were no previous data for comparison.

METHODOLOGY

During the week of November 7–11, 1994, Library Preservation Week, five observations were completed. The exhibition was mounted on the Thursday before the promotion week, and the observations actually began the following Sunday in order to tally a weekend day immediately after the exhibition was mounted. A tally form was created using segments of 15 minutes for each count. Anyone entering or exiting the lobby was counted, except readily identifiable employees of the library. The actual cases viewed were noted for the entire observation session.

In evaluating the exhibit, various times and days were used for observation to give a more accurate estimate of not only the traffic through the lobby but also the amount of interest in the exhibit. Monday, the first day of the promotion week and the day of the special guest lecture, two observations were carried out, both the hour before and the hour following the lecture. This may have skewed the results somewhat, given that six out of the total of eight persons, or 75 percent, looking at more than one case did so either before or after the lecture. The other observation times were in the early morning and late afternoon later in the week. The lowest numbers overall occurred in the early morning during the first hour the library was open. This time also had the fewest viewers of the cases. The behavior of those people looking at the display cases was noted, as well as a straight head count. Observation consisted of recording if people looked in more than one case, if they actually stopped to look, as opposed to glancing but not stopping. Table 3.1 shows the dates, times, and counts.

RESULTS

Out of the total 1,675 people walking through the lobby during the 300 minutes observed, 30, or 1.8 percent of the total number, looked at the exhibit. Eight, or less then half a percent (.0047) of the total number walking through looked at more than one case. Because no previous observation had been done, it is not possible to know if the subject matter of the display had an impact on the number of viewers or whether the viewing pattern was typical. Display Case I (see Figure 3.5), closest to the entrance gate, was looked at the shortest amount of time by any one patron. No one actually stopped to look; rather, they glanced while continuing to walk. It may be that patrons did not want to stop so close to the swinging security gate to view the display case, or it may be that since that display case had a poster with no graphics, just print, it did not catch their attention. The case (V) by the entrance to Technical Services was also not given more than a passing glance. The case beyond the stair and beside the Technical Services entrance door (case IV on floor plan) drew very little interest. In contrast, Display Cases II and III, and VII and VIII, which are also by the stairs but on the way to other public areas, had more concentrated viewing. People actually stopped and looked at these display cases. In every instance, if a person actually stopped to look at one case, they looked at another one (total of 8). Only on Monday, the day of the guest speaker, did anyone stop and look in all cases. These same people also attended the lecture.

CONCLUSION

So what was learned or can be surmised by this observation? Observations are meant only to record a particular behavior of people observed—in this case, whether or not people passing through the lobby stopped to look at, glanced at, or totally ignored the materials in the display cases. In this observation only 30 of the 1,675 or 1.8 percent of the people actually stopped or paused to look in the cases. Seventy-three percent of the 30 (22) glanced at the cases and did not stop walking through the lobby. These are the numbers, but an analysis of the observations also suggests other ideas about the space, arrangement, and design.

The cases are not particularly visible because they are set into the walls. In another setting, such as in a reading room, however, that might not be a deterrent. In a lobby, where there is nothing to hold a person in the area, the recessed cases may not be as noticeable. The lobby does not invite use beyond a path to somewhere else; there is no reason to linger. So high-traffic areas are not necessarily the best place for displays, especially for displays that try to teach. It

Table 3.1
Observation Data Chart

November 1994 DAY	TIME	People entering lobby	People looking at one case	People looking at more than one case
Sun. 6th	3:15-3:30pm	92	1	0
	3:30-3:45	86	4	0
	3:45-4	104	0	1
	4-4:15	120	1	0
Total	**60 min.**	**402**	**5**	**1**
Mon. 7th	11:40-11:55am	99	1	0
	11:55-12:10	133	2	1
	12:10-12:27	100	2	2
	12:27-12:40	60	0	0
Total	**60 min.**	**392**	**5**	**3**
Mon. 7th	2:05-2:20pm	125	3	0
	2:20-2:35	114	1	1
	2:35-2:50	102	0	1
	2:50-3:05	153	1	1
Total	**60 min.**	**494**	**5**	**3**
Wed. 9th	8:30-8:45am	22	0	0
	8:45-9	21	0	0
	9-9:15	30	0	0
	9:15-9:30	30	0	0
Total	**60 min.**	**103**	**0**	**0**
Thurs. 10th	5-5:15pm	62	1	0
	5:15-5:30	65	2	0
	5:30-5:45	80	0	0
	5:45-6	77	4	1
Total	**60 min.**	**284**	**7**	**1**
TOTALS	**300 min.**	**1675**	**22**	**8**

Figure 3.5
Floor Plan of Lobby Display Cases

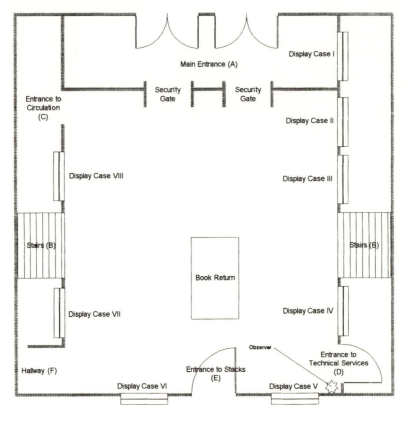

may be that space close to the information or circulation desk, where patrons might have to wait and could use their wait time to look at an exhibit, would be a more effective location than in an entrance. The few people who did linger in the lobby appeared to be waiting for someone and did tend to look at the display cases. This suggested that if someone was not just walking through, they might be more inclined to view the displays.

Large displays with graphics are more likely to catch people's eye. The less words and the larger the visual, the easier to see and register a meaning when walking past. The display cases beside the stairs, the traffic pattern for most of the people entering the lobby, had the most visual displays and also were viewed most frequently. Another behavior observed was that if someone was looking in a display case, a person passing by was more likely to look in as well. With recessed display cases, something to catch the attention and draw the viewer into the cases would probably increase the number of viewers; perhaps a mannequin positioned looking into one of the display cases.

Doing periodic observations and including surveys or interviews can provide information about the types of exhibits that elicit positive responses. It may not in fact be cost-effective to produce displays in the way that libraries commonly do. There does not seem to be any information about what the actual cost is to design and mount exhibits, either in time or supplies. Given that libraries are being asked to do more with less, the cost-effectiveness of many services is being examined, and exhibits and displays need to be analyzed for effectiveness as well. It may be that the displays and exhibits as passive information distribution vehicles are working, but only more evaluation of the behavior of passersby and viewers can verify that as true.

NOTES

1. Barbra Buckner Higginbotham, *Our Past Preserved: A History of American Library Preservation 1876–1910* (Boston: G. K. Hall, 1990), p. 43.

2. M. B. Alt and K. M. Shaw, ''Characteristics of Ideal Museum Exhibits,'' *British Journal of Psychology* 75, pt. 2 (1984): 25–36.

Tracking Book Damage

Patricia E. Palmer, Virginia Commonwealth University, Richmond, Virginia

User education has been incorporated into preservation programs across the country on the premise that much of the damage by library users occurs as a result of ignorance. A common method of education used by many types of libraries is to provide bookmarks, plastic bags, posters, and table tents with printed messages to remind users of simple actions that can help reduce damage to library materials. In the case of the plastic bag, the item itself can "preserve materials" when offered to patrons to protect library materials from wet weather. An expected outcome of such education strategies is a reduction in damage to library materials, but it is difficult to evaluate the effect of such strategies in terms of behavioral change in the library user community. While surveys might be done to elicit the response of users seeing preservation messages, this could not be linked to future behavioral patterns. However, tracking book damage prior to and following educational efforts can provide clues to education effectiveness and help to validate the effort.

One valuable source of data for the Virginia Commonwealth University (VCU) Preservation Program has been the Damage Assessment Report. While the primary purpose of the report is to document damage and assess fines for damage done, the reports also provide data on the rate and types of damage in a given time period.

The Circulation Department initiates the report when a damaged book is returned. Damage must be identified prior to discharge because once the item is discharged, the patron record attached to it is lost, and the damage fee cannot be collected. Damage is obvious if the book is wet or the cover is torn, but sometimes it is not so apparent. Circulation staff are instructed to examine every book, looking at both sides of the cover and flipping through the textblock before scanning it for discharge.

When it appears that the returned materials were damaged by the current patron, Circulation staff begin the report process. Patrons may bring existing damage to the Circulation staff's attention upon checkout, and the staff person will make a note on the date due slip so that that patron will not be held responsible when the materials are returned. Patrons are not held responsible for normal wear and tear on the books. Damaged books that come into the book repair unit from stacks maintenance staff who identify damage while sorting and shelving are not counted as part of the damage report process. The numbers thus reflect only current damage to circulating materials that are identified by Circulation staff upon return.

The Damage Assessment Report form is 8 ½" × 11", with the top third identifying the book, patron, charge date, and the circulation staff person completing the form. Once that portion of the form is completed, the book is discharged from the patron record and charged to the mutilation pseudopatron record. The rest of the form is used by the head of Preservation to describe the damage in detail along with the type of repair and charges. The completed form is returned with the damaged item to Circulation. The patron is notified of the fee and has 30 days to appeal in writing. Appeals are reviewed and forwarded by the head of Circulation to the Fines Appeal Board. Items remain charged to the mutilation pseudopatron during this period, and unless they are wet upon return, they are kept in the damaged condition. Wet books are dried and disinfected in Preservation prior to being sent back to Circulation with the form. After resolution either through payment or appeal, the book is returned to Preservation for treatment.

For the appeals process, it is very important to report in detail the type and extent of damage and, if irreparable, why. Damage is described in three parts starting with the textblock, then the case, and ending with the covering material. The most common types of damage are water damage and mutilation done by dogs. Nonwater stains, generally resulting from spills, make up the majority of the third category. Damage data from the reports are accumulated on a July–June fiscal year basis. Table 3.2 shows the complied data.

Maintaining this table proved valuable when the Friends of the Library were approached to financially assist the library in purchasing plastic bags early in 1992. I was able to show that the amount of water-damaged books had doubled that year and express my concern that it might be a trend. In a presentation to the Friends, I showed examples of water damage and why it was often irreparable or expensive and labor-intensive to treat. The Friends voted unanimously to fund the initial purchase of plastic bags, and the bags became available at the Circulation desk in the fall of 1992. In the fiscal year 1992–1993 water damage decreased by more than 50 percent from the previous year, from 51 to 23. The

Table 3.2
Damage Assessment Report Summary

Fiscal Year	Water Damage (Volumes)	Dog Damage (Volumes)	Stains, Spills, Stolen and/or Marked Pages (Volumes)
1990-91	23	9	5
1991-92	51	25	11
1992-93	23	7	0
1993-94	21	24	2
1994-95	9	8	1

next year, 1993–1994, water damage decreased slightly from 23 to 21, and in fiscal year 1994–1995, water damage decreased significantly from 21 to 9. In comparing the figures of 1990 and 1994, a 61 percent decrease was seen. I reported to the Friends of the Library that the number of water-damaged books being returned was decreasing. The reason for the decrease cannot be determined with any exactness; it may have been a result of the distribution of the plastic bags, or the weather conditions, or public awareness, or a combination of these, but the fact is the number decreased. Tracking damage will continue in the years ahead to determine if this downward trend continues, cycles, or stabilizes. It could be that the high number in 1991–1992 was simply an aberration. Analysis of the individual forms showed that there was not a large number of books damaged by one person, which might have had a confounding effect.

While the data were only informally gathered and cannot show causal effect, it was sufficient to convince the Friends to assist with funding the plastic bags. A sampling of all returned books might be done to ensure that a high percentage of damaged books are being identified during the check-in procedure. Such a sampling would help to validate the numbers, if it was found that most of the damaged materials are identified.

Tracking book damage is a worthwhile activity that can help justify providing plastic bags or organizing other preservation education efforts. While it may not be possible to obtain causal results given the number of variable factors that might influence damage levels, the collecting of data over long periods of time can be useful to suggest the impact of efforts and to argue for continued education programs targeted to reduce damage by library users.

Using Student Employees to Focus Preservation Awareness Campaigns

Diane Kaufman, Virginia Tech, Blacksburg, Virginia, and Jeanne M. Drewes, Michigan State University, East Lansing, Michigan

Program evaluation can be qualitative or quantitative. The two preceding case studies in this chapter are examples of quantitative methods. Both used numbers to evaluate programs. In the case of the Virginia Commonwealth University (VCU) study, Palmer used the numbers of water-damaged materials to suggest the value of offering plastic bags by showing a reduction in damaged materials after introduction of the bags; and in the case of the observation, numbers were used to evaluate the impact of a exhibit. While quantitative methods provide factual information based on raw data and percentages, they do not evaluate human reactions. Qualitative methods gather words and observations to evaluate rather than using numbers. Examples of the qualitative method include interviews, surveys with open-ended questions, and focus groups or open group discussions. Focus groups, like other qualitative methods, are used to obtain information from a predetermined and limited number of people. Like quantitative methods, there are three points in time when qualitative methods can be used for evaluation: before, during, and after a set time. The time might be for a program, such as a lecture series; for a visual display, such as an exhibit on care and handling; or simply for a determined period of time, such as before and after a class research assignment. The value of doing evaluation before a program or exhibit is that the information can inform the development and planning. Evaluation during a program allows changes based on audience perceptions, and evaluation done after a program is useful for future planning and for evaluating the success of the effort.

Since the 1930s, focus groups have been used in the private sector, mostly by product manufacturers and marketers, to determine the perceptions, feelings, and manner of thinking of consumers regarding products. Since the 1980s, service groups and nonprofits have used focus groups to determine perceptions, feelings, and manner of thinking of a select audience for services and/or opportunities.[1] Librarians have used focus group interviews for "determining users' expectation of a library, for evaluating the performance of the library and for identifying areas of user satisfaction and dissatisfaction."[2] If evaluation is only done using the perceptions of the library peer group, that is, librarians and support staff, then there is no sure way to translate those perceptions to the audience at large, that is, the library users. In order to know the perceptions of the library users, questions have to be asked of them. Focus groups are low cost and relatively easy to do and provide results very quickly. The disadvantage of focus groups is that you cannot easily generalize to the larger population. However, they do help to determine perceptions and allow a means to correct or reinforce assumptions about a particular audience.[3] A ready-made focus group for college and academic libraries is the population of student workers they employ.

FOCUS GROUP

At the Virginia Tech Libraries the student workers in the Preservation Department were enlisted to help with the design of the preservation awareness program. The student workers in the Preservation Department at Virginia Tech's Newman Library come from a variety of disciplines and are in various stages of completing their degrees. Some have worked for over a year, and others are new to the department. They became the focus group representing a cross section of the student population. The aim was to tap into the concerns and interests of a large part of that population on the assumption that those students bent on vandalizing the collection were in a minority and that the largest proportion of the students probably did damage out of ignorance or thoughtlessness. Of course the student workers had been educated to the library concerns, which made them not entirely a cross section of the general population; however, their general interests and attitudes were used to determine appropriate strategies for highlighting the problem of mutilation for the Preservation Awareness Week. The cost of replacing materials and the impact of those costs on the entire university became the theme, based on student suggestions. The students also helped to produce the posters. Two architecture students created the designs that were used for the posters displayed throughout the library and prominently in the lobby during the demonstrations of repairs. Large posters using photographs showing the damaged materials were also displayed in the lobby during that time.

The idea for using students for ideas came from six years of listening to the student workers' concerns. Tapping into their ideas and suggestions for the exhibit allowed them to be a part of the education of their peers. Preservation

Week was in October 1994; however, we began planning a year before. The "we" means the Preservation Department and all the student workers who are employed there. We collected various examples as the year progressed, but when we had to discard 40 books in one month, including a reserve item that was damaged beyond repair in the two hours it was out of the library, we realized how vulnerable our collection was. After analyzing the Reference Department's estimate for replacing these 40 books, we realized one of the students in our area could attend Virginia Tech one semester as an in-state student for the same cost. We had our first poster idea (see Figure 3.6). One of the students who was a business major suggested using a huge dollar sign on the top of the poster as an eye-catcher. Once the audience stopped long enough to look at the dollar sign, there was the good possibility they would read more.

Another student suggested contacting the student newspaper and asking that consideration be given to an article explaining the problems we face on a daily basis as well as the cost to students. *The Collegiate Times* agreed to a front-page article including a statement announcing the upcoming Preservation Week.

Out of one of our discussion sessions came the idea to compile some statistics for the public. We wanted the library users to be aware of our concerns. We used the accumulated records for interlibrary loan requests for copies of the mutilated pages needed for replacements. We were amazed to find that there was a pattern to damaged materials. Four areas of study were most often guilty of vandalism: education, engineering, psychology, and law. Some humor was included with the poster that read: "There is something very wrong when pages are removed from these particular journals or books: *Addictive Behavior, Crimes & Punishment, Delinquency, Urban Lawyer, Ethics in Engineering, The Journal of Business Ethics*, and *Robin Hood*." We used the environmental concerns of the students in a poster that advised that taking pages from *The Timber Producer* or *American Forests* was not a way to conserve trees.[4]

The Preservation Committee was impressed with the posters from the department. The committee helped set up tables in the lobby the week of the exhibit, and one of the committee members and the Preservation Department students showed the public how library materials were mended. The displays included books beyond repair, including the stack of 40 items discarded in one month and the posters designed by the students. We answered questions and gave suggestions to library users who had personal library collection problems. Had it not been for the student assistants helping focus on student concerns, the week would not have been as successful as it was. They were the key to providing insight into the largest single user group in the library, the students.

In future years, we may enlist the input of faculty to learn what their opinions and perceptions are about preservation in the library, or we may continue to use more of our student assistants in other departments or perhaps even visit a class that is studying focus groups as methodology in order to stay in touch with our user base. Our first experience with using a focus group gave us the inspiration to try it again.

Figure 3.6
Preservation Week Poster

 Guess how many students could **attend Virginia Tech full-time** on the amount of money spent to replace **lost, mishandled or damaged** library materials in just **one year?**

Support Library Preservation Week September 11-15, 1995

In just one month, the library discards **an average of 40 books** because of general **disregard for their preservation and upkeep.** To replace just these 40 books over a twelve-month period, university libraries spend a total equal to a **semester's cost for 12 in-state tuitions.** That adds up to over **$30,000 in just one year's time.** The fact is that this tremendous expense can be avoided if each of us did his or her part in **helping to preserve all library materials.** Just ask any library employee what you can do to help.

Preserving library materials helps make them available when you need them most

NOTES

1. Richard A. Kreuger, *Focus Groups: A Practical Guide for Applied Research*, 2nd ed. (Thousand Oaks, CA: Sage Publications, 1994), pp. 9–11.

2. Richard Widdows, Tia A. Hensler, and Marlaya H. Wyncott, "The Focus Group Interview: A Method for Assessing Users' Evaluation of Library Service," *College & Research Libraries* 52, no. 4 (July 1991): 352–359.

3. For more information about developing the use of focus groups, see both of the previously cited references and Mary Wagner and Suzanne Mahmoodi's *A Focus Group Interview Manual* (Chicago: American Library Association, 1993).

4. See also Diane Kaufman, "Building Preservation Awareness." *College & Research Libraries News* 56, no. 10 (November 1995): 707–708.

4

Preservation
Education in School
Libraries

Selling Preservation in School Libraries

Normandy Simons Helmer, University of Oregon, Eugene, Oregon

A NEW CONCEPT

Once upon a time, school districts had funding that enabled them to build and staff new libraries and media centers and keep them filled with new materials. For many, that time is now just a memory; for others, it has never been more than a fantasy.

Budgetary crises are a reality for cultural and educational institutions across the country, and cutbacks, even eliminations, in staffing and acquisitions have devastated many school libraries. Preservation, although not traditionally a concern in school libraries, is an important tool that can help stretch shrinking dollars further. Consider the model of proactive health care: If you eat right and exercise regularly, you are likely to feel better and live longer. If you can avoid damage to books, you can spend less on repair and replacement. That saves precious money, and it simply makes sense.

It is important to realize that preservation can be much more for school libraries than just a cost-saving measure. Preservation can be an active partner in education, supporting curricula in literacy, history, art, and citizenship. A good preservation program teaches values, not rules. A good preservation program teaches staff and patrons alike that library materials deserve respect and care and protection, not for what they cost but for what they give us and what they represent.

[It] seems to me that it is high time for the problems of preservation to become the concern of a broad cross-section of the library field, not just of those dedicated to preservation of research libraries and their contents.[1]

Preservation is a new concept for many school libraries, but one that Sullivan stressed in her article. In the past, it has not been considered necessary or worthy of expense in time or materials. Library schools have not included preservation education in their curriculum for school librarians, and it is seldom included as a component in literacy campaigns. But the financial status of school libraries and media centers is eroding, and they need to embrace preservation as a cost-containment measure and resource management tool. Successfully *selling* preservation in school libraries requires a complete understanding of the benefits of preservation and a willingness to infuse preservation into as many aspects of the school as possible.

AN OUNCE OF PREVENTION: WHERE TO BEGIN

The first person who has to learn good preservation technique is the school librarian. It is not enough to say that preservation is important; the librarian must also know what good preservation entails and must reliably make pro-preservation choices in behavior. Students are notoriously good at mimicry, and what they see the adult do is what they will learn. It does no good to lecture on proper book-handling methods if your real handling technique is damaging. The habitual handling methods must be appropriate, or formal training for others will not be effective. Always model good behavior (see Figure 4.1).

Since library schools have not traditionally included preservation in their curriculum, many school librarians have received no formal education in proper material handling. Good handling is a combination of common sense and understanding of the media. Understanding how books function is essential to explaining why some practices are safe and others injurious.

Once the school librarian has improved book-handling skills, it's time to begin converting the other adults who work in or use the library—aides, volunteers, teachers, and any occasional visitor such as a storyteller. Basic preservation education should be included in the library's adult orientation presentation. It is difficult but crucial to convey your watchfulness as a positive experience for others, not as the beginnings of a police state. Preservation should not reduce library use; it should reduce library *mis*use, and it needs all the allies it can attract along the way.

SELLING TO ADMINISTRATORS

School administrators also have to care about preservation. Administrators who understand the value of preservation will support it and attempt to find money for book repair supplies, facility maintenance, and preservation education

Figure 4.1
Basic Do's, Don'ts, and Why's

What to Do	Why
Make sure your hands are clean.	Dirt is hard to remove. An unattractive book seems less deserving of careful handling.
Gently set the crease in when you open the book.	The book will open better and the binding will remain flexible and not crack.
When reading aloud, cup the book in your palm instead of doubling back the cover.	The cover will stay attached to the book.
Use a slip of paper to mark a page.	Objects, such as pencils, are too bulky and split the binding. Paper clips tear the pages and rust. Folded page corners break off.
Mark a book and close it when you stop reading. Don't flop it face down or set an object on top of it.	The binding will crack, and the pages can become soiled.
Keep pens and markers away from books.	It's too easy to accidentally mark the book and very hard to remove the marks.
Take notes on paper instead of underlining or highlighting in a library book.	What is important to you may not be important to the next reader. It is very hard to read a book that someone else has marked up.
Keep books away from pets.	A puppy can destroy a book in just a few minutes. Some books are made with glues that have attractive scents, and even well-behaved dogs can forget their manners. Chewed books are hard to repair.
Keep books away from babies and toddlers. Give them durable board books instead.	Babies like to chew on books. Toddlers have difficulty turning pages without tearing them and will use any handy crayon or marker to adorn books. Make sure that small children have books strong enough to withstand their attention and make reading an altogether time.

Table 4.1 Continued

What to Do	Why
Leave repairs to the experts.	Adhesive tape turns brown with age and stains the paper. Libraries have special repair methods that last a long time. *Never* use duct tape or electrical tape or any other household materials to repair a library book. You will cause even more damage.
Use a photocopier when you want to keep something from a library book or magazine.	Tornout pages take time and money to replace, and the binding of the book is weakened by page loss. Often more pages are loosened and will fall out soon.
Keep food and drink away from books. This includes water and coffee cups.	Books are easily soiled and food residue attracts vermin.
Keep books dry in wet weather. Have a plastic bag available. Don't read library books in the bathtub.	Wet books quickly become mildewed. Mildew spreads through books like the plague and presents a serious health risk to some people.
Use bookends.	When books lean, their bindings are torqued and weakened. A book that is not shelved properly can pull itself out of its binding.
If books are too tall to stand upright, shelve them so their spine is down.	If the spine is shelved up, the textblock hangs unsupported and will tear itself out of the binding.
Photocopy gently. Don't smash the binding onto the glass.	A smashed binding can break, and the pages may fall out.
Keep books away from open windows and heaters.	Books are sensitive to humidity and heat and their life span can be shortened by exposure to environmental extremes.
To transport lots of books, use a box or book truck.	Books are heavy and often slippery. When they fall their bindings can break.
Grasp the book by the middle of the spine, not the head cap, to remove it from the shelf.	The headcap will tear and the spine may come off.

programs. Administrators, teachers, and parents share concern about the cost of education. It is important to make them all understand that preservation is a wise investment in education.

Preservation programs do not have to cost a lot of money. Training staff and patrons to handle with care is one of the most effective and least expensive components of a program. If you can reduce the amount of damage to materials, you can also reduce your repair and replacement costs. The more people who understand and practice that, the more noticeable the results. And when you have staff and parents and students who value preservation, you will see each one teach one. Your converts can initiate a grassroots campaign for preservation that is as effective and visible as antismoking campaigns.

Preservation programs can provide data to support facility maintenance and upgrades. School boards may not allocate money for a new roof just to keep a carpet dry. But when you tell them how much the value of the collection is, show them the cost of insuring the collection, and get estimates for abatement of the mildew caused by a leaking roof, you have hard facts. Preservation data can be useful ammunition when seeking support for funding. Preservation data can be elaborate and statistically significant, such as a carefully sampled survey of the condition of a collection. It can be as simple as a sheet of paper at the check-in desk, with tick marks showing how many books have been returned with visible damage. Automated catalogs can be used creatively to identify materials that are frequently checked out or to keep track of how many times a title has been repaired or replaced from wear. As with any data collection, it is important to decide exactly what questions you want your information to answer.

Preservation programs include disaster response plans. As with any disaster or contingency plan, people come first. After the safety of children and staff are assured, the preservation part of the plan can be initiated. These plans may help lower insurance costs, serve as starting points for resource sharing, and can provide the basic steps to protect and recover library collections and facilities in the event of a disaster.

School libraries face the same financial problems as other libraries. Materials have become more expensive to purchase, in part due to a significant increase in the cost of paper. Materials have become harder to replace because publishers can no longer afford to maintain the large inventories required by a full backlist. What schools have, they need to keep, and taking good care of the materials is one way to meet that need.

Preservation education makes good economic sense because it helps to stretch limited funds. Repair of damaged materials has its costs, too. Supplies, tools, and staff trained to perform the repairs can be expensive. If improved handling methods decrease the amount of repairs required, those financial resources can be used in other ways.

Preservation is a proactive approach that can raise your profile in the community and encourage participation and support from parents, volunteers, and benevolent organizations. People can see the difference made by effective preservation programs, as well as the difference their own contribution can make.

Preservation can also be a great fund-raising tool as the need and the results can be graphically demonstrated. Before and after examples are very arresting. Since almost everyone has books in their own home, they can relate to the need for book preservation more easily than, for example, nonmusicians can appreciate the cost of band uniforms. Preservation is so visual that it is easy to design eye-catching displays that almost speak for themselves (see Appendix 1). Additionally, book repair is an intrinsically fascinating process. People will be entranced if given the chance to see a bookbinder at work. Set up a repair work table in the lobby of a building or under a tent at a school fair.

SELLING TO STUDENTS

Selling preservation to schoolchildren is only a little different from selling it to adults. It is probably easier because children will buy into preservation on its emotional merits and are not particularly impressed by supporting statistical data. Kids can also relate on the level that they like to borrow books that look good. The first challenge is to instill a sense of the value of the material, which is the foundation for gentle treatment and protective behavior. The second is to systematically reinforce and renew that sense of value.

Children are easy to teach; the harder part is creating an environment that supports their continued participation in the protective role toward books. As with any kind of education, the most successful lessons are those that are reinforced at home. The children of reading parents are likely to be readers; so, too, are the children of careful book handlers more likely to show care. School library staff need to actively promote preservation to the parents of their young users, as well as to all the adults who work in or make use of the library.

Children need to learn that their actions have consequences and that the consequences will affect them. In Cheryl Holland's presentation on this subject during the 1994 American Library Association (ALA) conference in Miami,[2] she discussed her success at showing illustrations of poor book handling, as shown in library posters. This can present an interesting problem for preservation advocates in that the proliteracy and prolibrary children's graphics produced by ALA and others sometimes depict semihumorous situations in which books are being physically put at risk. Proliteracy messages show children climbing on piles of books, reading in the bathtub, reading to pets.

To reach out and grab hold of a group of students, the game show approach that Holland uses is very effective. To prepare your own presentation, you need to compile illustrations of good handling practices and bad. Sources of posters include ALA Graphics; catalogs of general library suppliers such as Demco, Brodart, and Gaylord; and Kidstamps, which specializes in rubber stamps and other graphic materials featuring popular fictional characters.[3] The recent compilation of Children's Book Week posters is also a useful resource.[4] As commercial poster series are often available for a limited time, you will need to watch for other sources and be prepared to tailor your presentations to materials that are available at the time.

Assemble your audience and talk about how books work and why gentle handling is necessary. Explain the basic book-handling rules. Then put out the posters and ask the students to point out "What's wrong (or right) with this picture?" A classic example is the magnificent *Lazy Lions* poster, which illustrates L in Graeme Base's *Animalia*. The lions are lying atop piles of books, and one has a book in its mouth. Children are quick to see this as an illustration of the rule that pets should be kept away from books. Another example Holland uses is the Muppet poster that shows Miss Piggy standing on books to reach a high shelf, which illustrates the rule that books are made to be read and should not be used in other ways. This approach is fun, engaging, visual, and therefore very effective. It also points out the importance of what kinds of posters are displayed around the school library. Take a look at what decorates the walls in your library, media center, or classroom and see what kind of preservation message is being sent.

Hold sessions that talk about bad book handling. Hold up a book that's been chewed by a dog, then ask the children, "What happened to this book?" Show them the damaged pictures and talk about what is missing and whether the book *feels* different when you read it because of the damage. Show what happens to a book that has gotten wet. Hold up a book that has been colored in or scribbled on and talk about how the actions of the drawer have changed the way you feel when you read the book. Graphic reinforcement of good handling techniques is important for students as well as for adults. Other ways to display preservation messages:

- Select commercially produced posters or hold design competitions among the students (or parents). Mount them in a rotating display within the library or in other areas of the school.

- Provide printed bookmarks (commercial designs or students' designs) when books are checked out. Or make your own, incorporating ideas such as those shown in Figure 4.2.

- Find a display case or an old aquarium and every month put in a new example of a book damaged by carelessness.

- If any prizes or motivational items are issued for reading programs, make sure that they illustrate good preservation and not book damage. A wonderful example of a propreservation message is Wallace Tripp's *Kind Rabbit* bookplate, which says: "Please be kind to this book. It is my friend."[5]

- To get additional suggestions for preservation graphics, place postings on Internet listservs that reach children's and young adults' librarians.

Make time for preservation orientations. Good times to do this are at the beginning of a story hour, during library tours, during library orientation sessions

Figure 4.2
Ideas for Bookmark Messages

Basic	! Wash your hands before handling books.
Book	! Keep pets and small children away from books.
Rules:	! Keep food and drink away from books.
	! Keep books out of the weather and out of the bathtub.
	! Books are for reading. Don't use them as furniture, ladders, or rain hats.

in classrooms, or when students receive a borrower's card. A presentation can be refined to take 5 to 10 minutes, and a handout can be used to help reinforce the training and to remind students and parents that the library does care about its books. You can also provide students with a more formal certificate to recognize that they have participated in learning about proper care and handling techniques (see Figure 4.3).

The preservation education efforts outlined above do not require a significant investment in materials or time, but if they are carefully maintained and repeated at every opportunity, they can convert enough students to gentle book handling to make a visible difference. Creativity and commitment, combined with a sense of humor, are the most important tools in effectively selling preservation to students. If you look hard enough, you can find a preservation angle in all kinds of activities.

SELLING TO TEACHERS

Schools have a second set of important adult models, teachers, who also need to understand and convey the value of preservation. Teachers are an essential element in the development of literacy, and if the teachers handle books gently, they can convey an appreciation for the physical elements of the book as well as for the language in it. Books are more than words, and teachers who understand that can teach it, too.

Many school districts have had to reduce or even eliminate library staff positions. Teaching staff, aides, and volunteers are absorbing the workload. In many cases, it is no longer possible for one person to have full responsibility for overseeing use of the collection, which increases the need to distribute the knowledge, respect, and responsibility for preservation among all users. Proper use will be more effective and long lasting if you can distribute the knowledge

Figure 4.3
Library Preservation Certificate of Instruction

LIBRARY PRESERVATION CERTIFICATE OF INSTRUCTION

Awarded to_____

For participation in an orientation program in the proper care and handling of library materials and school books.

Library preservation extends the life of the material and ensures its availability for others.

_____
(Grade)

_____
(Date)

_____
(Librarian)

_____
(Teacher)

_____
(Principal)

widely. If all teachers know how books should be handled, any teacher who happens to be in the library can intervene appropriately and prevent damage.

All teachers who use the library or media center should receive preservation orientation. They need to be able to reinforce the preservation message among their students by interceding when necessary, and they need to be able to model good handling techniques. Some subjects are very good candidates for partnership in preservation, and with a little creativity, teachers in other areas may be able to incorporate preservation lessons, also.

The most obvious partnerships are with art and reading. The creation of books, their typography and illustration, has obvious connections to an appreciation of the book as an object. Anyone who appreciates the labor that goes into a well-made book is likely to handle it with respect. Students who have made their own books can transfer their interest in book structure and design to commercially produced books. The development of movable type, commercial production of paper, and the invention of the photocopier have had enormous impacts on literacy, communication, and political events. Hands-on experience with the physical differences in production by the old-style versus the *new* technology can help underscore and enrich students' understanding of historical trends and watershed events.

Any activity that involves book-related arts should be considered part of a preservation program. Students can make their own books to use as journals in creative writing. Students can illustrate stories they write for English or for art classes. Students who work on yearbooks or school newspapers can gain an appreciation of typography, layout, and bookbinding. History classes may choose to experiment with papermaking, typography, or hand-copying or photocopying texts, in order to demonstrate the impact on literacy, communications, and politics engendered by the invention of commercial papermaking, Gutenberg's movable type, and the photocopier. If the school librarian can support all these aspects of book arts, a community of respectful book handlers can emerge.

PARENTAL PARTICIPATION

Parents are partners in education and should also be considered partners in preservation. Parents who volunteer or serve as aides should be given formal training in good book-handling practices. They may also serve effectively as liaisons to parent-teacher organizations, school booster groups, or benevolent associations. Meetings of these groups may provide good opportunities for distributing preservation information, including preservation concerns in book-related ventures or outright fund-raising for preservation and collection development. Offer them *adoption* opportunities, to replace or repair a worn set of encyclopedias or to buy a book-friendly flush-edge photocopier. Solicit donations to purchase book presses and tools to be used for book repairs as well as book arts activities.

Parents who do not participate directly in library activities also need to receive information about preservation. The financial justification is obvious—parents have to pay when their children damage books, so they should know how to avoid incurring fines. Parents should also understand that when they and their children take good care of school property, they stretch their education dollars further.

What can parents do at home to preserve books? Many things, most of which do not cost them anything except forethought. First, parents should come right out and tell their children that books are valuable and need to be handled carefully. It is very important to emphasize that books are treasures to be cherished, not fragile things better left untouched. Second, parents should be given instructions on how to provide a secure place for books. Bathrooms are not places where library books should be kept, nor are backyards, kitchens, or garages. Good places to keep books are places that are reliably dry and clean. Parents also need reminders that small children and pets can damage books, so a book-safe place is one where pets and toddlers are constantly monitored or not permitted.

Finally, parents need instructions on how library materials should be handled, such as how to open tightly bound books and safe ways to mark pages. Parents should also be given information about the fees charged for damaged or destroyed materials and what to do when damage does occur. (Answers to frequently asked questions: Return a damaged book to the library staff and show them the damage, so it can be fixed promptly. Keep a wet book in the freezer to prevent the growth of mold until the book can be returned.) Provide book-handling information for parents in a way that encourages them to introduce good practice in the home as well as in the library. Help parents build a home library; it is a foundation for literacy as well as for support of public and school libraries.

Parents who understand the value of preservation can become valuable library supporters. A Friends of the Library organization can be a great partner in supporting the library through directing its energies toward preservation or by involving parents interested in preservation in activities that provide wider support for the library. For a small fee, a library that puts plastic covers on the dust jackets of its own books may do the same for personal books with support from a parents' group. The group could also apply laminates to paperbacks purchased through a book fair. Encourage parents to give children covered books instead of toys as birthday presents. Another birthday tie-in that helps the library is the "Buy-a-Birthday-Book" campaign, in which parents give the library a book in honor of their child's birthday. This helps the library by building its collection and generally increasing its visibility and value to parents. To link the activity to preservation awareness, include a preservation bookmark or bookplate such as the *Kind Rabbit* plate mentioned earlier.

PRESERVATION AND THE FAMILY LIBRARY

- *Give children a place to keep their own books.* The best place is a low shelf easily monitored by parents while relaxing in the living room, using the table, or working in the kitchen. Books are thus an immediate choice when it's time for a new activity: Reading books is more prominently suggested than playing with toys.
- *Store art supplies and scissors away from the books.* This prevents use of library books for coloring or cutting of pages. Do not let kids use play dough or paint until all books are put out of harm's way.
- *If a child becomes rambunctious with books, intervene quickly* with a reminder about being gentle with books, with a gentle pat for the hurt book as well as one for the child.
- *Handle books gently when reading to the children.* Support the book on a lap or in a hand, open it carefully, and set in a gentle crease to assist in keeping it open. Turn pages by lifting, not dragging or using a damp finger.
- *Celebrate illustrators.* When reading aloud, include the name of the illustrator as well as the author and talk about how the pictures were made. (Collages by Eric Carle, Ezra Jack Keats, and Leo Lionni are particularly wonderful examples for this.) Compare different books by the same illustrator, which may be in the same style or very different. Collect images by favorite illustrators, which may be available as posters, T-shirts, rubber stamps, or buttons.
- *Buy hardcovers when possible.* It is more expensive, but the books are easier to handle and last much longer. Consider using clear plastic laminate (such as self-adhesive shelf liner) on paperbacks or on the dust jackets of hardcovers or purchase library-style polyester dust jacket covers.

- *Remove damaged books immediately.* When a page has a little rip, it is very tempting for a child to investigate and thus increase the tear. The sooner damaged books can be repaired, the better the chance to minimize damage. (Do not use regular adhesive tape, as it will turn yellow and stain pages as it ages. Look for archival book repair tape in library supply catalogs or art supply stores.) Use erasers to remove pencil marks.
- *Let children see adults enjoying their own books,* handling them carefully, and choosing to read instead of doing something else. Children can enjoy reading to each other and selecting books to be read to them.

The choices outlined above are not possible for all families. Many families do not have the luxury of bookshelves just for their children or can barely afford to set aside enough money to buy an occasional paperback. This should not be an obstacle to creating a book-friendly household. It costs nothing to set limits for children on where they may keep their books, whether borrowed or owned. All children can, and should, be taught to handle books gently. As an exercise in citizenship, children should value and care for the books owned by their school or public library as they do their own.

PRESERVATION, BOOK ARTS, AND LITERACY

Maurice Sendak wrote recalling his first book experience:

My sister bought me my first book, *The Prince and the Pauper.* A ritual began with that book which I recall very clearly. The first thing was to set it up on the table and stare at it for a long time. Not because I was impressed with Mark Twain; it was just such a beautiful object. Then came the smelling of it. I think the smelling of books began with *The Prince and the Pauper,* because it was printed on particularly fine paper, unlike the Disney books I had gotten previous to that, which were printed on very poor paper and smelled poor. *The Prince and the Pauper* smelled good and it also had a shiny cover, a laminated cover. I flipped over that. And it was very solid. I mean, it was bound very tightly. I remember trying to bite into it, which I don't imagine is what my sister intended when she bought the book for me. But the last thing I did with the book was to read it. It was all right. But I think it started then, a passion for books and bookmaking. I wanted to be an illustrator very early in my life; to be involved in books in some way—to make books. And the making of books, and the touching of books—there's so much more to a book than just the reading; there is a sensuousness. I've seen children touch books, fondle books, smell books, and it's all the reason in the world why books should be beautifully produced.[6]

One of the most important campaigns for any library is the support of literacy. For public libraries, encouraging literacy among adults is considered a service; for school libraries, literacy is part of the curriculum and therefore a highly visible and easily targeted commodity. It is curious that literacy campaigns often promote the text of a book without equally promoting the book as object.

Literacy campaigns usually stress writing and performance rather than book creation. The fact is that some people are visually oriented rather than auditorily oriented. They latch onto pictures instead of words. Paying attention to the design of a book, including the illustrators, can help visual people make connections to the words. Words can be easily reproduced, but illustrations cannot. This connection to the physical book is directly beneficial to preservation, where the language connection may not be. It is important, then, to include an appreciation of the physical book into any literacy effort. This is most effective among children because publishers generally put more effort into the appearance of a book designed for children. How can this happen?

Encourage children to make their own books. Ed Hutchins's "Guerrilla Bookmaking" in Chapter 5 presents a number of approaches for bookmaking with children. Chapbooks can be readily made by stapling or sewing sheets of folded paper together. The cover can be decorated by the student, and the pages can be used for writing or for further illustration and decoration. A person who has labored to make a book will naturally have more appreciation for the labor put into a commercial book by an illustrator or a publisher. Provide other opportunities to work with paper crafts. These can include origami, pop-ups, marbling, painting, or papermaking. Eric Carle has a video that beautifully conveys how he decorates paper and then uses it to create pictures to illustrate his books.[7]

Appendix 2, "Books for Children, Teachers, and Parents," provides a resource list for increasing children's awareness of the value of books, how they are made, and their proper care and handling. Libraries should inspire a passion for books. The process of bookmaking is fulfilling, rewarding, inspirational, and just great fun. The clever preservation advocate can turn bookmaking into yet another effective tool in the growing arsenal of preservation education approaches.

Figure 4.4 provides a checklist of what libraries can do to reinforce preservation. School libraries can reap as much benefit from preservation awareness as public and research libraries. Preservation can cut down on repair and replacement costs for materials, and advance planning may greatly reduce the overall damage in the event of a disaster. Most importantly, the preservation message can reach beyond the school and its families into the community, generating enthusiasm, understanding, and support for the library and for literacy. Use preservation awareness to protect your books, but use it also to protect your library.

Figure 4.4
Checklist: What Libraries Can Do to Reinforce Preservation

1. *Make sure all school staff and volunteers are trained in the proper handling* of library materials, and that they specifically understand that their actions, not just their words, will serve as models for the students.

2. *Keep all library materials in good repair,* and set up work flows to catch damaged books as they are returned.

3. *Formally train children in handling of books.* A quick session when the child receives the first library card might be an appropriate time. Give refresher sessions at least once a year to all classes during story hours or in classroom visits.

4. *Reinforce all preservation education with graphic materials* (posters, bookmarks, buttons, bookplates) and educational handouts and mailings for teachers and parents.

5. *Specifically reward the child's valuation of library materials.* Some methods: certificates of good handling, prizes, such as the bookplates "Please be kind to this book. It is my friend" offered by Kidstamps.

6. *Help children understand the labor that goes into producing a book.* Talk about the author and the illustrator, ask students if the illustrations remind them of another book, ask how they think the pictures were made. Hold activity sessions that let the children make their own books: albums, cards, simple pop-ups are all possibilities.

7. *Hold sessions that talk about bad book handling.* Show damaged books and talk about how a reader's experience of the book has been changed by the damage..

NOTES

1. Peggy Sullivan, "Preservation & Judgment," *School Library Journal* 36, no. 7 (July 1990): 16–17.

2. Cheryl Holland, "Selling Preservation: What to Say to the Customer" (presentation to the ALCTS/LIRT Program, ALA Annual Conference, Miami, FL, June 27, 1994). Audiotapes of the program are available from the American Library Association (ALA) (Tape no. 454).

3. ALA Graphics (1-800-545-2433); Demco (1-800-962-4463); Brodart (1-800-233-8959); Gaylord (1-800-634-6307); Kidstamps (1-800-727-5437).

4. *75 Years of Children's Book Week Posters* (New York: Alfred A. Knopf, 1994).

5. Available from Kidstamps #D4005, 40 for $4.95.

6. Maurice Sendak, interview by Virginia Haviland, "Questions to an Artist Who Is Also an Author," *Quarterly Journal of the Library of Congress* 28 (1971): 262–280.

7. Eric Carle, *Eric Carle, Picture Writer*, produced by Searchlight Films (New York: Philomel Books/Scholastic, 1993), VHS.

Teaching Preservation to Elementary School Children

Freida Hammett, Centerville Elementary School, Anderson, South Carolina

BACKGROUND

Students may come to the Centerville Elementary School media center to check out books at any time during the school day. In addition, each child is instructed in a class setting for 11 days in a row every nine weeks, in a 25-minute period each day. The majority of teachers are not involved in the curriculum that takes place in the media center. A preservation awareness component of the curriculum grew out of my own concern for the lack of care children exhibited for the books in the media center. It was developed for presentation to kindergarten students but has also been used with second graders.

MATERIALS

- A gallon jug one-half full of pennies (takes about 4,000).
- Damaged books (a variety of differently damaged books, choosing ones that have greatest appeal to children). Types of damage to include: fire (especially cigarette), water (especially mildew), tears, marks (preferably across illustrations), food damage, chew marks from animals, and missing barcodes.
- A metal trash can.

TECHNIQUE

With the above listed materials available, assemble the children and tell them that you want to show them a book that you think they will enjoy. Choose a book to read to them that does not show damage until you are into the book. For example, I have a copy of Eric Carle's *The Grouchy Ladybug* that has torn pages toward the end. When I get to the damaged part of the book that we are enjoying (*enjoying* is the key), I show them the problem. I then ask a question related to the situation such as, "I'm sorry. Do you know why I can't read any more of this story?" I then show the book and reiterate that pages are partly missing. Then I say, "Do you know what I am going to have to do? I am going to have to throw this book away!" I make a very sad face, and I proceed to throw the book in the trash can, making as loud a noise as possible. The students usually gasp! "Do you know how many pennies this book cost? Fifteen hundred pennies!" I then take the gallon jar and show them the pennies and pretend that it is the amount. I realize it is not precise, but I am after the effect. I let each child hold the jar. We discuss how many pennies it is in their terms—"a lot," "that many," and so on. I also let them know that their parents, friends, and relatives are the ones who supply the pennies for the books and that the books are not mine.

I proceed to go through each type of damaged book I have prepared ahead of time, discussing what caused it and how the children feel about books that were treated poorly. It furthers their involvement in the session by asking questions such as, "Do you like looking at a picture with all the scribbles on it?" Students make comments such as, "That makes me mad. I am sad. They shouldn't do that" after each presentation.

After this part of the preservation awareness unit, the time is usually up. I continue with other components at later times, including a lesson in proper page turning. The students then have to demonstrate this procedure correctly to me, and if successful, they are called to line up. I also do the same with carrying books properly. Petunia, Roger Duvoisin's goose from the book by the same title, can be used as a role model for carrying books.[1] We then pretend to take a trip home, have the book read to us, find a safe place to keep it, and then bring the book back and place it on the return cart.

For the final lesson in the preservation unit, the students are asked to illustrate on paper a good place to keep a book at home. We discuss some good places before they draw the pictures, such as a bookshelf or dresser. Pictures of good places that they have drawn are then displayed in the media center. We also review what are not good places like under a bed, in a toy box, or on top of the refrigerator!

FOLLOW-UP

Media center staff check each book for damage as it is returned and still manage to reshelve all 250 to 350 books each day. The staff emphasize with all students that we do not maintain that they do any damage. Students are reminded that they are responsible for looking at a book for damage and showing it to the staff before checking it out. After checkout they are to report damage to staff and pay for any damage that occurs while it is checked out to them. They are charged $.25 per page unless they can repair it themselves, with our supervision, as in the case of erasing pencil marks.

EVALUATION

The response of the students during the preservation unit has ranged from gasps in response to damaged materials to several students offering to donate their allowance for books. Although no official study of the condition of the media center books has been done, I find myself appalled at the condition in some of the other local media centers that I have visited. The staff attribute the good condition of our books to our education program and to the fact that we pull damaged books from circulation, thereby raising the quality standards for our students. In addition, we do not give damaged books to teachers for use in their classrooms.

In the future, it would be useful to have all new students at the school attend a library orientation and have this preservation lesson be a part of the session. We would also like to find ways to involve the teachers in reinforcing the preservation education sessions.

NOTE

1. Roger Duvoisin, *Petunia* (New York: Knopf, 1950). Petunia discovers a book in the meadow and thinks that she will be wise if she carries it with her. She carries it tucked under her wing and walks very straight and tall.

Instilling Preservation Awareness and Book Handling Skills

Andrea Rolich, University of Wisconsin, Madison, Wisconsin, and Evelyn Burke Weible, Northside Elementary School, Middleton, Wisconsin

When dealing with elementary school students, kindergarten through grade six, the librarian encounters a wide variety of book handling habits—from those of kindergartners who have not been exposed to many books at all, to those of children who have had the opportunity to interact with books since infancy. The goal of the librarian is to gauge the awareness level of each child and devise a means of imparting good book handling skills, so that library materials are well cared for and accessible to all who need them.

BACKGROUND

Northside Elementary School in suburban Middleton, Wisconsin, has 400 to 500 students from a variety of family backgrounds—farming, professional, blue collar. The library of approximately 13,000 volumes is a focal point of activity in the school. It is located in a central area without walls and is staffed by a full-time librarian and an aide. Students may visit the library at any time, with their teacher's permission. In addition, students in the primary grades (K–3) have one scheduled library session per week as a class, while older students' use is tied to classroom assignments, small group projects, and individual research. The librarian uses all contacts with the students as an opportunity to demonstrate and foster proper care of materials, through a combination of formal education sessions built into class library time and commonsense procedures and practices that have been integrated into library routines.

Retention policies have a direct impact on the library's preservation policies. While the collection includes reference materials and children's classics that are kept over the long term, the majority of materials belong to a well-balanced collection of currently popular children's literature. Since there is no attempt to create a comprehensive historical children's literature collection, older or less used materials are periodically weeded from the collection to make room for more popular titles.

Another factor bearing on preservation practices is the librarian's experience that unattractive or overly worn books are typically ignored by the children. Therefore, while books are kept in good condition as long as possible through careful handling, many eventually become tattered from repeated use. In an atmosphere where reading is encouraged by whatever means, the attractiveness factor is given full consideration, and when possible, damaged items are replaced rather than repaired. The librarian will even go so far as to purchase several copies of a popular title when she finds it remaindered, so that she will have fresh copies on hand. To help keep books intact and attractive, the dust jackets are retained along with a protective plastic cover.

METHODOLOGY

Preservation education begins at the kindergarten level, when students are introduced to the picture book collection. They are shown how to turn pages, not by lifting with their thumbs from the lower edge of the page near the binding (which is more likely to result in tearing) but by carefully lifting the lower right corner or fore-edge of each page, then using the palm of the hand to help turn the page.

Practice in turning pages is combined with practice in other skills that young students must master in the school environment. The librarian asks the children to sit in a circle so that they can be observed easily. They are given books and are asked to read for three minutes. As they are reading, the librarian notes their interaction with the books and encourages effective use of the material on a number of levels. Students are reminded of how to turn pages properly and are praised for doing so. If a child pages rapidly through a book and seems not to have given it much attention, the librarian may ask that he or she look through the book again and try to find a particular picture (e.g., the kitten eating). In this way, appreciation of the content of the book is combined with instruction in proper handling and with practice in focusing on a task for a given period of time.

To build an awareness of some of the misfortunes that can befall library materials, the librarian also maintains a small collection of damaged books and shows the children signs of careless and improper handling—torn, dirty, or scribbled pages or a dog's chew marks. The librarian tells students not to repair materials themselves but to report such damage so that it can be repaired properly with special materials. She virtually ensures that this will be done by reacting with understanding ("accidents can happen") and humor ("even Northside dogs love books!") rather than with strong disapproval. At the same time, the librarian reminds students to keep their library books in a place where they are protected and can be easily found when it is time to return them.

Library organization is also related to the care of and access to materials. When children reach the third grade, they are given formal instruction in use of the card and online catalogs. Even younger children are introduced to the special arrangement of their library as they are guided in finding all the works of a given author, in seeking other authors whose names begin with a particular letter of the alphabet, or in arranging titles in alphabetical order. In this way, students become aware that the library is an organized entity, rather than an assortment of books on shelves, and that each item should be in a particular place so that everyone will be able to find it. To prevent books from being misshelved or badly shelved, children are asked to place books that they have used on the tops of the shelving units. Students in the Library Helpers Club assist the librarian or an adult aide by reshelving volumes so that the spines are showing and books are not overcrowded on the shelves. This in turn allows volumes to be found and easily removed from the shelves without pulling and tearing the headcaps.

Students are also taught that large, heavy books must be given special treatment. Smaller children are told that such volumes can hurt their fingers or fall on their toes and that the books themselves can be damaged if they fall to the floor. The younger children are always given help in transferring big books to a table where they have proper support and can be used easily. Books that are large and heavy, especially if they are expensive to replace, cannot be checked out and must be used in the library.

Other large format books, which may not be particularly heavy but are oddly shaped or have fold-out or pop-up pages, can be checked out, but the librarian ties them closed with a crocheted length of brightly colored yarn to help prevent damage, should they be dropped. In general, children are encouraged to transport all books in bags or backpacks to minimize exposure to the elements and other potential hazards, and bags are given out in inclement weather. Magazines are placed into paper envelopes for protection at the time of checkout.

To help preclude such habits as turning down corners, placing the book face down, or using pencils or other damaging bulky items to hold the place, bookmarks are always available for the taking. Every effort is made to provide attractive bookmarks purchased from commercial sources or created in-house in connection with a special event. For example, when an author visits the school, he or she is asked for an autograph, which is then reproduced on bookmarks. Themes from special units of study are also reflected in the bookmarks.

Messages about proper care of library materials are taken more seriously and given greater meaning when students learn to enjoy many different aspects of the book. The librarian and teachers work together to cultivate appreciation of texts, illustrations, and the settings of books, while relating this to the authors' biographies and experiences. This is done through concentrated study of an Author of the Month or through comparison of many different illustrated versions of often retold tales such as *The Owl and the Pussycat*. Music classes echo favorite stories with programs of songs based on *Charlotte's Web, The Tale of Peter Rabbit*, and episodes from *Tom Sawyer* and *Huckleberry Finn*.

Appreciation is further enhanced through papermaking demonstrations by visiting artists or artists-in-residence at the school. In connection with the study of papermaking, a prominent industry in Wisconsin, students at the fourth-grade level also make their own paper. At the sixth-grade level, students write and illustrate their own books in an annual competition for in-house Newbery and Caldecott Awards. In this age of desktop publishing, students also create books to be used in the classroom or publish the products of their research projects. Some of these Northside School publications are bound and added to the library's circulating collections.

Preservation efforts also extend to computer equipment located in the library. Students are given formal training in its use and generally work with the online library catalog or with preloaded programs. An aide is responsible for preparing the machines for use so that students are not required to handle any discs. This particular library circulates no audio- or videotapes to students, though these are available for teachers.

The general environment of Northside School also reinforces proper care of the collections. The library itself is kept neat and clean, which encourages the students to take responsibility for helping to keep it that way. This may be due in part to the fact that there are no hidden spaces where messes would go unnoticed. The library is in a central location that is visible to passersby and the surrounding classrooms, and the librarian is able to see the entire area at a glance.

Students have a strong sense of identity with their school. Though there is fairly typical family mobility in the community, most of the students tend to remain in the school for a number of years. They attend after-school programs in the building; they use the playground equipment and playing fields on evenings and weekends; and many parents are actively involved in school affairs. The librarian believes that the students' general sense of pride in their school and their sense of ownership carry over to good treatment of library materials.

CONCLUSION/EVALUATION

The librarian has a good rapport with the students and a relaxed approach to guiding the children in both reading and care of library materials. Book handling is taught through modeled behavior and through sensible routines established and practiced in the library. Most formal instruction is presented to kindergarten through third grades, with informal reminders given as necessary to all grade levels. The children catch on quickly and treat materials well, and the librarian finds that she does not have to constantly verbalize her message to get the point across. School pride seems to motivate students to take care of their learning environment and its tools. In return, they receive praise for keeping their school, their library, and its materials in good condition.

Kids Don't Go for Dirty Books

*Sally H. Snyder and Doris Garlow, Nebraska
Library Commission, Lincoln, Nebraska*

The physical appearance of reading material affects its appeal, especially to children and young adults. Children can receive a negative message about the value of reading just from the presentation and condition of books at the library or school. In one case a mother was dismayed to hear her young daughter complain about having to spend time at her kindergarten's reading center. This was a surprise to the mother since whenever the two went shopping, they spent time looking at books. They often visited the public library, always staying there longer than planned, and frequently checked out children's books.

What was wrong with the books at the reading center? Nothing was wrong with the content of the books, some of which the family owned and read often. The problem was in the presentation. The covers were in need of repair, the colorful book jackets were missing, and many pages were worn and torn. In addition, the display shelf allowed only the top few inches of the books to be seen. The child was telling her mother those books were not worth the time to read.

When the children's collection is poorly weeded and unkempt, there is an unclear message to children about the importance of reading. This applies to classroom reading centers and to school and public libraries. Many schools do not have a book budget for classroom collections, and all must acknowledge

The authors originally published a shorter version of this case study in *Nebraska Library Association Quarterly* 20, no. 1 (Spring 1989): 27.

the need to stretch the book budget as far as possible. Books are expected to last through many loans. However, it is important to keep an eye on each book's condition and make retention decisions.

When weeding a library collection, one of the criteria for removing a book should be its physical condition. At this point, replacement becomes a selection issue. Consider it as you would any new book purchase; replace the worn and torn copy of a popular book. Is the book one you would like to have in your collection? While past popularity will play a role in considering replacement, try also to determine if you would rather purchase this book over another, or is a battered copy better than no copy? The reaction of the child to the reading center mentioned makes it clear the latter is not necessarily the case. If the book is worth having in the collection, that value should be reflected in the physical condition of the book and its cover or jacket.

A book in reasonable shape but missing a dust jacket can be made more appealing to children with a program sponsored by the school or public librarian or the classroom teacher. Children can create a dust jacket for a book they themselves have selected and read. Libraries using this type of program report an interest in the newly covered books, which they attribute to the colorful cover and the obvious interest another child has shown in the book.

The following guidelines provide an outline for libraries and media centers to sponsor a book cover project:

1. The books are placed in a box or special display on the counter with a sign advertising the project.

2. Instructions for the students are listed on a one-page handout next to the display. The instructions should include any requirements the library may have for the cover. For example, the title and author of the book must be written on the front cover.

3. The students select the book they want to read and for which they will design a new cover.

4. The student brings the book to the librarian or volunteer to have paper cut to fit the book. Alternately, paper could be cut ahead of time and attached to the book. Check with the local newspaper office or printers; they will often donate end rolls of paper.

5. Students are given a certain amount of time in which to complete the project.

6. Protect the new dust jacket with a clear plastic cover and attach it to the book as you would any dust jacket.

7. A sticker could be placed in the front of the book, indicating the name and grade level of the child and the date the cover was completed.

8. The project could include having the child write a book summary for the dust jacket as well.

9. A special display of the newly covered books gives participating students recognition and advertises the *new* books.

Teachers and media specialists unable to organize such a project might contact the art teacher at the middle school or high school. Their students could design new covers for books as an art project for the year.

In addition to giving some books new covers, do your best to display your library or classroom books in an appealing way. Interest is sparked by seeing the entire cover of the book. If possible, display them so children can see most, if not all, of the covers.

It is important to send a clear message to children if we want them to value books and reading, both for pleasure and for information. Take a few minutes to look, as a child would, around your reading area or library and see what messages are being sent.

Preservation on Career Day Reaches Young Minds

Patricia E. Palmer, Virginia Commonwealth
University, Richmond, Virginia

BACKGROUND

Career Day has been an annual event in the spring for all third through fifth graders at Johnson Elementary School in Richmond, Virginia. At this level, information is conveyed to create general awareness about future careers. Students spend a week learning about different careers and career resources. Careers represented are determined primarily by available adults, parents often being the first to be asked.

I heard about this opportunity when the Virginia Commonwealth University library director was contacted for librarians to participate in Career Day. Presenters would have about 15 to 20 minutes for a presentation to a class of around 20 students and present several successive sessions. Such a presentation interested me and provided an opportunity for user outreach in a new and different way.

After talking about my work responsibilities with the Career Day coordinator, she decided to list me as a *preservationist* rather than as a librarian. A reference librarian was also participating, and the coordinator did not want to cause any confusion.

PREPARATION

To prepare, I first thought about how children learn and what they would want to know. Having some experience being a Junior Girl Scout Leader with

10- to 12-year-old girls, I knew their attention spans were short but, when interested, very intense with lots of questions. To help direct and organize my presentation, I wrote a list of basic presentation skills:

1. Use simple words.
2. Speak in simple sentences.
3. Involve the audience.
4. Ask questions they can answer.
5. Walk into the group to show things.
6. Sit with them when sitting down, not in front of the room.
7. Keep moving.
8. Make them laugh.
9. Be flexible.
10. Have fun!

First I would cover the profession itself, how much people earn, what preservation people do all day, what levels of education people have, and where the opportunities are for employment.

Then I compiled a list of items that would be of interest to the students:

• A brittle book with a 1960 imprint (the rationale for this item was that while it was too old to be in their lifetime, perhaps they could relate the date to a parent's lifetime)
• Acidic ink transfer on paper, 1858 imprint
• Water damage to an art book
• Dog damage, both massive and minor
• A book in the process of being recased in its original cover
• A mutilated book with pictures missing and underlined text

In retrospect, I advise others to be careful to include examples that are as familiar to children as possible, such as old children's books or classic titles. Don't make the mistake I did of taking a Mary Cassatt art book that had the painting of *Reine Lefebvre Holding a Nude Baby* on the front. It was very embarrassing when one of the children asked why I was showing them pictures of naked people! It didn't occur to me ahead of time that they would focus on the picture rather than on the severely water-damaged book.

Finally, to keep it simple, my remarks would center around what it takes to keep library books in good condition so they can be read and to show examples of damage to make the children aware of what affects the readability of books. With so much to show and tell, there was no need for a canned speech. Knowing that kids of all ages love free stuff, bookmarks and plastic bags would be provided for everyone to take home.

PRESENTATION

On the day of the event, I placed posters around the room that were simple and brightly colored with messages such as:

Books and food don't mix.

Please protect your books from rain. Water damages books and causes mold and mildew.

Please don't mutilate or highlight in books.

Library books are a shared resource. Please pass them along unchanged.

On the blackboard, I wrote the word *PRESERVATION* so big and long it took up the whole board. This was to bring it to their attention and to help them learn the spelling. At the front of the room, I arranged two tables with my props. One table was labeled *Repair*, the other *Damage*. The repair table had the parts of a book displayed with tools used in book repair. Examples included before and after repairs of replaced pages, spines, and endsheets. The damage table had the wet art book with a plastic bag. Four 8 ½" × 11" cards described damage with large, easy-to-read type and bullets of information:

Wet
- Pages stick together
- Pages get wavy
- Mold grows
- Stains

Dogs
- Chew up books
- Don't know any better

Mean People
- Don't care who else uses the book
- Tear pages and pictures out of books on purpose
- Write in books

Chemistry
- Pages turn yellow
- Pages break when you turn them
- Pages get holes

When the bell rang, the school plaza came alive with hundreds of kids talking at once and racing toward doors. A few raced into my room, then a dozen, and as the bell rang again, a few more. They were all sitting down, a good sign. After introducing myself as a preservationist, a person who helps take care of library books, we looked at the word *preservation* on the board and talked about what it meant. Because they could relate to preservation of the environment and taking care of their favorite toys and family photographs, I told them people preserved lots of things, not just books, but the idea was the same. Then I talked about salary, education, and employment opportunities in Virginia.

Asking them questions about how they used library books helped them to understand my role in the library. Had they found some of the sample kinds of damage in the libraries they used? Had they or their dog done any damage to a library book? If so, what were the consequences?

Each presentation, six 15-minute sessions in two hours, was different. In one session, the children were interested only in how to choose a career. While emphasizing how important it was to choose something you genuinely enjoyed, I showed my examples and explained why preservation suited my interests— my love for books and reading and art; my ability to work with my hands; and my curiosity about why/how books and paper age. We talked about choices— making a little money at something you really like doing or making a lot of money at something you don't like doing; choosing work that is both stimulating and can provide a comfortable living; and choosing what a comfortable living is. The questions and comments were surprisingly good and led to interesting discussions.

In one class an early arrival came up to the repair table and began looking at the tools. She was my helper for that session and, with only a little prompting, held up the correct tool, and I discussed how it was used. Her classmates were impressed.

EVALUATION

In retrospect, I realize there was too much to cover in a short 15-minute session. I could have focused on just water and dog damage. Chemical damage was beyond their interest level, and after the first session, I deleted it from the presentation unless questions were asked. By having lots of props, I could let the audience direct the session, allowing whatever direction it took to be interesting. The plastic bags and bookmarks were all gone by the fourth session because the children would take extras for their friends and family.

The value of presenting information on care and handling of books to those of an impressionable age can be priceless if it is reinforced by school librarians, teachers, and family. All the children claimed to love books and liked seeing them undamaged and readable. Several questions related to the impact of technology on books; in particular, why repair a damaged book when it can be put on a computer? This led to more discussion on choices and the decision-making process used in preservation. I asked, "If you had a choice of fixing a really interesting book that you looked at only once in a while or another book that you needed to use a lot for your class, which one would you fix?" Answers varied, and this helped illustrate for them how there is no right answer, just different answers, for this kind of decision. While the age group may not be ready for the decision trees used in libraries, I think a simplified example is helpful to explain why certain books are treated and others are not.

There was no formal or individual evaluation prepared by the school. A thank-you letter from the coordinator was received along with four letters from children who attended my sessions. They thanked me for coming, said they enjoyed hearing me talk about restoring books, and hoped I would come back again. I hope to be invited back, and next time, I will take extra plastic bags and bookmarks and be careful of the pictures in the sample books!

Preservation of Materials in the Elementary School Media Center

Lynn E. Rohrs, Westwood Elementary School, Stillwater, Oklahoma

In light of major budget constraints facing public school library/media centers, an ongoing program of education and prevention has been initiated with students, parents, administrators, and staff. Through the establishment of standard policies regarding the loss of books, overdues, care of books, processing of new materials, and purchasing decisions, these groups within our school community are becoming partners in the appreciation and preservation of the media center collection.

BACKGROUND

Westwood Elementary School is located in a university community, with a student population of 500 in grades kindergarten through fifth. The families represent a wide range of socioeconomic levels, as well as a significant international population served by our English as a Second Language program. The media center provides both rigid and flexible scheduling, including weekly checkouts for each class as well as classes every other week for kindergarten through second grade and third through fifth grade. These half-hour classes focus on discussions of appropriate authors and illustrators, as well as genres, research, and library skills.

The media center collection, including print, audiovisual materials, and equipment, contains approximately 21,000 barcoded items. The center uses the Follett Unison automation program. Frequent changes in media center staff in recent years had resulted in an absence of a consistent policy in collection management. Inventories revealed a significant number of lost or missing books, as well as many examples of damaged and worn materials. But most importantly, the students showed a lack of concern and awareness in their handling of the collection.

Through discussions with the library assistant, teachers, and the principal, I set out to implement a plan to improve collection management policies and collection care education. As proposals were developed involving written communication to parents and teachers along with integration of care and handling instructions for students, official approval from the principal was obtained at each point.

The establishment of a collection management policy that will encourage users to be conscientious and responsible in their handling of materials was made easier by my being new in the position. I was able to generate support and enthusiasm for my suggestions by making the physical presentation of the collection more attractive and inviting. I sought out the advice and support of administration and frequently consulted with media center staff and teachers to better understand previous practices.

The implementation of the collection management policy has been gradual in order to foster and maintain schoolwide support. One focus is on educating and communicating with the students, parents, and teachers. The other focus is on new procedures for processing and managing the collection by staff members.

COMMUNICATING WITH THE STUDENTS, PARENTS, AND TEACHERS

Student education begins at their first visit to the media center, with introductions and a discussion of library policies and book care. In grades three through five, I use new books to demonstrate various aspects of book care and review the policy of using shelf markers to mark the location when searching for books on the shelves.[1] We discuss how books are organized on the shelf in preparation for learning how to use the new online catalog system. Students are given group instruction on the use of the automated search system and its connection to the organization of the shelves by specific call numbers.

Kindergarten through second graders are first introduced to the media center and staff, shown where the picture books are located, and hear stories about a favorite character (e.g., Clifford, Curious George). During the class, they learn how to locate and check out books.

During their next class session at the media center, the focus is on book care. Students discuss posters made in-house on book care that emphasize how to handle a book and safe places to keep a book away from young children, pets, food, and rain. The students are shown books that have been damaged by markers, coloring, water, and pets. They see that in many cases the book is unreadable and very unattractive. The students are asked to close their eyes and picture a safe place in their home to keep a library book. Then they watch a demonstration of proper ways to turn pages of a book to prevent tearing, as well as when to use a bookmark to save their place. Finally, the class watches a video or filmstrip story of their character and then makes bookmarks featuring a sketch of that character. These will be laminated and given to the students to use with their library books, reinforcing the book care principles.

At this time they are able to check out their first book for the year. Letters are sent home to parents of kindergartners and first graders to encourage parental support of these lessons. The letter includes the importance of reading to and with children and invites the parents to visit the media center and to check out books themselves. The following book care message is included:

This year your children will be checking out books from the Westwood media center. They will be learning to be responsible for these books and will begin to realize what it means to *share* library books.

During the first weeks of school, we will be discussing how to check out books and how to take care of books both at the media center and at home. Below are the main guidelines for taking care of books at home:

1. Find a special place at home to keep media center books so they won't be lost or damaged.

2. Be sure hands are clean before you read.

3. If your book is accidentally damaged (including torn pages), do not try to repair it at home. Bring it to the media center and we will fix it.

4. Return the book as soon as you finish reading it so that others may read it, too. As soon as you return yours, you may check out another one to share at home.

5. On rainy or wet days, have a plastic bag to use for carrying the book to and from school.

During the first few classes of the year, I point out new titles and series that have been bought for the collection, encouraging students to check them out. I remind them about proper book care and about returning books on time or renewing them. I also inform them that the average price of a new hardback book is about $16 and that the inventory completed over the summer indicated that about 350 books were missing without being checked out, and over 100 books were lost after being checked out. We do not charge fines but require that students with a lost book return a form signed by a parent before they check out another book. If the lost book is not found by the end of the year, they are sent a bill. Payment for lost books is encouraged but ultimately is voluntary.

One attempt to raise an awareness of the problem of missing books in a positive way is to publish an article each fall in the school newsletter that goes home to parents. Titled "We're Going on a Lost Book Hunt!" (a parody of *We're Going on a Bear Hunt*), the article includes all of the places that students have reported finding lost books in the past (see Figure 4.5). A natural tie-in for the hunt is in conjunction with National Children's Book Week in November. The Follett Unison program allows us to include titles, call numbers, and barcodes of missing books. Students who return a lost or long overdue book are rewarded with a piece of candy.

Figure 4.5
"We're Going on a Lost Book Hunt!"

We're going on a lost book hunt.
We're going to find a lot of them.
We're excited about our hunt!

Oh-oh! Where can they be?
Under the couch,
Behind the cushions,
On top of the dresser,
Under the bed,
Up on the refrigerator,
Behind the TV,
In with the other books,
Mixed up with the magazines,
Left in the car (on the seat, under the driver's side),
In the toy box,
At the bottom of the trunk,
At Grandma's house,
Under the laundry,
Left in day care,
Turned in to the public library or CML,
Left in the school desk (do we dare look?),
Under the dresser,
In my sister's (brother's) room,
Stuck in my backpack,
On the coffee table,
In a box or a bag or a sack,
At the back of the closet,
Under the shoes—clothes—toys—old school papers,
At my friend's house,
In the classroom with the teacher's books,
Up high on a shelf,
At home in the study.

On, yea, we found one!
Let's hurry and return it!

We'll put it in our backpack
And take it back to the library.
We'll put it in the book drop,
And be sure to tell the librarian.
She'll give us a piece of candy
For being such good book finders.

So let's go on a lost book hunt!

COLLECTION PROCESSING AND MANAGEMENT

Due to a significant cut in the media center budget as well as an increase in technology costs, a conscious decision to buy more paperback books, as opposed to hardcover, has been made to ensure that the collection will have copies of as many highly reviewed and popular titles as possible. While proper care of hardback books and the use of mylar jackets on dust covers have been emphasized, there has also been a need for the media center staff to explore various ways to protect paperback covers and extend the life of these books. Book tapes and clear adhesive covers have been utilized.[2] Such protective methods are reasonable in terms of cost and time and do not require extensive training to perform successfully.

The repair and maintenance of the collection is of great importance to school library staff. Trade-offs made due to time constraints, cost limits, and lack of trained repair staff often limit the use of accepted preservation repair techniques. Parent volunteers frequently provide the book processing and repair in a public school setting. Karen Williams, the former Westwood librarian, developed a preservation policy and trained media center staff and parent volunteers in care and handling and book repair. Her efforts created an atmosphere of increased awareness within the public school library community.[3]

The public school collection also needs to remain flexible and current, reflecting changes in school population, curriculum focus, and the publishing industry. It is important to maintain the quality of the collection through weeding obsolete, outdated, and worn-out materials. Students will be more likely to take care of books that are in good shape, as well as appealing in content. They will also feel that their patronage is considered important if they know the library media specialist listens to their requests and considers their academic and leisure reading needs.

Students appreciate the opportunity to contribute to the media center collection through the donation of their own books, as well as through purchase of new books. During the annual Parent-Teacher Association (PTA)–sponsored Book Fair, a variety of paperback and hardcover titles that are on the media center "wish list" are displayed. Students and parents are encouraged to consider buying a book for the collection, which is then book plated to acknowledge the donation. Students take special note of these books in the collection when they find them. The donated titles are listed in the next school newsletter. This donation program can be continued throughout the year, advertised by various slogans such as the Birthday Book Club.

CONCLUSION

Many of the policies discussed above do not have clearly measurable outcomes. By observing student behavior in general, we can ascertain that many seem to be using shelf markers more carefully. Students regularly point out a ripped page in a book and give it to us to repair, thus encouraging preventive maintenance. They point out in dismay a book damaged by scribbling or water. Although specific statistics have not been kept, the frequency of damaged books due to careless handling has declined. And students are heard correcting peers on the use of shelf markers. They also point out books that are out of order.

The overdue book policy has resulted in a definite and measurable drop in weekly overdues. Records show that the average number of overdues is 50 to 60 books, as opposed to previous totals of well over 100. Teachers comment that their students put pressure on each other to return overdues so that their class can earn a reward. The classes with no overdues vary from week to week, indicating that more than one particular teacher's diligence is at work. Students are now more apt to ask when their books are due or check to see what titles are on their record.

The Follett Unison program allows us to keep daily, monthly, and yearly collection statistics. Over time these records will indicate how the collection is being used, areas that need development, and numbers of lost and missing books. By checking out books to repair, statistics are kept on the number of repairs being made in a current year. We continue to experiment with preservation materials for paperbacks to determine which are the most cost-effective and long lasting.

Above all, the key to maintaining a successful collection management program is frequent and positive communication with all segments of the school community. If the students, faculty, parents, and staff see the school media center as *their* collection, they will become partners in its care, preservation, and development.

NOTES

1. Shelf markers are thin strips that are inserted in the location where a book is removed. They are used if a child intends to replace the book on the shelf. They can be made out of plastic or paint sticks or purchased from library supply catalogs.

2. Alternatives that seem to offer more protection than applying book tape on book cover edges include: Kapco® library products, such as Easy Cover® by Kent Adhesive Products Company; Vistaflex Laminate or Demco Repositionable Laminating Film by Demco; and comparable Highsmith book care and repair materials such as Vistafoil® Vinyl Delayed-Action Laminate and Highsmith Repositionable Book Covers.

3. Karen Williams, "Preservation and Conservation in the Elementary Schools," *Conservation Administration News*, no. 52 (January 1993): 4–5, 7, 13.

Teaching Little Hands to Care for Books

Susan Middleton, La Jolla Country Day School,
La Jolla, California

What do *Beezus and Ramona*, scarred book stories, and paper- and bookmaking have in common? They are all approaches used to educate lower school (kindergarten through fourth grade) students at La Jolla Country Day School in California. The library serves the independent school of nearly 1,000 students in nursery through the twelfth grade. Care and handling instruction is geared to the lower school students, but all students see an annual display of *scarred* books as well as posters throughout the library, which promote good preservation techniques.

BEEZUS AND RAMONA

Beverly Cleary's Ramona books are an excellent series in which to introduce a truly noteworthy children's author, combined with a care-of-books message. In *Beezus and Ramona*,[1] the chapter "Beezus and Her Little Sister" stands on its own as a read-aloud where the enjoyment of libraries and responsibility for library books are the focus. When Ramona scribbles her name on every page of a library book, the two sisters return to the library to pay for the damage. The librarians in the book are friendly and helpful. (Mention can be made to the students that Beverly Cleary was a librarian.)

The reading lends itself to further discussion about how libraries are not bookstores. You cannot damage a book just so you can buy it when paying for the damages. You can commend Beezus for taking Ramona back to the library to point out the damage and pay for it and how you hope they will be just as responsible.

This session is conducted during a regular library visit, usually with a group of about 20 students. It is especially popular with second and third graders. Be sure to have plenty of Ramona books available to check out.

SCARRED BOOK STORIES

Some damaged books have quite a history! Showing actual moldy and chewed books leaves a big impression. To emphasize the point and to encourage children to tell stories, a session for each kindergarten through fourth-grade class is held to share *scarred book stories*.[2]

Keep a collection of damaged books that have been returned to the library. Break the class into groups of two or three students each and give a book to each group. Demonstrate what you want them to do by telling a scarred book story to the class. Set some ground rules for the stories and set a time limit. The idea is for them to use their imagination to think about kinds of damage that could actually happen, such as being left out at recess just before that amazing rainstorm hit or falling off the roof of the car and being run over by the neighbor's motorcycle!

Then enjoy walking around the room and listen in while the groups develop their own stories. The session can be combined with a written story if a teacher wishes to develop a creative writing exercise. In that case, short written stories can accompany scarred books in a library display to show damage to materials along with the stories written by the students.

The students remember this session and ask for it year after year. They remember both the storytelling and the specific damaged books. It is easily repeated annually as children see different perspectives as they get older.

PAPERMAKING

A papermaking session is presented each year to kindergartners. While making something beautiful, the students learn about the fragility of paper and the process of papermaking and recycling. The effort is considerable the first time, but after the needed materials have been assembled, it is a snap to do year after year. There are kits available in art, toy, and bookstores for papermaking. All that are needed are two strong wooden picture frames, wire screening, an old electric blender, construction paper, a large plastic tub, and water.

It is very easy to make your own screened frame by stretching and stapling wire screen across one of the wood frames. Leave the second frame without screening. A useful shortcut is to place an extra piece of loose screen on the screened frame that can be lifted off with the pulp. The pulp easily peels off the loose screen. If you have several pieces of loose screen, the dipping process can continue while others are removing the pulp from them. There are a number of books available on papermaking, such as those listed in Appendix 2.

To begin, have the children tear up sheets of construction paper into small pieces. Buzz the paper with water in the blender and add to the basin, which already has some water in it. As you dump buzzed pulp into the basin, take out more water, mixing until the consistency is good. A drying area should be prepared ahead of time. One way is to put masking tape with each student's name on the sidewalk. After making the paper, the students place it on the sidewalk to dry. Drying time depends on the weather, but in a sunny spot, it can be as little as 15 minutes.

Making bookmarks from the paper is popular. Make sure not to make the paper too thick for bookmarks so they do not cause more damage than good when used. They make lovely presents and can be enhanced with a decorative ribbon knotted through a punched hole or further decorated by the students.

BOOKMAKING

To encourage third and fourth graders to think about what *not* to do in the library or with books, a classroom visit by the librarian is developed around making a book of their ideas. The session begins with a reading of *Alexander and the Terrible, Horrible, No Good, Very Bad Day.*[3] Students are given time to think of all that could go wrong in the library or to think of things that could happen to a book that would damage it. They are encouraged to be as realistic as possible. Paper, die-cut in the shape of a book, is given to each child. They are then asked to begin a sentence with the phrase ''And then . . . ,'' followed by their *bad* idea. They can illustrate their page as time allows.

After the class concludes, the papers are put together by gluing them to blank pages to make a single book titled *Ms. Middleton and the Terrible, Horrible, No Good, Very Bad Day in the Library.*

The children really enjoy this project. The books remain in the library and are favorites to be looked at and borrowed. By thinking of what could (and does!) go wrong, we are all reminded of the right ways of caring for and using our books.

NOTES

1. Beverly Cleary, *Beezus and Ramona* (New York: William Morrow, 1955).

2. This idea comes from Vicky Reed, a storyteller and librarian in Chula Vista, CA.

3. Judith Viorst, *Alexander and the Terrible, Horrible, No Good, Very Bad Day* (New York: Atheneum, 1972).

5

Preservation Education in Public Libraries

On Target: Reaching the Public Through Preservation

Nancy Carlson Schrock, Conservator/
Consultant, Winchester, Massachusetts,
and Anne L. Reynolds, Wellesley Free Library,
Wellesley, Massachusetts

THE PUBLIC LIBRARY PERSPECTIVE: THE DIALOGUE[1]

The scene opens with a conversation between Tim, the technical services librarian who is responsible for preservation activities in the Middletown Public Library, and Jeannie, a public services librarian. Maud, the library's director, is mentioned.

Tim: Jeannie, guess what? Maud just showed me a $3,000 check donated for library preservation. She said that I'd earned it for the preservation program. You will never guess who the donors are.

Jeannie: The historical society? Or one of the Wentworth family members? The Thalian Club?

Tim: No—the VFW, our esteemed Veterans of Foreign Wars, of all people. I never in my wildest dreams thought that group would be making a donation to the library and for preservation of all things. Maud said that their president, Ray McDonald, just came in the door with the check. It certainly made her day.

Jeannie: What on earth prompted that? Are we preserving some World War II memorabilia? Don't tell me that we are getting stuck with some musty archives that have rotted away for years in someone's basement.

Tim: Actually, there are no strings attached—it is an unrestricted gift. I guess the hours that I put in with the volunteer book repair team and the rounds that Maud and I have made to various community groups have finally begun to pay off.

I understand that the VFW gift came about after a spirited supper table discussion in the McDonald house. Ray, of course, is very active in the Kiwanis Club and had heard Maud speak at one of their meetings. It is amazing how attitudes change when you can reach people on their level. Maud says that the minute she describes the collections as capital assets and stresses the importance of cost avoidance, those businessmen start to pay attention.

Jeannie: Well, your little coup with the Thalian Club must have helped. Isn't Louise McDonald a member?

Tim: She sure is, and she has been one of my most faithful volunteer menders.

Jeannie: Did I tell you that the president of the Thalians was in the other day and that she was positively bubbling about the rematting of all the club prints? When they had the mats and backing removed, they found considerable damage. Thanks to your expertise, the club has greatly improved the condition of their print collection. They have become believers. In fact, they are even going to loan me a few prints to use in the spring exhibit on preserving family treasures.

Tim: I was pleased about that project. You do know that Louise had a number of family pictures rematted. According to Maud, when Ray Jr. told them all about the book-handling video he watched during one of our library page training sessions, something just clicked. Ray Sr. made the case to the local council, and they approved the gift as their spring project.

I had forgotten that several of our firemen were VFW members who had assisted us with our townwide disaster planning workshop. At first they thought that wetting down all the books was pretty silly, but when they saw us going through the disaster drills, they were impressed. Best of all, if the VFW thinks that preservation is important, can our five-year proposal to the town's Finance Committee be far behind?

Jeannie: You're right! I think I'd better get going on developing that proposal in more detail for Maud.

THE PUBLIC LIBRARY PERSPECTIVE: THE BACKGROUND

Every librarian enjoys those rare days when someone comes in the door with an unrestricted gift. But rather than focus on the donation mentioned in this story, consider what it says about community attitudes and the role of preservation in every level of operations in this public library. It is preservation in the broadest sense—that is, the care of library collections as physical objects made of different materials and structures that have their own frailties, uses, and life spans. It encompasses the selection of bindings, jacket covers, and enclosures that extend the lives of books and audiovisual materials while presenting them attractively. Proper maintenance and repair, handling, and display are included as well as education of the public. A proper physical environment adjusted for light, heat, and humidity is also fundamental to every program.

In the public libraries, preservation education spans a range of areas. It includes the attitudes and commitment of library staff and a preservation program that extends to all levels of library service. Our dialogue concentrates on sharing preservation information and educating the public, a task often accomplished by contacts with individuals or through talks to community groups.

Before educating the community, however, public librarians must examine their own attitudes about collections management. Too often, when public librarians think about preservation at all, their thoughts turn to the local history and genealogical collections. The library's "treasure room" may receive climate control, and if any conservation measures are taken, they are reserved for these materials. Certainly local history and genealogical materials are important, but so too are circulating collections. Unfortunately, these are often considered expendable and not worth maintaining, even though an attractive and well-presented collection is more heavily used and speaks loudly about the attitudes of those responsible for it.

In summary, the primary requirement for a successful public library preservation program is to make certain that library staff at all levels understand its importance and are committed to including it in the library program. In our dialogue, the library director, a public services librarian, a technical services librarian, an adult volunteer, and a page all dealt with preservation at some level. For each of them, collections maintenance was part of their individual tasks. As a result, preservation was integrated into the library's overall program, and all library activities included a preservation component.

Staff invested in the physical management of collections take their responsibilities seriously. And it is here that public librarians need to make the case about the importance of collections early and often—from their cultural significance to actual dollars and cents values. Residents see their libraries as the intellectual foundation of their community, but the librarians hesitate to make this case. It is imperative that librarians continue to stress that collections are important—and ensure that they receive the best care that can be given to them. Part of that care is the physical maintenance of collections. It is far more cost-effective to perform a simple mend than to replace a badly damaged book, taking pressure off the acquisitions budget. Local funding authorities do understand the maintenance of capital assets. If repair and rebinding can be presented in these terms, a strong case can be made for funding collections maintenance.

Preservation provides an excellent opportunity for library staff to share their expertise with the community. If the staff understand and care for books, papers, photographs, and works of art, they can become a resource to help individuals to care for personal treasures and community groups to preserve their resources.

THE PUBLIC LIBRARY PERSPECTIVE: THE RESPONSE

In the public library environment, sharing preservation and educating the public are often done on a person-by-person basis through talks to community groups, general orientation sessions, and interaction at the reference and circulation desks. Formal instruction, as seen in school and academic settings, is far less likely to happen, although the advent of technology and automation may allow public libraries to incorporate preservation information into their own versions of bibliographic instruction. How can public libraries take advantage of all these opportunities, both formal and informal, *to sell* preservation? Consider the following seven commandments for the public library preservation education initiative:

1. *Be a believer. You can't sell it if you don't believe in it.* For many, believing that preservation has any role in public libraries is the greatest hurdle. Public librarians perceive preservation as a problem for research libraries with brittle books or for historical and genealogical societies with materials that are guarded in a treasure room. Their attitude may be summed up by the comment, ''Thank heaven I don't have to deal with it.'' This same colleague may loan a book with loose pages, with a cracked spine, or mended with oozing sticky tape.

''Preservation is the activity that attempts to keep what you want and need for as long as you want or need it.''[2] This pragmatic definition of preservation by Robert DeCandido of New York Public Library is one to which public librarians can more readily relate. It speaks to keeping videotapes in working condition, to extending the use of best-sellers until they lapse into obscurity, and to protecting all materials against theft, vandalism, and leaky pipes. Many items may ultimately be discarded, but all public librarians should maximize the investment that their communities have made in their library collections and buildings. This is the mission of preservation in most public libraries, not the conservation or microfilming of old books.

2. *Be an advocate for your collection, both for its content and its physical condition.* The view that public library collections are ephemeral and do not warrant preservation has been accepted as a truism far too long. The 1992 condition survey of book collections in four Massachusetts libraries showed that 10 percent of the holdings in all libraries were more than 30 years old, and a quarter were over 20 years old. Even the rural library and small city library that insisted they only collected current materials retained nonfiction and literature.[3]

Even if 40 percent of all books are discarded after 10 years, the use that they receive during those 10 years is substantial. Publishers' bindings are made for the private individual who will read them once or twice. In contrast, public librarians expect these same bindings to withstand at least 20 circulations and children's books to withstand 90. Moreover, local holdings are used by people throughout the state. Over 45,000 books circulated on interlibrary loan in eastern Massachusetts in 1987. Just 7 years later in 1994, that number had jumped to 1.5 million. No academic library subjects its collections (except perhaps for reserve materials) to the use and abuse that public library materials receive. These library materials require ongoing maintenance if they are to survive, even for a limited time.

Library collections are part of the public trust—the tools and the cultural icons of their communities. Public librarians are the advocates for collection materials when they plead for funding for acquisitions. These same librarians must be equally articulate when they ask for funds to house their collections properly and maintain them in usable condition through repair, rebinding, and replacement. Capitalize on the respect that people have for books and recorded knowledge to support funding requests and to seek donations and gifts.

3. *Speak in terms that your listeners understand.* While *preservation* may attract the attention of the members of the town's historical society, it is often more effective to avoid the "P" word altogether when speaking to other members of your constituency. Substituting *collections maintenance* will bring home the theme of ongoing care of all materials, including videotapes and nonprint media. For library colleagues, *providing access to scarce resources in a time of fiscal restraint* might make the point best. For businesspeople, try *maintenance of capital assets.* Underlying all these terms is a constant principle: Library collections represent a significant investment of community resources and should be accessible to the public in a usable condition. Preservation, or whatever you call it, makes this possible.

4. *Make certain that believers exist at all levels of your library, your community, and your state.* Unlike research or academic libraries, public libraries rarely have a preservation officer on their staff. Instead of a centralized department, preservation is more likely to be a shared responsibility. Be sure that preservation has an advocate among the upper administration to ensure financial support and advocacy among the decision makers. Too often, preservation is seen as simple mending and relegated to the basement. Involve all library staff. Repair is only one part of a more complicated decision-making process that involves weeding and replacement to build a collection that is in condition to circulate.

Bring the decision makers on board. The board of trustees should be the library's strongest preservation ally. Show them examples of new books that have fallen apart after one use and books that have been repaired and commercially rebound. Use similar tactics with the town finance committee but emphasize the cost-effectiveness of repair and maintenance. Demonstrate the value of mending titles at $2 per title rather than delaying repair with a resulting $10 commercial rebinding or a $45 replacement cost. Point out that overhead costs of maintaining well-repaired and well-weeded collections are lower because of space savings and higher circulation.

Community support is essential because citizens are the ones who use or abuse the collections and, through taxes, provide the funds to purchase and maintain the collections. Friends of the Library members and community volunteers can become the nucleus for a group of citizens knowledgeable about preservation. Through the type of outreach described in the case studies in this chapter, this core group can expand to yield wider community support.

Libraries no longer function in isolation, and online records are only as useful as the physical objects they represent. Local efforts to keep books in good condition will have limited effect if interlibrary loan sends the volumes off in flimsy bags to other libraries where no effort is made to care for materials. Involve colleagues in the preservation issues that impact networks, for example, proper shipping during transport, last copy policies, and shared collection development for at-risk titles.

Be an advocate for preservation on the state level, especially when budgets are developed. Contact state representatives. Help build a constituency for libraries, library collections, and library buildings. Political advocacy has become increasingly important as national programs are reduced and funding transferred to the states.

5. *Share expertise and encourage all staff to do so as well. Use enlightened self-interest to tell the preservation tale.* What are the first concerns of people after hurricane winds have abated? They make sure everybody is okay and then they ask, "What about the family pictures? What about the precious . . . ?" People are interested in their own collections, their family history, their photographs. Capitalize on these concerns to introduce the general principles of preservation to the public in a meaningful way.

Include books on conservation among new acquisitions. Art conservation, furniture restoration, historic preservation, as well as book and photograph conservation reinforce the theme of preservation. For example, *Conservation Concerns: A Guide for Collectors and Curators*[4] is an inexpensive basic text that covers a range of media. *Caring for Your Collections*[5] provides information on conservation, appraisal, and security, with beautiful color illustrations, while *The Art of the Conservator*[6] explains the science and historical analysis that underlie treatment. *The Permanence and Care of Color Photographs*[7] provides comprehensive coverage of one of the most pressing concerns of the public, the care of modern photographs, and *The Care of Fine Books*[8] gives practical advice for the book collector. These books will enable the public services staff to answer reference questions about preservation while increasing public awareness about the field of conservation.

Conservation can be a popular topic for public programs. Possibilities include "Preserving Family Documents" in conjunction with the local historical or genealogical society. Saving family photographs is of great interest, especially after the recent press focusing on the damage caused by storing color prints in vinyl *magnetic* albums. Enlist the services of a local bookbinder for a talk on binding or a local book dealer for a talk on appraising collections. Textile conservation has appeal, especially when it focuses on preserving a family wedding gown or christening dress. Although not directly related to library issues, such programs raise public awareness of the importance of proper care and storage.

The book arts can be the topic of workshops for both children and adults. Exhibits of papermaking, marbled paper, and hand bookbinding reinforce the concept that books are objects of craftsmanship and beauty. Exhibits of the book arts can also reinforce the need to care for these valued objects. Library display cases can be used to mount exhibits with examples such as "When bad things happen to good books." As the library staff become more knowledgeable about preservation, they are able to assist local groups with the preservation of their collections. School librarians and church groups share the public library's concern with book repair. The town clerk may need advice about repairing and/or microfilming ledgers; the local art society may ask for information about matting and framing. By meeting the preservation needs of the local community, the library staff can build support for the library collections. Remember that enlightened self-interest is a powerful tool.

6. *Educate, educate, educate.* Train the library staff. Instructions in care and handling should be part of basic orientation for all new staff members, whatever their level. Provide financial support so that staff can attend workshops on book repair. Send the person who does the actual repair, not an administrator. Place preservation topics on the agenda at staff meetings. Promote discussions about the condition of the collections and how decisions about processing, for example, will impact it.

Use every opportunity to educate the public about preservation. Training should begin with the young. Chapter 4 on school libraries contains excellent programs that can serve equally well in public library children's rooms. When high school students ask for help with papers, show them how to use the photocopy machine so that the spine of the book is not broken, and ways to take notes rather than writing in the margins of library books.

Incorporate preservation into library programs. When advising parents about books for their children, discuss the proper care of these books. When doing a book review, hold up the $75 art book and explain why it should not go through the book drop. Discuss the physical composition of library materials whenever possible so that people begin to see books, videotapes, and other media as vulnerable objects that can be damaged through poor handling and neglect.

Involve local government. Disaster preparedness is an excellent opportunity for the public library to join with local government agencies and neighboring libraries. Disaster response and recovery training and mutual aid agreements can provide opportunities for public libraries to participate in local preservation networks.

Work with your state and regional library associations to place preservation issues on the program at annual meetings and to sponsor workshops on book repair, disaster preparedness, and environmental monitoring.

Bring in experts to make your point. Some state libraries make funds available for preservation surveys of public libraries. Survey reports document problems and provide an excellent basis for long-term preservation planning. Regional centers such as the Northeast Document Conservation Center (Andover, Massachusetts), the Conservation Center for Art and Historic Artifacts (Philadelphia), and conservators in private practice also offer consulting services. Expert opinion can be effective for gaining the support of government and the community.

7. *Persevere. By taking many small steps, you can achieve a great deal.* An effective public library preservation program cannot be imposed from above. It

is the cumulative effort of personal contact, example, and hard work. Since support and funding ultimately come from the public and since the public are the ones who use library materials, it is the public whose attitudes, opinions, and behavior must be changed. As the introductory dialogue and the following case studies show, the process is gradual and cumulative.

NOTES

1. Adapted from Anne Reynolds's talk at the program "Selling Preservation: What to Say to the Customer" (presentation to the ALCTS/LIRT Program, ALA Annual Conference, Miami, FL, June 27, 1994). Audiotapes of the program are available from the American Library Association (ALA) (Tape no. 454).

2. Robert DeCandido, "Out of the Question," *Conservation Administration News* no. 38 (July 1989): 24–25.

3. Nancy Carlson Schrock, "A Collection Condition Survey Model for Public Libraries," in *Advances in Preservation and Access*, Vol. 2, ed. Barbra Buckner Higginbotham (Medford, NJ: Learned Information, 1995), pp. 210–233.

4. *Conservation Concerns: A Guide for Collectors and Curators* (Washington, DC: Smithsonian Institution Press, 1992).

5. *Caring for Your Collections* (New York: Harry Abrams, 1992).

6. *The Art of the Conservator* (Washington, DC: Smithsonian Institution Press, 1992).

7. Henry Wilhelm, *The Permanence and Care of Color Photographs: Traditional and Digital Color Prints, Color Negatives, Slides and Motion Pictures* (Grinnell, IA: Preservation Publishing Co., 1993).

8. Jane Greenfield, *The Care of Fine Books* (New York: Nick Lyons Books, 1988).

CASE STUDIES

Preservation Education Workshops: A Public Library Approach

Jane Mueller, Fullerton Public Library, Fullerton, California

BACKGROUND

In 1990 the Fullerton Public Library initiated a program of ongoing workshops focusing around the care, handling, and treatment of the personal collections of library patrons. The goal of the program was twofold: to provide patrons with information about specific preservation problems with their personal materials and to create a public awareness of the need to care for information recorded on varying types of media.

Originally, patrons requesting information about specific preservation problems with personal materials—wet and moldy books; torn pages; aged and damaged photographs; proper care for phonograph records, audio- and videotapes, CDs, and computer disks—were directed to shelved library preservation information or to the Reference Department staff. Librarians, as well as patrons, were frustrated by the lack of public-oriented information sources. The need for more available information was considered, and the proposal for a preservation education program was initiated.

METHODOLOGY

The Fullerton Public Library is a single library of 220,000 volumes with 32 full- and part-time staff, serving a population of 200,000. The major organizational responsibility for setting up the preservation education program has been assumed by the adult services librarian with 15 years of preservation training and experience. She has collection preservation and local history responsibilities and teaches the preservation education sessions such as "Preservation in a Nutshell: Protecting Your Family Archives" and "Hands-on Old Paper Preservation."

Staff from other departments are also involved. The Reference Department, which receives most inquiries for preservation information, provides input on patron needs and interest levels. The library administration provides the needed support including publicity, staff release time, and an atmosphere that encourages user education and outreach. The library community services department promotes and advertises the programs and ensures that necessary approvals and space needs are obtained.

The target audience is the public at large, which has the need for information on basic paper and audiovisual preservation methods. Most participants are library users from the local area, although patrons from surrounding libraries also participate. The information is directed toward the nonlibrarian; however, several public, special, and academic librarians have attended.

Some of the workshops include a hands-on component and require more advance planning and space. After receiving administrative approval, the librarian who implemented the program used the following task list to organize each workshop:

- Declared focus/subject and drafted an agenda.
- Set a date and coordinated space availability.
- Conferred regarding promotion with community service librarian—flyers for distribution, newspapers, city newsletter, and so on.
- Created appropriate handout drafts and session evaluation form.
- Developed supply list from catalogs and set supply fee.
- Accepted reservations and fees for supplies (no charge for class).
- Ordered supplies, finalized handouts, and prepared displays.
- Compiled handouts in binders.
- Organized supplies, along with samples and binder, and assembled them into individual acid-free boxes for distribution to each attendee.
- Selected preservation video to be shown before session.
- Conducted session.

Enthusiasm for the workshops was generated by the public's interest. The library distributed flyers to users and ran announcements in the city newsletter and local newspapers. As regional newspapers picked up the story, inquiries were received from outside the immediate area. The library expected to conduct programs from time to time, but with the overwhelming public response, they have become a regular outreach program.

EVALUATION

The public is fascinated with the information presented and gratified since these programs have never before been offered. Participants include collectors, genealogists, business people, students, family historians, and others who have specific preservation needs.

The result has been increased community awareness of the preservation issues and proper care surrounding both paper-based materials—books, documents, photographs, and memorabilia—as well as audiovisual items such as video- and audiotapes, CDs, and computer disks.

A printed evaluation is distributed requesting such information as: opinion of session presentation and format, most convenient time and best location, and interest in future preservation information. Comments received on these evaluations and from the experience and observation of the instructor indicate that there are several improvements that can be made to make the workshops more effective.

All sessions should be limited to 10 or 12 participants instead of the 35 to 40 who attended the original programs. Each session should cover one area— paper and books, photographs, or nonprint materials—for a two-hour session, rather than trying to cover all three in one three-hour session. Also, the logistics of the programs would be improved by asking for volunteers to assist with handing out the kits and other supplies and to record registration and fees. These tasks take a great deal of time during and outside of library hours.

As an adjunct to the workshop series and to aid future preservation education outreach to area libraries, a preservation guide is being assembled. It will include updated workshop handouts; the illustration and indexing of the handouts; and a list of additional resource materials.

In addition, a proposal is being developed to create and distribute bookmarks and handouts that will advise the public on measures they can implement to care for library materials—proper shelf removal; improper use of pens and pencils; care at home and in the car; the damage caused by food and drink; protection from animals and small children; and their responsibility when materials are lost or damaged.

CONCLUSION

The preservation workshop approach in a public library can be rewarding not only as a successful education and outreach effort by the library but also as a satisfying professional development opportunity for library staff. The personal interest of individual staff members can be encouraged and developed for the benefit of the library and community. Hands-on workshops can be further expanded to in-house demonstrations along with a preservation exhibit or be tied to a children's room story hour. Administration support and guidance for these efforts will allow them to develop in many directions with far-reaching library and community benefits.

User Education in Care and Handling of Audiovisual Materials

*Susan E. Annett, Santa Monica Public Library,
Santa Monica, California*

What does the library employee say to the user who returns a melted cassette? How does a staff member respond to the patron who complains about video distortion and then looks blank when asked if the tracking was adjusted? How does the librarian explain a policy when challenged by a customer about whether the previous borrower was penalized for not rewinding a tape? These are the practical, day-to-day situations that challenge audiovisual (AV) staff to achieve balance among institutional values of providing excellent customer service, implementing library policies and procedures, marketing and maintaining media collections, and promoting user responsibility, education, and enjoyment.

The Santa Monica Public Library's audiovisual collections consist of approximately 4,500 videos, 4,000 CDs, 7,000 audiotapes, and 2,500 books-on-cassettes and circulate from the 1,500-square-foot Audiovisual Services Division. This division is staffed by two full-time equivalent (FTE) librarians and four FTE clerks and pages. As with many media departments, the starting point for user education is the library's Audiovisual Regulations. This letter-size, double-sided flyer is given to all new borrowers of AV materials, and the staff are trained to verbally reinforce major policy features. In the video section, for example, are these basic care instructions:

- Use a VCR [videocassette recorder] that is in good operating condition. Problems are often resolved by consulting your VCR manual. Adjusting the video tracking mechanism may resolve image and sound distortion.

- Keep videos away from dust, dirt, humidity, sunlight, and heat. Do not leave them in cars, as even brief periods can result in heat damage.

- Do not keep videos near magnetic sources, such as stereo speakers or electric motors, as they can erase tapes.

There is also a statement acknowledging what has been called the inherent vice of audiovisual media: "The Santa Monica Public Library is not responsible for damage to borrowers' equipment or any costs of repair resulting from use of library materials." Although not too frequently invoked, this caveat is a precaution against users holding the library liable for expensive repairs usually associated with removing a video stuck in the VCR's tape transport mechanism.

If such a problem is reported before any costs are incurred, staff tries to walk the patron through removing the tape from the equipment. If this is not possible, staff apprises the borrower that the library's damage charge is less than a trip to the repair shop. Staff will then urge the patron to check the VCR's operating condition using a personal tape. The employee may also advise the patron of the importance of having a VCR regularly serviced and cleaned, especially if a lot of videos from the library or video rental outlets are used.

Should a patron demand that the library pay an equipment repair bill, the librarian must refer to the limitation of liability clause mentioned above. As a salvo to the often incensed patron, the librarian may offer to waive the damage fee. Experience has shown that this is not an opportune time to instruct users about equipment maintenance, when they are generally convinced that it is the fault of the "bad library tape" (which it may well be) and not of their "new, top-of-the-line VCR."

The Santa Monica Public Library often uses labels to educate borrowers in the care of AV collections. For example, labels caution borrowers: "Do not put this item in the outside book return. It is fragile and subject to damage from heat." Until recently, the library also put the following 2" × 3" bright yellow label on the outside of each CD jewel case:

Basic Care of the CD

- To remove from container, press on center and lift by the edges.
- Always handle by the edges. *Do not touch CD surface.*
- Do not place on hot or abrasive surfaces.
- Return to container immediately after use.

This label has been replaced by a similar Compact Disc Care sign posted in the collection area. There were several reasons for this change. The library had previously displayed the liner notes in the public area while housing the CDs behind the service desk but has changed over to an open shelving system where the intact CD is locked in a plastic security case that can be detached when the item is checked out. Because the liner notes are no longer available for examination, the care label was eliminated in favor of the marketing consideration of making the note covers more visible. Moreover, technical services staff needed to streamline their work flow by skipping the labor-intensive step of applying the label. Finally, CDs have been in the marketplace more than a decade, and staff believe that the public no longer needs such basic care instruction as they did when the format was new.

The greater need now is to educate patrons about what to do when a library CD occasionally skips. With any item that is reported defective, AV staff tell the patron that the material is visually inspected and then played on library equipment if the damage is not obvious. Staff will run videos through an industrial-grade, inspector-cleaner unit or clean CDs with a clean cloth before checking the play quality. Even though most borrowers know to handle the disc by its edge, many still believe the adage first touted by the recording industry about CDs as a virtually indestructible medium. Certainly staff and users alike who recall the chronic playing problems plaguing library record albums can attest to the superiority of CDs as a circulating collection over albums. However, borrowers sometimes need convincing that neatness with respect to CDs still counts.

Audiovisual staff inform patrons that problems with CDs are often resolved by cleaning the disc. They may demonstrate the proper cleaning technique of using a soft, lint-free cloth to gently wipe the CD in a radial motion from the center of the disc out to its edge. For those patrons who used to borrow albums, staff emphasize the importance of using a radial, rather than circular, motion in cleaning CDs. Once these clients understand that circular cleaning can etch a harmful groove into the CD that compromises the reading of the digital data, they are less likely to revert to their old album-cleaning habits. Other troubleshooting tips include alerting customers who experience frequent skipping with several CDs to the possibility of dirt or dust on their player's lens. Use of a dust blower, such as those used for cameras, may remedy this equipment malfunction.

The importance of this close interaction between specialized staff and media patrons cannot be overemphasized in pointing to recurring problems that require remedial action. A few years ago, it became apparent that a disproportionate number of costly unabridged books-on-cassettes were being returned with heat-warped tapes and vinyl containers. Santa Monica, a beach community located on the western edge of Los Angeles, rarely gets as hot as the Los Angeles basin or valley areas. There is often the misconception among clientele that leaving books-on-cassettes in their cars during the loan period is not harmful because of the more temperate climate. Without evidence of a meltdown, it is difficult to convince patrons that heat plays havoc with any tape media. Excessively hot cassettes and players contribute to poor, echoing sound quality and promote tape stretching.

An environmental approach was taken in tackling this problem. One approach might have been to present a comprehensive conservation/preservation flyer divided into format categories. But since books-on-cassettes are mostly played either in the car by commuters or at home, a focus on user environment provided the structure for the handout. It also takes into account Southern California's extended summer weather season, between March and November, and a notorious aspect of the region's famed car culture—theft from automobiles. In the hope that the flyer will actually be read, it is printed on only one side of a half sheet of bright yellow paper:

SUMMER'S HERE . . . ! CARE OF AUDIOVISUAL MATERIALS

In Your Car:

- On sunny days, and even when overcast, parked cars (and trunks) can become ovens. When transporting AV materials to and from the library, we urge you to minimize the time they are in your car.
- When listening to cassettes, take only as many as you expect to hear on your trip. Borrowers have lost costly AV materials after having their cars broken into.

At Home:

- Handle AV materials carefully. Avoid touching tape surfaces. Handle a CD with your fingers around the outer edge.
- Avoid placing cassettes and videos near magnetic fields found in speakers, TVs, computers, etc.
- Keep AV materials in their protective storage cases when not in use.
- Keep your playing equipment clean. Clean/demagnetize your tape heads every 24 hours of playing time.
- Please report problems with AV materials to library staff.

As the Santa Monica Public Library launches into lending another new format, multimedia CD-ROMs, the care and handling of this technology are of as paramount concern as determining selection, cataloging, processing, packaging, and circulation policies. The experiences of other CD-ROM users and vendors provide us with a starting point from which to develop our policies. The article "CD-ROM Disc Maintenance and Care"[1] confirms that many of the same disc care practices already in place for audio CDs are also recommended for CD-ROMs. The advice of colleagues on the Audiovisual Committee of the Metropolitan Cooperative Library System, a consortium of 31 public library systems in Southern California, is being solicited. Trusted media vendors and sales representatives are also being queried about selection and return problems with multimedia products.

In the library, CD-ROM drives are being added to staff computer workstations, and staff will be trained to check discs for data errors and to troubleshoot problems with text or software that are reported by end users. The AV regulations are being updated to include CD-ROMs.

Finally, just as with users of videos, CDs, and other media, staff will learn from questions posed by CD-ROM end users, and the library's policies and procedures will be adjusted accordingly. As part of collection development and maintenance responsibilities, this attention to the care and handling of materials is crucial. Promoting user education relates also to the broader public library mission of meeting the needs of each person for information, education, and recreation. The student who needs a Shakespeare play on video, the senior who wants a classical music CD, and the child who checks out a multimedia encyclopedia should all derive the greatest benefit possible from a carefully selected and well-maintained media collection.

NOTE

1. "CD-ROM Disc Maintenance and Care," *OLAC Newsletter* 10, no. 1 (March 1990): 27–28.

The Library Lock-In

*Ann Ridout, University of Michigan, Ann Arbor,
Michigan, and Jeanne M. Drewes, Michigan
State University, East Lansing, Michigan*

BACKGROUND

Public libraries often provide space for local civic groups to meet. Sometimes the meeting rooms are available for a fee, but often the room is free. Making the entire library building available to a local group is much less routine, but that is what the Ann Arbor Public Library in Michigan did for a local fourth- and fifth-grade Girl Scout troop. On a Saturday night the troop was *locked in* the library. By next morning when the doors were unlocked, the girls had fulfilled the requirements for the Girl Scout "Books" badge, while relating to libraries and librarians in a new and more informal environment.

Working together, the librarians and Scout leader provided activities for the girls in a sleep-over setting at the library. They handled the logistics and prepared several activities that were an excellent entrée to learning preservation principles. The girls were responsible for bringing their own sleep gear. The troop supplied food, cookies, and milk in the evening and bagels, cream cheese, and juice in the morning. While food is not ordinarily allowed in the library, an exception was made in this instance. The Girl Scout tradition of leaving a site better than you found it provided the necessary emphasis for the girls to clean up after themselves, and the food presented no problems. The library provided personnel for the night to teach and supervise activities and to provide security.

BOOKS BADGE

The requirements for the "Books" badge are outlined in the *Girl Scout Badges and Signs*. Six activities were selected to fulfill the requirements, going from more active ones appropriate for the beginning of the evening to more passive ones for when the night wore on. All of the activities listed below were based on the badge requirements. Additional suggestions have been made to enrich the experience.

- *Explore the library resources and make a poster to encourage use of the library.* The library catalogs provide the starting point. In addition, the Web can be surfed, visiting such pages as the Library of Congress and its Preservation homepage (http://lcweb.loc.gov/preserv/preserve.html) or searching "Girl Scouts" through one of the search engines (there are lots of entries).

- *Design a set of bookmarks based on Newbery and Caldecott books.* The librarian, or one of the troop parents with a little research, can do a "show and tell" about a selection of the books. The girls will likely be able to add a lot to the discussions, telling about other award winning authors and illustrators.

- *Bring a book with you to donate to a shelter for battered women and children.* This community service aspect of the badge can be repeated throughout the year as other troop activities lend themselves to it.

- *Find out about careers with books.* Librarians made presentations, and books on the topic were available for the girls to read. Other guests could include newspaper writers and editors, who are often willing to spend 30 minutes speaking to a group. Even a high school or college student, who is writing while pursuing a degree in journalism, would make an interesting speaker. Try making the guest's profession a mystery and let the girls start the program by asking yes/no questions to guess the career.

- *Perform a service project suggested by the librarians.* The project had a nice preservation tie-in as the girls cleaned the covers of a number of children's books. Other possibilities are having the girls mount a display about their favorite books or helping to decorate for an upcoming holiday, such as Halloween or Thanksgiving during the fall. Or libraries can always use help sorting or reshelving books!

- *Make a book.* This was organized by Ann Ridout, a bookbinder for over 20 years. While not a public library employee, she volunteered her time to help with this portion of the evening. The rest of the case study is devoted to her presentation and the project she organized for the girls.

PRESERVATION HINTS

The presentation started with a short talk on the care and handling of library materials. It consisted of a short demonstration on how to properly remove a book from the shelf: "By pushing back the books on each side of the chosen book, you can remove the book by gripping the spine." The demonstration of this technique emphasized how pulling the book off the shelf by the top of the case caused the most common damage to the cases. Ridout's talking about how many books had passed through her hands because of people pulling on the headcap and damaging the book was a real learning experience for the girls. Since many people don't know the proper way to take a book off the shelf, she asked the troop to help her educate people about the methods she had just taught them. She made the point to protect their books from the weather, keeping them especially out of water and emphasized how important it was when taking library books home to keep them away from pets and younger brothers and sisters. The troop especially enjoyed the idea of keeping *their* library books away from their younger brothers and sisters. There were lots of books handy for the troop to practice the correct way to remove a book before moving on to their own book project.

MAKE-A-BOOK

The next part of the evening was devoted to making a simple single signature sewn-in pamphlet. The materials were prepared ahead of time. Materials for each book included: five pieces of paper cut 7" × 9" wide, folded in half and punched with three holes in the fold, one in the center and one equal distance from center to each edge; two strips of book cloth two inches wide and the length of the pages plus two inches (one of those pieces also had three holes punched to match the holes in the signature); two pieces of lightweight board for the covers cut the size of the folded paper; and needles and thread.

In Ridout's presentation the parts of the book were related to comparable body parts to make the book structure more understandable—spine, front, back, fore-edge, and textblock. Each piece of the book was explained as it was used in the construction. The folded paper became the signature/textblock, rather than just some folded paper. The boards became the front and back cover, and the book cloth became the spine.

The first step was to sew the signature to one of the pieces of book cloth using a figure-eight stitch (see Figure 5.1). Pass the needle through the center hole and include the piece of cloth with the holes punched to match the signature holes, pass the needle out through the upper hole, come down past the center hole on the outside of the signature, and go in through the bottom hole. Bring the needle back out through the same center hole and tie a square knot around the thread using the two loose ends. Cut the cloth to fit the length of the signature.

The next step was to make the case. Fold the open piece of cloth in half lengthwise and use that line for a guide. Glue a piece of board on each side of the fold, lining up the top and bottom edges (see Figure 5.2). Then fold over the cloth top and bottom and glue that to the inside of your case (see Figure 5.3).

The last step was to hang in the sewn signature pamphlet by gluing the book cloth sewn of the signature to the inside of the case (see Figure 5.3). Then fold the book, place under weights, and let dry for about an hour. Later, the girls

Figure 5.1
Figure-Eight Sewing Pattern

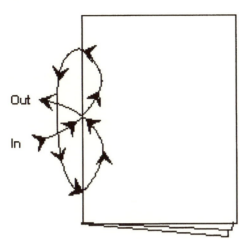

removed their books from the weights. There was time to write in them or to move on to other activities.

EVALUATION

While the focus of the lock-in was not specifically preservation related, the end result was a group of girls who had a fun experience in the library, who made a simple book structure, and who learned some of the most basic care tips for handling library materials. The girls were given the mission of caring for library materials and left the presentation with a sense of their own part in prolonging the life of books.

While lock-ins are not a regular service of libraries, they are a natural user outreach event for both school and public libraries. If libraries can find creative ways to cope with limited staff resources for supervision, the event is an unparalleled community service opportunity. Both Boy and Girl Scouts and summer reading program awards lend themselves to providing these young people with a new look at the library and preservation education as a bonus.

Figure 5.2
Assembling Cover

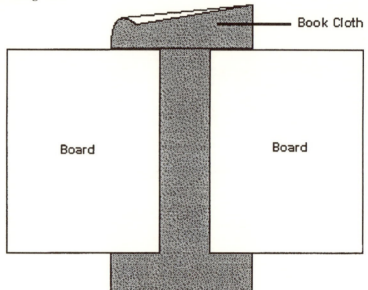

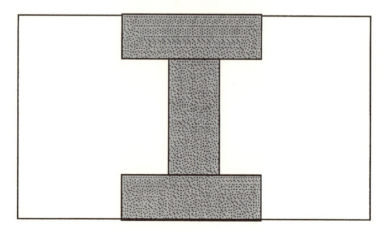

Fold over book cloth, even with board edges, and glue.

Rub down cloth around boards.

Figure 5.3
Hang Signature to Cover

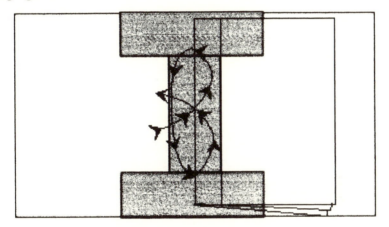

Glue cloth sewn to signature onto cover.

Preservation Education Campaign at the Côte-des-Neiges Library

Danielle Keable, Bibliothèque Côte-des-Neiges, Montréal, Québec

BACKGROUND

In the fall of 1993, the Bibliothèque Côte-des-Neiges, a public library branch in Montréal, Québec, took action against the mutilation of books. The library coordinated its activities with a public awareness campaign organized by Tandem Montréal, a community organization of Montréal and in collaboration with the 23 branch libraries of the Montréal library system. The goal was to make the patrons of the Montréal public libraries more aware of the damage being done to the library collections and to bring about a change in their care and handling of the books they borrow.

A display of a library's mutilated books and the production of a promotional bookmark were the two main events of this campaign, called "Un livre aussi peut être malade" (A book can also be sick). In the spring of 1994, the awareness campaign was expanded by the Côte-des-Neiges branch to focus on children's awareness of book-damaging habits.

METHODOLOGY

Damaged books and magazines that were part of the Côte-des-Neiges branch collection were displayed to show the unfortunate experiences in their lives.

The editors gratefully acknowledge the assistance with translation from the French by Jacynthe Blanchet.

Eye-catching graphics and thought-provoking slogans were included that both children and adults could understand. The graphics were displayed along with the damaged materials, as well as being posted and available throughout the library system. Slogans included: "If you really want to write in a book, why don't you write one yourself." "The scissors maniac has struck again." "Devour a book only with your eyes" (in French, it is said that those who read a lot of books are devouring them). A bookmark was developed that told people to be careful to prevent "sickness" such as "underlinitis" "cutitis," and "corneritis." The names were made up from the problem and the medical suffix for infection. The remedy says: "Two spoonfuls of good citizenship and three tablets of education" (see Figure 5.4).

When the preservation awareness campaign turned its focus to combating mutilation of materials by children as well as adults, additional procedures were developed. When a patron comes to the circulation desk, the employee asks him or her to check the condition of the books to be borrowed. The patron tells the employee of any damage—scribbling, tears, cut pages or photos, stains, or pages ruined by water. (In some cases, the staff make the damage assessment.) If the book is mutilated, the employee writes the specific problem near the due date slip, then initials and dates it. The patron is then informed that if some other or new damage is noticed when the book is returned, a fine may be assessed. The library has a written sheet of fines that may be charged. The fines are assessed only if there is no doubt that the last user was responsible for the damage.

EVALUATION

As a whole, this project has enhanced patrons' awareness of caring for borrowed books. The patrons' comments are mostly positive. Many parents have told us that they think it is an excellent way to make children sensitive to caring for books for the public good. However, it was also some of the parents who presented the greatest resistance to the project. Those parents are opposed to the idea of having the children check the books before taking them or making them pay a fine if the book is damaged when returned.

Another outcome of this project has been that employee workload and the number of repairs have increased since the books are being systematically examined. The benefit is that the collection looks better, and the users can have more enjoyment from the materials. Ideally, this project should have started earlier, when the collection was in a better state as a whole. When the project started, a number of the books were already badly damaged.

As for future plans, we will soon be using rubber stamps instead of writing in the damaged books. The stamps will include the words: *crinkled, stained, underlined, annotated, other*, and *do not repair anymore*. The employees will still add their initials. The stamps will have the advantage of preventing patrons from writing in an annotation after damaging a book.

In late 1994, a year after beginning the initial public awareness campaign,

Figure 5.4
Preservation Education Campaign Bookmark

Figure 5.5
Preventive Measure: Self-Adhesive Stickers

Cutting is prohibited. This document is checked on return.

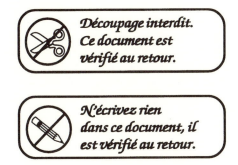

Do not write in this document, it is checked on return.

the Côte-des-Neiges library Committee against Vandalism met to discuss what had been accomplished and to suggest recommendations for the future of the project.

ESTABLISHING A LONG-TERM POLICY

A clear policy is essential to ensure the smooth operation of any program that seeks to heighten public awareness of preservation issues and to prevent mutilation of books. For example:

- Employees must receive clear guidelines regarding the interventions expected of them.
- Clear and precise evaluation criteria must be established in order to make an accurate evaluation of a book's condition and to apply an appropriate fine, if necessary.
- A consistent policy must be established for all the branch libraries of the Bibliothèque de Montréal since some patrons use more than one branch library.

PREVENTIVE VERSUS COERCIVE METHODS

It is better to use preventive measures rather than coercive ones. Here are some preventive measures that are being implemented:

- Self-adhesive stickers are affixed inside the cover of items with an inscription mentioning that it is forbidden to write in or cut from this book (Figure 5.5). These are presently used for workbooks or in books that have questionnaires and are very effective in deterring damage.
- Certain books or series are labeled in order that a thorough examination can be made

at check-in and check-out. This approach is used for items that are frequently damaged or mutilated.

- Efforts are made to clean book covers from time to time.
- At the time of registration, new patrons are verbally informed about the problem of damage and vandalism, advised of the fines, and given a list of library rules.

The library plans to organize another preservation education campaign. There is interest in producing a humorous questionnaire about damage to materials, as well as holding another display of damaged books (always popular with the public). Coordination with Tandem Montréal and systemwide cooperation with preservation education campaigns will make for the best results and improvement of the condition of library collections.

Book Repair as Preservation Outreach: Two Massachusetts Public Library Approaches

Nancy Carlson Schrock, Conservator/Consultant, Winchester, Massachusetts

Book repair is often hidden away in the basement of public libraries where a staff member does repair when other responsibilities permit. Limited budgets often curtail the development of an effective collections maintenance and repair program. Yet book repair can be developed as part of a library volunteer program, especially if it is combined with staff education and public outreach. The work lends itself to volunteer efforts because people can work independently and at their own pace once trained. It also capitalizes on public interest in the craft of bookbinding and conservation. However, such volunteer programs should be limited to circulating collections; historical collections and more valuable materials require the skills of a trained bookbinder or conservator.

WINCHESTER PUBLIC LIBRARY

The Winchester Public Library in Massachusetts implemented a book repair program that combined staff and volunteer training over a three-year period. Winchester is a suburb of Boston with a population of 20,000. Its public library has 105,000 volumes with a staff of 19.5 full-time equivalents (FTES). Like many public libraries, it had suffered staff cutbacks, and there were shelves filled with a backlog of damaged books awaiting review and treatment when the program began.

The project was initiated by a local bookbinder who had been volunteering her time to repair books in a local elementary school. Her proposal to give lessons to library staff was eagerly accepted by the associate director, who suggested a joint staff and volunteer project. Several of the more reliable volunteers were approached, along with staff from technical services and the children's room. Candidates were asked about their experience with crafts and hobbies that required attention to detail and precise hand skills.

Four volunteers and two staff members took part in the initial training. Sessions took place once a month for the first six months. Participants made a commitment to practice their skills weekly between sessions. After initial training, three or four sessions were held during subsequent years. There was some turnover, but a core team emerged, with two of the most experienced volunteers providing training for the replacements. Four people proved to be a good number to train and supervise. Moreover, they were able to keep up with the flow of damaged books.

Training began with simple procedures such as hinge tightening, hinge repair, and replacement of damaged dust jacket protectors. Sticky book repair tape was replaced with book cloth, following procedures in Robert Milevski's *Book Repair Manual* (see "Readings on Book Repair" at the end of this case study). More complicated procedures were gradually added as competency improved. One of the most common problems was hardcover fiction books that had split in half. Because there was no commercial binding budget for rebinding, the staff followed the procedures in the Milevski volume to tip in loose pages, consolidate the textblock, and reinforce the spine.

The second year of the project focused on children's books, since these materials were also a major preservation problem. The volunteers repaired damaged books as they were returned from circulation and also began a routine review of the stacks, refurbishing mysteries and cookbooks, both areas of heavy use in the circulating collection. During 1993, volunteers and staff repaired 688 volumes. Older historical materials, such as Winchester's town atlases and the Civil War collection, were outside the scope of the repair program.

The new repair program was publicized in the local paper, which ran photographs of the volunteers at work. As a result of the publicity, a local resident made a bequest of $1,000 toward supplies and equipment. A used book press was purchased with some of the funds and refurbished by a town hardware store at no cost. Other library volunteers asked to receive repair training when places became available. It was a boost to the morale of library staff to see well-repaired books returned to the shelves. As they began to know the limits of repair, staff found it easier to make weeding decisions based on physical condition. Before the repair program began, there were eight shelves of damaged books. With the repair program there are no more than one or two.

The program has been successful for several reasons:

• The local bookbinder was able to provide continued training in new skills and review of techniques. The training sessions also kept volunteers motivated.

- The assistant library director scheduled meetings and oversaw the program so that it did not languish from lack of direction. She also attended the training sessions.

- A library staff member was assigned to book repair in order to serve as a resource person for the volunteers and to evaluate badly damaged items to see if they should be weeded before making extensive repairs.

- The gift of outside funds provided supplies and materials. Another source of funds would have been the Friends of the Library.

- The volunteers are exceptionally devoted to the project. They give many hours of dedicated service. They enjoy the flexibility of their schedule and the satisfaction of seeing on the shelves the results of their hard work.

WELLESLEY FREE LIBRARY

A slightly different approach was taken in a larger Boston suburb. The Wellesley Free Library is a subregional reference center for the Eastern Regional Library System. It has a collection of 233,000 volumes and a staff of 38 FTEs. When a 1987 survey of book condition revealed that 22 percent of its holdings were damaged, the library enlisted the services of a preservation consultant, staff, and volunteers to improve and expand book repair.[1] The consultant taught new techniques to the part-time repair person, planned a new work space, and recommended new supplies and equipment. As in Winchester, work focused on minor repairs. Unlike Winchester, the town of Wellesley provided supplemental funds for commercial rebinding and replacement, based on survey findings that 12,000 volumes were too damaged to be repaired or used.

The Wellesley Service League agreed to add book repair to the list of projects that met the service requirements for new members. During the first year, participants received instruction from the consultant, but the program quickly became self-sustaining under the library's preservation/processing assistant and the head of technical services. The library has become a popular choice for volunteers, and since new members turn over regularly, the number of citizens who know about book repair and understand the effort it takes to maintain collections increases each year. Since 1988, about 50 volunteers have mended an average of 7,570 books per year, making it the most productive public library repair program in the state. The condition survey was repeated in 1993; results showed that damage had dropped 5 percent, and fewer mends were required per book. The director reports that the condition of the collection looks ''profoundly different.''

As at Winchester, the Wellesley program had the enthusiastic support of the library administration and the guidance of a preservation professional during its early stages. However, the size of the Wellesley program required a greater investment of staff, space, and supplies. Its success is the result of several additional factors:

- The Wellesley Service League provides a steady stream of intelligent, dedicated volunteers who select book repair and make a commitment to work a specified number of hours. Library staff do not have to spend time recruiting replacements.

- The library has set aside a basement room for the volunteers. Large work tables have workstations for four people, each equipped with tools, supplies, and good lighting.

- The preservation/processing assistant works 30 hours per week and is therefore available to train and advise the volunteers on an ongoing basis.

- Volunteers are scheduled to work in groups of two or more. They learn from each other and enjoy the social contact.

- One volunteer contributes a significant amount of her time to book repair, providing the library with the equivalent of a half-time employee with high-level repair skills.

CONCLUSION

The Winchester and Wellesley repair programs have had an impact beyond the mere number of books repaired; they have also helped to educate library staff. Both programs require that circulation staff be able to identify damaged materials so that there is a steady stream of work for the volunteers. The rapid turnaround of repaired materials provides further incentive. As they become knowledgeable, the circulation staff advise patrons not to make repairs themselves, to point out damage to materials, and to protect books in inclement weather. All staff learn the criteria for identifying books that should be repaired and those that are so damaged they need to be weeded. The volunteers become community advocates for collection care. But the best advocate for preservation is the appearance of the collections themselves. Books that have clean dust jackets and clear labels and that don't fall out of their covers or split in half show that a library cares for its collections and encourages users to do likewise. Posters, videotapes, and other education efforts have little impact if collections are shabby and worn.

Librarians who wish to expand their repair programs should first learn more about current repair techniques and select procedures that are appropriate to their collections. They should also encourage staff to take advantage of workshops and programs that teach proper book repair.

Preventative maintenance is most effective, but repair will always be necessary in a heavily used collection. Sound repair takes longer than applying tape, but through education and effective use of volunteers, a public library can develop an improved repair program, especially for those portions of the collection that are heavily used by the community.

NOTE

1. Anne L. Reynolds, Nancy C. Schrock, and Joanna Walsh, ''Preservation: The Public Library Response,'' *Library Journal* 114, no. 3 (February 15, 1989): 128–132.

READINGS ON BOOK REPAIR

Gaylord Preservation Pathfinder No. 4: An Introduction to Book Repair. Syracuse, NY: Gaylord Bros., 1995.

Greenfield, Jane. *Books: Their Care and Repair.* New York: Wilson, 1983.

Lavender, Kenneth, and Scott Stockton. *Book Repair: A How-to-Do-It Manual for School and Public Libraries.* New York: Neal Schuman, 1992.

Milevski, Robert J. *Book Repair Manual.* Carbondale, IL: Illinois Cooperative Conservation Program, 1984. Also published in an abridged form as part of *Illinois Libraries* 67, no. 8 (October 1985): 648–684. Reissued in *Illinois Libraries* 77, no. 2 (Spring 1995): 76–112.

Morrow, Carolyn Clark, and Carole Dyal. *Conservation Treatment Procedures: A Manual of Step-by-Step Procedures for the Maintenance and Repair of Library Materials.* 2nd ed. Littleton, CO: Libraries Unlimited, 1986.

Guerrilla Bookmaking: Preserving Your Community's Heritage

Edward H. Hutchins, Book Artist / Teacher,
Cairo, New York

An important preservation opportunity exists for libraries everywhere that is more than just taking care of existing materials. It is the creation of new books that record and preserve the stories and visions of the communities being served. Guerrilla bookmaking is the discovery that the stories of the people can be recorded and preserved using simple skills and ordinary materials.

Libraries are sometimes thought of as bringing knowledge to a community. But in every community surrounding a library, there exists a unique set of customs, traditions, experiences, and viewpoints that are often overlooked. These are the imaginations of the children, the hopes of the teenagers, and the experiences of the adults. The local library, in whatever setting, has the opportunity to record these aspirations and preserve them for the future.

WHY MAKE BOOKS?

With all the books being produced, why encourage more? Bookmaking is a great equalizer in our vastly competitive world. Not everyone will achieve success on an athletic field. Not everyone will succeed in business. But everyone has had a unique experience, and that gives them a personal, one-of-a-kind story. Everyone is a potential bookmaker.

LIMITATIONS OF MASS-PRODUCED BOOKS

Everyone has a story to tell. However, it may not be a story that will be of interest to everyone else. There is a common perception that books have to be mass-produced. When a book is offset printed, the difference in cost between printing 50 copies and 1,000 copies is not great. But what do you do with 1,000 copies? Thoreau said that he had over 1,000 books in his library, and he had written most of them himself. It was one book that didn't sell!

In the book industry, the current philosophy is to arbitrarily select potential best-sellers, print up thousands of copies, put them up for sale, and after a relatively short period, dump or remainder every copy that has not sold. What a waste!

Even with self-published books, there is a danger in producing a large edition. It is natural to be proud of your first effort and to want to see a copy of it in everyone's hands. Alas, there is an agony in being forever surrounded by a bottomless supply of your first effort. My first literary effort was not very good. As my literary talents improved, I realized that it would make sense to create small editions of first efforts and save larger editions for improved work. Mass-produced books are not always successful on the national level. On the personal level, they are a recipe for disaster. Let's rethink the model.

RETHINKING BOOKS

Consider the option of making much smaller editions by hand. Imagine the pleasure of creating an edition of 30 copies of a special, handmade book that can be shared with the people who will value and appreciate it most. Handwritten books are the ultimate small editions. But when you have something worthwhile to say, reproduce the text mechanically so that you can share your message with more people.

If we are going to produce our own handmade smaller editions, we have to reconsider how books are made—how they are printed, assembled, distributed, and preserved. We need to explore how we can produce a better book. We want to end up with a book that is special and uniquely ours. We want a book that is so representative of our talents and abilities that it not only is *not* mass-produced but *couldn't* be mass-produced.

If not handwritten, we can start by considering how our books should be printed. Offset printing will probably be ruled out. The process of setting up the press, getting it running, and cleaning it up afterwards encourages longer printing runs. But there are other options.

The photocopy machine is quick, easy to find, easy to use, and inexpensive. Even the cost of color copies is coming down to the point where they can be used for small editions. A good idea is to copy the text pages on a regular copy machine, leaving spaces for the color parts. Gather up all of the color illustrations on one sheet, copy that sheet, then cut apart the pictures and paste them in their respective places.

Gocco printing provides another option for producing color in small editions. Developed in Japan, this type of printing begins with a stencil made by using flash bulbs. Ink is added inside the stencil, and the press operates like a giant stamp pad. It is possible to print more than one color at a time. Most large craft supply stores carry gocco printing outfits, and they can also be purchased by mail order. A set including everything necessary for printing a 4" × 6" area currently costs under $100.

Other ways to reproduce text and images include rubber stamps, silkscreen, block prints, stencils, sponging, collage, mimeograph, ditto, and Xerox transfers. It is still possible to find tabletop letterpress printers. Nothing discourages wordiness like having to set each word in type, letter by letter!

While we are rethinking books, let's take a second look at the structure of books. We tend to think of books as pieces of paper folded in half and attached somehow between cardboard covers. But there are a lot more possibilities.

Pages can be unusual shapes. They can have pockets for fact cards, minifolders, even paper puppets. Pages can unfold to the side, top, or bottom. Pop-ups can be added. Holes in pages can reveal images and text before the page is turned. The edges of the page can be torn, crinkle-cut, or folded to give an interesting effect. Tabs can be added to make parts of the page slide, swivel, or unfold.

The binding for the book can be elaborate, but it does not have to be. It might be as simple as a punched hole with a key chain through it. It is possible to glue the pages together or to use several different decorative sewing stitches. Paper fasteners and staples can be used. Most copy centers have a comb binding machine that allows you to combine different colors, sizes, and types of pages in one binding. Pages can be interwoven to stay together. They can be held together with tabs. It is even possible to take one sheet of paper and cut and fold it into several different book structures.

Books can take many forms. There are tunnel books, star books (with pages that unfold like petals), shape books, miniature books, oversized books, action books, pocketbooks, collage books, journals, diaries, scrolls, accordion folded books, cloth books, *dos-a-dos* (two books that share one of their covers), time-lines, flip books, and rotating wheel books. The possibilities are limited only by the imagination.

THE JOY OF BOOKMAKING PROGRAMS

If everyone has a story to tell and everyone should make a book, what part does the library play in encouraging, promoting, and preserving these efforts? As the community center for preserving and presenting information, libraries are a natural facility for bookmaking programs. And it is a win-win situation. The materials are inexpensive, the instructions simple, and the results overwhelming.

MATERIALS ARE INEXPENSIVE

I believe in keeping bookmaking simple. Paper and materials can be found at an office supply store, and basic tools such as a pencil, ruler, scissors, glue stick, and something for folding are all that are necessary to produce simple editions. A bone folder would be wonderful, but the back of a plastic picnic knife (the nonserrated edge) suffices.

Some instructors favor using only the best handmade and decorative papers. The argument is that if students have the best materials with which to work, it will encourage their best efforts. I think it is important to show people that making books is within their reach and can be accomplished with materials close at hand. There is something to be said for using materials that you will not feel badly about destroying if a mistake is made.

At the point of materials selection, you can talk about the longevity and preservation of the materials being used. Decisions about acid-free paper and archival glues, as well as the type of binding chosen, can be connected in a very real way with the library's preservation efforts.

Simple bookmaking leads to more involved bookmaking. If you can get people hooked on making books, once they gain confidence, they will search out better materials and more complicated structures. But start simple first.

INSTRUCTIONS ARE SIMPLE

Fine bookbinding, like fine letterpress printing, is a complicated art form requiring study and practice—lots of it. But that is not what guerrilla bookmaking is about. It is the process of putting simple bookmaking skills into the hands of everyday people. Put aside conventional ideas of what a book is and look for innovative ways of putting the stories and visions of people into book form. As librarians, you can obtain instructions easily. Either go to the stacks and pick an instruction book off the shelves or place a couple of the titles from ''Bookmaking: An Annotated Bibliography'' (see end of this case study) at the top of your next book order.

THE RESULTS ARE OVERWHELMING

How do you evaluate a bookmaking program? The answer is to look at the books produced and at the people who created them. Look for stories recorded for the first time and in unusual ways. Look for people that radiate happiness, the result of seeing their first book produced. They have just taken part of themselves and put it into a form that preserves it and allows it to be shared with other people. This is library preservation at its best.

A fourth grader came up and proudly presented the book she had just made. ''I'm going to save this,'' she announced, ''and show it to my daughter when she is in the fourth grade.'' This is the essence of preservation and making books. And if you think there is pride in the first book, wait until you see the satisfaction that comes from the vast improvement on the second try.

EXCAVATING FOR CREATIVITY

In the course of our education, many things are educated into us. Unfortunately, some things are nearly educated out of us; creativity is one area that often suffers. How can children start out so full of excitement and inspiration and end up as insecure adults? But creativity is never lost; it just needs encouragement. And making books is a wonderful way of developing and promoting creativity.

EVERYONE HAS EXPERIENCE

How many writing sessions have started off with the complaint, ''I have nothing to write about''? Everyone, including children, has an experience about which to write. Someone may have experience growing up with a houseful of brothers and sisters, while another may have experience growing up as an only child. Someone may have tried many different occupations, while another may have the in-depth knowledge that comes from concentrating on one area for a long period. Someone may have a lot about which to write because they always have something to say; another may because they are always listening. Everyone has something about which to write.

EVERYONE CAN DRAW

If you ask a group of third graders to draw a horse, without a moment of hesitation they will all start drawing horses. And what a wonderful herd of horses emerges! Not one will look like any of the others, and no one notices or cares. But somewhere in the middle grades the situation changes. Given the same instruction, the pencils get put down and the wail starts to rise, ''I can't draw a horse.'' Somewhere we have learned that unless we can draw like everyone else, sing like everyone else, dance like everyone else, we can't draw, sing, or dance. If someone said, ''You don't talk like us,'' would we shut up? Of course not. And we should not let others stifle our artistic talents either.

An argument can be made that you cannot draw like everyone else. But then, they can't draw like you! Like everything else, the more we draw, the better we get and the more comfortable we will be with our talents. I did not start drawing seriously until I was in my late thirties. It took me that long to overcome the mistaken belief that I could not draw. People may not feel comfortable with the present state of their talents. But that does not change the fact that everyone *can* draw. A little encouragement often reaps surprising results.

You do not even have to draw. There are other ways to add illustrations to your books. You can ask a friend who is more comfortable with their drawing skills to help. There are books of copyright-free clip art on every subject. You can also use rubber stamps or clippings from magazines.

BALANCE BETWEEN WORDS AND PICTURES

In the early grades, we learned to combine words and pictures. Somewhere along the way, the two areas separated. We learned that the art teacher has to teach art and the English teacher has to teach writing. In fact, the two areas have a lot in common. If you can visualize a picture, you can write about it. If you can describe it in words, you can also illustrate it.

The great quality about a blank book is that you can fill it in any way you want. People who like to write put in lots of words and may leave just enough room for spot decorations. People who like to draw may create big illustrations, leaving just enough room for captions. However it is done, it is helpful to recognize the relationship between words and illustrations and to strive for a balance that recognizes the importance of both.

DON'T FORGET THE ADULTS

Children's librarians will find this case study helpful. Other librarians may be tempted to skip over it, thinking there is nothing here for them; they are wrong. Children bring a lot of enthusiasm, inventiveness, and imagination to the book arts. Adults bring experience, perspective, and knowledge. And they bring a willingness to share this information with others. Adults, particularly men, have an initial reluctance to get involved. Do not be fooled. Once the joys of recording and sharing life experiences through books is understood, there follows an outpouring of enthusiasm and productivity.

I taught a series of bookmaking workshops at the Phoenix Public Library. The workshops for children filled up quickly. The evening adult workshop did fill, but only at the last minute. All through the workshop, I noticed curious adults poking their heads through the door to check out what we were doing. After the class, as we were putting our materials away, several other adults came in to look at the books we had created. Then, in the parking lot as I was loading my car, I was overwhelmed by adult library patrons wanting to know more about how they could make a book and when more classes would be offered. Adult workshops are a hard sell, but the results are worth the effort.

A PRESERVATION OPPORTUNITY

A library is more than the sum of its books. It is the total of all of its programs for preserving and sharing knowledge in the community. Making books is an opportunity for the library to go beyond preserving physical items, to preserving information and experiences on the grassroots level. It is a way to get people interested and excited about all books. It is a way to make the library an unforgettable and appreciated part of a community's existence.

BOOKMAKING: AN ANNOTATED BIBLIOGRAPHY

How-to Books for Young Readers

Chapman, Gillian, and Pam Robson, *Making Books: A Step-by-Step Guide to Your Own Publishing*. Brookfield, CT: Millbrook Press, 1991.

Divided into two sections. The first section contains instructions for making a variety of book structures, including cloth, zigzag, scrolls, sewn, and pop-up books. The second section is devoted to planning, designing, printing, and decorating the finished book.

Stowell, Charlotte. *Step-by-Step Making Books*. New York: Kingfisher, 1994.

Carefully drawn illustrations and colorful photos of finished projects show how to create many types of books including novelty notebooks, zigzag, pop-ups, mechanical, and peek-in (carousel) books.

Walsh, Natalie. *Making Books Across the Curriculum: Pop Ups, Flaps, Shapes, Wheels and Many More*. New York: Scholastic Books, 1994.

Not as colorful as the other books but loaded with ideas. The instructions are divided into shape books, minibooks, and dozens of folding books.

Traditional Bookbinding

Johnson, Pauline. *Creative Bookbinding*. Seattle: University of Washington Press, 1963. rev. 1980 and 1990.

Includes a history of books and a discussion of materials, tools, and procedures. The instructions that follow go from simple folders all the way up to full leather bindings. There is also a good section on paper decoration.

Shepherd, Rob. *Hand-made Books: An Introduction to Bookbinding*. Turnbridge Wells, Kent, England: Search Press, 1994.

A thin book, but with over 100 color photos, it contains easy-to-follow, step-by-step instructions for creating many traditional book structures such as single section, multi-section, and single-leaf bindings.

Exploring Innovative Book Structures

Gaylord, Susan Kapuscinski. *Multicultural Books to Make and Share*. New York: Scholastic Books, 1994.

Dozens of book structures are divided by geographic areas: Africa, the Americas, Asia, and Europe. The structures describe six basic book forms: scroll, accordion, palm leaf, slat, Oriental stitched binding, and Western stitched binding.

Johnson, Paul. *A Book of One's Own: Developing Literacy Through Making Books*. Portsmouth, NH: Heinemann, 1990.

Johnson, Paul. *Literacy through the Book Arts*. Portsmouth, NH: Heinemann, 1993.

Not only do these two books show how to make interesting structures, many from a single sheet of paper, they also show how to bring out the natural creativity of people.

LaPlantz, Shereen. *Cover to Cover: Creative Techniques for Making Beautiful Books, Journals and Albums*. Asheville, NC: Lark Books, 1995.

This book is loaded with bright photographs, detailed instructions, and step-by-step illustrations to make an overwhelming variety of books. The major categories are pamphlet stitch, basic codex, stitches, stab bindings, fold books, combination books, and unusual bindings.

Webberley, Marilyn, and JoAn Forsyth. *Books, Boxes & Wraps: Binding and Building Step-by-Step*. Kirkland, WA: Bifocal, 1995.

The author has pulled together ideas from many sources to compile a handy sourcebook with instructions and diagrams for making a multitude of book structures and cases to hold them.

For the Advanced Student

Ikegami, Kojiro. *Japanese Bookbinding*. New York and Tokyo: Weatherhill, 1979, 1986.

This is the first book in English with instructions for making all of the major, historically important Japanese bindings: basic four-hole binding with variations, accordions, ledgers, and scrolls. Among the procedures described is how to back ordinary fabric so it can be used as book cloth.

Smith, Keith A. *Structure of the Visual Book*. Rochester, NY: Keith Smith Books, 1984, 1992.

Smith, Keith A. *Text in the Book Format*. Rochester, NY: Keith Smith Books, 1989.

Smith, Keith A. *Books without Paste or Glue: Non-Adhesive Binding*. Vol. 1. Rochester, NY: Keith Smith Books, 1990.

Smith, Keith A. *1-2-& 3-Section Sewings: Non-Adhesive Binding*. Vol. 2. Rochester, NY: Keith Smith Books, 1995.

Smith, Keith A. *Exposed Spine Sewings: Non-Adhesive Binding*. Vol. 3. Rochester, NY: Keith Smith Books, 1995.

All available from Keith Smith Books, 22 Cayuga Street, Rochester, NY 14620-2153; 1-716-473-6776. Eventually everyone involved in the book arts comes around to discovering Keith Smith's books. He covers how to organize a book as a visual object, how to use and present text, and more imaginative ways to put pages together without using glue than anyone thought possible. The books are very technical, but the results are well worth the effort.

6

Preservation Education in Academic Libraries

Approaches for Preservation Education in Academic Libraries

Lorraine Olley, Indiana University,
Bloomington, Indiana

INTRODUCTION

Preservation is central to the mission of the academic research library. During the course of recorded history, libraries have served as repositories for the protection of and access to recorded knowledge, regardless of medium or format—clay tablets; papyrus scrolls; codices on animal skins and, later, paper; and more recently, electromagnetic tape and disk, optical disk, and electronic files. Preservation concerns go beyond the physical well-being of materials that serve as the substrate for information. Preservation is now understood to mean ensuring continuing access to information of enduring value by protecting the original artifact, creating a facsimile, or copying the information onto a more stable substrate.

In this age of electronic resources, online access, and the information super-highway, library users and librarians are lulled into a feeling of "information security." The glut of CD-ROM, Internet, and other electronic resources makes it hard to imagine being without information on virtually every topic—more information than we can handle. However, there are early warnings that we are losing information and cultural resources as quickly as we create new ones. For example, there was no footage from the first five years of the *Tonight Show* included in Johnny Carson's farewell broadcast because none had been preserved. At an Internet conference in 1994, it was announced that the Archive of Rock Lyrics had closed off Internet access because the demand for network access was too heavy for the host system to support. This is the equivalent of destroying every copy of a book but one, making the Rock Lyrics Archives perhaps one of the first ''rare'' electronic resources. On the World Wide Web, URLs (Universal Resource Locators) change or vanish with alarming frequency.

Electronic publications are another example of the precarious nature of these data. Discussion of electronic journals usually includes recognition of the necessity to ''archive'' the files in order to provide continuing access. But there appears to be no standard protocol for assigning the responsibility and providing for the expense of maintaining the backfile—what would on paper be the ''bound run.'' Does that burden reside with the publisher, a designated subscriber, a commercial document delivery service, or with each library?

With this in mind, it becomes imperative to alert the future librarians, scholars, technologists, and citizens that pass through our institutions of higher education about the importance of preservation for the growth of knowledge and the continuity of our cultural heritage. Consciousness is being raised in surprising ways. For example, two cable television channels, Nickelodeon and the American Movie Channel, advocate preservation in their commercial spots. Nickelodeon announcements talk about the importance of preserving our TV heritage. In 1994, the American Movie Channel launched its ''Film Preservation Festival,'' an annual fund-raising telethon for the preservation of motion pictures.

Since, as members of the general public, academicians and students are already aware of the deterioration problem inherent in cultural artifacts, they should be more understanding of and receptive to messages about preserving all materials, including information resources. However, the prevalence of electronic resources in academic libraries has given rise to the misguided notion that ''everything will be digitized anyway'' and a consequent disregard for materials in the traditional paper format.

PROMOTING PRESERVATION AWARENESS

Despite the growing role of academic libraries as gatekeepers for electronic resources, they are still basically storehouses of information contained primarily in the traditional format of print on paper. Books, documents, and other media all deteriorate over time. The goal of the library's preservation awareness program is to promote an understanding of the causes of deterioration and of the ways to retard it for as long as possible.

Bibliographic instruction and reference librarians, since they are on the front lines, are in perhaps the best position to promote preservation awareness among library users. And it's understandable that they might balk at being asked to add one more topic to the plethora that they must cover in a rapidly changing information environment. However, there are many ways in which preservation awareness, particularly the importance of proper care and handling of the paper-based resources that comprise the vast majority of research library collections, may be incorporated into informal and formal bibliographic instruction in a relatively painless way. This discussion will focus on three approaches: (1) training the trainers; (2) incorporating preservation concerns into bibliographic instruction, regardless of audience or topic; and (3) presenting stand-alone formal preservation awareness activities.

Training the Trainers

All librarians and staff are responsible for promoting preservation awareness, particularly the importance of proper care and handling. Consequently, it's important for all librarians and staff to be conversant about—not necessarily expert in—preservation issues (e.g., causes of deterioration, importance of proper environment, proper handling techniques for all media, safe photocopying).

Unfortunately, most library school curricula offer little, if any, education about preservation, and most academic libraries lack a preservation administrator. Consequently, librarians interested in combating deterioration in their collections must take the initiative to educate themselves. Beginning with Lisa L. Fox's *A Core Collection in Preservation*,[1] the librarian can select readings for background and to suit immediate interests or needs. (For additional information on patron education, see Appendix 4.) Subscribing to several of the general interest periodicals in the field, which are listed in the *Core Collection*, will help the librarian keep abreast of trends, technology, programs, and ideas. Frequent visits to the CoOL (Conservation OnLine) Web site (http://palimpsest. stanford.edu/) and a subscription to the related *Conservation DistList* (consdist-request@lindy.stanford.edu) are essential for up-to-the-minute information about conservation science and technology and news of the preservation field. Throughout the year, many national, regional, and local agencies offer preservation workshops, often in conjunction with professional conferences. These workshops present opportunities for hands-on training and networking with other preservation professionals.

The knowledgeable librarian can then disseminate information throughout the local library, through the library's newsletter or other communication tools, staff training, and informal encounters. Educated staff are better able to answer users' questions (e.g., "Why are the pages breaking when I turn them?") and provide the rationale behind bothersome regulations, such as the prohibition against food and drink in the library.

When library staff educated about preservation work to create and maintain a proper environment—neat book stacks, materials in processing units handled with care—their efforts convey a professional respect for library materials that impresses and influences users. There is anecdotal evidence that neat stack areas tend to stay neat, and disorganized or untidy areas tend to degenerate into chaos.

Routine training of student workers, especially shelvers, may be seen as a form of bibliographic instruction. Students educated about the causes of deterioration of library materials and the importance of proper handling will exercise more care when they perform their tasks. They may also promote proper care and handling among their peers.

Including Preservation Awareness in Bibliographic Instruction

The second approach is to incorporate preservation concerns into routine bibliographic instruction (BI). Again, the librarian's spoken concern and unspoken care for materials can send a powerful message. For example, during the course of an orientation tour, the librarian can briefly describe the "brittle book" problem, demonstrate how to remove and reshelve a volume safely, point out where to get help loading a microfilm reader, and indicate posted instructions for nondestructive photocopying. If the library has a preservation department or a book repair workshop, it can be added as an interesting and informative stop on the tour.

The Indiana University (IU) Libraries offer tours to parents and incoming freshmen during summer orientation and to all students each fall. The Conservation Unit of the Preservation Department has been included in these tours during the past few years, and the response has been positive. It should be noted that there is no attempt during orientation to discuss causes of deterioration or to do "care and handling" training. Tour guides bring the group into the conservation area, which has big, exotic-looking equipment such as board shears and a portable fume hood, as well as computer workstations. Using a script prepared by the head of collections conservation, the guide gives a very brief description of the activities that go on in the unit. The guide also describes the examples of damaged materials and repaired counterparts (labeled "problem" and "solution") that are set out on a small book truck. These examples include a book with a partly detached "loose" spine and one with a repaired spine; a book with detached boards (captioned "loose spine allowed to circulate—continues to deteriorate") and its counterpart in a new cover; a brittle book in a phase box; and a water-damaged book that has been freeze-dried. Several books damaged through negligence are displayed as well. The most amusing one of these is a cookbook with the rings of an electric range burner scorched into its front cover. There are also examples of death by photocopier and by dog, and books permanently marred by pizza grease and chewing gum.

Informal canvasing of the tour guides indicates that they feel comfortable with the level of information they are expected to convey and that the tourists are very interested and impressed by the damaged materials, the repairs, and the equipment. It wasn't until the Wei T'o Freezer-dryer was moved out of Conservation that the guides disclosed that it had been one of the most popular attractions on the tour. It should be noted that this particular education effort is virtually no-cost (after all, someone else went to the trouble to destroy the books) and reaches a large number of library users and potential supporters.

Preservation education can also be incorporated into one-on-one reference interchanges. The librarian who is conversant about preservation issues can answer user questions about the fragility of a particular volume, the overall poor condition of materials in the user's subject area (e.g., Slavic or African imprints, music published in France), or the library's choice of less user-friendly formats (e.g., microfilm rather than bound volumes of newspapers). When removing a reference volume from the shelf or loading a CD-ROM into its drive, the librarian sets an example by handling materials with care. Unusual actions, like grasping a volume at midspine rather than pulling the headcap, even if unexplained, will make an impression on the user, provoking thought and perhaps questions about care and handling.

Ideally, preservation would be a topic in every bibliographic instruction session and lecture. Practically, the BI librarian works against the clock and the short attention span of students to convey as much information about print and electronic resources as possible. But preservation can be incorporated into classroom sessions with relative ease. For example, one bibliographic instructor prepared a transparency of cockroaches swarming on the overhead projector, with the caption "ROACHES EAT BOOKS." This had great shock value, as it popped up unexpectedly in her series of transparencies about reference resources. When it did, the instructor would briefly explain that food is not permitted in the library because it draws bugs that attack library materials. On the other hand, the approach can be as subtle as simply handing out bookmarks or flyers with preservation messages along with other materials distributed to students.

If a course on library research is offered, it is possible to devote all or part of a class session to preservation. At the IU Libraries, librarians teach a one-semester undergraduate course on library use. The head of collections conservation presents one class session on preservation. She reports that contrasting the strong flexible paper in an eighteenth-century book to the crumbling paper in a late nineteenth-century book makes a strong impression on the students.

If there is no preservation specialist on staff, the BI librarian can turn to a number of effective audiovisual resources. It's important to preview the presentation and gear its level to the audience. For undergraduates, the 15-minute *Murder in the Stacks*[2] gives good basic care and handling information in a slightly campy, entertaining format. For more sophisticated audiences, the 33-minute version of *Slow Fires*,[3] although slightly outdated, is still an effective tool for educating users about the causes of deterioration and the importance of preservation measures for books, photographs, motion pictures, electronic, and other media. (For more video resources, see Appendix 3, Videography.)

Surrounding the library user with preservation messages in other formats can strengthen the impact of formal instruction. Take-away information, such as flyers in information packets distributed to faculty and students or bookmarks inserted in books as they are checked out, will prompt users to remember and consider preservation issues. The IU Libraries Preservation Department prepared a flyer, "Caring for the Libraries Collections," which is one of the series of general informational leaflets available in reference areas and distributed to users. Displaying engaging graphical reminders, such as posters and exhibits, will reinforce preservation awareness. There are many sources for the content of bibliographic instruction about preservation, including this publication, publications from the Association of Research Libraries, and information from LOEX Clearinghouse for Library Instruction (see Appendix 4) and from individual libraries.

In all bibliographic instruction on preservation, a few basic points should be hammered home. First, all library materials are fragile and endangered. Paper tears and crumbles, books fall apart, microfilm breaks, videotapes wear out, compact discs scratch, electronic files become unreadable. Second, each library user has an impact for good or ill on the condition and longevity of the library's collection. Third, repair and replacement are expensive activities that decrease the library's capacity to purchase new materials and services; consequently, the user benefits by taking care of the collections.

Preservation Awareness Activities

The third approach to teaching preservation awareness is to develop stand-alone programs. These events can reach a broader audience more effectively than bibliographic instruction. An example of this approach is the IU Libraries Preservation Awareness Week, which incorporated many types of activities to focus attention on preservation.

Preservation Awareness Week was presented during National Library Week in 1992, but planning began fully 19 months earlier. All of the activities and materials were developed by the Libraries' Preservation Committee, which is made up of volunteer librarians and staff from all segments of the library system. A tremendous amount of time and hard work went into planning and presenting this very ambitious week long event, but individual activities can be used effectively with much less effort.

The most exciting part of the planning was developing the graphic materials package to be introduced to the Libraries during the week. The Preservation Committee arranged to work with a class in the IU School of Fine Arts to develop original graphics. To make it a more valuable experience for the students, the committee acted the role of client negotiating with the students as graphic designers. During the initial meeting, the committee gave a brief overview of the issues of library preservation and outlined the goals of the graphic design element of the campaign. The primary goals were to create an identity for the Libraries Preservation Program and to focus attention on the impact of proper and improper handling on the longevity of library materials. Resources available to the class included samples of materials from other libraries campaigns and access to committee members for consultation. A few weeks later, the class members made formal presentations of their designs to the committee. There were over a dozen really engaging designs, all of them on target in terms of the messages conveyed. It was very difficult to make a final choice. The selection of a package of materials based on the design element of a bold sans serif capital *P* was made because all the materials were self-explanatory and consistent as a series and because, being two-color, they were inexpensive to print. Ten bookmark designs, four poster designs, a book bag, a table tent, and a photocopy charge card envelope were produced and distributed. The IU Libraries Preservation Program logo—two interlocking *P*'s—that appears on all of the items mirrors the infinity symbol (see Figure 2.1). (Samples of some of the bookmarks and posters may be viewed on the IU Libraries Preservation Department home page (http://www.indiana.edu/~libpres).

The week's activities were supported by the IU Libraries and the School of Library and Information Science (SLIS). The week was planned to have great visibility and broad appeal, with 12 programs in various formats. Publicity appeared on all eight campuses of the university and in the local and Indianapolis newspapers. The dean of the University Libraries mailed invitations to George Cunha's keynote address and reception to all the librarians in the IU system and SLIS faculty and students.

Four exhibit areas in the main library lobby, which is the highest traffic area, gave the greatest visibility to the event. One exhibit highlighted the schedule of the week's events. The second illustrated the work of the Preservation Department, with photos depicting various treatments displayed along with smaller tools and presses and eye-catching swatches of book cloth and marbled paper. The third, "The Enemies of Books," educated users about the causes of deterioration of library materials, with a display of the usual grisly examples of brittleness, insect damage, user abuse, and the like. The fourth, "Daily Disasters," reinforced the notion that careless handling and deliberate vandalism can be as harmful as fires and floods. The examples included torn and mutilated pages and volumes, pages with illustrations cut out, highlighted texts, and other damage resulting from users' negligence or action. The preservation graphics materials also premiered at circulation desks and in exhibits during this week.

George Cunha, the late director emeritus of the Northeast Document Conservation Center and one of the founders of library preservation, gave the keynote address, titled "Library Conservation: The 1990s and Beyond," to an audience of librarians, library staff, SLIS faculty, and students. Cunha emphasized that conservation is an inseparable part of the overall management of libraries. Contrary to those who predict that libraries will soon cease to exist, he countered that "book-filled libraries as we know them now will be around for a long, long time, and with them the requirement for conservation management of the traditional materials plus solutions for the new problems that are inevitable as the new technologies are absorbed into the overall scheme of things." The printed text and videotape of his talk were added to the SLIS Library collection and so are available for continuing education purposes.

Besides the preservation graphics, exhibits, and keynote address, a preservation "Film Festival," with such classics as the aforementioned *Murder in the*

Stacks and *Slow Fires*, as well as videos with a more local appeal was presented. A video tour of Heckman Bindery[4] gave library staff a view of the operations of the current commercial binder for the IU Libraries. A special presentation was the documentary *The Mark of the Maker*[5] which features the Twinrocker hand papermaking business in Brookston, Indiana. This film had great local appeal, since it was about an Indiana business. Also, since it had been nominated for an Academy Award, it drew film studies students as well as the general audience.

By far the most popular feature of the week was "Doctor Book." For this, head of collections conservation Jo Burgess set up a workbench in the main library lobby and gave diagnostic consultations to people with "sick" books. She explained causes of problems, discussed possible treatments, and referred people to local businesses and conservation suppliers for materials and assistance. Besides the people who brought books in for the Doctor to evaluate, there were many students and other library users who, curious about the sewing frame on the workbench, engaged in lengthy conversations about preservation issues.[6] The talent and energy that went into planning and presenting Preservation Awareness Week was rewarded by the IU Libraries receiving the John Cotton Dana Award for Public Relations in 1993.[7]

It is important to repeat activities to keep preservation visible, and the library should plan at least one event every year. It may be advisable to choose a time other than the beginning of the school year so the message is not lost in the information overload that occurs at that time.

In reviewing Preservation Awareness Week, the committee decided that using National Library Week in April was too late in the school year to have the desired impact. The IU Libraries 1995 preservation campaign was presented in November, near the middle of the first semester and after all orientation activities were over. Focusing on promoting a sense of respect and care for library materials, its theme was "The Life of a Book: It's in Your Hands." A new poster illustrated various types of user abuse—cut-out pictures, a dog-chewed volume, food-stained pages, defaced texts, and the like. An exhibit in the main library lobby illustrated the tasks, resources, and costs involved in repairing user-caused damage. Conservation staff set up shop in the lobby for eight hours during the week to demonstrate treatments and answer questions. A video kiosk showed *Murder in the Stacks*, the Heckman Bindery tape, and a segment from the campus TV station newsmagazine *Studio 6* highlighting the Preservation Department. Publicity appeared in local news sources, some library publications, and on the Libraries Web site. See the Vaughan case study in Chapter 2 for more details on the 1995 campaign.

CONCLUSION

Preservation education can be incorporated into library use instruction in many ways and with varying degrees of intensity. The example set by knowledgeable librarians and staff, the information about preservation that is available for distribution, and exhibits and posters are the least labor-intensive ways to increase preservation awareness. Preservation can also be effectively folded into bibliographic instruction and can certainly be the focus of attention for a special event or activity.

Perhaps in selling preservation to all library users, we can take a lesson from society at large. Preservation is not usually seen as a library service but as a burden and restriction on the user. We need to promote the idea that preservation, especially proper care and handling, is a vital service that users can provide for each other and for the future. Like recycling, which takes extra time and effort, but is acknowledged as a universal good, preservation can be presented as an individual responsibility that has lasting benefits for society. the Hard Rock Cafe admonishes us to ''Save the Planet''—let's save the books, too.

NOTES

1. Lisa L. Fox, comp., *A Core Collection in Preservation*, 2nd ed. by Don K. Thompson and Joan ten Hoor (Chicago: American Library Association, 1993).

2. Columbia University Libraries Preservation Committee, *Murder in the Stacks*, (New York: Center For Biomedical Communications, College of Physicians & Surgeons, Columbia University, 1987), 1 videocassette (15 min.).

3. *Slow Fires: On the Preservation of the Human Record*, (Santa Monica, CA: American Film Foundation, 1987), 1 videocassette (33 min.).

4. *The Heckman Bindery, Inc.*, (Indianapolis, IN: USATeleproductions, 1989), 1 videocassette (12 min.).

5. *The Mark of the Maker: Twinrocker Handmade Paper*, (Chicago, IL: McGowen Film and Video, 1991), 1 videocassette (28 min.).

6. For more information about this event, see Lorraine Olley, ''Indiana University Libraries Presents Preservation Awareness Week,'' *Conservation Administration News* no. 53 (April 1993): 10–11.

7. Connie Vinita Dowell, ''An Award Winner Brings Preservation Out of the Lab,'' *College & Research Libraries News* 54, no. 9 (October 1993): 524–526.

CASE STUDIES

Jammin' with Preservation and Preservation Awareness Month

Becky Ryder, University of Kentucky, Lexington, Kentucky

During October 1993 the University of Kentucky Libraries staged a monthlong preservation education event in an effort to broaden the university community's understanding of library preservation concerns. The event, "Preservation Awareness Month," also known as PAM, was designed to orient new staff and students to basic preservation routines. Additionally, the exhibits, displays, handouts, and book repair demonstrations were geared to appeal to the Libraries' patrons. The Libraries' Preservation Committee, composed of librarians and support staff from the entire library system, coordinated the event, which took nine months to plan.

PLANNING

In planning for the event, the Preservation Committee enlisted the assistance of the staff in the Binding/Book Repair Unit and the Microfilm Center. In January 1993, this combined group assembled for a brainstorming session. Although there was administrative support for the planning efforts, only minimal resources were available for advertising and publications. With this in mind, the group tried to think of events and exhibits that might have significant impact, without incurring significant cost. The group also considered that prior efforts to promote preservation were only moderately successful due to the tight scheduling at public service desks in the main and branch libraries. Many staff simply could not leave a desk area to attend a preservation slide-tape presentation, and for those who could attend, a forum for discussion was not available because of time constraints. This dilemma begged for more flexibility and variety. As a result, the committee planned a monthlong series of activities, most of which would "replay" during the course of the month. In addition, the group was certain that a monthlong preservation "media blitz" via E-mail, flyers, handouts, television, and radio spots would certainly permeate the consciousness of nearly every employee and many library patrons. By February, the event had taken shape and Preservation Awareness Month was on the drawing board.

PAM: THE EVENTS

After eight months of planning, Preservation Awareness Month came together as a cohesive and varied event. It included several major features:

1. Speaker Series
2. Preservation Video Festival
3. Book Repair Demonstrations
4. Book Problem Diagnosis Session and Book Value Assessment Session
5. Tours of the Special Collections and Archives Department
6. Tours of the Microfilm Center

The Speaker Series occurred once a week during PAM. The late George Cunha, then a resident of Lexington and an adjunct faculty member at the University of Kentucky College of Library and Information Science, agreed to provide the first lecture, titled "Library Conservation: 1990s and Beyond." Others speakers included the Libraries' preservation librarian, who documented the Libraries preservation planning program; the audiovisual archivist, who discussed and demonstrated the challenges of nonprint media; and the associate director for facilities, who related the efforts to involve preservation principles in the planning of a new central library.

The Book Repair Demonstrations were set up in the lobby of the main library. Staff and students from the Book Repair Unit conducted seven four-hour sessions. They worked together demonstrating page repairs, spine and endsheet repairs, pamphlet binding, box making, and diagnosis techniques. Four two-hour Book Diagnosis and Book Value Assessment sessions were held. The Book Repair and Book Diagnosis/Assessment sessions were immensely popular. People brought in treasures and trash for evaluation. They watched spellbound while students wielded scalpels and PVA (polyvinyl acetate) to create book repair magic. Catalogs from preservation supply companies, handouts with simple directions for caring for personal collections, bookmarks, and Heckman Bindery pencils were used as giveaways for those who spent time at the demonstration areas.

The Preservation Video Festival included showings, sometimes "double features,'' of a variety of preservation videos. Most videos were shown at least two times, with *Slow Fires* being shown three times. *The Inside Track to Disaster Recovery* was paired with a 15-minute demonstration on how to dry out a (1) damp, (2) soaking wet, or (3) soaking wet, muddy book. UMI's video titled *Caring for Your Microfilm Collection* was paired with Preservation Resources' video *MAPS: The Future of Preservation Microfilming*, after which a 15-minute discussion ensued about microfilm and digital technologies. All videos were introduced by a Preservation Committee member. Brochures or informational flyers were distributed at the end of each showing.

The tours of Special Collections and Archives provided a glimpse of the efforts to preserve rare and unique materials. In addition to seeing specialized materials, the tourists also saw the Liebert units, hygrothermographs, and compact shelving. The Microfilm Center also provided tours of its facility. The staff set up examples of the prefilm preparations, demonstrated the filming of newspapers and books, and explained the processing and quality control routines. In addition, they compiled a photo exhibit of the filming processes, and they prepared handouts detailing the history and the mission of the Libraries Microfilm Center.

EXHIBITS

During PAM, two exhibits were mounted in the main library. One exhibit focused on the factors leading to the deterioration of library materials and what can be done to prevent damage. Examples of pre-1850 books in excellent condition were displayed alongside early twentieth-century books. The durable paper contrasted profoundly with the embrittled pages. A hygrothermograph was set up in the exhibit case to demonstrate climate monitoring, examples of preservationally sound book repairs were presented, and archival products were displayed. The second exhibit focused on the food and drink problem. Empty exhibit cases were lined with books, all of which were withdrawn from the collection. Then the library was toured for food trash. Within two hours, enough food trash and dead bugs were accumulated to cover the books in the cases. Two plastic rats were added as an extra gross touch. A large banner over the exhibit case exhorted patrons to observe the food and drink policy by stating: ''Your 10-Minute Snack May Cause Centuries of Damage.'' That exhibit and several smaller exhibits mounted at the Medical and Law Libraries generated many comments.

The impressive panel exhibit rented from the Commission on Preservation and Access was on display for two weeks. The panels featured excerpts from *Slow Fires* and drew attention to preservation and access issues faced by libraries and archives. This exhibit served as a backdrop for all of the book repair demonstrations and book diagnosis/appraisal sessions.

COSTS

The library provided funding to rent the Commission on Preservation and Access exhibit. They also provided $200 to produce the 1,500 copies of a flyer that served as the day-to-day schedule and description of events. These 11" × 17" flyers were distributed to all university faculty and library staff. They were mailed to library directors at nearby academic and public libraries, and they were sent to branch libraries to post and display in their buildings. The university's public relations department was notified, and they, in turn, took the lead in alerting newspaper, radio, and television contacts. One of the local television stations sent their weather expert to do a special feature on climate control and brittle books, while the university television station interviewed George Cunha and captured footage of the exhibits.

Two members of the Preservation Committee, both fairly skilled with graphic design and Pagemaker software, created a new brochure that provided pointers on how library patrons could assist with preservation care. This brochure was inexpensively copied on pink and blue stock and folded into brochure format by the committee. These brochures were widely disseminated to branch libraries and public service desks in the main library. Additionally, they were distributed at all video showings and other special events (see Figure 6.1).

EVALUATION

Following Preservation Awareness Month, the committee met to evaluate its efforts. No formal evaluation tools had been used, although head counts were tracked for all demonstrations, video showings, and tours. Informal feedback from library staff and patrons was overwhelmingly positive. A suggestion was made to mount this type of monthlong campaign on a biannual basis. In the intervening years, it was recommended that the committee sponsor a scaled-down, weeklong event. The committee observed that attendance at the video sessions comprised mostly main library staff. Few branch library staff and students attended. To remedy that, the committee suggested that the videos be circulated to all branch libraries for viewing and that in future planning more "remote" sites should be set up for viewing. Also, in planning for another large-scale event, the committee suggested that the event be coordinated with the local public library system, the community college library, and two nearby college libraries.

FOLLOW-UP EVENT

In the spring of 1995, the committee followed up with a four-day event titled "Jammin' with Preservation: How Well Preserved Are You?" The committee created the "Jammin' " theme, then designed a logo that featured a large straw-

Figure 6.1
Preservation Committee Brochure

Caring for Your Library's Collections

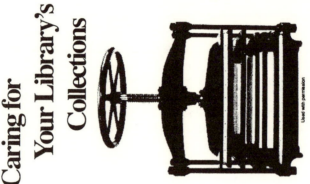

Used with permission

How Everyone Can Help

University of Kentucky Libraries
Preservation Department
301 King Library North
Lexington KY 40506-0039
(606) 257-4445

*Our Collections
Are In Your Hands*

For more information concerning
preservation issues, call:

Preservation Department
(606) 257-4445

Special Collections
(606) 257-8611

Brochure originally produced for
Preservation Awareness Month, 1993.

∞ Printed on **Permanent Acid-Free Paper**

YOU Can Help!

*Six easy steps YOU can take to
help protect our imperiled library
collections:*

1. Handle books with care.

2. Shelve books upright.

3. Report all disasters or potential
   disasters (e.g, water leaks).

4. No food or drink in the library.

5. Photocopy library materials
   with care.

6. Return damaged books to
   someone at the Circulation
   Desk instead of using a book
   drop.

The inside of this double-fold brochure gives additional care and handling information for library users.

berry, dancing "California Raisin-style" on a stack of books (see Figure 6.2). The logo was used on mailing labels, video sign-in sheets, posters, and other notices. The bright red strawberry immediately caught the eye of passersby as they glanced at the posters on the library bulletin boards. The posters listed the schedule of events, which included one three-hour book repair demonstration in the lobby of the main library and video showings at several sites. The committee put together a "Preservation Information Packet" containing several articles and brochures and a preservation bookmark. These were mailed to every library staff member. The preservation librarian posted a "Preservation Puzzler," a self-test, on e-mail every day. The questions ranged in scope from true/false statements about food and drink policies, shelving practices, microfilm, and digital technologies to "choose all that apply" questions about disaster response procedures. The "extra credit" question dealt with vinegar syndrome. Answers were posted the next day with new Preservation Puzzler questions. The concluding event for "Jammin' with Preservation" was a drawing for "Best-Preserved Librarian." To be eligible for this prize (a jar of strawberry jam!), folks had to attend at least one of the video sessions.

This entire event took no more than six weeks to plan and only a minimal amount of time and resources to mount. Photocopying articles and distributing the information packets consumed the most time. Composing the Preservation Puzzlers took very little time, and electronic mail proved to be a wonderful means to reach many people with some basic and entertaining preservation facts.

CONCLUSION

At this juncture, the University of Kentucky Libraries has not scheduled another Preservation Awareness Month, although plans are under consideration to link a preservation awareness event with the opening of a new central library in 1997. The Preservation Committee, however, will continue to provide a basic preservation orientation program in the form of a weeklong event every 12 to 18 months. It is gratifying to have library staff inquire about the plans for the next preservation event. This is perceived as a positive sign that preservation awareness events are of significant value to the entire library system.

Figure 6.2
Preservation Flyer

Join the fun
March 6-9!

Jammin'
with
Preservation!

How Well Preserved Are You?

Brought to you by the friendly folks on
the Preservation Committee.

Student-Designed Bookmarks for Preservation Education

Anthony J. Amodeo, Loyola Marymount University, Los Angeles, California

The opportunities to present preservation information to patrons can differ from institution to institution. Some academic librarians teach information literacy via required courses; some have the opportunity during subject courses team taught with regular faculty. For many, however, other than on a one-on-one basis at the usually busy reference desk, a 50-minute ''one-shot'' library session may be the only opportunity for many students to learn about the library. The latter is the situation at Loyola Marymount University (LMU).

Given the almost endless multiplication of technologies in recent years, more and more information about technology has had to be included in the same 50-minute time slot. This reduces the time available for several other topics, including preservation, to be covered.

The purpose of this project, then, was to make basic information about library preservation widely available to patrons, whether or not they had had formal library instruction at LMU. Additionally, the library is heavily used by both high school and college students from other institutions as well as walk-in community patrons. It was therefore hoped that the information would reach a greater proportion of patrons via something freely available, especially at the Reference Desk, which is situated to be visible and accessible to anyone entering the building.

BACKGROUND

For several years, at least some ideas regarding library preservation have been included in tours and classroom instruction at the LMU Von der Ahe Library. The instruction coordinator, a firm believer in preservation, provided the impetus, including the introduction of a few slides into the standard orientation package. The other librarians agreed to include at least some information on the importance of careful handling in their classroom presentations. Depending on the presenter and the type of presentation, some combination of slides, oral information, or hands-on demonstration was used to convey information about careful handling.

In order for patrons to be information literate these days, librarians have an obligation to cover new technology information in even the most basic instruction sessions. Yet even before this new information had become so necessary, instruction librarians were grappling with time constraints and the amount of information to be taught in the restrictive one-shot session.[1] Recently, at the Von der Ahe Library, a combination of low turnout for orientation tours, higher demand on librarians' time for upper-level instruction, and the learning curves for new technologies led to some changes. An audiotape cassette tour was introduced as a substitute for the standard orientation slide show or walk-around tour for new students. The standard one-shot session had to be modified to include Boolean logic and information about CD-ROM indexes. Therefore, presenting preservation information in a different way became a pressing need.

METHODOLOGY

In the spring of 1993, the coordinator of instruction decided that bookmarks with a preservation message would be a good way to reach patrons. Even if not read, the bookmarks would prevent some damage to heavily used reference books being caused by patrons. Patrons often marked their places in reference materials with notebooks, pens, pencils, and other thick objects—even other books—before carrying them upstairs to the photocopy room. After writing out about a dozen messages, the librarian showed them to Carm Goode, who teaches graphic design at LMU. After some discussion, Goode agreed to incorporate the design of some of the bookmarks as an assignment in his current class. The assignment is reproduced in Figure 6.3.

Criteria included a strong visual appeal without the use of color, a *look* that would appeal to college-age students, and the incorporation of the university's name or logo. The coordinator readily agreed that the given wording of individual messages could be modified or shortened, as long as the basic preservation message was evident.

The formal assignment embodied both the mechanical and philosophical/aesthetic issues involved. Goode selected one message for all the students to work with and gave them a choice of a half-dozen others. To make the assignment

Figure 6.3
Graphic Design Assignment

Loyola Marymount University
Department of
Art and Art History

Art 360	Graphic Design
Instructor:	Carm Goode
Semester:	Spring 1993
Project:	Number 3

Project Title: Bookmarks with Dyadic Symbols

Objectives:

1. To design a set of functional bookmarks to be given away by the LMU library.

2. To make a bold visual statement within an extemely small format

3. To use a visual dyad to illustrate the copy

Procedures:
Design a visual symbol and the accompanying text of a set of bookmarks for the LMU library. Use the copy supplied. See copy on a separate handout sheet. Before seeking reference material, analyze the written material into an A+B dyadic set, for instance, book + worm, book + highlighter, book + vandal, etc.

Restrictions:
Black and White, one side only, 2" x 7 1/4" Each bookmark must have a visual element in addition to typography. (However, typography might, in some cases be made into a visual symbol by the way it is treated.)

First steps:

1. Research: Find 3 good source images per each design. Be creative in your selection of reference imagery. Use photographs or scientific drawings, (no illustrations unless they are at least 40 years old) Actual objects can be used but only under certain circumstances. (Check with instructor.) Present your research neatly and in xerox form, all images within the approximate area of a 4" square, paired on an 8 1/2 x 11" page. This material too, will be assessed for the clarity of its basic form from 20 feet. Before you bring the material to class, look at it from 20 feet away and edit out images that lack silhouette interest and clarity.

2. Roughs: Choose two source forms, combine and simplify. Use principles from the dyadic chart supplied. Identify specific dyads used as structural models. Make sure images will reduce to the specified size.

At least one rough out of each three for each text must feature the image (or symbol) reversed out of a simple piece of geometry. To design the reversal, first design it in positive form, then reverse it out a simple black geometric shape. In order to insure figure and ground interest, make the form break out of the geometric form where possible, without destroying the definition or boldness of the forms. By all means,"give the viewer some work" in making visual continuances, or creating illusionistic effects.

Create 3 roughs of ideas for each symbol. Work to size. Because the success of the symbol depends on clarity at a small size, you must make use of simple geometry, even the initial roughs can't really be very rough. In order to gain simplicity, you must eliminate any "illustrative" detail. Select one out of each set for final-presentation. Any details or forms that are in the slightest way unclear must either be simplified or deleted. However, try to retain some significant feature from your research material in order to retain definition and to give your image some unique and eidetic (memorable) quality.

Final Presentation: at final presentation, turn in initialled xeroxes of research, initalled roughs (3 different ideas each) and comps, (3 refinements each) and the final versions for three bookmarks. Finals should be neatly mounted, tissued and flapped in black, and all material in a clean white or manila envelope. A duplicate unmounted set is included to give to the library for their actual use in reproduction.

as real world as possible, he had the class treat the librarian as a studio client. The librarian inspected the first draft mockups and commented on them. He was pleasantly surprised to find a board full of a variety of workable designs, many of them quite professional in concept and execution. A few designs were slightly off the mark, but almost all were pertinent, often clever, some humorous, and almost all drew in the viewer. Some were judged quite good for a special collections environment but too "classical" or bookish to meet the criterion of appeal to college students. The librarian made it clear that there was at the moment no funding for printing the bookmarks but that the designs would be used to sell the product.

Not many days later, the librarian returned for a final critique and selection. Only a few designs could be "finalists"; the students were told that many more were worthy of printing but that the printing budget would probably be very limited. Not even all the finalist designs could be printed at once, though it was hoped that money would eventually be found for more. What pleased the students (and, it was hoped, comforted the nonfinalists) was the librarian's asking for permission to make slides of all entries for use in an upcoming workshop on preservation for librarians involved in library instruction.[2] All students gave their permission, and slides were made. At the workshop, the slides generated favorable comments, some delighted laughter, and even applause from the librarians present. At the end of the semester, the librarian returned to the class with dessert and sparkling cider to thank the students for their efforts.

With input from both colleagues and library student workers, the final cut was made. The university librarian, G. Edward Evans, who had been shown the first culling, sought funds for printing. He was able to come up with sufficient funding for the thousand copies of each of the five designs that were eventually printed. Four of the bookmarks are regularly available for pickup at the Reference Desk. Sometimes librarians use one to make a point with a patron disobeying the pertinent rule. The bookmarks are also laid out with the handouts to be picked up at library classroom sessions. The fifth bookmark is distributed (along with plastic bags) at the Circulation Desk when rain threatens.

CONCLUSION/EVALUATION

The preservation messages represented in the final printed designs included:

- Not marking/writing in library materials: "Please, one author per book!"
- Not bringing food or drink into the library: "A Tiny Threat."
- Not exposing materials to moisture: "Keep It Dry!" (see Figure 6.4).

Due to a tight budget, the design with the following message will be printed in the future:

Figure 6.4
Preservation Messages Bookmark

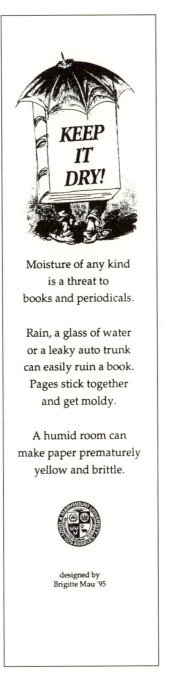

KEEP
IT
DRY!

Moisture of any kind
is a threat to
books and periodicals.

Rain, a glass of water
or a leaky auto trunk
can easily ruin a book.
Pages stick together
and get moldy.

A humid room can
make paper prematurely
yellow and brittle.

designed by
Brigitte Mau '95

- Not using excessive force when photocopying [wording visually pushed to the bottom of the bookmark by an elephant].

Because both the design instructor and the students had been involved in the choice of messages, and library personnel in the final selection, two of the five bookmarks were not about preservation but rather

- Encouraging patrons to seek assistance at Reference: "Make My Day: Ask Me."
- Asking patrons to keep reference books in the reference area: "And where do you think you're going?"

The bookmarks were printed in black ink on textured business card stock at the campus printing office. I would have preferred alkaline stock and a larger size so as not to disappear in larger books. But the basic criteria of visual impact, clear message, and inclusion of the school logo were met.

In the future, the following would be desirable:

- A larger budget, available before the project is begun. This would generate more enthusiasm among the students and ensure that materials and printing would be optimal. It would also improve the overall process.
- A wider variety of messages.
- More control over the messages chosen.

These could be accomplished through further negotiation with the faculty member and by having a planned budget. It would have been nice to have been able to give more students the satisfaction of having their worthy designs chosen, printed, and available for inclusion in their portfolios.

- More timely printing and wider distribution.

Several students graduated before the bookmarks were printed. Holding the project in the fall semester with an existing budget would have remedied this. A larger printing run would also mean we could spread bookmarks around the library and in particularly pertinent locations, such as on the shelves and in the photocopy room and (a suggestion that came out of the California Clearinghouse on Library Instruction [CCLI] workshop) in the elevators.

Overall, I think this project was successful as a first effort. Our students do pick up the bookmarks and use them. Visitors, including adults and high school students, have asked to take one or more home with them. When I mention them in classroom sessions, students perk up their ears when they hear that the bookmarks were designed by their fellow students. I'm looking forward to adding more designs in the future, especially the cautionary one on photocopying—illustrated with an elephant!

NOTES

1. Tony Amodeo, "A Debt Unpaid: The Bibliographic Instruction Librarian and Library Conservation," *College & Research Libraries News* 49, no. 9 (October 1988): 601, 603.

2. "Preserving the Future: How to Teach Preservation to Library Users" (a program of the California Clearinghouse on Library Instruction [CCLI-South], presented by Tony Amodeo, Julie Page, and Michele V. Cloonan at the California State University at San Bernardino, April 30, 1993).

Preservation to the People! Mainstreaming Preservation into Instructional Sessions at an Undergraduate Library

Duffy Tweedy and Esteban Valdez, University of California–San Diego, La Jolla, California

The Undergraduate Library (UGL) at the University of California at San Diego (UCSD) has a unique mission on campus. Rather than focus on a group of disciplines, its materials cover all subject areas and are focused on the course-related needs of UCSD's freshmen and sophomores. It has more study space than any other library on campus and houses most of the reserves material.

A large part of UGL's mission is its function as a gateway to the other more specialized and often more complex campus libraries, to ease new students into the intricacies of university-level research. UGL's collections and services are simply arranged and easy to use. The undergraduate instruction program focuses on the core writing classes, the courses through which most undergraduates must pass, in order to impart vital library skills early in the students' studies. Those skills are taught in a more intensive way in a two-credit library research class offered at UCSD.

Until the early 1990s, however, these core competencies did not include preservation in any systematic way. With UCSD's hiring of a permanent preservation librarian came increased awareness of preservation as a necessary component of library use.[1] The undergraduate instruction program is an obvious place to introduce preservation to the heaviest users of the library system. The challenge of where and how to insert discussion of these issues in a busy bibliographic instruction (BI) syllabus is apparent, especially in a quarter system. Instructors are hesitant to give up even a single 50-minute session, and librarians must be highly selective in choosing material to include in that single session.

In a one-shot session as well as in the quarter-long library course, students are focused on meeting deadlines and completing projects, so preservation must be pitched so as to engage their interest—and preferably their self-interest. How this is done in the two very different settings is described below.

PRESERVATION IN A FOR-CREDIT COURSE

Contemporary Issues 50 (CI50), ''Information and Academic Libraries,'' is a 10-week, two-unit course designed to instruct students on how to wend their way through the maze of information available to them. The course is taught through the UCSD Muir College Interdisciplinary Studies program, and instructors have traditionally been librarians from the Undergraduate Library. Though the course is a lower-division course intended primarily for first-year students, CI50 is open to all UCSD students.

In the early 1990s, in conjunction with UCSD's preservation librarian, CI50 instructors began to make a concentrated effort to incorporate discussion of preservation issues into the CI50 curriculum. Instructors realized they had a golden opportunity to instill awareness of preservation onto a—for lack of a better word—''captive'' audience. Unlike the traditional one-shot, 50-minute bibliographic instruction session where attendance is usually mandated, students in CI50 are presumed motivated to learn library issues simply by enrolling in the class. Again, unlike a standard BI session, a for-credit course provides enough time for the instructor to prepare and present issues beyond the core skills usually discussed in a BI session.

Preservation concepts are presented at the very beginning of the class. On the first day, after discussing the syllabus, course objectives, and instructors' expectations, work begins on introducing students to the variety of information networks available. Before plunging into the areas of topic formulation, search strategies, controlled vocabularies, and other advanced concepts, the instructor takes a few minutes to introduce students to the proper handling of library material.

It is easy to stand before the students and delineate the do's and don'ts of preservation. It is much harder to actively engage the students in discussions of why the do's and don'ts are so important to them. One instructor found that the easiest way to begin discussion was to give a small multiple-choice test on preservation issues. The questions are taken from four bookmarks prepared by the UCSD Libraries Preservation Program. The questions address issues dealing with torn pages, handling books when interrupted, precautions in rainy weather, and dealing with spilled food and liquids. The instructor found discussion could be started by asking the questions and asking for a justification of the students' answers.

As the quarter progresses and students begin to gather material for their annotated bibliographies, the instructor generally has preservation interludes during regular class time. Students are encouraged to report any problems they are having in accessing material due to torn-out pages in journals or pencil markings in reference books and indexes. In this way, students see the importance of the do's and don'ts discussed in the first class session. The abstracts of preservation principles are brought home in a way that evokes their personal interest.

During the final weeks of the quarter, a full class period is set aside for preservation. At this time, the preservation librarian is invited to give a presentation of how preservation affects all users of the library. The video *Slow Fires* is shown, accounting for 33 minutes of the class time. The rest of the period is devoted to student reaction to the video and the preservation librarian's presentation.

Having the preservation librarian present the issues has been very successful. CI50 instructors have been gratified by the response of students after the presentation. A particularly effective device used by the preservation librarian has been giving students a page of brittle paper. The very act of holding the page and crumbling it has a profound effect on the students—they see firsthand the reasons why librarians are so concerned with preservation. Discussions with the preservation librarian cover a wide range of issues. Students' questions have concerned their own role in preservation, publishers' roles and responsibilities, and the effects of electronic/digital technology.

PRESERVATION IN A ONE-SHOT SESSION

In 1992, UGL librarians began incorporating preservation into their one-shot bibliographic instruction sessions, as part of a librarywide initiative that included displays and orientation newsletter articles. Though there are serious time constraints in these sessions (50 minutes is the norm), in some respects they are an ideal forum for introducing preservation—and research skills—to students. Most of the sessions involve writing classes or other very low-level courses, so the audience is new to the campus and to universities. Also attractive is the fact that a large percentage of UCSD students pass through these courses. This means that librarians have a chance to influence a large number of library users at the beginning of their college careers, introducing good materials-handling habits early.

Of course the difficulty in including preservation discussion in these one-shot sessions is obvious. Fifty minutes is an unreasonably short amount of time in which to teach even the rudiments of university-level research, especially in the age of automation. The decisions regarding what material to include and exclude were already painful. Deciding between or balancing important components such as basic library familiarity, search strategy concepts, online demonstrations, hands-on practice, and course-related subject areas had led to a packed 50 minutes. It proved difficult to find space for anything else.

There was also a concern about fitting preservation in philosophically. UGL instruction sessions had always made a great effort to be as course related and topically relevant as possible, with a minimum of abstract theory. A 10-week

Figure 6.5
UCSD Libraries Newsletter Plea for Preservation

Your Gift to Future Generations?

Your role in preserving the Library's collections is critical. UCSD Libraries volumes are subject to over one million uses per year: such handling takes a great toll on their physical condition. When you take care of the Library's books and journals, you assure that they will be available for your future use, and for the use of future generations.

Observe the "No Food and Drink" policy in library buildings. Spills and stains permanently damage materials, and food attracts pests and rodents that destroy paper and bindings. Keep food and drink away from library materials that you have checked out, too.

Treat library materials with care. If a book's binding resists being pressed flat, do not force it. Settle for a less than perfect copy when using photocopiers. Or ask about our "preservation sensitive" copiers located in most libraries.

Limit the use of bookdrops. Books take a beating when dropped, especially when other books land on top of them. Return books to the Circulation Desk whenever possible; if you use a bookdrop, placing a rubberband around books before depositing them can lessen the damage they sustain.

Use a proper bookmark to mark your place. Please don't "dog-ear" pages or use "Post-It Notes" or metal clips. These items can be permanently damaging, leaving stains or tearing pages.

Never mark, highlight, tape, or cut library materials. If you find materials that are missing pages or in need of repair, turn them in at the Circulation Desk so library staff can replace or repair them. Never try to make repairs yourself.

quarter forces students into an academic pace that doesn't allow for much wasted time or effort, and they tend to ignore anything that doesn't promise a concrete payoff. So instructors always use sample topics from the course to illustrate exactly how a systematic search strategy can lead to better results more quickly. Nothing is included in the sessions that can't be demonstrated as being useful to the term project for the course.

In contrast, preservation information is often presented as an appeal to be considerate of others, or in displays that graphically show the results of carelessness, infestations, or environmental catastrophes. The preservation librarian created a short article titled "Your Gift to Future Generations?" for the UCSD Libraries Orientation Issue, a newsletter which goes out to all incoming freshmen and transfer students and is used by the campus personnel office. This article stresses the damage that can be done by negligent handling and use and asks readers to be more thoughtful (see Figure 6.5). UGL and Geisel Library have hosted displays with lines of plastic ants crawling over candy wrappers onto books; items that have been dropped into bathtubs or run over; and other abused materials. These displays draw much attention and, like the newsletter entry, largely appeal to the students' consciences. While this is an appropriate and effective method in those situations, such an approach would be out of place in an otherwise very directed course-related instruction session, which appeals more to students' short-term survival instincts (while, of course, sneaking in lifelong learning skills where possible).

So the question was how to include preservation in a session that discussed library familiarity and subject-specific sources in the context of a particular class and course assignment. The answer was to add it to the section on finding articles and books, introducing it as the solution to a problem all the students could relate to: the unavailability of crucial materials due to misuse or neglect.

After describing and demonstrating a sample search on a topic relevant to the class, the students are shown how to find the material. Then the instructor lets the students know that, sooner or later, they are likely to be frustrated by a bound journal volume out for repairs, pages missing from a book, or a missing monograph. The point is then made that the patrons who damage materials aren't necessarily villains. This is a good lead-in to a description of all the routine acts of carelessness that can be destructive. The instructor emphasizes that while an individual drink spill or candy wrapper seems innocuous, multiplied by 600,000—the nine-month gate count at the tiny Undergraduate Library—these same acts can ultimately do enough damage to render library materials unusable. So the books saved now may be the ones needed later. And of course the instructor deviates from appeals to students' self-interest long enough to invoke the Golden Rule to get them to think about the future students who will need access to these same documents.

This approach has a two-part effect. By starting personally and a bit negatively (''You could be the victim'') the students' interest and indignation are aroused. Then, by turning it around (''You could be the perpetrator''), they are prodded into realizing that most of the damage isn't done by ''bad guys'' but by ordinary patrons like themselves who simply haven't thought about their library habits or who did something under desperation without thinking about the effect on others.

Unfortunately, time in these sessions doesn't allow for much more than a simple listing of bad habits: marking in books; using ''removable'' adhesive notes, paper clips, and other objects instead of bookmarks; leaning on books at the photocopier; food and drink; and so on. Where possible, the instructor follows the usual practice of phrasing these points positively, for instance, by noting the availability of drop-edge photocopiers. As a final appeal to the students' personal interest, the section ends with a reminder that stealing or mutilating library materials is actually punishable by law and can have dire academic repercussions as well. While positive appeals are often preferable, this last warning is important. In a way, it reminds students that they are adults and will be treated as such by the university, for better and for worse.

CONCLUSION

While many factors differ in the above examples, in both settings a strong effort is made to arouse the interest, and if possible the self-interest, of the students. It is easy to determine the success of this in CI50, where there are 10 weeks of contact. In a session lasting less than an hour, there is time only for fleeting impressions, as no further contact with the students is likely. In neither case was any sort of quantifiable measurement done, either to record heightened interest or to explore a connection between increased awareness and a change in behavior.

Anecdotal evidence—strong anecdotal evidence in the case of CI50—suggests that many students will pick up on preservation principles if they are engaged in a variety of ways: from appeals to their own best interests to warnings of legal repercussions to discussion of widespread threats facing the world's intellectual heritage. If as many of these perspectives are covered as time allows, students will get the message, and instruction librarians will make a difference.

NOTES

1. See also the case study in Chapter 2, "Preservation Orientation for Library Staff."

Integrating Preservation Information into Basic Library Skills

Sara Williams Trapolin, Tulane University,
New Orleans, Louisiana

General book-handling and preservation information was integrated into a library instruction program for English 101 students at Tulane University in the academic year 1994–1995. The English 101 program is an excellent vehicle for reaching a majority of incoming students at Tulane, since virtually all freshmen take the course, and about three quarters of the classes participate in the library skills program. Our objective was to provide a means of educating as many of our users as possible about proper materials handling, users' responsibility for preservation, and the value of maintaining library materials for future generations.

BACKGROUND

Classroom instruction in basic library skills at Howard-Tilton Library is currently designed to promote an awareness and general understanding of the mission and design of the research library. (The mechanical, technical, and directional aspects of library usage are addressed with self-paced worksheets and an optional online catalog workshop.) Students are introduced to a brief model of "the scholarly information system" and guided through a decision-making process for library searching, based on their new knowledge of how research is engendered, distributed, validated, and packaged in the scholarly environment. Preservation education becomes an integral part of this curriculum as it addresses the pragmatic aspects of every user's role in maintaining the materials that promote and make possible this scholarly conversation across the centuries. Preservation information was deemed a compatible, even integral part of this type of approach to library instruction. The idea for the inclusion of preservation information came from the coordinator of user education, who also designed the classroom curriculum. The coordinator discussed her ideas with a member of the library's Preservation Committee, who was most supportive, and offered suggestions for materials.

METHODOLOGY

The library owns copies of the preservation video *Murder in the Stacks* and also a slide-tape presentation *Handling Books in General Collections*, produced by the Library of Congress. All librarians involved in the instructional program viewed these two titles and decided unanimously to use the Library of Congress (LC) slide-tape show in the English 101 classes. The chair of the Collection Maintenance Unit Task Force supported the decision and indicated that she had used it with great success as a part of her student worker training program. She noted that several of her students had said of the presentation, "Everybody ought to see this." There was a clear consensus that the *Murder in the Stacks* video was a bit too "cute" for the audience, with its use of a Sherlock Holmes character to convey the message. All agreed that the freshman audience would be sensitive to any presentation that appeared to be aimed at youngsters rather than adults. The LC slide-tape presentation is aimed at library employees and a general audience of library users. Another criticism of the video was its failure to address photocopying techniques. Both the video and the slide-tape presentation met our requirements for length, with 20 minutes or less to set up, introduce, and view.

The slide-tape presentation was shown early in the two-and-a-half-hour class session, mainly for logistical reasons of pacing the lecture portion, equipment setup and exchange, class discussion, and tours. (The sessions vary somewhat in content, depending on the library instructor and the wishes of the classroom instructor, but online demos, brief tours, and visits to special collections may also have been included in the sessions.) Librarian instructors were asked to introduce the slide-tape presentation by emphasizing the unique role research libraries play in the scholarly communication system as preservers of materials that support the exchange of scholarly findings and ideas and materials that document the scholarly and popular culture. It was suggested that they make some comparisons to other libraries the students had used most recently—for example, pointing out that many public libraries buy multiple copies of best-sellers, only to deselect them when they are no longer popular. Research libraries, on the other hand, will buy one copy, if any, and will expect that copy to last virtually for generations as a cultural artifact.

EVALUATION

Students evaluated the library skills program at the end of the semester. In answer to the question, "What was the least useful part of the session?" students were nearly unanimous in their opinion of the preservation slide-tape presentation. There were no positive comments, and many comments were outright hostile. The most common complaint was that it was boring, with the comment that it was condescending ("We learned this in third grade"; "We already know this stuff") running a close second. We make note here that the class session is quite long (two and a half hours). In retrospect, there is little surprise that the preservation information, which was the least germane to the students' immediate needs for retrieving materials for their assigned papers, was the most criticized. Indeed, the strongest criticism in the second semester, when the preservation component was dropped, was that the session was too long. (There was no general consensus on what part was least useful after the preservation information was omitted.)

CONCLUSION

We feel certain that these students do not "already know this stuff" but postulate that the information was viewed as "preachy," and perhaps it sent the (unintended) message that we had assumed that we were dealing with naughty youngsters who had no better manners or sense than to destroy library property. This persistence of young students to insist that they "already know how to use a library," even in the face of overwhelming evidence to the contrary, is legend among instruction librarians. It was somewhat puzzling that the student workers who had viewed the presentation several times in the past were quite enthusiastic about it. It is hypothesized that the difference lies in the age and experiences of the two groups. The student workers were older by a few years. They had the advantage not only of chronological maturity but also of scholarly maturity; many had probably encountered problems due to materials damage and loss. It is further postulated that freshmen, at an average age of 19, are at a developmental stage at which they may be hypersensitive both to authority and to any behaviors that appear to be patronizing or that brand them as neophytes. Proper methods for photocopying or removing books from shelves may not seem to them to be college-level concerns.

The plan is to provide another means of presenting this information to the freshman audience or to provide another audience for the presentation. This librarian's suggestion is to provide a permanent display in the instruction room, which would address preservation issues; the information would be highly visible, and clear, without the "preaching." Another idea is to use brief live demonstrations instead of a video or slide-tape presentation. A second direction may be to look to another audience for classroom preservation education in the library, perhaps history or art students, who would have a stronger interest in preservation issues. And a third direction may be to take preservation education out of the classroom altogether and to develop, instead, other ways to spread the message. One way might be the use of an information kiosk, including a brief video that could be viewed by individuals. A preservation information fair, held once a semester, is also a possibility.

Preservation Education: Case Western Reserve University

Sharlane Gubkin, Case Western Reserve University, Cleveland, Ohio

The Preservation Department of University Library, Case Western Reserve University in Cleveland, Ohio, has been involved since its inception in a wide variety of preservation education efforts. The focus of our projects and efforts has been directed toward educating both library staff members and patrons of University Library in the care and proper handling of books and other library materials. While several educational strategies are employed, providing "point of use" instruction is a strong component of the overall effort and provides a continuous reminder for proper handling.

STAFF EDUCATION

Staff education is an important function of the Preservation Department. If student workers and staff are taught the proper care and handling of library materials as a part of their initial job training, they are less likely to develop damaging habits that are more difficult to alter later on. Because all incoming books are handled many times by staff in the Technical Services Department even before circulating, and because so many books seemed to be weakened or damaged by Circulation and other staff members through improper handling and shelving practices, the department introduced the following staff education programs:

Video presentation. The idea for a presentation originated with the assumption that if staff are educated to understand why certain policies are in place and to know that their own individual efforts can make a difference in the future condition of the books and materials they handle, they will follow recommended practices. In 1987, the department wrote and produced an instructional slide presentation, *Handle with Care* (see Appendix 4 for complete citation). It was converted to video and is mandatory viewing for all new staff and student assistants. The 19-minute video conveys through narration and still photographic images the correct way to remove a book from the shelf, book-shelving procedures including oversized books, nondamaging placement of books and other materials on book trucks, handling of CDs and records, handling of maps and other oversized materials, placement of security strips, photocopy procedures, stamping and placement of date due slips, handling of microfilm and -fiche, and operation of the readers. Examples of types of books that should not circulate until reviewed or treated by the department are also included.

Open house. With the approval of Library Administration, the Preservation Department has a periodic ''open house'' and invites other staff to see firsthand the wide range of activities carried out by the department. While this activity has been directed toward staff, we intend to publicize the next open house with signs and a notice in the campus paper to encourage library patrons to attend as well. Displays are set up during this activity to show samples of different types of damaged materials, completed and in-process repairs routinely performed in-house on books and paper, and types of materials sent to the commercial bindery. In addition alternative means of providing access for brittle materials through reformatting and environmental monitoring equipment are presented. Students taking classes in library science at a nearby college are routinely given tours of our department, and we take advantage of exchanges with other local library preservation departments to compare practices and learn from each other. The open house, departmental tours, and exchange of visits are intended to provide an increased understanding of the essential functions of library preservation and to encourage open relationships between our department and other staff and institutions.

Handouts and posters for staff. While the video and open house are interesting ways to teach staff about preservation issues and encourage proper handling of library materials, the point-of-use placement of posters provides a constant reminder for staff actually performing the tasks that can cause damage. In addition, since the Circulation Department staff identify materials routed to the Preservation Department, it is critical that they are versed in the types of damaged materials that need attention.

To help Circulation staff recognize the types of books that should not be shelved or allowed to circulate until they are treated, the Preservation Department made posters using photographs of different kinds of damaged materials that should be routed to them. A chart with photos of books with detached cases, torn spines, torn headcaps, worn cases, missing pages, and obviously brittle books is posted at all circulation desks. Also, in-house posters showing illustrations of books placed correctly and incorrectly on trucks and shelves are posted in the preshelving areas. The staff of the Access Services Department are responsible for packing and shipping books requested from storage, other libraries on campus, and other institutions through interlibrary loan. They have one-on-one training at the time of hire by preservation staff to identify and route to the Preservation Department books too fragile to be transported or circulated. In addition, they are shown the correct way to pack books in boxes and crates for shipping and transporting. Reminders of procedures are included in the posters (made in-house), which are displayed in all areas where books are processed for shipping and in the office of the library storage facility.

EDUCATION OF LIBRARY PATRONS

Patrons of University Library are exposed to information on proactive preservation. The focus is on increasing the patrons' awareness of their own role in preventing damage through proper handling, use, and treatment of collection materials.

Open house. As mentioned in the staff education section, we intend to include patrons in the next open house of the department.

Exhibits. With permission from the library administration, the department regularly uses the glass cases in the front lobby to display different exhibits with a preservation theme. Past exhibits have included "Enemies of Books," showing both inherent problems (acidic paper causing embrittlement of books, breakdown of materials, insects, mold) and preventable damage; "You Are Being Robbed," illustrating the time-consuming process of replacing pages torn by patrons from books and journals; and an exhibit on different styles and types of binding. The phone number of the department is included in the displays with a note to call with any questions or comments. We have received calls from a variety of patrons who have told us that they have gained knowledge from these exhibits and/or have changed the way they now handle books. For example, one patron told us he did not realize how much time went into replacing torn-out pages and stated that our display should be exhibited in other Cleveland libraries.

Posters and signs for patrons. We use a combination of commercially available and made in-house posters and signs to encourage proper practices and handling of books by library users. These visual reminders are strategically located at the point-of-use for patrons.

Small "Save a Book" posters from the Illinois Cooperative Conservation Program are mounted at the ends of many stacks throughout the library, illustrating the proper way to pull a book off the shelves (not by the headcap.) We also purchased "Save a Book" posters using before and after photographs to exemplify the damage caused to a book's spine by squashing a book down on a photocopy machine and posters conveying the message not to cut or tear pages from books. These are posted over the public copy machines. "No Food and Drink" signs were made in-house by the department and are posted throughout the library and at the entrance. All library staff are responsible for reminding any student they notice bringing or using food or drink in the library that it is prohibited.

Bookmarks and brochures. The Preservation Department designed acid-free bookmarks with basic information for patrons on preventive preservation and small brochures with similar information (see Figure 6.6). The bookmarks are printed with different colored inks on off-white thin cardstock. The brochures are printed on coated paper and have an eye-catching black and white photo on the front of a student trying to use a book so damaged its pages are falling out in her hands. Both encourage patrons to handle books with care. They include reminders not to remove books from the shelves by the headcap, to refrain from underlining or marking books, and to observe the no food and drink policy. The brochure also urges use of a thin paper bookmark instead of a pencil or thick object and waterproof bags to transport books. These items are distributed at the circulation desks and are available at the point of checkout. Our department's phone extension is listed on the handouts and bookmarks, and patrons are encouraged to contact the department with any questions or comments. It is hoped that these handouts are read by a large percentage of library patrons who will eventually assimilate and act positively on the information.

EVALUATION

It is difficult to evaluate the effectiveness of the patron education efforts. It is especially hard to determine if education has significantly helped to improve patron care because we have an older collection with a high percentage of previous damage, including both inherent and preventable human abuse. Also, although it can be minimized, heavily used or poorly bound newer books will inevitably suffer damage with use even if handled carefully. We cannot police the stacks to see how people remove books from the shelves or use the copy machines. However, the various instructional posters placed throughout the library are constant reminders that there is a proper way to do even the simplest task. An increase in the number of books coming to the department needing treatment can well mean not that more materials are being damaged but that staff and patrons are more aware of the need to report damage so materials can be treated.

In some areas, there are more obvious indications that an educational effort or policy has proven successful. The food and drink situation has vastly improved since signs were displayed at the time the policy first went into effect. Food and drink containers, once a common sight on tables in study areas or in wastebaskets, are now rarely seen. Brochures and bookmarks placed at circulation are depleted on a regular basis. We are always pleased when patrons ask questions or respond to an exhibit, whether they come to the department or call because that indicates to us that patrons are aware of library preservation issues.

An important question is, To what extent does having knowledge of proper care and handling actually curtail damaging practices? Patrons know they are

Figure 6.6
Preservation Department Brochure on Preventive Preservation

Transporting the book:

- Use waterproof bookbags or backpacks, especially in snowy, rainy weather. University Libraries provides plastic carry bags at the circulation desks for transporting books.

- Try not to cram a book into an overcrowded bookbag.

- Do not carry too many books at one time. They are easily dropped and damaged.

Handle books with care and use common sense. They will last longer and provide more use to you and to other patrons. You are really protecting your own interests when you treat books with respect.

Thank you for helping to preserve the university's research collections.

If you have any questions about the information provided in this brochure, please contact Case Western Reserve University Libraries Conservation Department, 368-3465.

Case Western Reserve University
University Libraries

Having trouble studying?

The inside of this double-fold brochure gives additional care and handling information for library users.

damaging books when they rip out pages, underline, or spill drinks on them. How can their behavior be modified?

It is the library's responsibility to make things as easy as possible for the patron to use the collections without causing damage. If food and drink is not to be consumed in the library, do not have vending machines with food and drink located in a lounge or room within the library. Books should be shelved loosely enough so it will not take a struggle to remove them from the shelves. Book-friendly flush edge copy machines could replace standard models so patrons can obtain an acceptable copy even into the gutter without needing to put undo pressure on the spine of the books. The cost of copies should be kept at a minimum to encourage copying versus mutilation of materials. A supply of cotton gloves kept in the microform areas would invite their use while handling film and fiche. Plastic book bags made available for patrons would help them to protect books from the elements while transporting them to and from the library. In all of these examples, having point-of-use instructions can assist in obtaining the final result of proper care and handling of library materials.

There will always be an uncaring element of people in any situation involving the use of shared, borrowed materials. However, preservation education must continue. We believe that if staff and patrons are shown how they can help prevent damage to the library materials they use, the majority will try through careful handling practices to keep the collections available far into the future.

Creating an Interactive Multimedia Training Program

Elayne Bond, Northwestern University, Chicago, Illinois

The collections of Northwestern University library represent the library's most valuable investment. The Preservation Department's mission has been to maintain and protect all library collections in all formats. Education is considered one of the more cost-effective preservation activities because (1) education is proactive in preventing damage rather than correcting it after it happens, and (2) education has the potential of reaching and influencing large numbers of people who handle library materials for better or for worse. Our objective has been to educate users (faculty, staff, and students) by promoting an awareness of issues through preservation activities. We also wanted to impress upon the users the importance of the role they play in caring for the collections. The total population to educate was large so it was decided to focus on targeted groups using different appropriate educational methods. Brochures geared toward faculty were made and distributed, and displays were regularly created on the topic of preservation. Rain bags were designed and purchased for patrons to protect their books during wet weather. While these methods followed the usual path of preservation education in academic libraries, the department has taken a slightly different approach in training staff and student workers in the library.

BACKGROUND

The 15-minute video called *Murder in the Stacks*, produced at Columbia University in 1987, addresses the general care and handling of library materials.

This video touches on the correct way to remove a book from the shelf, to fill a book truck, to shelve books; and the hazards of eating in the library. Until 1995, the Preservation Department regularly showed the video five times during the fall quarter and three times during the winter and spring quarters. Group showings were held and a short introduction and talk was given by the preservation education coordinator (the coordinator is an assigned task within the Preservation Department) before the showing, and discussion was encouraged afterwards. Staff announcements were sent as reminders to all staff and students. We recorded the number of people attending each session and realized that while we were targeting enough people, not enough were actually attending. One problem was scheduling: no matter how many sessions we scheduled, there were people who could not attend. We needed a new strategy.

METHODOLOGY

The college generation has embraced the changing technology as readily as anyone. Bibliographic instruction librarians comment on the fact that students will sit for hours at an automated index searching for citations and even wait in line to use a busy machine, while the paper indexes go begging. This interest in and facility with computer aided instruction became the focus of the training initiative when it became clear that our current methods were not reaching the intended audience.

With the new technological possibilities afforded by our Media Center facilities and staff, we could create a replacement for *Murder in the Stacks*. We talked about the advantage of creating something that was made at Northwestern depicting our students, our stacks, and our buildings on campus (both interior and exterior). We also wanted this program to cover book-friendly photocopy machines, and the fact that our library is a smoke-free building, a fairly recent development. We wanted something that would be available from any library department computer, and finally and most importantly we wanted something that would be interactive—not just a presentation in front of an audience, but something that kept the users clicking and thinking as they proceeded through the program.

Based on discussions within the department and with the Media Center, the plan was to produce a dynamic program that addressed Northwestern's preservation issues directly and that could be updated periodically. The initial step was to create a short general program. Later, we intend to add modules directed to specific audiences such as interlibrary loan or stack control staff. With experience gained in the area of staff education, we plan to branch out to more general user education. We know that technology is constantly changing, and we view this program as never actually being completed—there will always be new software and new ideas that we will want to try.

Before embarking on the care and handling training, we decided to learn with a smaller issue to gain experience with our choice of software, HyperCard. In the fall of 1993 we began to work on a small HyperCard script with the idea of learning from that experience in order to move on to the larger project. The beginning topic was a short training program for preservation student employees on how to program a reel of microfilm. (Our students are trained to program our grant-funded microfilming projects as well as our use-based microfilming.) We hoped that this would be a more interesting way for them to learn some of the basic guidelines, and we also saw it as a time-saver for the supervisors. As we developed this short HyperCard program, we learned about several software applications including Adobe Photoshop, HyperCard Color Tools, and Ofoto (a basic scanning application). The completed program was tested and became part of the training routine for new students. While not taking the place of the supervisor walking the student through the process and actually demonstrating the steps, it does provide beginning training for the student with one-on-one follow up.

After learning from the development of this small HyperCard program completed in the fall of 1994, it was time to begin the a more ambitious program that would take the place of *Murder in the Stacks*. Drawing on years of experience presenting various educational programs to staff and students, I began to compose the outline and script for the new program. I met with several of the staff in the Media Center who have expertise in the use of HyperCard and learned more about the software, both limits and possibilities.

Determined to have all the bells and whistles that the cards could hold—quick time movies, sound, color images, and so forth—I used a work study student who was majoring in video production, along with several student ''actors'' and ''actresses,'' to shoot videos showing the right and wrong way to load a book truck, to shelve a book, where to smoke, how to photocopy, and where to eat in the library. We shot many rolls of film from which we selected the best and most appropriate negatives to be made into slides that were scanned and inserted in the program. We also scanned images—happy people who would pop up on the screen to reward the users when they clicked on the correct button/answer and angry/sad people when the user chose the wrong button/answer.

We finished this program in the fall of 1995—while interactive, it was not entirely satisfying because it took a long time to come up on the screen. HyperCard was just not the best software application for handling all these different techniques as well as not being compatible with the WWW—for, by this time, the library was heavily into departmental home pages, and ''surfing the World Wide Web'' was a phrase heard all over campus. Now we needed this program to be accessible through the Preservation Department home page (http://www.library.nwu.edu/preservation/).

As quickly as one program becomes familiar, another one is on the market to take its place with even more features. HyperCard was no exception. At just about the same time we were launching the HyperCard program, the staff in the library's Media Center had purchased Macromedia Director, a cross-platform application which allows users to create interactive, multimedia worlds incorporating text, images, video and sound in a single portable environment. This new program appealed to us because not only could it provide animation features that HyperCard could not, but it was also compatible with HTML. Using talented students and staff in the Media Center, we transferred the HyperCard program to Macromedia Director. The design and production had taken the better part of a year; the transfer was accomplished in about six months.

CONCLUSION

"The Care and Handling of Library Materials" program is available on hard drives within the library or via the Web. The Web page (http://www.library. nwu.edu/preservation/care.html) has a brief explanation of the program with Macintosh and Windows icons so that users will be able to access either version directly from the preservation home page. A short "read me" file was created for the specific Web page warning the user of the file size (30 megabytes). At this writing, the Windows version is not yet accessible,

During the testing phase a sample group of 20 staff were used to evaluate the program. This focus group was helpful both in terms of content and level of instruction needed to "work" the program. We found that a few of the people had no experience with using a mouse, and that the screen had to have very explicit instructions, such as "click on the picture to continue." Our goal was to create an interesting and humorous way for staff and student workers to be made aware of the importance of handling the library's collections with care. Currently, the locally loaded program is used for new staff. A paper evaluation form is given to everyone who views the program. The 60 questionnaires returned so far suggest that we have accomplished our goal. Some of the comments follow:

"It was nice to watch something with a sense of humor!"

"Real-life photographs and the voice made the program interesting."

"It's humorous; easy to follow! The point comes across clearly."

Of course, not everyone liked the program. Some viewers wanted more cartoon animation, some more sounds. Phase two (and three, and four . . .) will build on our experience as we develop more modules for training and introduce modules for user education. In the near term we want to automate the evaluation form, add a counter to the Web site, and create buttons to move around more easily. Each improvement and newly developed module will bring us closer to the goal of heightening the awareness of careful handling practices.

7

Preservation Education in Special Collections and Archives

Preservation Education for the Library User: The Special Collections Perspective

Kenneth Lavender, University of North Texas, Denton, Texas

BACKGROUND AND CONTEXT

Special collections and archival collections offer unique resources within the larger library, institutional, or global context. To the researcher, what most obviously distinguishes these collections is the presence of rare and fragile materials that are not available at all elsewhere or that are not available as a collection elsewhere. In the first instance, the sources are unique or very rare and are often used in and of themselves. This is particularly true of manuscript, archival, and early printed book collections. In the second instance, while the sources may also be rare, their importance lies in the collection as a whole; that is, many examples will be consulted side by side, and these provide a more complete picture of the subject under study. Collections devoted to individual authors, local history, or a specific genre and period often are of this type. Because these collections contain unique materials or aim to be inclusive, they traditionally hold a wide variety of formats, both paper-based (e.g., books, manuscripts, documents, maps) and non-paper-based (e.g., artifacts, photographs, and works on vellum and parchment). The justification for special collections entails not only the permanent custodianship of these diverse materials but their continued availability to the public.

Access to rare and archival materials always carries strong preservation consequences; the handling of such materials necessarily involves risk. Yet access has increasingly become the keyword for the survival of many special collections, whether they be rare book collections, archives, or special libraries. This paradox is keenly felt by both curators and conservators, who have often approached the custodianship of these materials from divergent perspectives. The increased use of special collections by researchers and the public at large is now seen as necessary for continued existence; yet this use may contribute to the destruction of these materials. This paradox is heightened as collections become more widely known through electronic network resources and as more users are alerted to their availability.

The above discussion establishes the broad context within which special collections must exist today and within which their preservation must be considered. The question of access has, in fact, become central to defining the role of special collections. A sense of urgency has arisen because of the decreasing financial support for institutions and their specialized resources. All types of special collections, whether they be part of academic or public libraries, are at risk. Academic administrators, for example, want to see these collections better integrated into the general informational resources of their institutions. This ''mainstreaming'' is seen as the key to survival: ''In my view, special collections in a research library must be in the mainstream. . . . Because of increasingly limited resources, most university libraries must have 'working' special collections, i.e., collections that support the instructional and research program of the university faculty and students'' (Bengston, p. 92). This idea of mainstreaming can also become one aspect of the programs of quality assessment that are the result of the new emphasis on productivity.

The leaner and meaner environment of higher education is leading to renewed preoccupation with productivity and certainly to attempts by administrators to improve efficiency by imposing change from the top down. Special collections librarians must intertwine themselves and their operations thoroughly with other units both inside and outside the library, so that they are more completely integrated into the broader systems of the library, of the university's academic community, and of the scholarly world at large (Jones, pp. 88–90).

This active search for a broader audience entails, however, its own contradictions. First, the development of electronic catalogs and other guides may bring researchers from afar to use collections, but these users are not part of the ongoing support needed within the particular institution: ''[T]hese peripatetic scholars are not visible sources of support to campus or even library administrators'' (Jones, p. 89). Second, their use of the material brings consequences for preservation, even though their actual support for such needs may be only minimal.[1] But electronic access also holds a great promise for preservation by providing full-text retrieval of rare materials. Even though it may be a long time before most texts are entered and all scholars have their own workstations, such productions as Project Gutenberg clearly show the potential of this technology. Reformatting, of course, has long been used for both access and preservation purposes, most obviously with microforms, photography, and photocopying. On a more immediate and practical level is the increasing availability of various electronic imaging technologies involving scanning, videodiscs, or digitization. These have been of particular use with fragile maps, documents, architectural drawings, photographs, and scrapbooks.[2]

With all forms of reformatting arise the question of access to the original materials. Because most special collections do not lend original materials through interlibrary loan systems, they have long made available photographs, photocopies, and transcriptions of fragile and unique materials as part of their service to off-site researchers.[3] In addition, many such collections have provided photocopies, reprints, and reading copies for use in place of the originals to on-site researchers. The justification for these "substitutions" is that the original is too valuable or fragile to be used under normal circumstances. The curator and researcher are often at odds over these restrictions, so many archives and libraries have established policies that detail the types of enquiries that would permit the researcher to have access to the original.[4]

A policy should also be established regarding the use of original items when preservation photocopies or microfilm are available. Access to an original should be permitted only if physical examination of the item will provide answers to questions that cannot be answered by the reproduction. Legibility is obviously an acceptable use. Verification of the authenticity of a document and examining the paper (watermarks, chain and laid lines, etc.) to help date or locate the item's origin are needs that casual researchers will not have. Researchers who insist that they cannot gain a true understanding of the intellectual content unless they are allowed to use and handle the material in original format should not be indulged (Ritzenthaler, p. 114). The preservation concerns that might necessitate restriction of original materials can be identified in the initial handout given to researchers. This procedure alerts them to the reasons for the policies and thus acts as a possible deterrent to their objections.

INTELLECTUAL PURSUITS

Since special collections librarians must balance the desires for access and the needs of preservation, they are more than usually affected by new fields of study that may suddenly make their holdings prominent. It is in their best interests to anticipate needs and thus to integrate these new items into ongoing preservation programs. This foresight also has the advantage of alerting the librarian to the condition of the holdings in a particular field. A discussion of the condition should be made part of the initial interview with the user. One particularly broad field of study that has recently taken center place in modern scholarship has far-reaching consequences for preservation.

Since the mid-1980s a large body of important scholarship has been produced in contextual studies, especially in the area known as "book history," which examines such aspects of culture as reading, education, publishing, and their impact on society. The main thrust is to place the book in its cultural context, illuminating both by analyzing their relationship. Whereas the "New Critical" approach studied a text as disembodied from the facts of its creation or publication, this approach emphasizes the importance of these aspects. Thus, scholars are looking at the various appearances of a novel, at second-rank serious works, at popular works, and at the development of the publishing industry (Studwell and Huang; Winkler). The ramifications for special collections lie in the fact that these pursuits often depend on a work in its *original* form: "Reproductions cannot retain all evidence of the original text or of the form in which the text originally appeared. Further, the original form of the preservation of print is itself a cultural object and has scholarly merit and value in its own right" (McCorison, p. 85). No reprint, no photocopy, no electronic transmission can adequately represent what the scholar needs. Thus, the preservation of the original formats is essential, but in very many cases, these publications are produced on the most acidic paper and in the flimsiest bindings.[5] "The current state of ferment in literary studies is matched by similar ferment in other disciplines. Scholars in many fields turn to texts and materials they would not have dreamed of looking at just a few years ago. They do not need the obvious texts they already know about, the texts whose stature and status have long been recognized. They need the rubbish" (Traister, p. 37).

The above example serves to demonstrate the impact of intellectual pursuits on preservation programs. Other subjects have always been of concern (children's literature comes to mind) because of the fragile nature of the materials. The special collections librarian or curator must be aware of these fields that are part of the collections and make the caution known to the researcher. This should become an integral part of the initial interview in which the researcher discusses his or her needs and the staff member attempts to meet them. Such an awareness on the part of the researcher often encourages the consultation of reproductions, except when examination of the physical object is actually essential.

STRATEGIES

Introduction

Special collections are distinctive among library collections because of such factors as age, scarcity, value, beauty, and fragility. These factors also form the basis for policies concerning the care and handling of special materials. These same factors also necessitate the careful item-specific conservation that is indicative of special collections treatment. User education in the handling of these materials is unique among library collections because the approach is always with the individual at time of use, whether or not there may be additional broader methods that have been employed. This one-on-one strategy allows the staff member to present preservation rules and to discuss them in relation to the specific items the user is interested in. This step follows the initial interview in which the researcher discusses need and in which the staff member may comment on the general condition of the materials and other relevant matters, such as the availability of reproductions or electronic imaging programs.

Many users of special collections are favorably predisposed toward careful handling of the materials they are investigating. First, many researchers are already familiar with rules for handling materials in special collections. They have used other collections, and thus they come to a specific collection expecting to adhere to policies for security and handling. This expectation often helps put a ''positive'' spin on preservation education efforts. Second, most special collections are housed in restricted areas within the library building. This segregation helps to emphasize the value of these materials and consequently to underscore the need to preserve and protect them. Third, the fact that the reading room is constantly monitored makes the user more aware of maintaining proper security and preservation practices. Fourth, the age, beauty, and fragility of many rare materials are intrinsic reasons for special care and handling. All of these factors aid the staff member in educating the researcher about good preservation practices in general and about those that are specific to the materials requested. If the researcher, on the other hand, is not familiar with general practices of special collections or if he or she simply remains antagonistic, the staff member must use the interview to emphasize security and preservation concerns.

The Interview

The special collections interview compares to the general reference interview in that it seeks to establish what the patron is interested in and how the resources available may satisfy his or her needs. The staff member may suggest specific titles in addition to those the researcher already knows about or may suggest alternative methods of finding information (such as electronic catalogs and databases). The special collections interview differs from the general reference interview in that special conditions relevant to the materials requested (e.g., preservation concerns or other restrictive factors) are an integral part of the discussion and recommendations.[6] This helps make the patron receptive to more specific rules about careful handling and to possible restrictions, such as photocopying and tracing.

It is important that this interview be conducted with intelligence and tact. It is good to remember that most patrons may already be favorably disposed toward appropriate security and preservation practices. But if the patron is already very familiar with the subject and is thus requesting only specific items, they may resent a set speech about research techniques and basic handling of rare materials. And if a patron is just beginning research, they may be overwhelmed by a plethora of sources and myriad of restrictions. A correct approach at this point is especially important because it lays the foundation for appropriate behavior and for subsequent efforts at preservation education. The obvious importance of the materials and the environment that surrounds them often aids the staff member in establishing a spirit of cooperation.

Policies

Written policies concerning security and preservation should be presented to the user sometime prior to the handling of materials. Security policies are often given to the patron at the time of registration, the preservation policies at the end of the interview and prior to the use of the materials. The appearance of these rules has an impact on the user. The better they look, the more likely it is they will be heeded. Three formats are widely used in rare book rooms and archives. The first is a clearly printed sheet of paper, perhaps encapsulated and matted, that is placed on the reading table. The second is a card that is on display at each individual reading station. The third is a bookmark that is given to the user and that may be placed in the material requested.[7] With each of these formats, the rules should be clearly visible and succinctly stated. Explanatory notes should be kept to a minimum: "Taking notes: Take notes in pencil. Stray marks made by pencil are far easier to remove than those made with ink. Pencils are provided for your use. Tracing from Rare Book Room materials is not allowed."[8]

Policies: Security

Security is a necessary part of the use of special collections. It is also a point of potential conflict between staff and users. Patrons sometimes initially object to having to present identification and to having to follow explicit rules of conduct. After the staff member has presented these rules in written form, however, a few moments of explanation often show the reasonableness of these precautions and alert the user to the unique qualities of the materials that are being made available. Most rare book rooms, archives, and other types of special collections have security procedures that are specific to their situation, but these procedures aim at a few basic tenets of conduct:

All researchers entering the archives reading room should sign a daily register. A secure place near but outside of the reading room should be designated for hats, coats, umbrellas, briefcases, large purses, backpacks, and the like, none of which should be allowed at reading tables. As a security precaution, the archivist or reading room supervisor should require positive identification of the researcher as a formal part of the reference interview or other registration procedure. At this time, potential users also should be informed of all regulations regarding access to and use of materials. These rules should be posted in a prominent place. . . . These preliminary procedures should take place before the patron is given access to any material. (Ritzenthaler, p. 113)

The staff member may also point out that some security measures, such as placement of personal objects, have preservation reasons as well. The fewer items that are crowded on a reading table, the less chance of casual damage to fragile pages and bindings.

Policies: Care

While these procedures may not be obvious to the user, they do affect the materials and the environment. Staff are responsible for them and need to know how and when to relate them to the patron.

Environmental control. Special collections often have employed methods to stabilize humidity and temperature, lessen the harmful effects of light, and reduce pollution in the atmosphere. If the room is consistently cold, for example, it helps to explain the reasons to the user.

Examination. Staff should examine the condition of each item before it is brought out to the patron:

Before records are served to researchers, a staff member with preservation training should review the materials to ensure that they are in stable enough condition to be handled. The review process, which can be carried out relatively quickly, can incorporate basic preservation actions that will protect the records. While major rehousing cannot be accomplished as a part of this preservation review, fragile or vulnerable materials can be placed in folders or polyester sleeves. . . . [T]he preservation review provides a mechanism for intervening and withholding from use records that because of their condition or format simply cannot be handled until they receive preservation attention. (Ritzenthaler, p. 113)

In the case of items that are withheld because of condition, the staff member should try to find alternatives for the researcher. Catalogs at other regional institutions, available in printed format or accessed through electronic networks, can identify copies that the researcher might be able to use on-site. In addition, national electronic databases, such as OCLC, are helpful in locating copies at institutions that might be able to accommodate the researcher through lending or copying. Such searching should be considered part of the staff member's duties. This effort often educates the researcher as well as bringing goodwill to the special collection that has just been forced to refuse them access. A discussion of the condition and of the reasons that the item has to be withheld is an aspect of preservation education that is too often ignored.

Enclosures. Most archival materials and many rare books are stored in protective enclosures, such as drop-front boxes, clamshell boxes, sink mats, map folders, and pamphlet holders. Material must be removed from these enclosures before it can be studied, and the staff should educate the patron in the proper techniques and provide assistance if necessary. Tight enclosures, such as book wraps, slipcases, and the like, should, however, be removed by the staff member. Replacement of materials should always be done by the staff, since there is too much danger of damage, especially of fragile books and documents. Some materials, such as broadsides and maps, may be encapsulated in polyester film to enable them to be handled. This type of enclosure should be explained to the user, and if photographing the item is part of the project, then the staff member may be asked to remove it. Because of the wide variety of formats normally part of a special collection, other types of enclosures may be used and will need to be handled by the staff member. Artifacts, prints, photographs, and recordings all have specific enclosures that the staff member should discuss when presenting the material to the researcher.

Policies: Handling

It is at the point of handling special materials that the greatest need for preservation education exists. The staff member must be convinced that the user knows how to handle the materials correctly or be prepared to provide instruction. There are a variety of ways to present this instruction, but it is usually a combination of hands-on demonstration and written procedures. Some procedures may be specific to the library or archive; some may be specific to the type of material. Whatever the format or the specificity of the policies, they most commonly cover the following general practices:

Please be sure your hands are clean and dry.

Please handle fragile books *very* gently.

Please use our acid-free bookmarks to mark your place.

Please take notes in pencil.

Notify a librarian of damaged or missing pages.

Never force a book to do anything.

Give a book all the support you can. (Greenfield, p. 107)

Printed sheets, place cards, and bookmarks are common written formats to use in educating the researcher about preservation, and they have the advantage of being available for consultation throughout the use of the materials. More extensive written instructions may also be given to the user prior to their handling special materials; there may, in addition, be a handout in a group presentation.[9] These serve as reminders of good preservation policies. It is the individualized instruction, however, that makes the most impact on the user; thus, the careful attention given to this aspect will greatly aid the staff member in maintaining sound preservation practices.

Instruction: Individual

Instruction in the proper handling of materials is the most important aspect of preservation user education in special collections. It must be based on the written policies presented to the user, but it must also be adapted to the needs of the particular situation. The specific procedures and examples discussed below are meant both as sound responses to their specific needs and as guidelines for additional preservation procedures. It is important that the staff anticipate

Figure 7.1
Wedges with Walls Supporting Joints of Cover

the handling requirements of their collections, including format, condition, and other relevant factors.

Supports. All books in codex form should be used with some type of support. The most common support is a wedge, or wedges, often of foam rubber or other material covered in felt, such as barrier board or four-ply mat board. They may be made in many sizes, of different heights, and at varying angles. In order for the book to receive the proper support, however, the joint (or outer hinge) must not sag (see Figure 7.1). This is particularly important if the hinge is loose or torn. Wedges with no hinge wall should be used only with flat-back books or very thin books with no perceptible shoulder.

Book cradles of the type made for exhibits should not be used for consultation support since they are tailor-made for a specific book opened to a specific place. They are not interchangeable, as wedges are. Book stands, however, may be adapted to such a purpose, provided that the book itself is properly supported. Of particular use here are the stands that are designed to hold books horizontally. They are often made of metal and Plexiglas and may be adjusted to different angles.

Large, thick books pose a particular problem. The angle of the opening shifts radically as the leaves are turned, and the binding structure is often not strong enough for the weight. The cradle may thus have to be frequently adjusted to provide the correct support. The easiest method is to place wedges on top of each other to attain the proper angle and height (see Figure 7.2). Because of the weight of the book and the angle of the opening, however, they tend not to lie open. If a patron wishes to consult a particular page for any length of time, it may have to be secured with a book snake or band of polyester film.

The staff member will need to provide the required support(s) when they present the material for the patron to use. At this point the staff member should explain the reasons for the support and demonstrate how to use it. The staff should also discuss any additional preservation concerns, such as fragile paper, loose pages, weak hinges, and the like. Most patrons will then understand how to use the supports and will continue to use them with other books they will be examining. It is always good, however, to monitor the use of special materials, since differing circumstances may arise frequently. This is particularly important with fragile materials.

Figure 7.2
Wedges Placed on Top of Each Other Supporting a Heavy Book

Turning Pages. The staff must demonstrate the proper way to turn pages,[10] since most patrons will continue to use the same techniques they use at home. By talking about the fragile nature of paper and the specific qualities of the books being consulted, the staff member can prepare the patron for these basic lessons. The correct procedures can perhaps best be presented as a list of do's and don'ts:

Don't flip a page by its corner.

Don't grab an edge between thumb and forefinger.

Don't flip a page from the bottom edge.

Don't wet a finger for a better grip.

Do place a hand behind the page to give it support.

Do turn the page gently.

Do follow through to make certain the page lies down flat.

Do turn pages carefully.

Large bound books present a particular problem because the pages flex more severely and thus need greater support. In such cases, both the hand and the forearm should be slid behind the page and used to turn it over gently. This "follow-through" motion will help keep the page from bending and thus possibly creasing or breaking, if it is fragile.

Works in portfolio format need special instruction to be opened properly. They are often large and cumbersome, thus requiring extra care in handling. The distinguishing features of this format are the protective enclosure and the separate leaves. If the enclosure is a slipcase, the staff member must remove the leaves as a block so that they may be handled safely. The leaves may then be carefully shifted one at a time, using hand and forearm for support, from the right-hand stack to the left, in reverse order. If the enclosure is a fold-over case or a box,[11] the leaves may remain in the right-hand side of the open enclosure and be shifted with the above procedure (see Figures 7.3 and 7.4). When the patron finishes with the portfolio, the leaves are then shifted back one at a time to the right side of the enclosure. They are now in their original order. The

Figure 7.3
Fold-over Case with Flaps Open

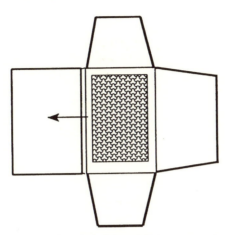

Leaves should be shifted, one at a time, from right to left, in reverse order.

leaves are *never* flipped over as in a bound book, as this could cause severe damage to the edges as well as to any fragile artistic medium. If it is necessary for the patron to look at the back side (verso) of a leaf (for manuscript notes, plate impressions, watermarks, and the like), they should be instructed to ask a staff member to turn it over for them. This is done with the same technique of sliding hand and forearm under the leaf but supporting it on the front side (recto) with a piece of acid-free mat board. This procedure gives the support necessary to keep the leaf from bending.

Securing Pages. Many books will not stay open at a particular place because the binding is too tight or the paper too stiff. The user must be instructed not to force a book open in any way and to ask a staff member for help in such a case. There are generally two methods used to hold a book open. First, weights may be placed on the pages to hold them open. These should be covered in soft cloth and filled with pebbles or shot. A particularly effective type is the book snake, which has the advantage that it may be placed in the gutter of a book (see Figure 7.5). Weights are also easy to use and require little instruction. Second, bands of polyester film may be wrapped around the page to hold it open in place (see Figure 7.6). Polyester film is virtually transparent, so the band may be placed over the text and not hinder the user. It is important, however, that only a staff member perform this procedure because of the possibility of damage to the paper and the binding.[12] This would thus need to be done each time the user wished to turn the page. In the case of very delicate paper, it is possible to lay a sheet of polyester film over the entire open area, the weight often being enough to hold the pages open. If the book still will not remain

Figure 7.4
**Portfolio Box without Spine Walls, Allowing Shifting of Leaves from Right
to Left**

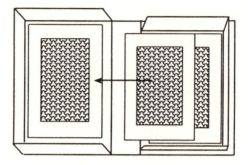

open, the sheet of film may be made larger than the book and secured to a piece
of mat board beneath the book. If one side is secured with double-sided tape,
the other side may be weighted down, thus allowing the sheet to be lifted easily
when a page needs to be turned. A disadvantage of these two methods comes
from the reflective quality of polyester film, which often necessitates reposi-
tioning the books and film away from direct glare.

Gloves. Cotton gloves are often worn by special collections staff in handling
certain types of materials, such as fine bindings and photographs. Generally
speaking, gloves are worn with materials that would be immediately damaged
by oils in the skin. Leather bindings are very prone to soiling by greasy fingerprints, as are photographic prints and negatives. With paper objects, however,
the wearing of gloves is problematic and should be determined on a case-by-
case basis. Brittle paper or paper with fragile deckled edges is particularly subject to damage from the nap of even the finest cotton gloves. On the other hand,
soft or older paper absorbs oil very readily and should be used, whenever possible, with gloves. The user must be provided with the proper gloves and instructed when and how to use them. In this regard, teaching by example is
important.

Note Taking. One of the strictest rules with special collections materials is
that pens must never be used for taking notes. Tracing should also never be
allowed, since it damages the surface of the book or print. Many patrons do not
immediately understand and, in fact, may resent the insistence on these precautions, so it is helpful to explain how difficult it is to remove a stray ink mark
from paper. Even though these concerns may be mentioned in the policies presented to the user at time of registration, they should be explained and reinforced
through individualized instruction.

In the past, many special collections made provision for the use of typewriters,

Figure 7.5
Pages Held Open with Book Snake along Gutter

but the arrangements were often cumbersome because of the noise level. Today, most special collections have felt it necessary to provide for the use of personal computers, primarily for the retyping of text but sometimes for the scanning of images. These computers are most easily accommodated at separate stations, but the scanning of images should be overseen by a staff member. Leaving aside the possible objections from copyright and artistic rights infringement, the scanning of text or images may bring the same type of structural hazards as photocopying: the binding may crack, the hinge may separate, the paper may crease or tear. As with photocopying or photographing, this type of computer use should be discussed in the interview.

Photocopying and Photographing. Photocopying is so prevalent in libraries and other public institutions that when a patron is told that a particular book may not be photocopied, there is likely to be an immediate and strong reaction. Some archives and special collections libraries do not photocopy materials for the individual reader at all, but most public and academic libraries generally treat it on a case-by-case basis. User education at this point is thus critical to establishing cooperation on the part of the patron and also to maintaining the long-term support of researchers.

Staff members in special collections should be trained in recognizing the preservation criteria for photocopying a specific item.[13] These include both the general concerns that apply to all materials and the specific requirements of different formats. Staff members must also be familiar with the types of photocopying machines available to them, since the features of a particular machine will help determine how well it will accommodate special materials.[14] For example, an edge-copier will accommodate a tighter binding than will a flat-copier. Preservation concerns in photocopying may be summarized as follows:

Figure 7.6
Pages Held Open with Bands of Polyester Film

- *Condition of paper.* Fragile paper may be severely damaged by handling.
- *Effect of light and heat on paper and images.* Paper may become brittle, and delicate images (e.g., watercolor) may fade.
- *Type of binding.* A tight binding requires an edge-copier or the spine may crack.
- *Condition of binding.* A loose binding may be damaged by handling.
- *Size of object.* Maps and large folios may require several exposures, thereby increasing the risk of damage both from handling and from light and heat.
- *Weight of object.* A heavy book may be damaged by handling.

During the interview, the staff member should explain the general policies concerning photocopying, emphasizing the need for protecting the materials. The patron will thus have a context for inquiring about the photocopying of a particular item. If the answer must be a refusal, the staff member should explain the basis for the decision (e.g., tight binding, fragile paper). If necessary and appropriate, alternatives may be suggested, such as professional photography, videotaping, availability of a reprint, or interlibrary loan of microfilm.

Photographing of special materials is a frequent occurrence, either because of the images needed by researchers or because of the use of the collections in publicity and other publications. Many special collections have established routines for photographing and filming. In general, the major concerns are the handling of fragile materials and the heat and light of photographer's lamps. For delicately colored prints, flash bulbs may also pose a problem. For photography the basic props should include a properly mounted copy stand, appropriate cradles for the objects, and cloth for backdrops. All things being equal, the photography is best done within the collections themselves. If this is not feasible, packing, transportation, security, and handling requirements must be considered before the items may leave the collections.

Instruction: Group

Preservation education for the user of special collections may also take place in a group setting, although this is not nearly so effective as the interview and point-of-use instruction. It is possible to present basic instruction to a number of patrons at the same time using overheads and other audiovisual techniques. The proper handling of materials may be demonstrated and the basic policies outlined. Further individualized instruction may then be given as needed or as monitoring indicates. This group presentation may be accomplished in one of three ways. First, a number of patrons may be brought together at the beginning of their research. This session is then prerequisite to their use of the collections. A staff member may discuss basic preservation concerns and handling procedures, with demonstrations, videotapes, overheads, and the like. Second, preservation guidelines may be part of a bibliographic instruction program. An introductory class in library research contains a segment on the proper handling of books, with consideration of the extra care needed for fragile and special materials. Since this type of class is most often taught by general library staff, however, it is not usual to stress the nature of special collections. Nevertheless, general preservation concerns may be effectively introduced at this level. Third, proper handling procedures and basic policies may be discussed as part of the introduction to research using the resources of special collections. These classes are most often centered on a particular research subject. Since this introduction is presented by special collections staff utilizing examples from the collections, it is easier to integrate specific and appropriate preservation procedures. This group presentation is followed, of course, by individualized instruction at time of use.

Instruction: Exhibits

Another method of preservation instruction is exhibits, although this is generally limited to presenting generalized statements and examples. Nevertheless, exhibits may be effectively used in presenting the context within which the user of special collections must apply specific procedures. A ''consciousness-raising'' exhibit, for example, may make the patron more receptive to the strictures imposed in his or her use of rare and fragile materials. Thus, exhibits may provide the right climate for the patron to be receptive to the importance of preservation instruction during use of the collections.

Some of the topics most usually covered in exhibits on preservation include proper handling of books; damage by pests, water, or people; inherent deterioration of materials; and disaster recovery. Posters and pictures reinforce the message; handouts may be consulted later when materials are actually being used. Such exhibits emphasize to the user the importance of preservation concerns and procedures.

CONCLUSION

Special collections and archives today are faced with a potentially damaging dilemma—that of the paradox of access and preservation. Access is seen as survival, yet this may help cause the destruction of the very materials that make such collections unique. Curators of special collections thus must anticipate conservation needs and integrate user education into their research assistance procedures. The most effective method of education is individualized instruction at point of use, because it allows for specific procedures relevant to the materials being handled, logical and detailed explanations, and reinforcement through monitoring. Written policies must also be made available to the user. User guides, group instruction, and exhibits are additional means of information and support for the proper care and handling of special collections materials. A good user education program is the best answer to the dilemma posed by access and preservation.

NOTES

1. An exception may be found with those collections that have received preservation grant support because of their national importance and wide usage among scholars.

2. For example, AVIADOR (Avery Architectural Library), National Geographic Society's Photo Library, and the Photo CD project at Cornell University. See Dorothy Wright Moore, "Survey of Electronic Imaging Projects," *ALCTS Newsletter* [Part One] 5, no. 5 (1994): 64-67; [Part Two] 5, no. 6 (1994): 86-91.

3. See *Rare Books & Manuscripts Librarianship* (fall 1988) for several articles on the growing debate concerning the lending of rare materials.

4. See also "ALA-SAA Joint Statement on Access to Original Research Materials," *College & Research Libraries News* 54, no. 11 (December 1993): 648–649.

5. See also "Selection of General Collection Materials for Transfer to Special Collections," *College & Research Libraries News* 54, no. 11 (December 1993): 644–647. These guidelines point out the relationship between conservation and bibliographic research.

6. We are not concerned in this chapter with other possible restrictions, such as copyright or donor conditions.

7. For example, see *Presevation Education in ARL Libraries*, SPEC Kit 113 (Washington, DC: Association of Research Libraries, Office of Management Studies, 1985), pp. 78–80.

8. Quoted from the "University of North Texas Rare Book Room Policies."

9. For a particularly good example of a user's guide, see *User's Guide to the Conservation of Library Materials* (Stanford University Libraries, 1980), in *Preservation Planning Program Resource Notebook*, comp. Pamela W. Darling; rev. ed. by Wesley Boomgaarden (Washington, DC: Association of Research Libraries, 1987), pp. 175–184.

10. In this and following paragraphs, the term *page* is frequently used in preference to *leaf* as this is the term that the user would best understand. Technically, however, *leaf* is the correct designation.

11. This is possible only if the box does not have inner walls along the spine edge. If it does have these walls, it is treated as though it were a slipcase.

12. Only chemically inert polyester film should be used, such as Mylar® D or Melinex® 516. A thickness of .003 (3 mil) is recommended.

13. Sometimes, because of the makeup of the staff at any given time, it may be wise to designate only certain individuals to have the authority to make photocopying decisions. This option is particularly helpful if student assistants or volunteers are left in charge.

14. The same considerations apply, of course, to other methods of image reproduction (e.g., microfilming, scanning).

REFERENCES

Bengston, Betty G. "Navigating the Mainstream: Key to Survival." *Rare Books & Manuscripts Librarianship* 8, no. 2 (1993): 92-96.

Greenfield, Jane. *The Care of Fine Books*. New York: Nick Lyons Books, 1988.

Harris, Carolyn. "Trends in the Preservation of Rare and Special Materials." In *Rare Books, 1983–1984: Trends, Collections, Sources*, ed. Alice Schreyer. New York: Bowker, 1984, pp. 121–127.

Hickerson, H. Thomas, and Anne R. Kenney. "Expanding Access: Loan of Original Materials in Special Collections." *Rare Books & Manuscripts Librarianship* 3, no. 2 (1988): 113–19.

Jones, William Goodrich. "Leaner and Meaner: Special Collections, Librarians, and Humanists at the End of the Century." *Rare Books & Manuscripts Librarianship* 8, no. 2 (1993): 80–91.

Lange, Thomas V. "Alternatives to Interlibrary Loan." *Rare Books & Manuscripts Librarianship* 3, no. 2 (1988): 107–111.

McCorison, Marcus A. "Statement on Conservation." *Abbey Newsletter* 14, no. 5 (August 1990): 84–85.

Oram, Richard W. "The New Literary Scholarship, the Contextual Point of View, and the Use of Special Collections." *Rare Books & Manuscripts Librarianship* 8, no. 1 (1993): 9-16.

Preservation Education in ARL Libraries. SPEC Kit 113. Washington, DC: Association of Research Libraries, Office of Management Studies, 1985.

Ritzenthaler, Mary Lynn. *Preserving Archives and Manuscripts*. Chicago: Society of American Archivists, 1993.

Studwell, William E., and Samuel T. Huang. "The Rare Book Room: A Marvelous Resource for Research in Popular Culture." *Popular Culture in Libraries* 2, no. 1 (1994): 73–80.

Traister, Daniel. "What Good Is an Old Book?" *Rare Books & Manuscripts Librarianship* 7, no. 1 (1992): 26–42.

Winkler, Karen J. "In Electronic Age, Scholars Are Drawn to Study of Print." *Chronicle of Higher Education* (July 14, 1993): A6–A8.

Wooley, James. "Special Collections Lending: A Reader's View." *Rare Books and Manuscripts Librarianship* 3, no. 2 (Fall 1988): 121–125.

CASE STUDIES

When "Treat It as Though It's Your Own Book" Isn't Good Enough

Charlotte A. Tancin, Hunt Institute for Botanical Documentation, Pittsburgh, Pennsylvania

We are always looking for new ways to communicate to our library users the need for careful handling and to instruct them on how to handle collection materials carefully. In this way, we try to provide as much access to the collections as we can while limiting handling damage as much as possible.

BACKGROUND

The library of the Hunt Institute for Botanical Documentation at Carnegie Mellon University is a research collection containing a sizable proportion of rare books. In addition to controlling how our books are stored and maintained, we pay close attention to how they are handled. Because so much of the collection is rare, old, or otherwise valuable, we are frequently faced with the necessity of sensitizing our library users to the appropriate care and handling of such materials. Finding ways to communicate this information directly yet diplomatically and to ensure that the library user actually gets the message are ongoing challenges. Beyond our official procedures, outlined in the next few paragraphs, there is often a need for subjective judgment regarding how much instruction, if any, should be conveyed to the user and how it should be done. I have found that this subjective dimension of library instruction is not frequently addressed in the literature, so I thought that some explicit discussion of implicit thought processes and associated actions might be useful to others.

METHODOLOGY

Visitors who come to use the library are instructed in careful handling and supervised by a librarian throughout their visit. A sheet listing a basic set of rules for use of the collections is read and signed by first-time users of the library as a contract signifying their agreement to comply with our conditions. In addition, we follow up with them by emphasizing selected rules, such as the use of pencils only for taking notes (we make exceptions for laptop computers), as well as by giving other handling instructions as needed. With repeat visitors, we usually just remind them of a few key rules and point out any condition-specific characteristics that they should be careful about.

The library's closed-stack access arrangement reduces wear and tear, prevents misshelving, and reduces security risks. In the case of rare books, we are also sometimes able to minimize wear and tear and maximize security by acquiring reprints or copies in other formats, which in many cases can be consulted by library users in place of the original publications with no loss of information or compromise of scholarly value. Most frequently, however, the library visitor uses original materials; often, there are no reprints or copies available, or in some cases such facsimiles are available, but the user may need to consult the original work. For most modern publications, no instruction or comment is necessary, but in situations involving older materials, we often feel the need to provide some handling guidance for the user. The type of material that the visitor has asked to see is one factor that helps us to decide how much, if any, instruction is warranted.

When we retrieve the requested items, we briefly assess the condition of each one in order to draw the user's attention to specific characteristics as necessary, for example, a loose board or a detached page. We provide felt-wrapped bricks against which the boards of an open book can be leaned for support if needed, and we let the user know if there is an angle beyond which the book should not be opened.

Beyond offering this sort of initial, condition-specific instruction it is occasionally necessary to further sensitize the user to the possibility of damage that can be caused simply by turning pages, moving the book on the desk top, or other routine handling. This level of interaction calls for careful judgment and considerable diplomacy, as some users are more mindful than others, although virtually every user appears to believe that he or she is appropriately careful in the way they handle library materials. Consider the following statements:

"This book has survived all this time just fine, so why worry about it now?"

"These books are here to be used; otherwise, why have them in the library?"

"This is a book, not a relic."

"I've handled innumerable rare books and have never had a complaint."

"I was at [a major research library] last year, and they let me make photocopies from
their medieval herbals myself."

At this point my readers may be wondering to themselves whether people
who make those statements might not be the wrong people into whose hands
one might place something like a medieval herbal. However, attitudes toward
rare books vary widely, and some of the statements above were made by scholars
with good credentials who appeared to feel a proprietary familiarity with the
works they had come to consult. Also, condition varies from copy to copy, and
perhaps they had previously consulted a particularly hardy copy and now were
faced with a more fragile one.

In my early days on the job, statements like those quoted above made me
feel as though I were being overly cautious (if not outright paranoid) if I was
at all uneasy about the way books were being handled. After all, in some cases
these were scholars who may have handled more rare books than I had. I vac-
illated between total nonintervention and anxious hovering. However, learning
more about preservation allowed me to develop a better sense of what constitutes
appropriate handling and to become more comfortable in assuming responsibility
for the ongoing well-being of the books in my care. With this confidence came
a desire to learn to provide on-the-spot handling instruction combined with consciousness raising at the right level for the situation and without alienating the
user.

Shown below are a few techniques used singly or in combination. In most
cases, once it is ascertained which books are needed, retrieved, and given to the
researcher, I will remain there for a minute or two, chatting about the research
or the books and observing the researcher's handling style. If what I see makes
me feel concerned or uneasy, one or more of the following methods of communication are brought into play.

1. Note existing deterioration, for example, of binding or paper. One of the
easiest ways to get people to pay closer attention to how they handle things is
simply to alert them to an existing condition and then briefly indicate or describe
both what would exacerbate the problem and what type of handling would not
be likely to cause further damage. For many users, this, or this plus a brief
cautionary statement about microdamage, is sufficient.

2. Introduce concept of microdamage. There's damage and then there's damage. Beyond the obvious examples of torn pages and split bindings, there are
the more subtle types of damage such as strain, abrasion, or minute tearing or
weakening, which users can easily cause unknowingly but which have a cumulative effect, eventually resulting in more visible deterioration.

3. Relate my own experience. The evolution of my own understanding over
time has made me more sensitive to the potential need for users to be given
appropriate information to enable them to handle rare materials responsibly.
Often, a user will be unaware that he or she is doing something potentially
harmful, such as leaning on an open book or making little creases in the paper

when turning pages. Therefore, I sometimes try to induce mindfulness through descriptive example and personal anecdote.

4. *Cite age/value/condition of item.* This is a bit like situation ethics; I might talk briefly about how standards for careful handling vary depending on context, condition, value, age, rarity, and so on. Some people respond very favorably to the idea that they are being asked to handle an item with particular care because it has special characteristics.

5. *Note my responsibility for the well-being of the collection.* On rare occasions, there is simply no other choice than to volunteer to do the handling oneself or else regretfully withhold or limit access to an item. Sometimes I make this decision at the time I retrieve the item (e.g., in the case of a book with high artifactual value that is only being consulted briefly), and in such cases, the user handles the book minimally or not at all. At these times, I don't present an option but just do the handling myself as though that were the usual state of affairs. But there have also been several occasions when I have intervened and taken over the task of turning the pages of a folio volume for a user who was either steadfastly resistant to behavior modification or just apparently incapable of assimilating the instructions. This is an extreme circumstance that arises infrequently, but such intervention does remain an option, and one must be willing to intervene. When this happens, I try to make it clear that it's nothing personal but that I'm responsible for the well-being of the collection, that the item in question is particularly susceptible to damage, and that if damage occurred inadvertently at the hands of the user, we would both feel terrible. I try to convey the idea that my intervention has less to do with the user than with my curatorial responsibilities. It should be noted, though, that such intervention won't work in a situation where the user simply wants to sit and read. In that case, one really is dependent on achieving a mutual understanding on the level of careful handling required.

These various considerations may give the impression of inherent mistrust of library visitors, but this is not the case. Rather, I believe that people in general want to do the right thing but that sometimes they do not have enough information to enable them to do so. How many of us are born with the knowledge of how to handle rare books? This, like so much else in life, is something that is learned, and one of the ways it is learned is through situation-specific instruction.

Central also to these considerations is the concept of trust. There is a certain amount of risk involved in handing over rare materials that are under your care to someone whose primary connection with them is the wish to use them. The risk is lessened if there is a level of mutual understanding (a "comfort level") between the librarian and the user such that a certain amount of knowledge about careful handling is understood and agreed to by the user. How such a comfort level is achieved varies. Of course, one could just shrug off the notion of risk and assume that no damage will occur. However, my own experience is that both the concept and the reality of careful handling are subjective and variable, potentially falling anywhere along a wide continuum, with deliberate and mindful care at one end and careless page flipping at the other. Seeing this, I have chosen to work on ''keying people in'' to a few basic ideas:

- *Book opening.* If a book would be harmed by its being opened beyond a given angle, I explain that and explain why, showing how far to open the book.

- *Page turning.* Whether paper is pristine rag or brittle, careful page turning is warranted for rare books, and I often give a brief demonstration (sometimes using a separate sheet of paper) of how and how not to turn pages, explaining why.

- *No excess pressure on the book.* I discourage people from leaning on books and particularly on open books. It's interesting to observe how many people lean on books without thinking about what they're doing. Stacking too many books also falls under this category.

- *Photocopying.* Photocopying has become a fact of life in libraries, but it is also a prime cause of book damage. In recognition of this, as well as for security reasons, all photocopying for researchers at our library is done by the librarians as a matter of course. We provide photocopies when we can, but only if we can do so without damaging or endangering the item in question. If the researcher accompanies me to the edge platen photocopier, I will usually make a comment about why those copiers are designed that way and why we often prefer not to open books flat to copy them.

CONCLUSION/EVALUATION

Generally speaking, the results of these various ''behavioral experiments'' have been favorable. As time goes on, I am continually honing my communication style, finding subtler and more laid-back ways to accomplish my objectives. Eventually, I hope to become so adept at this sort of instructional communication that it will be completely subliminal, and while ostensibly I will have been standing there chatting about the flora of Greece, in actuality there will have been implanted in the researcher's mind the desire to turn the pages as delicately as if they were flower petals. In the meantime, brief and carefully stated observations about condition and handling must suffice, hopefully sufficient to the situation.

Care and Handling Education for Patrons

Charlotte B. Brown, UCLA, Los Angeles, California

INTRODUCTION

Implementing effective and ethical care and handling practices is the obligation of every institution that retains materials designated as special collections (rare books, manuscripts collections in any format, and archival collections in any format are often considered to be primary research materials and, therefore, designated special collections). Care and handling routines are practical, they reflect standard library and archival practice, and they contribute toward satisfying the institution's ethical obligations as the custodian of materials that are often fragile and unique.[1] The following case study will describe the methods used by a department of special collections to educate their patrons in the appropriate care and handling of rare books, manuscripts, photographs, and architectural drawings—all types and formats of special collections materials.

It is important to note that the care and handling routines described in this case study reflect standard practice as it applies to special collections materials, no matter the type of library or repository. Furthermore, this case study is a useful example of a special collections unit attempting to satisfy two, frequently divergent, goals of library service: providing patron access to materials that are rare, valuable, or unique versus the physical preservation (protection) of these materials to minimize deterioration as a result of use.[2] The resolution of this situation lies in educating patrons to handle special collections materials appropriately.

BACKGROUND

The Department of Special Collections of the University of California at Los Angeles (UCLA) was founded in 1946 and from its beginning experienced a phenomenal period of planned and opportunistic acquisition of special collections materials. As a result, UCLA currently maintains significant rare book, manuscript, and archival holdings; administers a scholarly publications program based upon the department's holdings; and has established an active and highly regarded oral history program.

The UCLA University Research Library (URL), in which the Department of Special Collections is housed, implemented a preservation program in 1986. Consistent with the library's preservation goals, the Department of Special Collections has designed and implemented a customized subset of the overall library preservation program that supports the unique physical and administrative requirements of special collections materials. In addition, the department willingly serves as a test site for the development of new librarywide preservation initiatives. The design and implementation of condition surveys for selected holdings is one example.

Care and Handling at UCLA

Once properly arranged, described, physically protected . . . and stored, collections are ready to withstand the rigors of research use. It is this area of activity that collection materials are most susceptible to damage or loss.[3]

Educating the patron is only one component in the department's overall care and handling routines. First, appropriate storage and handling, from acquisition to final shelving, must be addressed. The following list describes each of the department's care and handling stages and the steps taken to achieve a preservationally sound collection.[4] The stages are in sequence and reflect the department's processing work flow.

- *Stage 1.* When a collection is first acquired, it is inspected for pests and mold; a preliminary preservation condition survey is conducted and information entered into the collection database.
- *Stage 2.* The unprocessed collection is stored under stable HVAC[5] conditions; the collection is stored in a secure area; the collection is assigned a priority in the department's disaster recovery plan.
- *Stage 3.* Based upon the results of the preliminary condition survey, individual items and/or an aggregate of materials—for example, several folders of manuscripts within a box—are identified and prioritized for off-site conservation treatment; the collection is intellectually processed and physically stabilized using the following techniques: rehousing, separation by format, preservation reformatting (microfilming, photocopying), and basic conservation item treatments; the collection is located in a secure area during processing.

- *Stage 4.* The physically stabilized processed collection is stored under stable HVAC conditions; the collection is stored in a secure area; the disaster recovery priority of the collection is reassessed and reassigned, if necessary.

- *Stage 5.* Access to the processed collection by the patron is monitored in the special collection reading room; the collection is stored in a secure area during use; the patron is monitored while consulting the collection; the collection is checked for completeness and condition after use.

As the previous list clearly demonstrates, successful care and handling practices do not occur in a vacuum. Rather, they are supported by an overall preservation program.

EDUCATING THE PATRON

The dichotomy between providing access to materials and the preservation of materials has already been noted. What has yet to be mentioned is the frustration often experienced by the patron from the conflicting library service principles of access and preservation. To address this issue, UCLA's patron education procedures are designed (1) to convey the department's consistent attention to proper care and handling and (2) to obtain the patron's ongoing cooperation.

Patron Registration and Informational Handouts

UCLA's Department of Special Collections is a public repository, and the materials are available to everyone. All patrons who wish to consult special collections materials begin the process by registering as a researcher with the department, a process intended to orient and educate new patrons and to remind returning patrons of the department's established routines (see Figure 7.7). The registration form (Figure 7.8) serves three functions: (1) It documents the identity of the patron for security purposes; (2) it documents that the patron received the department's informational handouts; and (3) it documents the amount and type of anticipated use of the collections by the patron.

All registered patrons receive a copy of "Access to UCLA's Special Collections Materials" (Figure 7.9) and a copy of "Departmental Rules" (Figure 7.10). It is the "Departmental Rules" that describe for the patron the department's care and handling expectations. When the patron identifies collections to be consulted, a paging call slip (Figure 7.11) is completed and signed. In signing the paging slip, the patron acknowledges that they will abide by the department's rules for use.

Taken as a whole, the registration and paging processes establish a verbal and written contract between the patron and the department: It is understood that patron access is dependent on proper use. The expectation of appropriate use and its definition are stated in the written handouts. Appropriate use is also encouraged through the consistent application and enforcement of these proce-

Figure 7.7
Registration Guidelines

```
Department of Special Collections-URL
UCLA Library
Los Angeles, CA
```

Registering a First Time Patron

```
Reference Desk:
```

   The following - in priority order - are the steps to register a patron
   who is using UCLA's special collections materials for the first time:

   1. Before completing a paging slip or the "Access Form," patron must
       show a valid, non-expired UCLA library card or a current UCLA
       student registration card.

       If patron does not have a card, refer them to the URL Circulation
       Desk to obtain one. Tell the patron that they will be asked to
       present a photo-I.D. before being issued a library card.

   2. After verifying the validity of the library card, give the patron the
       "Access Form" to complete and sign (in ink); completed form is
       returned to the reference desk staff, initialed (on back) by
       staff, and filed.

   3. Give patron copies of the "Access Policy" and "Department Rules."

   4. Explain "Policy" and "Rules" to patron; be sure to mention fees
       if the user is not affiliated with UCLA or the University of
       California system.

   5. Patron may proceed to consult finding aids and/or request materials
       by completing a paging slip.

       Please Note: for conservation reasons, page slips should be
                     completed using pencil, not pen.

```
Dec 1993/cbb
```

dures by the department's staff, with few exceptions. Though there is no guarantee that patrons will carefully read and comprehend the informational handouts, the texts serve to document what will occur. Ideally, once the patron is registered and interviewed by the reference staff, there should be no surprises either for the patron or for the department when special collections materials are being consulted.

Reading Room Configuration and Procedures

Patron education received during the registration and paging process is reinforced by the physical configuration of the department's reading room and by

Figure 7.8
Registration Form

Name (please print): _____
                     Last   First

* * Special Collections Access Form * *
University of California, Los Angeles Libraries
Los Angeles, CA 90095-1575

NOTE: The information on this form is considered confidential; you are
      asked to verify the information every Fall Quarter.

                                        Date: _____

Signature in full (in ink): _____

Permanent Address: _____

                   _____

                   _____

                   Permanent Phone: (   ) _____

Local Address (if different from permanent address):

         _____

         _____

         _____

         Local Telephone: (   ) _____

UCLA Library card / bar code: _____

                    / stat. cat.: _____

What is the purpose of your research?

     ____ Class Assignment:
                 College/Univer. _____

                 Professor _____ Course No. _____
     ____ Master's Thesis
     ____ Doctoral Dissertation
     ____ Publication or Production
     ____ Personal Interest
     ____ Other _____

If for publication/production, please indicate format (book, film, other):

_____

Would you like to discuss you project with a librarian? yes ____ no ____

Figure 7.8 Continued

```
[OPTIONAL]  Subject(s) of current study or project (this information
            will be used to assist our collections development staff):


            _____


May we mention your name, address, and research topic to others doing
similar work?

            yes ____    no ____

            (please initial and ask to complete a research card)


---------------------------------------------------------------------
Office use only

Registered by: _____

Div./Librarian(s) to be notified: _____

Forms distributed to user:
            ____    Access (policy)
            ____    Departmental Rules
            ____    Photodup. Services (gen. policy)
            ____    Photodup. Restrictions
            ____    Photodup. (form)
            ____    Copyright Compliance (form)
            ____    Perm. to Pub. (policy)

Comments:




                                               9 Jan 1995/cbb
```

the room's security procedures. For example, the arrangement and furnishings of the reading room are designed to facilitate compliance with the "Departmental Rules." The room contains six large tables; each accommodates two patrons. Each table is supplied with several foam book cradles and a set of book weights, and the tables are configured so that patrons sit with their backs to the walls of the reading room, always using the materials in full sight of the reading room attendant. The attendant's desk, located at one end of the reading room next to the entrance, is on an elevated platform and offers a full view of the reading room. The reading room entrance has a door that is locked and unlocked by an electrical system operated by the reference desk staff, outside the reading room entrance, and by the reading room attendant. No materials—not even pencil or paper—can be taken into the reading room without prior permission and inspection by the reference desk staff. All materials brought out of the

Figure 7.9
Guide to UCLA's Access Policies

Department of Special Collections-URL
Room A-1713
University of California, Los Angeles
Los Angeles, CA 90095-1575

ACCESS TO UCLA's SPECIAL COLLECTIONS MATERIALS

"...recognizing its role as a unique regional, state, and national resource, the [UCLA] Library provides access whenever possible to the rarer and more specialized items in UCLA's collections, since these may be available only at UCLA."

"Guidelines for Access"
UCLA Library

I.   POLICIES

The UCLA Department of Special Collections-URL is committed to providing basic Reading Room use of the collections free of charge.

All researchers are expected to abide by the Department's standard rules and regulations which are designed to maintain the integrity of the collections and to ensure their preservation.

To assure continued access for years to come, collections held by the department cannot be checked out nor can items be borrowed or requested through Interlibrary Loan.

Availability of Materials:
Materials housed in the Department may be consulted by all registered researchers of the UCLA Library. For identification and security purposes, researchers consulting special collections materials are required to be registered. A registered researcher is a person who has presented a valid UCLA Library card and completed the Department's researcher form.

On occasion - usually due to a lack of space in the Reading Room - researchers not affiliated with UCLA, the University of California system, or with other UCLA contractual agencies may be asked to delay consulting the department's collections.

Priority of Service:
The stated mission of the Department is to give *priority of service* to researchers formally affiliated with UCLA or with the University of California system. The Department's service policies reflect this priority.

Commercial Projects/Commercially Financed Research:
Researchers involved with commercial projects are expected, when asked, to identify their projects as such.

On-site commercial researchers may, on occasion, be requested to limit the number of items consulted. Such a request is most often the result of staff shortages or of unusually heavy use of the collections by UCLA-affiliated researchers.

Figure 7.9 Continued

II.   ON-SITE PROCEDURES

A researcher wishing to consult the Department's collections must present any one of the following to the person at the Department's Reference Desk:

           1) a valid UCLA library card;
           2) a UCLA student ID card with a library bar code & a
               current validated registration card.

Obtain a UCLA library card:
Library cards and library bar codes may be obtained at the following circulation service areas:

University Research Library [URL] Circulation Desk - first floor; cards may be obtained during regular library hours, up until fifteen minutes before closing; a photo ID must be presented.

Biomedical Library Circulation Desk; cards may be obtained during regular library hours, up until fifteen minutes before closing; a photo ID must be presented.

Complete the "Special Collections Access" form:
First time researchers will be asked to present a UCLA library card and given a short form to complete. The information on the form remains confidential. Forms are renewed every year at the beginning of Fall Quarter.

III.   PHYSICAL ACCESSIBILITY

Researchers requesting special accommodations are asked to contact the Department at least five working days in advance. Reasonable accommodations will be provided upon request. Proxy Borrower Cards are also available in the name of the researcher.

UCLA-affiliated researchers may contact the following campus resources offices:

UCLA Office for Students With Disabilities,
      (310) 825-1501/voice; (310) 206-9688/TDD

UCLA Disabled Staff Outreach Program, (310) 206-2942/voice;
      (310) 206-2947/TDD

IV.   FEES

There are no fees charged to registered researchers for basic Reading Room use of the Department's collections.

Service fees:
Fees will be charged when researchers request photoduplication services, permission to publish text or images, the lending of materials for exhibition, or permission to set up camera/video shoots. Handouts listing the services and fees charged are available upon request.

9 Jan 1995/cbb

292

Figure 7.10
UCLA Special Collections Rules

Department of Special Collections-URL   Hours: 9 am to 5 pm
University of California, Los Angeles   Mon. to Sat.
Los Angeles, CA 90095-1575   Phone: 310/825-4988

Departmental Rules

The Department of Special Collections was established in 1946 to bring together collections of rare books, manuscripts, and other scarce or unique materials so as to insure their safekeeping and appropriate use. The Department's collections are available to all registered researchers of the UCLA Library.

Information about the collections and how to access them is offered at the Department's reference desk. A guide (1992) describing the Department and its holdings is also available at the reference desk.

                                *   *   *

The following rules have been established to preserve the Department's collections and to ensure that they are accessible.

-       Items held by the Department of Special Collections are provided to registered readers in the Department's reading room; collections cannot be checked out or used in other parts of the University Research Library.

-       The reading room is reserved for registered readers using Departmental collections.

-       Registered readers should complete a call slip - available at the reference desk - for each item requested. Requested items are brought to the reading room by Department staff on a regular schedule. Readers should ask the reading room desk attendant for their requested items.

-       Readers will also be provided with paper and pencil. Readers may not take personal materials (e.g. pens, notepads, books) into the reading room.

-       Laptop computers (out of cases), reference books, and architectural tracing paper are permitted in the reading room. These items are subject to search by the reference desk staff prior to entering the reading room.

-       Keyed lockers are provided to store briefcases and other personal items.

-       All materials must remain on the reading room tables during use. Nothing may be placed on Special Collections items except book weights and plexiglass overlays provided by the Department.

-       The arranged order within folders and boxes of the manuscript collections must be preserved. Please notify the desk attendant if you suspect that a collection is out of arranged order.

-       Material may not be left unattended in the reading room. If it is necessary to leave the room, arrangements must be made with the desk attendant. When work is completed, material is to be returned to the reading room desk and checked in by the attendant.

-       Please notify the desk attendant should you encounter uncut book leaves (pages) so that we may open them for you.

-       On occasion, arrangements can be made for Department staff to photograph or photocopy materials. All requests for copying are reviewed by the staff. (see: "Reproduction Guidelines...")

-       All papers, computers, and reference books brought out of the Reading Room by readers will be searched by the reference desk staff.

                                               10 Jun 1995/cbb

Figure 7.11
Paging Call Slip

Department of Special Collections ∾ University Research Library		
CALL/COLL. NO.	AUTHOR _____	
	TITLE _____	
VOLS./BOXES:	EDITION INFO/ NEG. NO.: _____	
PRINT LAST NAME:	*I am familiar with the Department rules and agree to abide by them.*	
STAT CAT._____	*Signature:* _____	
(Dept use only) IN USE:	RETURNED:	NOTES:
BY:	BY:	SRLF: *Already paged for:*
University of California, Los Angeles ∾ 90095-1575		

reading room by the patron are subject to search. Pencils and pastel salmon–colored paper are available in the reading room for use by patrons.[6]

Ensuring that special collections materials remain under completely secure conditions is of utmost concern for UCLA and an essential aspect of patron education. Close monitoring is required while the collections are in use. UCLA's security procedures assume that an occurrence of theft or mutilation may be attempted. As a result, the department's procedures are designed to prevent such an occurrence by recording patron use (in writing) and by providing uninterrupted surveillance of the reading room.

Only patrons having materials waiting for their use are allowed into the reading room. Upon entering, the attendant locates the patron's materials and documents in writing the call number of the item, the patron's name, the time that the item was first used, and the time of day the item was returned. The department also places a limit on the number of items a patron may have on the reading room table at any one time; in most cases, the limit is one bound volume or one manuscript folder. In addition, the reading room attendant visually monitors the use of all reading room materials. Should the attendant suspect that an incidence of theft or mutilation has occurred, UCLA has written public service security procedures for the attendant and reference staff to follow.[7]

CONCLUSION

Are there gaps in UCLA's care and handling procedures? Yes, there are gaps. For example, UCLA has yet to establish a systematic routine for checking the physical condition of collections before use. Due to the large number of books and manuscripts brought to the reading room on a given day, the department would have to design a quick and effective method for checking condition that would not unreasonably delay patron access.

UCLA's Department of Special Collections patron education in the care and handling of materials is well documented, consistently applied, constantly reviewed, and effective. Should a patron comment on or complain about the department's routines, the reference staff is instructed to acknowledge the patron's concerns and to offer a detailed explanation of the department's preservation procedures, as stated in the "Departmental Rules." Patron concerns are also reviewed at the department's biweekly reference meetings. On occasion, and to emphasize the need for vigilant security procedures, we will show patrons the department's reference desk file of suspected book and manuscript thieves. This information is regularly updated by the UCLA Library Security Officer and from postings on the archives and rare books Internet listservs.[8]

UCLA's special collections are withstanding the "rigors of research use" because of the importance UCLA places on patron education.

NOTES

1. "Standards for Ethical Conduct for Rare Book, Manuscript, and Special Collections Librarians, with Guidelines for Institutional Practice in Support of the Standards," 2nd ed., 1992, published in *College & Research Library News* 54, no. 4 (April 1993): 207–215.

2. For additional information on the issue of access versus preservation for special collections materials, see Association of College and Research Libraries, "ACRL Guidelines for the Preparation of Policies on Library Access: A Draft," *College & Research Library News* 53, no. 11 (December 1992): 709–718; American Library Association–Society of American Archivists (ALA-SAA), "Joint Statement on Access: Guidelines for Access to Original Research Materials," *Archival Outlook* (September 1994): 8–9; and "Appraisal, Protection and Arrangement (Section VI) in Code of Ethics for Archivists" (Chicago: Society of American Archivists, 1992).

3. Mary Lynn Ritzenthaler, *Preserving Archives and Manuscripts* (Chicago: Society of American Archivists, 1993), p. 112.

4. According to Ritzenthaler (ibid., p. 6) the core preservation program elements for an archival repository are preservation policy formation, preservation planning, staff and researcher training, holdings maintenance, environmental control monitoring, disaster control, preservation duplication, and conservation treatment.

5. The term *HVAC* refers to the environmental control system of a building that partially consists of heating, ventilation, air conditioning. See ibid., chap. 5, pp. 51–66, for a detailed description and discussion of environmental control systems.

6. Providing patrons with colored note paper is part of the department's reading room security program. Pastel salmon was the color selected by the special collections staff; it is a readily visible color and a color that allows the photocopying of penciled notes.

7. See "ACRL Guidelines for the Security of Rare Book, Manuscript, and Other

Special Collections,'' *College & Research Libraries News* 51, no. 3 (March 1990): 240–244; ''Guidelines Regarding Thefts in Libraries,'' *College & Research Libraries News* 55, no. 10 (November 1994): 641–646; Vincent A. Totka, Jr., ''Preventing Patron Theft in the Archives: Legal Perspectives and Problems,'' *American Archivist* 56, no. 4 (Fall 1993): 664–672.

8. The UCLA library has a designated Library Security Officer (LSO), as per the recommendations of the ACRL Rare Books and Manuscripts Section (RBMS) Security Committee. The LSO regularly copies the Department of Special Collections' announced library thefts and physical descriptions of alleged thieves. For a more detailed listing of the LSO functions, see Section I of the ACRL ''Guidelines Regarding Thefts in Libraries,'' *College & Research Libraries News* 55, no. 10 (November 1994): 641.

Preservation Education Initiative in an Archive

Kenneth White, Archives of the Catholic Diocese of Pittsburgh, Pittsburgh, Pennsylvania

The purpose of the preservation education initiative at the archives of the Catholic Diocese of Pittsburgh is to ensure that visitors and staff are aware of the proper procedures for handling archival material. By restricting what patrons may and may not do in the research room, we hope to reduce the wear and tear on the documents and to ensure against their loss or damage. The target audience for the preservation initiative is twofold. One is the individuals who come to the Archives to do research. The other is the staff who provide research room security, many of whom are volunteers with no formal archival training or experience.

BACKGROUND

The Diocese of Pittsburgh was created in 1843. The Archives was established in 1917 to preserve the historical records of the diocese's central administration, parishes, and schools. For many years, the Archives was managed by diocesan personnel who had little or no formal professional training or experience. Documents were not collected systematically. Those documents that had been collected were not adequately processed or preserved. In 1993, the sesquicentennial of the diocese, a total reorganization of the Archives occurred. The preservation education initiative was developed during this reorganization. The first step taken was the development of diocese-wide policies and procedures for the handling and management of records. As part of this step, policies for the research room were developed by the newly hired director of the Archives and approved by diocesan management.

METHODOLOGY

Two policy documents have been developed for the research room. One is targeted to the researchers and explains what they may and may not do in handling the records. The other policy document is targeted to staff members assigned to the research room. This document is a supplement to the researcher policy and informs staff of their specific responsibilities. Developing a separate document for staff has helped ensure that unpaid volunteer staff act professionally in the research room and answer questions on research policy accurately. For example, before the staff policy document was written, one volunteer frequently initiated casual conversations with researchers. The explicit policy against that curtailed this activity. Both documents are printed in hard copy and kept in the research room.

When a researcher arrives, they are given the copy of the research room policy to read. This is reinforced by the staff member who verbally goes over the rules. The patron is then required to fill out a patron analysis and regulations form, which requests their name and address and includes a signed acknowledgment that the researcher has read and understood the policies. The staff member then records the items the researcher uses so that we can identify who has handled a file, should a problem arise. Fortunately, no problem has arisen to date that has required the Archives to locate a researcher.

The policies that researchers are required to follow are standard archival practices. Researchers must leave items they bring with them, such as coats and briefcases, with the research room attendant. These are stored until the researcher is ready to leave. No more than two boxes of records are brought to the research room at a time, and the researcher is required to use only one file folder at a time. Pens may not be used in the research room (pencils are provided by the Archives). Eating, drinking, and smoking are prohibited. Researchers are cautioned to handle the documents themselves with care. This caution is done verbally by the research staff person. "Do not lean or write on top of documents; do not bend or fold the paper." Researchers are also advised to gently handle paper that may be brittle, although the most brittle documents have been either photocopied onto acid-free paper or closed to researchers.

The staff is instructed to linger nearby as the researcher pulls out the first file folder. If the researcher handles the documents carefully, the staff member returns to their desk and periodically observes the researcher. If the researcher does not handle the documents carefully, the staff member gives additional instruction. To date, the only additional instruction that has been generally necessary has been to remind the researcher not to use a pen.

The policies for the staff are also written and a copy kept at the staff desk in the research room. All employees or volunteers who are assigned to work in the research room are given a brief orientation of approximately 30 to 60 minutes as to their duties and responsibilities. Because the number of volunteers is small, this orientation has always been given one on one. They are also given a personal copy of the applicable policies. The staff's main preservation responsibility is security. The staff member is required to stay in the research room the entire time that the patron is there. If the staff member must leave the room, they must get another staff member to cover. The staff member must make sure that the patron reads the policy document, go over it verbally, and secure the signed patron analysis and regulations form. They must also observe the patron to ensure that the policies are being followed. Once the patron is finished with the material, the staff member must briefly examine items to verify that there are no obvious problems. The staff member must also ensure that the patron analysis and regulations form is on file so that if a problem does later become obvious, responsibility can be determined.

If the staff member discovers a researcher violating a rule or mishandling a document, they are instructed to politely remind the individual of the research room requirements. If the individual ignores the request or attempts to argue, the staff person is instructed to immediately call the archivist or the director of the Archives for assistance. So far, this problem has not arisen. In the few instances when a researcher has violated a rule, such as trying to use a pen, a single reminder has solved the problem.

CONCLUSION/EVALUATION

The preservation education initiative as described above is the first step in a two-part process. The purpose of the first part is to help ensure the preservation of the archival materials already in the Archives by informing staff and patrons as to the proper method for handling these records. This part has so far proved to be successful, as the policies have been implemented without problem.

The second part of the initiative is yet to be accomplished. This is to ensure that diocesan personnel outside the Archives are aware of the preservation needs of archival records. The bulk of the records that come to the Archives are generated by the diocese's schools, parishes, and administrative offices. Many of them must be kept in the office of origin for years for administrative purposes. Some archival records will not be transferred to the Archives until 70 years after creation. Records that have been held in originating offices for long periods of time often arrive in poor condition. In many instances, the condition of the record reflects the damaging environment in which the record was stored.

To remedy this, the Archives plans to develop a training program for the diocesan staff on the care and handling of records. Particular emphasis will be given on the use of acid-free materials and the environmental conditions necessary for the long-term preservation of material. This training will be done through workshops developed by the Archives, supplemented by leaflets or pamphlets on preservation.

Local Records Management: One-on-One Preservation Education

Carolyn K. Collings, Missouri Local Records Program, Jefferson City, Missouri

Providing advice through demonstrations, presentations, and one-on-one consultations is part of the responsibilities of the archivist position in the Local Records Program, a division of the Office of the Secretary of State, Missouri. The program began in 1990 after a successful pilot program from 1986 to 1990, and provides assistance to county and municipal officials and other public-funded entities such as community colleges and public libraries in order to preserve permanent documents and provide access to public records as required by Missouri law.

BACKGROUND

Nancy Kossmann, city clerk of Union, in Franklin County, Missouri, had heard about the program through my presentation at a city clerks' meeting. An initial on-site visit was scheduled following her telephone request for assistance. As Local Records Archivist, I examined the Union storage space, a basement room approximately 50 feet by 18 feet with 52 metal shelving units. Records, for the most part, were organized in a cohesive system for the city clerk and other officials in city hall; however, supplies and equipment were interspersed with record boxes. The crowding led to less-than-adequate standards for archival storage. A systematic retention check was not in effect. Preservation concerns included security, care and handling, housing and storage, environment, and disaster planning.

Using the *Missouri Municipal Records Manual* published by the Office of the Secretary of State to determine which records were past retention, the archivist determined that nonrecords needed to be cleared out and suggested separating the supply area from the records area. After the initial visit and recommendations, the Local Records Program, the city clerk, and the Board of Aldermen of Union agreed to work together for the organization and preservation of the permanent records.

METHODOLOGY

Shortly thereafter, work began to reorganize and refine the records storage system and to begin preservation initiatives. Initial supplies and vendor and supply lists were furnished by the Local Records Program. Preservation techniques were discussed with one-on-one demonstrations using the supplies and equipment. Standard-sized boxes, cotton gloves, paper cleaning supplies, and archival mending tape for repairing documents to be microfilmed were provided. For maps and other broadsides the advantages of encapsulation over lamination were discussed. As record series were identified, and boxes containing permanent and long-term retention records were reorganized, the archivist continued including preservation strategies during preparation of materials. Just as important as the assistance in preparation of materials was the training using examples at hand for illustration. This method of one-on-one instruction using local situations for specific examples to show the process is used with varying success, but in this case, the clerk took all the comments to heart and began thinking about how to incorporate sound preservation methods in all aspects of her records management program. By listening to understand the perception, and providing a prompt answer, the archivist encouraged clear understanding of concepts. Conveying the concept by including background and rationale helped to provide solid understanding. Defining terms and clarifying the relative importance of each preservation concept provided the clerk with enough information to make sound preservation decisions on her own.

The archivist assisted the clerk in identifying records according to the *Missouri Municipal Records Manual* published by the Office of the Secretary of State. The clerk decided to construct a database using the existing dBase program but included all the necessary local records fields, including a physical condition field. The inventory sheet used by the Local Records Program is shown in Figure 7.12. The data could be sorted by any of the fields. For example, location order was used for an inventory check. Future conservation treatments could be batched by this sorting method. The physical condition field of the inventory sheet provided codes on the condition of the materials and the type of material, such as bound volume, map, or paper. The definitions of some of the physical condition codes are shown in Figure 7.13. The code book was provided and the terms discussed. As the various condition codes were explained, the archivist took the opportunity to talk in general terms about pres-

Figure 7.12
Local Records Inventory Sheet

MISSOURI SECRETARY OF STATE

Local Records Computer Inventory Sheet

County [＿＿＿＿＿＿]   City [＿＿＿＿＿＿＿＿＿＿＿＿＿＿＿＿]

Office [＿＿＿＿] Vault [＿＿＿＿] Unit [＿＿＿＿] Unit_Section [＿＿＿＿＿]

Tier [＿＿＿＿]   Till_Section [＿＿＿＿＿]   Tills [＿＿＿＿＿]

===

Title [＿＿＿＿＿＿＿＿＿＿＿＿＿＿＿＿＿＿＿＿＿＿＿＿＿＿＿＿]

Subtitle[＿＿＿＿＿＿＿＿＿＿＿＿＿＿＿＿＿＿＿＿＿＿＿＿＿＿＿＿]

Volume Number [＿＿＿＿＿＿＿＿＿] Volume Code [＿＿＿＿＿＿＿]

Begin_Date [＿＿＿＿＿＿＿＿＿＿] End_Date [＿＿＿＿＿＿＿＿＿]

Format [＿＿＿＿＿＿] Medium [＿＿＿＿＿＿＿] Arrangement [＿＿＿＿＿]

Physical Condition: *(Please check mark conditions that apply)*

L P	B B	M C	L C	R R	T R	M T	S O	S T	B P	Y W	M D	I D	W D	T P	V R	L B	L E	M S	F D

Inches: Height [＿＿＿＿＿＿]   Width [＿＿＿＿＿＿]   Depth [＿＿＿＿＿＿]

Box Number [＿＿＿＿＿＿]   File Number [＿＿＿＿＿＿]   Archivist [＿＿＿＿＿]

Date of Inventory [＿＿＿＿＿＿＿＿＿]   Microfilmed Y/N [＿＿＿＿＿]

Permanent Y/N [＿＿＿＿] Retention [＿＿＿＿＿＿＿＿＿＿＿＿＿]

Remarks:＿＿＿＿＿＿＿＿＿＿＿＿＿＿＿＿＿＿＿＿＿＿＿＿＿＿

_____

_____

(Explanation about codes & conditions please refer to the Local Records
Inventory Database Code Manual)

Figure 7.13
Physical Condition Codes Definitions

CONDITION:

LP   **LOOSE PAGES** *(bound volumes)*: pages which have detached from binding.

BB   **BROKEN BINDING** *(bound volumes)*: binding with broken threads and/or loss of adhesive so that covers have pulled away from the pages along the spine.

MC   **MISSING COVERS** *(bound volumes)*: all or part of one or both covers is missing.

LC   **LOOSE COVERS** *(bound volumes)*: cover is loose but binding is not broken.

RR   **RED ROT** *(bound volumes)*: leather binding is dull, rust-colored, powdery and surface rubs off easily.

TR   **TEARS** *(any material)*

MT   **MISSING TEXT** *(any material)*: information missing due to losses to support paper on maps or documents and/or lost pages in bound volumes.

SO   **SOIL** *(any material)*: loose dust, dirt or soot.

ST   **STAINS** *(any material)*: blemish left by a liquid-based material.

BP   **BRITTLE PAPER** *(any material)*: paper which breaks on three repetitions of folding and unfolding a small corner.

YW   **YELLOWING** *(any material)*: discoloration caused by inherent acidity in paper and/or exposure to light.

MD   **MOLD DAMAGE** *(any material)*: active growth of mold spores or staining from previous mold growth.

ID   **INSECT DAMAGE** *(any material)*: losses to text, paper, cloth or leather from insect attack and/or stains, droppings, cocoons or dead insects on material.

WD   **WATER DAMAGE** *(any material)*: stains, discolorations, adhered pages and/or blurred inscriptions caused by exposure to water.

TP   **TAPE** *(any material)*: pressure-sensitive tape and/or stains from such tape.

VR   **VARNISH** *(maps)*: protective coating sometimes applied to maps which may deteriorate by flaking and/or yellowing.

ervation principles, concerns, and solutions. For example, the issue of brittle paper and the need for microfilming records was easy to illustrate when the paper at hand was falling apart. Red rot on leather cases could easily be seen and solutions to protect the adjacent materials were discussed.

Under the advice of the archivist, supplies and other nonrecord items were confined to one area, opening adequate storage space for the records, allowing for uniform housing and even leaving space for a table and chair to be added so that records could be safely viewed on-site. Some records were rehoused in more appropriate containers. Large bankers' boxes and expensive lidded containers were in use. Inexpensive cubic foot boxes, similar to the ones used in the Missouri State Archives, were supplied to demonstrate ease of handling and better fit on the shelves. Maps were gathering dust on the open shelves, but purchase of an enameled metal map case was not an option for the clerk. Instead, the clerk and archivist were able to wrap the rolled maps in acid-free paper and, when possible, place each one in a box to fit the size of the map. Loose papers were tied with cotton tape, clearly labeled as to record series, inclusive dates, and retention information, and stored in smaller acid-free Hollinger boxes for more efficient storage.

During the inventory, the archivist continued to talk about preservation issues. Temperature and humidity could be monitored with moderately priced equipment and controlled somewhat by existing heating and air-conditioning units. Other topics included security measures, disaster planning concepts, and preservation microfilming of permanent records. Since the actual rehousing was done with the assistance of the archivist, there was ample opportunity to demonstrate proper handling procedures and to explain the reason for such measures.

CONCLUSION

The awareness level of the clerk as records manager dramatically increased as the archivist introduced management and preservation subjects. Organization of records, proper care and handling of materials, record management procedures, and environmental considerations all became a part of the joint planning between the clerk and the archivist. Another outcome from the consultation in Union was the development of a manual for the city clerk and the other officials in city hall, providing information on new procedures for security of the records and how to access them. The purpose stated in the introduction of the manual was "to provide safe, efficient storage of city records, provide a methodical approach to records management, free up valuable file space in crowded offices, provide for destruction of documents meeting their retention requirements, and ensure that historically valuable documents would be stored in the proper manner." The clerk designed a Document Request Form, a Records File Storage Form, and a File Removal Form to provide control of records being borrowed.

The archivist's final report summarized the project and organized the informal discussions into storage recommendations specific to Union, stating problems and offering solutions including short-term and inexpensive options. The clerk was encouraged to think of additional options for her specific needs. The topic of preservation was ever present along with the records management component.

On March 3, 1993, the annual city clerk's conference was held in Columbia, Missouri, featuring the Local Records director, the Local Records conservator, the Franklin County recorder, the city clerk of Union, and myself as archivist for the Union project. The idea of sharing the experience to encourage other local clerks to take advantage of the service has worked well. In the same way that the Union project began as a result of seeing a presentation, telephone calls followed this presentation as municipal clerks initiated more preservation projects.

The Union clerk declares that a seemingly impossible task was made possible through the assistance provided by the staff of the Local Records Program. Certainly, the preservation knowledge of the clerk has been increased to a great extent, and the Union records have a much better chance of surviving for their required use.

Preservation in a "Historical" Setting

Annita Andrick, Erie County Historical Society, Erie, Pennsylvania

The Erie County Historical Society was founded in 1903 and has been collecting local history materials since that time. As a library and archives in a county historical society setting, we have a special commitment to the protection and care of the materials in our custody. We share this preservation ethic on a daily basis by one-on-one contact with patrons who use materials in the reading room of the History Center. We also educate organization representatives when the opportunity presents itself through the Collection Care Center program, which expedites access to preservation materials at cost by organizations and individuals in the community.

BACKGROUND

The Library and Archives of the Erie County Historical Society is a local history research collection utilized by many different types of researchers with varying levels of experience in using materials with special needs. Schoolchildren, adults eager to find family history, and college students working on research papers usually are not acquainted with the special challenges of making local history materials available yet secure for future generations. Much of the collection, housed in over 8,800 square feet of space at the History Center, is a mixture of old, delicate, sometimes unique, one-of-a-kind resources. Materials include out-of-print genealogies and Erie imprints, fragile glassplate negatives, ambrotypes, albumen prints, paintings, architectural plans, business records, city directories with delicate spines, vertical files of clippings, and manuscripts dating from the late 1700s through the recent past. There are special considerations for these local history materials, because of their location in a local history repository, that others in similar situations may find useful.

METHODOLOGY

The Erie History Center, which opened in July 1992, was designed and constructed with long-term care of materials in mind. Special shields for fluorescent lighting protect materials used in the reading room and stacks. The entire building is humidity and temperature controlled to extend the life of the documents in its care. A Collection Care Center is set up with simple tools and materials to provide long-term care for the collections. The arrangement of office space is designed with a small staff in mind. The staff consists of two permanent staff members—a librarian and archivist and a library assistant—and a changing cast of work-study students, loyal volunteers, and an occasional intern. The staff is the first line of protection for these special materials. A register is kept for statistical and security reasons. Each patron is shown a list of regulations to be followed. For example, no food and drink are allowed. No direct tracing of drawings or maps is allowed. Limited copying of materials is permitted on a case-by-case basis. The staff performs copying duties for the patrons. A reference interview is conducted at the point of service contact. As a special subject research library, we house a majority of our published books in the reading room for direct patron access. The dictionary card catalog provides intellectual access to the collections. A reference collection of finding aids, atlases, county histories, as well as standard genealogy research tools are easily available to patrons. The microfilm collection is accessible directly by patrons under the watchful eyes of the staff. Vertical files of research materials on local topics, maps, architectural drawings, business records, manuscripts, serials, oversize books and special collections of books, Works Progress Administration (WPA) transcripts, photographs, postcards, stereoviews, and slides are kept in archival storage where there is controlled access by staff only.

Intellectual access to photographs is provided by a subject heading list, special finding aids, and a collection's list. When materials are retrieved, special instructions accompany materials. For example, when patrons look at photographs from the collections, they are allowed two folders at a time for review. This procedure reduces the possibility of accidentally mixing images out of order and provides the opportunity to more closely supervise the patrons' handling of images. Cotton gloves are worn by the patron when viewing negatives. The prints, postcards, and stereoviews are protected from hand oil and dust by placing them in polypropylene sleeves. Materials are also placed in acid-free file folders. Photo albums are housed in acid-free boxes to provide support and to protect them from light and from other negative environmental dangers. Careful, attentive supervision is provided by the staff, as patrons are assisted in finding the image or images they want.

Glassplate negatives (GPNs) have their own preservation challenges. Educating the patron to the delicacy of handling glass can be critical to the survival of the artifact. The Historical Society's collections are now housed in the glassplate negative storage room, located adjacent to the darkroom in the basement of the History Center. Over 13,000 GPNs are stored in acid-free paper sleeves, and specially designed acid-free boxes, on metal shelving designed for very heavy load capacity. When a patron selects an image for viewing, the staff retrieves the GPN and carefully supervises viewing by the patron.

To speed retrieval and to increase selectivity in what is needed by patrons, finding aids are developed for archival and manuscript material. In addition to being standard archival practice for description of holdings, this is an effective preservation technique because having a finding aid in place reduces wear and tear on collections, as well as saving the staff. Collections are less vulnerable to accidental damage if smaller amounts are retrieved and used by patrons on a selective basis. This technique becomes harder to achieve as use statistics rise and time for processing diminishes.

Although our rare books are relatively few in number, they can provide some preservation hurdles. The problem of weak bindings and separating hinges coupled with eager patrons can cause unintentional damage. Whenever time will allow, phase boxes and other enclosures are constructed for these special materials. In addition to providing physical support for the artifact, it sends a clear message to the patron that special handling is needed.

Educating the research public on the need for preservation of history materials and the mandate of keeping history materials forever, or as close to forever as we can achieve, is a constant challenge for the staff. Aggressive educational programming with high schools has led to special opportunities for the staff to introduce students to primary documents and their care and handling. It is a preservation education opportunity to explain what a primary document is, why it is important, and why gentle, attentive handling is imperative for it to survive for others to appreciate and use. Erie's bicentennial celebration last year provided many opportunities to educate the public on the types of information that were important to save for the future. It was also an opportunity to give straightforward information about preservation.

Such questions as "Do I keep my mother's love letters in the tin box in the attic?" "Where can I get the family Bible rebound?" "Should I throw away all those unidentified photographs?" and "How can I mark those newer photos with the plastic paper that's hard to write on?" were typical questions with direct answers. In addition to on-site individual and class instruction, off-site opportunities are maximized. We have developed two slide shows with a library archives slant. *Fish, Floods, and Fantastic Buildings* is a slide show developed with heavy use of primary documents, including account books, atlases, photographs, postcards, personal letters, city directories, maps, and efficiency time reports. Content includes information on a fish company, the Erie Millcreek flood of August 3, 1915, and local buildings. It is used as an educational tool to explain what a primary document is and what local history content is all about. One section of the presentation deals with the History Center's Collection Care Center. In addition to sharing information on how the staff of the History Center treats its materials, information is provided on how the audience can care for materials in its custody. To reduce barriers to personal care, and in some instances, institutional care of materials, the Library and Archives has purchased preservation materials in bulk. These materials may be purchased by the public, in small quantities, at cost. The Collection Care Center is promoted as the last sequence in the slide show.

The second show's topic is women's diaries, *The Battles and Grubb Women: Local Diaries*. Numerous examples are presented that reveal characters as presented by these primary documents. The conclusion of the program discusses care of the materials at the History Center and also emphasizes how audience members can care for their primary documents. These two slide shows have been shown to a wide variety of groups including the Sertoma Club, American Association of University Women, PTA groups, senior citizens' groups, and the Historical Society's membership.

Both shows were produced in-house as part of the Library and Archives program. These shows have been designed with content specific to the geographic area. When the Erie History Center opened in 1992, a conscious effort was made by staff to attend the showing of programs in the community. Members of the audience thus had the opportunity to ask questions about their own materials, personalizing the experience. *Fish, Floods, and Fantastic Buildings* has been shown widely. The slide show on women's diaries is used frequently during Women's History Month. In addition to introducing the Erie History Center and the Library & Archives program, these slide shows have led to donations of books, business records, and photographs. More people have taken advantage of the Collection Care Center's preservation materials and preservation advice as a result.

CONCLUSION

The Erie County Historical Society has recently adopted a major broad-based preservation initiative to discover, collect, and preserve collections "at risk" in the community over the next five-year period. Acquisition of a very large Great Lakes Maritime Collection including 10,000 photos, 6,000 negatives, 40 charts, 300 books, and other materials has increased organizational awareness of what may be lost in the community every day. We have begun to approach people in the community to increase their awareness of materials that may have historical value but may also be lost for future researchers without intervention and action by the History Center. Our department will continue to play an activist role in educating the general public and others who work with these materials every day on the importance of their preservation and the techniques to save these materials for the future.

Appendixes

Appendix 1

Effective Graphics for Displays and Handouts

Brenda Clark and Jeanne M. Drewes, Michigan State University, East Lansing, Michigan

"Kids, don't try this at home," carped motorcycle daredevil Evel Knievel. "I am a professional."

Library staff might feel a sense of trying to catapult over several buses when confronted with the complicated problem of conveying a message via a display or printed matter. While some libraries may have a graphic designer on staff or may use a professional agency, most of us have to come up with a less costly solution to get our message across. There really are only two ways to get it done: find someone else to design your message, or do it yourself. When possible the best course is to go with a pro. But, how do you follow along in the process of creating the design? Or, if a limited budget means working the project entirely in-house, how do you create the best possible visual effect without professional help?

The answer to both questions lies in understanding the principles of good design. It's not a short cut to developing the intuition and skills that designers acquire over the years, but it can provide a map that will help you work your way through the puzzle. This appendix features ideas about accessing professional designers even with a minimal budget, designing publications and displays in-house, and understanding basic design steps.

The steps for design follow the same steps one takes to prepare a published article: gather information, organize it, present it in a way that appeals to your audience, and do this within the required time allowance. For a design project an additional issue is cost. These components are part of the process whether or not you design with the help of a professional.

ACCESSING DESIGNERS EVEN WITH A LOW BUDGET

Organizations operating on a shoestring budget still have avenues for coming up with professional or near-professional quality work. Community college, college or university graphic design programs, publications offices, and freelancers frequently offer less-expensive resources for creating a design piece. Larger design studios are frequently willing to donate talent and resources to nonprofit groups.

Keep in mind that instructors are often looking for real-life design problems to challenge their students. Contact art, communications, or advertising departments at colleges and universities to get in touch with their student design programs and ask to speak to the appropriate professor. The professor should be available to consult with the client (that's your role) and supervise the project through to completion. An educational institution might also be willing to provide the name of an independent student design club or the names of students or alumni interested in donating time in exchange for experience and a completed piece to show for their efforts. If you envision a string of projects over a few months, consider taking on a design student intern. The intern benefits from the experience; the library gets an in-house ''pro'' working under the tutelage of a seasoned mentor.

Regardless of whether you intend to work with a class or intern, it is best to initiate contact with the school before a new semester begins. This allows the project to be incorporated into a syllabus or an internship schedule. You will have to cover the costs of materials for a project, but consider, too, a donation of some sort to the student or the program in return for a job well done.

College or university publication offices offer convenience and reliability, usually at an economical rate. They will usually supply you with an editor and a designer. These offices also tend to be very busy and will not drop everything to work on a new project. Nevertheless, there's an advantage to working with an office where client and designer are familiar with each others' needs and routines. That could be a plus compared to working with a new set of students each semester.

Another option is to work with a freelancer or a commercial design studio. These resources can be found in the Yellow Pages or by a referral from a satisfied client. A fee will be required for the work, unless services are donated. But, not only do you get the experience and professionalism (remember, the reputation of the designer or studio is on the line), you can also rush a job, although there may be extra charges.

DESIGNING PUBLICATIONS AND DISPLAYS IN-HOUSE

As a librarian or library staff person appointed to produce a publication or create an in-house display, you are your own critic, information-gather, and organizer. You may not be a professional designer, but there are concepts you can apply to help you produce a good vehicle for your message. The purpose of design is to communicate a message. To communicate cost-effectively with wit, economy, and elegance is good design.

The key to delivering your message is to relate it to something already in the viewer's knowledge base. This gives the short-term memory a chance to relate an image to something in long-term memory. Otherwise, the image held by the short-term memory fades and is replaced by the next image the eye sees.[1] Associative images are often used to grab the attention of a spectator and begin the process of forming mental connections or bonds between sensations, ideas, or memories. Emotional responses are another useful tool for creating those bonds. These are frequently used elements to catch the attention of the reader/viewer long enough to hold their attention.

Once the reader/viewer is attracted enough to look, there has to be more to hold their attention. The first layer of information must convey an easily grasped message. This is done by expressing a broad concept, often a visual one. The second tier of information is usually text. For example, a library display might be composed of a larger-than-life book. The attention-getting first layer is the unusual scale of the piece. The second layer of information might be the text explaining the point of the piece, or it might be a slightly more complex set of graphic images. If the latter, then a third tier of information could be the text.

The graphics must allow the viewer to quickly grasp the general concept and focus on areas of interest. Whatever the second layer of information is, it usually demands more participation. The idea is to interest the viewer first with a visual presentation, and then draw the viewer into the more-detailed data.

A page full of text is a page full of gray. And it's rarely interesting enough to get a viewer's attention. Something in the heading or the layout should provoke a response by being aesthetically alluring and well-positioned to attract interest. Otherwise, it might not stop the viewer long enough to be read.

BASIC DESIGN STEPS

No matter how a piece is designed, whether by a professional designer or through in-house efforts, there are some basic planning questions to answer before beginning a design project. The following checklist is drawn from Mark Beach's list in *Getting It Printed*.[2]

- *What is your purpose?* Do you want to entertain, inform, teach? Knowing what you want to convey to your reader/viewer and thinking about the best way to convey that is absolutely necessary to begin your design project. The first step in resolving a problem of design is defining the problem. Whatever you want to convey in terms of a message needs to address the problem. Is it informational? Are you hoping to change a behavior? Is the goal to attract people to a lecture? A workshop? Or is it to provide a self-teaching method to reduce the instruction load?

As the person sending the message, you must be able to clearly communicate the message to the designer or to your audience. A strong solution to the problem of communication develops out of clear understanding and defining the message, based on the desired outcome. If the message is not clearly defined, the recipient of the message can wind up confused or unaware of the message. Posters, exhibits, and handouts should be limited to what most patrons can absorb in a brief encounter. The message should be intentional and clear, with a strong idea that is memorable. The idea should come first, then the design.

- *Who is your audience?* How you convey your message is based on who your audience is. If your audience is on average over 55, then perhaps font size is an issue. If your audience is made up of children, then graphics become more important. It's likely that your audience has a very different perspective which should be taken into account. Once you've defined the message, knowing your audience helps you to clearly define the solution. For example, for the typical college student the message "Preserve the Human Record" probably does not translate to protect books in rainy weather. For a patron to know the correct behavior they have to be told in exact terms.

  The word "preservation" is often associated with saving animals or the environment, not necessarily books. Some library users may relate it to preserves or jelly (See Figure 6.2). The designer can use these ambiguous turns of phrase to produce a playfully creative solution. But a quick and clear translation of the message needs to follow or the intended message will be lost.

- *What text and graphics will your piece contain?* After answering the first two questions about message and audience it will be easier to decide on the balance between text and graphics. Remember, the more text you use the longer it takes to read, so if you are designing a sign or a display case in a heavy-traffic area, the less text the better. Large amounts of text should be grouped with white space to break the text. Using a large font will encourage reading.[3]

- How will your design look? Again, the answers to the first two questions will influence the look you want to convey. If you are working on a group of images then you want a theme to travel through all the pieces. If your design is to attract the attention of college students, then you want a look that will appeal to that audience. Using student workers for ideas and testing your concepts on them is a good idea before you proceed too far into a design project. Ask a sample of your targeted audience for reactions to a concept or elicit ideas from them to begin development of a piece.

- *How will readers use your printed product?* Is your piece something you want people to take with them, such as a bookmark? How long do you want it to last? Choice of paper is an important issue for longevity. If you want your patron to keep your information for future reference, then consider the size as well. What would easily fit on a bulletin board? Would a book bag with a drawstring be more likely to be used again than a bag with a handle?

- *How will your piece reach your audience?* Are you making your handout available as part of a group of other materials? If so, what will make your handout stand out and catch the eye? Are you including your information in a packet for freshmen? What will make the student read your sheet instead of tossing it? If you are giving away plastic bags for rainy days, consider a display that can be put up at appropriate times. Perhaps you want to offer a variety of bookmarks at the checkout desk so that your patron can choose their favorite design.

• *When do you need the job delivered?* Whether you are doing the job in-house or farming it out, you need to establish a deadline to get the work done in a timely fashion. Allow an appropriate amount of time to accomplish the project and include time for revisions.

• *How many pieces do you need?* Especially if you are having the printing done outside of the library, this is important to determine. There is often a cost break for larger numbers, but the cost break will not be a savings if the pieces sit so long on the shelf that they start to look old before they are distributed. This is particularly true if you use low-cost colored paper that will fade over time.

• *What quality do you need?* Using a printer instead of production in-house with a copy machine opens a variety of options, including color. If photos are necessary to convey your message, be sure that your final product will produce well. Getting a sample before the printing begins will assure that you have the quality you intended to have.

• *How much can you spend?* Even in-house there are costs associated with any design project. Using the right weight paper for posters makes a big difference in the final look. If you are spending time and effort in design, then your final product should be worth that effort. Find out what your options are before you begin. Most paper supply companies have free sample books so that you can see the range of available materials before you start your project.

A big budget is not necessary to be creative, although it has an impact on the quality of the materials used in the project. Not knowing or not paying attention to the budget can hinder creative solutions. One needs to know the parameters of the project, whatever the size. For in-house designs the costs are usually for paper: look at paper size, paper weight, toner application. For example, toner can smear on some types of paper.

Development of an Idea

The first step in developing an idea is researching the problem and stating your desired end result. Once you know what you're trying to accomplish, start jotting down ideas and sketching them out. These roughs can be useful when you are consulting with others on your project. These preliminary ideas may be very different than what you end up with, but they can start the discussion. No matter what, a visual idea should at some point be explored through drawing on paper or computer. These steps allow for quick analysis to decide if an idea conveys the message. If it doesn't fit, don't force it.

An ideal way to determine the appropriateness of your idea is to seek feedback from your selected focus group. For college appeal you can use student workers in the library; for a Friends group ask for comments from the Board; use a story time to test a children's campaign idea.

Later, any idea under serious consideration should be examined at the actual size at which it will be used. Remember, even if you're the only one who has to approve a concept, a review is still useful. What appeals to you may not be reaching your audience. Testing before production can save costly mistakes.

Design Elements to Consider

Think in terms of space, placement, texture, contrast, color, and shape. Most graphic design exists on a flat surface, but there is a lot you can do on that surface.

- *Space* can be the size of a stamp or the size of a billboard. Surfaces can make up a brochure or a display unit that can be broken by folds to define space. The surface space is generally the first production consideration because text and color rely on it. Creating the illusion of three-dimensional space on a flat surface is an interest element. Another illusion is to have an image go off the side of the surface. The human eye will fill in what is missing based on what it sees or look for more on the other side.
- *Placement* of type and graphics can be used to create patterns in your space, whether that space is a sheet of paper or a display case. Pattern leads the eye from one part of text to another or from one image to another. Don't clutter the space with too much or there won't be a place to rest. Remember that a single strong impression is more likely to remain in the brain long enough to form an association. Less is more, especially if the reader/viewer is in motion. Short messages are most likely to be retained.
- *Texture* can be used in displays but also in the choice of paper for a handout. The second sense utilized by a viewer is usually touch. Papers look and feel different. Be sensitive to the aesthetics of paper to heighten the message. Paper texture that is pleasing or interesting to the touch can hold interest long enough to hook the reader into reading more. Texture can also be visually interesting, especially for a larger piece such as a poster. Think of using textured paper both for bookmarks and for posters.
- *Contrast* is used to draw attention, intensify meaning, and simplify organization. Contrast is fun. It creates opposing forces in a piece: dark against light or one against many. Text can be broken into light and dark areas, using bullets to signify separate points.
- *Color* can work with contrast. Starting with the three primary colors, combinations can highlight information and create different emotional responses. Red is the most tumultuous, emotional, and active. Blue is passive and soft. Yellow represents light and warmth. Red becomes subdued by mixing it with blue. It becomes more active by combining it with yellow. If you have a small budget, don't expect to produce a full-color printed piece. But background color can be used effectively. The color of paper can enhance the importance of a message through contrast.
- *Shape* gives definition to design. It can be sharp and clean, or rough and diffused. Colors can define the shape or shape can be created by arrangement of text or object groupings. The three basic shapes are the square, the circle, and the equilateral triangle. The square is dull, but honest, straightforward, and workmanlike. The triangle evokes action, or conflict and tension. The circle is endless and protected.

These essential elements should be used with a specific intention in mind. That means, ''I thought it looked good,'' is not good enough when it comes to choosing design solutions. Using specific elements for specific reasons allows the message of your piece to remain clear and clean. It ensures that the elements of your piece or your campaign will work together to deliver a clear thought to your audience. The unity of your message can be enhanced using rhythm, repetition, and the design elements we've already covered. Emphasis, or a focal point, can be created through contrast, isolation, or placement. A focal point gives the viewer a place to start and should be disproportionate to catch the viewer's attention before the other elements. When reading a page from a book, we know to start at the upper left–hand corner. Focal point for a display should be obvious to start reader/viewers in the right direction.

At the same time that we are challenging the viewer, to draw his or her attention, we also want to make sure they stay with us. This is accomplished with balance. Balance can be formal or informal, symmetrical or asymmetrical. A design which can be folded down the middle—an image split exactly in half—is formal or symmetrical balance. A design composition which optically feels balanced, but has different proportions of weight on each side, is asymmetrical or informal balance. Balance does not mean boring. Be careful not to create "tombstone designs," where everything stacks down the middle of the surface. This is mundane and an instant signal of an amateur design job. Using asymmetrical balance is more interesting and can lead the reader/viewer from point to point.

TIPS WHEN WORKING WITH TEXT

Make sure the different typefaces you will use are discernible from each other. For example, if you use two fonts that are very similar but not exactly the same, your choice might wind up looking like a typesetting mistake.

Choose typefaces like you would choose the elements of a salad. Be bold—pull wildly different things from your garden to create something crunchy, tangy and filling.

Remember legibility. The smaller your typeface, the more white space is needed between lines. If you are using a lot of body copy, create breaks for the reader with white space and graphics.

Use as few words as possible, especially in headlines and subheads. And remember graphics. Everyone processes information in a different fashion. Some people work better with words, some with pictures and some with mathematical equations.

There are four design principles that will help make a text message more likely to be read and understood in a brief period of time: proximity, alignment, repetition, and contrast.[4]

- *Proximity* is putting similar ideas close together. Remember how memory works? Teachers know that linking new information to what people already know—even if the knowledge was acquired recently—helps students remember. Proximity also helps convey the message. Grouping allows the mind to see more readily the relationship between material.

- *Alignment* is placing text and information in such a way that it's easy to follow and process. Usually, a designer creates an imaginary line for the eye to follow, but there's nothing to stop you from drawing a real line to carry the viewer from start to finish.

• *Repetition* is deciding what you want people to remember and then repeating it in different ways. The idea, remember, is not to bore people by repeating the same message; it is to reinforce the central theme. Reinforce the visual with the verbal, perhaps with a sign. For example you might use a formula: "If [graphic of thunderclouds and rain], then [umbrella and bag] = protection for you and your books." A graphic design and text to reinforce the idea is repetition with variety.

• *Contrast* can also be used to help memory create links for the brain. Visual interest using contrasting images can be the hook that brings the reader/viewer in long enough to convey the information. Size, color, and spacing can all use contrast to good effect.

And there's one more thing. Don't overburden people with data. Give them enough to ponder and process and then move on.

In other words, *know when to quit.*

EXAMPLES

Figures A1.1 through A1.4 demonstrate some of the principles discussed in this appendix. Figure A1.1, bookmark from Pennsylvania State University, beautifully catches the attention of the patron because of its unusual imagery and creatively written text. The insects are the dominant element, so the pictorial element dominates in this case. The back panel reinforces the message on the front. The strong diagonal emphasis on the front panel tempts the viewer to turn the bookmark over to then be drawn to the contrasting geometric box of text. The flickering tiny graphic borders on the top and bottom reinforce the connection of the front and back. Unity is achieved.

Figure A1.2, from Columbia University Libraries, Preservation Division, has conveyed a very simple message almost purely with the use of type as the image. The message to inform patrons not to eat or drink is conveyed without the use of a negative word. Instead, the undesirable behavior is casually conveyed through the use of a recognizable graphic symbol often used on signage. The symbol of the "x" represents "do not" in a less preachy manner. The text is mainly composed of a sans serif typeface (font) however, it is complimented by a heavy thick/thin font which creates emphasis in the overall layout. The arrangement of the text is placed slightly to the left with text aligned flush left for a more interesting composition.

In Figure A1.3, created by Neil Bryson, the cheerful illustration is placed at a diagonal and is lighter than the background which brings the viewer into the bookmark. This is an example of contrast. The diagonal directs the viewer to the "Clean Paws" text. Notice how the cheerful looking typeface works well with the illustration. A bold geometrical typeface probably would have appeared

Figure A1.1
Bookmark with Diagonal Interest

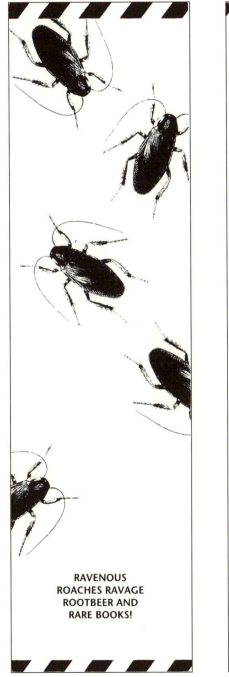

RAVENOUS
ROACHES RAVAGE
ROOTBEER AND
RARE BOOKS!

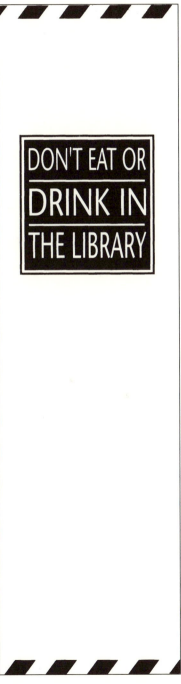

DON'T EAT OR
DRINK IN
THE LIBRARY

Figure A1.2
Information through Simple Text

In the library

PLEASE

READ

BROWSE

STROLL

~~EAT~~

THINK

STUDY

~~DRINK~~

SIT

LOOK

PONDER

MEDITATE

ENJOY

COLUMBIA UNIVERSITY LIBRARIES

Figure A1.3
Instructional Bookmark

Figure A1.4
Guidelines for Photocopying Special Collections Materials

Guidelines for Photocopying Special Collections Materials

Materials in the Special Collections Division may be photocopied when the condition of the material and copyright restrictions permit. Please present your requests for photocopies to a staff member. The Special Collections Staff has been trained in safe handling techniques for photocopying materials. Any photocopy request for an item which the staff judges to be vulnerable to damage if photocopied will not be honored.

The Special Colections Staff uses the following criteria when deciding what items may be safely photocopied:

1. **SIZE:** No bound book larger than 14 in. tall x 10 in. wide or 1 in. thick (35 cm. x 25 cm., or 3 cm. thick) may be copied. Large materials cannot be adequately supported while being maneuvered on the photocopy machine.

2. **BRITTLE PAPER:** Brittle books and periodicals may not be photocopied. Opening books flat for photo-duplication puts undue pressure on the spine, this will cause the paper to break at stress points and crumble. Brittle newspapers cannot withstand the extra handling required for photocopying.

3. **BINDING TYPE AND CONDITION:** A book which must be forced open to lay flat may not be copied. Age is not always s a determining factor in deciding which books may be safely copied. Books published within the last 20 years with adhesive bindings can crack when opened to 180 degrees for photocopying. Pages of tightly sewn books can tear if forced open.

4. **FOLD OUT MAPS AND PRINTS:** Fold out maps and prints are difficult to photocopy without damaging the materials. In the event that a fold out map cannot be copied, camera stand and lights are available for making photographs or slides.

* * * REQUESTS MADE WITHIN 30 MINUTES BEFORE CLOSING MAY HAVE TO BE FILLED * * *
THE FOLLOWING WORK DAY; LARGE ORDERS MAY TAKE LONGER

\seh\speccopy.pm3

cold in relation to the illustration. The message is completed by contrast of size in the typeface used at the bottom of the bookmark.

In Figure A1.4, the top sample is text-dominant in a bad way. It is too gray in appearance. This mundane-looking handout, which contains important photocopying information can be livened up through simply adding contrast and creating emphasis. The quick sketches illustrate how emphasis could be created by highlighting a word which quickly conveys the topic of information. Other ideas begin to break up the gray text into pockets of non-overwhelming text. Adding small graphics (even if circles or squares) can give the reader a starting point and breathing space. Form could be explored. Maybe the page should not be rectangular. A square handout that has text on two sides might be more unusual and convenient to stick in a datebook or wallet for future use. Or it could function as handout and bookmark.

NOTES

1. Paul Alter and Rita Alter, "Exhibit Evaluation: Taking Account of Human Factors," *Curator* 31, no. 3 (September 1988): 167–177.

2. Mark Beach, *Getting It Printed*, rev. ed. (Cincinnati, Ohio: North Light Books, 1993), p. 3.

3. Patterson Bitgood, "The Effect of Gallery Changes on Visitor Reading and Object Viewing Time," *Environment & Behavior* 25, no. 6 (November 1993): 767–781.

4. Robin Williams, *The Non-designer's Design Book* (Berkeley CA: Peachpit Press, 1994). The four principles for this section are all to be found in the Williams book.

DESIGNING GRAPHICS: AN ANNOTATED BIBLIOGRAPHY

Alt, M. B., and K. M. Shaw. "Characteristics of Ideal Museum Exhibits." *British Journal of Psychology* 75, pt. 2 (1984): 25–36.

Alt and Shaw present a method of classifying displays in terms of the ways in which they are perceived by museum visitors. The authors conclude that exhibitions that impart a clear, short message, displayed in a vivid manner, are most attractive to visitors.

Alter, Paul, and Rita Alter. "Exhibit Evaluation: Taking Account of Human Factors." *Curator* 31, no. 3 (September 1988): 167–177.

The authors analyze exhibit evaluation from the "human factors" perspective and find that exhibits often do not include the main components that have been demonstrated to foster learning and understanding. The authors encourage exhibitors to keep in mind that users do not necessarily come to the institution with the same background, experience, or cognitive skills and emphasize that displays should be designed to appeal to the audience they are attempting to reach.

Beach, Mark. *Getting It Printed*. Rev. ed. Cincinnati, OH: North Light Books, 1993.

This volume is a much-used textbook for beginning graphic design classes and provides a clear, easy-to-understand explanation of the process from design to printed product. It provides terminology and explains the necessary steps needed when working with a design company.

Bitgood, Patterson. "The Effect of Gallery Changes on Visitor Reading and Object Viewing Time." *Environment & Behavior* 25, no. 6 (November 1993): 767–781.

The author shows the effect of larger fonts and spaced text in retaining viewer interest in museum text accompanying displays.

Borun, Minda. "Assessing the Impact." *Museum News* 68, no. 3 (May–June 1989): 36–40.

In this article, Borun proposes that evaluation of how an exhibit has affected users is important for both educational and marketing reasons. Borun advocates using "process" evaluation in which users' needs, opinions, and expectations are measured before the final exhibit is mounted rather than summative evaluation, which surveys users once the exhibit has already been decided upon and mounted. Process evaluation includes pre-testing or front-end audience analysis and requires that institutions ask the following three questions: (1) Who is the audience? (2) What is the desired impact? and (3) How will the impact be measured?

Edsall, Marian S. *Library Promotion Handbook*. Phoenix: Oryx Press, 1980.
Edsall acknowledges that displays in the library are a time-honored and traditional activity but asserts that while there are "some very good reasons" for displays, there are also some bad ones. In the chapter "The Library on Display," pp. 105–114, she urges librarians to weigh the reasons for a display against the estimated expenditure of time and money. Edsall also advocates careful and thorough audience research and planning before mounting a display.

Garvey, Mona. "Display." In *Prepare: The Library Public Relations Recipe Book*, ed. Irene E. Moran. New York: New York Public Library, 1978, pp. 33–35.
In this brief essay, Mona Garvey (a public relations and educational display consultant) defines the library display, discusses the purposes of library displays, and provides guidance on materials and methods for mounting an effective library display.

Garvey, Mona. *Library Displays: Their Purpose, Construction and Use*. New York: H. W. Wilson Company, 1969.
Garvey begins by acknowledging the ambivalent relationship that librarians have with displays but emphasizes that displays can be an effective tool for conveying a message and/or generating interest in library materials. The author covers the display process from conception and planning through mounting the display. *Library Displays* presents the basic design principles of display and provides guidance on methodology.

Garvey, Mona. *Library Public Relations: A Practical Handbook*. New York: H. W. Wilson Company, 1980.
In Chapter 9 "Signs, Posters, and Bulletin Boards," Garvey offers tips for constructing these three forms of library displays. The author emphasizes that the most important thing about signs is what they say and how they say it. Garvey advocates putting displays right out front—in the entryway or even outside, if possible.

Hamilton, Feona. *Infopromotion: Publicity and Marketing Ideas for the Information Profession*. Brookfield, VT: Gower Publishing Company, 1990.
In Chapter 20, "Exhibitions," Hamilton discusses the purpose, methods, and planning process for library exhibits. The author provides guidelines for planning the details of location, content, purpose, tools and materials, costs, assigning responsibility, and publicity for an exhibition.

Hayett, William. *Display and Exhibit Handbook*. New York: Reinhold Publishing Corporation, 1967.
An illustrated guide to the display and exhibit process. Hayett's primer for exhibiting

includes the presentation and analysis of tools and supplies needed for mounting an exhibit and provides a glossary of exhibition terms.

Horton, Steven V., and Thomas C. Lovitt. "Construction and Implementation of Graphic Organizers for Academically Handicapped and Regular Secondary Students." *Academic Therapy* 24, no. 5 (May 1989): 625–639.

Horton and Lovitt present methods for constructing and implementing graphic organizers in an educational setting. These methods include dividing text with white space and images and putting information into an outline form. The authors also confirm past evidence that displaying information graphically facilitates comprehension.

Jacobs, Rita D. "Signage With Sense, Not Signature." *Graphis* 47, no. 274 (July–August 1991): 29–37.

This profile of the two graphic designers who designed the signage in the Louvre emphasizes that signage must conceptualize the idea behind the design and ensure that any messages conveyed are intentional and clear.

Klein, Larry. *Exhibits: Planning and Design*. New York: Madison Square Press, 1986.

Although aimed at large-scale exhibitors, Klein's *Exhibits* offers a detailed "how-to" and "why" of every aspect of mounting an exhibit. The author discusses the principles behind exhibiting and itemizes the proper equipment for every exhibition environment. Included are extensive color photographs of commercial and museum displays.

Rice, Danielle. "Examining Exhibits." *Museum News* 68, no. 6 (November–December 1989): 47–50.

"Examining Exhibits" exhorts exhibitors to take visitors' preferences and needs into account when designing exhibits. In order to expand the visitor base, Rice advocates that exhibitors provide materials that allow users to actively participate in the exhibit and foster learning.

Roth, Laszlo. *Display Design: An Introduction to Window Display, Point-of-Purchase, Posters, Signs and Signage, Sales Environments, and Exhibit Displays*. Englewood Cliffs: Prentice-Hall, 1983.

Roth's introduction to the concepts and methods of designing displays includes chapters on signs and signage and exhibit design. Roth emphasizes that displays are meant to draw the attention and provides extensive black and white photographs that illustrate this principle.

Schotz, Wolfgang, and Raymond W. Kulhavy, eds. *Comprehension of Graphics*. Advances in Psychology 108. Amsterdam: Elsevier Science, 1994.

Comprehension of Graphics is a compilation of 18 articles, divided into four parts, of which parts two and four are especially relevant for exhibitors. The articles in part two examine the importance of aspects such as layout and size in determining the effectiveness of graphics; the articles in part four examine the effectiveness of graphics as instructional aids.

Screven, Chandler G. "Learning and Exhibits: Instructional Design." *Museum News* 52, no. 5 (January–February 1974): 67–75.

In "Learning and Exhibits," Screven examines some ways in which the principles of learning and instructional communication might be applied to exhibits. Screven emphasizes that a successful exhibit changes the viewer in some way: The viewer *behaves* differently after seeing the exhibit. Screven advocates using postexhibit evaluation tools to measure the degree of change experienced by viewers.

Sheppard, D. "Methods for Assessing the Value of Exhibitions." *British Journal of Educational Psychology* 30, no. 3 (November 1960): 259–265.
An early examination of the problems related to evaluating the effectiveness of exhibits, Sheppard presents and critiques several methods of evaluation.

Sign Design: Contemporary Graphic Identity. New York: PBC International, 1986.
Sign Design examines the area of environmental graphic design through extensive color photography documenting effective signage in public settings, including retail, restaurants, hotels, corporations, and public works. The emphasis here is that signs not only should convey a message but also should present an image.

"Signage: Special Report." *Design* (January 1993): 35–41.
This article profiles new trends and concepts in signage and provides a visual overview through color photography of how effective signage incorporates good, uncluttered design with a clear message.

Visual Merchandising and Display: Designing for Retail Seasonal Campaigns. Tokyo: Meisei Publications, 1993.
Although this book is targeted toward retail display, it presents ideas for eye-catching and effective visual displays using both black and white and color photography. The selected displays were chosen for their ability to "sell" based on one of three criteria: (1) visual appeal of company principles, (2) visual entertainment of "customers," and (3) visual appeal of products. Each display chosen effectively demonstrates the goal of establishing corporate identity and customer loyalty.

Williams, Robin. *The Non-designer's Design Book.* Berkeley, CA: Peachpit Press, 1994.
Basic design principles for displaying text are explained, with many examples of each principle provided.

Willows, Dale M., and Harvey A. Houghton, eds. *The Psychology of Illustration.* Vol. 1, *Basic Research.* New York: Springer-Verlag, 1987.
The articles in *The Psychology of Illustration* discuss the use of images in instruction and evaluate the effectiveness of this practice. The authors provide in-depth information ranging from background explanations of how people learn to a review of the literature and report the results of research in this area. According to the editors, the book is meant to be an "omnibus reference."

Appendix 2

Books for Children, Teachers, and Parents: An Annotated Bibliography

Teaching proper care and handling of books at an early age is an important concept. Creating a sense of ownership with art projects where children make their own books can increase the careful handling of all books. Citations include children's literature, bookmaking guides, and information directed to parents. All can be used to increase awareness in children of the value of books and the importance of appropriate care and handling of library materials.

Teachers, librarians, and media specialists will find that there are ways to use the books included here across grade levels—particularly kindergarten to sixth grade. Picture books for primary children often hold detailed information that can be incorporated into curriculum planning displays and projects for children in upper elementary grades. "How-to" books geared toward upper elementary students and the middle years can often be adapted for younger children by simplifying processes. For these reasons, grade levels are not specified.

Aliki. *How a Book Is Made*. New York: Thomas Y. Crowell, 1986. 32 pp.

In Aliki's distinctive style, the story is told of how a book evolves from the germ of an idea to a bound product. Rich with illustrative detail, the message is clear that it takes more than author and artist to create a published volume. "Who made this book? We all did!''—author, illustrator, editor, publisher, designer, printer, production director,

Initial compilation was done with the assistance of Sandra Kortesoja, Renee McKinney, and Kathy Steiner, students in the "Preservation of Information Resources" class taught by Elizabeth Yakel at the University of Michigan School of Information during the 1995 summer session.

among others. Language experience is equally rich. The text is replete with commercial book production terms tied to the drawings: *contract, manuscript, dummy, typeface, galleys, color separations*, and more.

Bartlett, Susan. *Books: A Book to Begin On*. New York: Holt, Rinehart and Winston, 1968. 41 pp.
A classic and thoughtfully told story of the history of books and printing illustrated by Ellen Raskin. *Books: A Book to Begin On* starts with storytelling and ends with acknowledgment of Randolph Caldecott and John Newbery, annually recognized when the Caldecott and Newbery Medals are awarded for children's literature. In between, it describes how stories survived on clay tablets, papyrus, and parchment and in manuscripts, illuminations, and block books. This book captures the significance of the evolution of the book over centuries—quietly and eloquently.

Brookfield, Karen. *Book*. New York: Knopf, 1993. 64 pp.
The history and evolution of the written word is beautifully portrayed through the combination of photographs and text in *Book*. Photographs of historically significant artifacts show how the alphabet grew out of drawing and how papermaking and bookbinding developed over the centuries. Photographic examples of rare medieval Psalters, manuscript books, early children's books, books from Asia and Islam, as well as images of early mechanical processes tell the story of the book in a visually rich way.

Chapman, Gillian, and Pam Robson. *Making Books: A Step-by-Step Guide to Your Own Publishing*. Brookfield, CT: Millbrook Press, 1991. 32 pp.
Making Books describes a number of approaches to use with children in bookmaking, from easy-to-make booklets to more complex tactile books, scrolls, pop-ups, and sewn and bound books. The illustrative examples, while not the work of children, are plentiful and colorful. They show numerous ways original writings and original artworks can be combined to create keepsake products.

Cleary, Beverly. *Beezus and Ramona*. New York: William Morrow, 1955. 159 pp.
In the first chapter of this book, nine-year-old Beatrice (Beezus) takes her four-year-old sister on her first visit to the public library. When it is time to return the book, she is horrified to discover that Ramona has practiced writing alphabet letters with crayon on every page. This is a classic read-aloud story, long enjoyed by children, that will spark lively discussion on caring for library materials at home.

Cytron, Barry D. *Fire! The Library Is Burning*. Minneapolis, MN: Lerner Publications, 1988. 56 pp.
This is the story of a devastating fire in 1966 at the Jewish Theological Seminary's 250,000-volume library in New York City and the neighborhood that banded together to rescue as many of the remaining books as possible. Young children will identify with the kindergartners who held a bake sale to raise money for the library during the restoration process and older children with the volunteers who helped with the tedious and tiring work of moving and drying out precious volumes.

DiMaggio, Tanya. *Multi-Media Bibliography of Book and Paper Arts for Kids*. January 1996. Web site at http://fiat.gslis.utexas.edu:80/~tdimag/biblio.html.

Web site containing an annotated bibliography of books and media useful for teaching grades kindergarten through nine, with grades designated for each entry. May not be regularly updated but was current at this printing.

Gaylord, Susan Kapuscinski. *Multicultural Books to Make and Share*. New York: Scholastic Books, 1994.

Based on both contemporary and historical sources, Gaylord's manual includes 16 bookmaking projects from Africa, the Americas, Asia, and Europe. Presented from the simplest to the more difficult, each is a study of the book as an expression of culture and the exploration of creative possibilities in book form. Guidelines are presented for advance planning, and suggested related readings are included. All of the projects have been tested in classrooms, and each includes photographs of handmade books created by students.

Gibbons, Gail. *Paper, Paper Everywhere*. San Diego, CA: Harcourt Brace Jovanovich, 1983.

A picture book that simultaneously depicts the manufacturing process of paper while exploring its various uses, *Paper, Paper Everywhere* is the sort of book that will be read over and over again. Simple and clear illustrations accompany equally simple and clear text describing the papermaking process in a way that even the youngest child can understand. The book has an interesting interactive component—"paper puzzlers" are sprinkled throughout the pages, inviting children to find items made of paper in the drawings.

Greene, Carol. *How a Book Is Made*. Chicago, IL: Children's Press, 1988. 48 pp. with exhibits.

This excellent and informative 10-piece kit explains the commercial bookmaking process. The book depicts, in readable text and illustrative photos, the stages that a book goes through from author's idea to the finished book. The total kit includes samples from the book itself showing the steps involved in its manufacture. It contains 10 exhibits of edited manuscript pages, galley proofs, dummy pages from layout, blueprint pages, page layout for printers, poster showing color separation process, printed cover glued to boards and ready for binding, a press sheet, finished book ready to be cased in, and a complete bound copy of the book. The book and hands-on exhibit material in the kit are highly recommended as a source for teaching how a book is made. Glossary of terms. Index.

Grummer, Arnold E. *Paper by Kids*. Minneapolis, MN: Dillon Press, 1980. 109 pp.

Grummer, former curator of the Dard Hunter Paper Museum, dedicated this book to the "thousands of kids whose eyes grew wide with wonder as they watched paper being made." Clear and explicit directions are given for making handmade paper, "just for fun" and "like a craftsman." While geared to upper elementary students, all children will find the photographs of magnified papers and fibers fascinating.

Knowlton, Jack. *Books and Libraries*. New York: HarperCollins, 1991. 36 pp.

In attractively illustrated vignettes, this book tells the story of the development of books and libraries from the time of ancient cave paintings to the present. The rise and growth of libraries is told in a simple and readable way, with descriptions of the invention of the Dewey Decimal System, the formation of public libraries by Andrew Carnegie, and the establishment of the Library of Congress. Endpapers graphically illustrate the Dewey Decimal System.

Langley, Andrew. *Paper*. New York: Thomson Learning, 1993. 32 pp.

One of a series that introduces children to important world resources, *Paper* utilizes photographs and clear text to explore contemporary papermaking. Children will be particularly interested in the photographs of machinery used in the process and pages that discuss recycling and reforestation.

Levine, Shar. *The Paper Book and Paper Maker*. New York: Hyperion Books for Children, 1993. 56 pp. Guide to two-piece papermaking kit.

This small handbook is primarily a guide to the use of the Paper Maker Kit, which consists of a plastic mold and detachable deckle. The papermaking procedure is presented in easily followed graphic step-by-step order. Other applications are demonstrated, such as using plants and fabric, creating watermarks, making ink and dyes, binding techniques, and making personalized cards and gifts. The guide is interspersed with presentations of the development of bookmaking and descriptions of commercial papermaking techniques. Glossary of terms and list of environmental organizations are included.

Limousin, Odile. *The Story of Paper*. Ossining, NY: Young Discovery Library, 1988. 36 pp.

What can you do with paper? Did people always have paper? How was paper first made? How is paper made today? This little book makes effective use of a question and answer format to trace the history of paper from ancient times to the present. High-quality and detailed illustrations are rich with information. The last two pages give directions for making papier-mâché.

O'Reilly, Susie. *Papermaking*. New York: Thomson Learning, 1993. 32 pp.

Following a short history of papermaking and the uses of paper, a detailed step-by-step procedure for making handmade paper is given. Each step is clearly and simply described with excellent photographic illustrations of children performing the process. Shown are the making of the mold, the making of pulp from recycled paper, the forming of the paper sheets, and the using of special techniques. Highly recommended as a guide to handmade papermaking. Glossary of terms, selected bibliography, and index.

Perkinson, Kathryn. *Helping Your Child Use the Library*. Washington, DC: U.S. Department of Education, 1992. 26 pp.

One in a series of publications on educational topics tied to National Education Goals, this book focuses on ways the local public library helps parents encourage in their children a love of books and learning. Not ignored is the need to teach children the proper care and handling of library materials—materials that belong to everyone in the community. Parents are encouraged to instill in children of all ages the value of keeping books in good condition for other users to enjoy.

Stock, Carolmarie. *Sassafras Holmes and the Library Mysteries*. Hagerstown, MD: Alleyside Press, 1991. 61 pp.

Through the adventures in the library of young detective Sassafras Holmes and her friend, elementary students may learn about the Dewey Decimal System, the using of reference materials, the importance of reading, and lessons on library management and book care. Told in dramatic story form for eight different mystery cases. Glossary of library terms.

Suhr, Mandy. *Making a Book*. New York: Thomson Learning, 1994. 48 pp.

Presents in step-by-step order the process of making and publishing a handmade book. Text tells how to research, design, write, edit, typeset, prepare pages, and bind the books. The commercial publishing and printing process is described and illustrated. Color photographs largely depict children looking at and working on books, but actual handmade bookmaking processes are not illustrated in detail. Glossary of terms. Short bibliography. Index.

Swain, Gwenyth, with Minnesota Center for Book Arts. *Bookworks: Making Books by Hand*. Minneapolis, MN: Carolrhoda Books, 1995. 64 pp.

Presents a short history of books from ancient clay tablets to modern typeset books. Describes in readable step-by-step order the process of making books by hand: finding the story, planning the book, making handmade paper, binding the book, making fold-up and pop-up books, making the cover, and illustrating the book. Profusely illustrated with photographs of children making books in the Center's workshop and line drawings of the bookmaking process. Glossary of terms. Selective bibliography on bookmaking and resources. Index.

Walsh, Natalie. *Making Books Across the Curriculum: Pop Ups, Flaps, Shapes, Wheels and Many More*. New York: Scholastic Books, 1994. 112 pp.

This book begins with basic bookbinding and then introduces shape-books, minibooks, folding books, and pop-up books. Each project is geared toward a possible curriculum theme and includes a list of related children's books. There are patterns and templates throughout, which many teachers and librarians will choose to ignore. It is, however, a useful planning resource for connecting bookmaking to content areas.

Wilkinson, Jean. *Work with Us in a Printing Company*. Milwaukee, WI: Information Systems & Services, 1981. 47 pp.

One of a series on career awareness, this book utilizes photographs and drawings to help children imagine the world of work—in this case, at a printing company. Children are photographed taking on the role of estimator, production supervisor, typesetter, proofreader, keyline artist, camera operator, scanner operator, color artist, film assembler, folding machine operator, binding machine operator, plant superintendent, and more. The intricacies of book production are presented in ways that will wholly interest most children.

Appendix 3

Videos for General Preservation Education: An Annotated Videography

Julie A. Page, University of California–San Diego, La Jolla, California

More comprehensive listings of audiovisual sources can be found in the following publications:

Palmer, Joseph W. "Audiovisual Programs Related to Preservation: A Mediagraphy." *Collection Building* 13, no. 1 (1993): 7–20.

Swartzburg, Susan G. "Audiovisual Aids on the Preservation and Conservation of Library and Archival Materials." *Conservation Administration News*, no. 49 (April 1992): 8–13.

Books Are Not for Bashing
Providence, RI: Brown University Library Preservation Office, [1990].
1 videocassette (10 min.): sd., col.; ½" VHS
Basic information for academic library users about appropriate handling of library materials. Includes humorous examples that may appeal to a secondary school audience as well.
Availability: Brown University Libraries Preservation Office, Box A, Providence, RI 02914, $40 sale.

Handle with Care
Produced with the assistance of students at New York University's Department of Film and Television.
New York: New York University, [1988].
1 videocassette (4 min.): sd., col.; ½" VHS
A young man demonstrates the wrong ways to treat books as a satiric off-screen

narrator comments on the action. Useful to promote discussion in a class setting, from secondary to college level. The continuous loop can be used in an exhibit or lobby setting.

Availability: New York University Libraries Collection Management Office, 70 Washington Square South, New York, NY 10012, $39 sale (28 min. continuous loop, $45).

Handle with Care: Library Materials
Cleveland: CWRU Educational Media Dept., [1990].
Case Western Reserve University; University Libraries Conservation Dept. A CWRU Libraries Preservation Education Film.
1 videocassette (19 min.): sd., col.; ½" VHS
Explains the proper way to handle and care for various library materials and the function of the Conservation Department. Originally made in slide format.
Availability: Not for sale. Request interlibrary loan from: Case Western Reserve University Library, 11161 East Boulevard, Cleveland, OH 44106.

Handling Books in General Collections: Guidelines for Readers and Library Staff Members
Washington, DC: Library of Congress, National Preservation Program Office, 1984.
Originally produced in a slide-tape version (79 slides) in 1984. Edited video transfer retaining original narration, made by University of California, San Diego, 1994.
1 videocassette (12 min.): sd., col.; ½" VHS
Suggests handling and shelving practices that will prolong the life of books in general collections. Aimed primarily at staff but can be used for student groups and volunteers.
Availability: Slide/tape show: Library of Congress Sales Office 1-202-707-5112, $60 sale; SOLINET Preservation Program, $20 rental. Videotape: Preservation Department, Geisel Library 0175N, University of California–San Diego, 9500 Gilman Drive, La Jolla, CA 92093-0175, $15 sale; no interlibrary loan.

Los Libros: Uso y Cuidado (See *Use and Care of Books*)

Materials at Risk: The Preservation Challenge
Originally produced by the National Archives and Records Administration (NARA) and the Library of Congress National Preservation Program as a slide-tape show. Later produced in video format.
1 videocassette (10 min.): sd., col.; ½" VHS
A quickly moving program good for raising awareness of preservation concerns in libraries and archives. Useful as a general introduction for groups seeking cooperative solutions to preservation problems.
Availability: Contact the Library of Congress Sales Office (1-202-707-5112) or the National Archives and Records Administration Sales Office for availability and pricing.

Murder in the Stacks
Columbia University Libraries Preservation Committee. New York: Center for Biomedical Communications, College of Physicians & Surgeons, Columbia University, [1987].
1 videocassette (15 min.): sd., col.; ½" VHS
A presentation by Sherlock Holmes and Dr. Watson on the shelving and handling of library books. The point is made that books are a shared resource and should be handled carefully in order to prolong their life. One of the most frequently used videos for teaching preventative preservation to both staff and library users.

Availability: Columbia University Libraries Gifts and Exchanges, 104 Butler Library, New York, NY 10027, $35 sale; University Products (1-800-762–1165), $68 sale; SOLINET Preservation Program (1-800-999-8558), $20 rental.

Slow Fires: On the Preservation of the Human Record
Prepared with the support of the Council on Library Resources, the Library of Congress, and the National Endowment for the Humanities.
Santa Monica, CA: American Film Foundation, 1987.
1 videocassette (33 min.): sd., col.; ½" VHS. Also available in a 58 min. version and as 16mm motion picture.
One of the best-known videos for raising awareness of preservation issues. It describes the loss of the world's intellectual heritage through the deterioration of library and archival materials, focusing particular attention on acidic paper. Assesses the situation, demonstrates preservation and restoration techniques, and suggests ways to prevent deterioration in the future. Especially useful for public and academic programs as well as staff education. For nonstaff audiences, the 33-minute version is more effective. Bound transcript available.
Availability: American Film Foundation, 2021 North Western Avenue, P.O. Box 2000, Santa Monica, CA 90406. $40 for 33 min. version; $60 for 58 min. version. 16mm film longer version, $750 sale; $95 rental. 16mm film shorter version, $550 sale; $65 rental. AMIGOS Preservation Service (1-800-843-8482) has the 33 min. version available free on interlibrary loan.

Turning to Dust
Toronto: Canadian Broadcasting Corporation, 1990.
1 videocassette (45 min.): sd., col.; all video formats
Produced for a Canadian television science series, it shows how scientists and librarians in the United States and Canada are seeking solutions to preservation problems in the deterioration of library and archival materials. Useful as an alternative to *Slow Fires*.
Availability: U.S.: Filmmakers Library, 124 East 40th Street, New York, NY 10016; 1-212-808-4980, $395 sale; $65 rental. Canada: CBC Enterprises, $99 sale.

Use and Care of Books
[s.l.]: Centron Films, 1979.
Cornet Films and Video (School Citizenship Series)
1 videocassette (13 min.): sd., col.; ½" VHS
Well-done video introducing some basic techniques of properly handling library books and textbooks for elementary school children. Culturally diverse classroom and library users. Effective use of humor, with books themselves speaking in a combination of animation and live action. Best used for the lower elementary grades. Also in Spanish: *Los Libros: Uso y Cuidado.*
Availability: Coronet Films and Video, Simon & Schuster, 4350 Equity Drive, Columbus, OH 43228 (1-800-777-8100), $29.95 sale.

Use or Abuse: The Role of Staff and Patrons in Maintaining General Library Collections
Carbondale, IL: Produced by the Illinois Cooperative Conservation Program at the SUI Broadcasting Service, [1986].

1 videocassette (24 min.); sd., col.; ½" VHS

Describes the role of staff and patrons in maintaining library collections. Illustrates typical mishandling, the damage it causes, and describes correct practices for care and handling. Includes repair of library books. Filmed at the Carbondale Public Library.

Availability: Not available for sale. Request interlibrary loan from: Illinois State Library, 300 South Second Street, Springfield, IL 62701 (1-217-785-5531).

Appendix 4

Staff and User Preservation Education: An Annotated Bibliography

Amodeo, Anthony J. "A Debt Unpaid: The Bibliographic Instruction Librarian and Library Conservation." *College & Research Libraries News* 49, no. 9 (October 1988): 601–603.

Amodeo's article is an appeal for extra effort—on the part of reference librarians in academic libraries—toward preservation education. In the space of a page and a half, he dramatizes patterns of book abuse by users, the irreplaceable value of many books to the library, and the general lack of training for students. He acknowledges both the reality of time constraints and the natural inventiveness of bibliographic instruction people, then cheers on those librarians who have the most contact with students to make the extra effort in preservation education.

Anglim, Christopher. "The Special Collections Program at the South Texas College of Law Library." *Conservation Administration News* no. 49 (April 1992): 4–5, 25.

Commemorating the dedication of the newly renovated library at South Texas College of Law, Anglim's article describes the Special Collections program and the anticipated preservation benefits of the renovation—which was also accompanied by efforts to create a preservation plan for the collections. He stresses the need to maintain the awareness of users and staff of appropriate ways of handling books, and notes that a librarywide publicity effort is planned to alert users to the possible damage to materials caused by abuse or neglect.

Initial compilation was done with the assistance of Sandra Kortesoja, Renee McKinney, and Kathy Steiner, students in the "Preservation of Information Resources" class taught by Elizabeth Yakel at the University of Michigan School of Information during the 1995 summer session.

Bansa, Helmut. "The Awareness of Conservation: Reasons for Reorientation in Library Training." *Restaurator* 7, no. 1 (1986): 36–47.

In this English text version of a paper given August 20, 1985, at an open meeting of the International Federation of Library Associations and Institutions (IFLA) Section on Library Schools and Other Training Aspects, the author argues that education for a new consciousness of librarianship is needed. Based on his experience in Germany, he strongly recommends that the awareness of conservation should infiltrate and penetrate all other subjects taught, being raised intensively and often, in order to create a new behavior that will influence everyday professional life.

Bloomfield, B. C. "The Librarian as Custodian; Or, A Policeman's Lot . . . ?" *Journal of Documentation* 40, no. 2 (June 1984): 144–151.

This is one of the earliest articles to stress the importance of training on how to handle library materials correctly. Briefly describing the role of the librarian in general and the focus of library schools in the United Kingdom, the author also emphasizes that both library staff and readers need to be trained to handle books carefully as a matter of course, noting that such training can easily be started in primary schools when children are first taught the use of books and libraries.

Boomgaarden, Wesley L. *Staff Training and User Awareness in Preservation Management*. Washington, DC: Association of Research Libraries, 1993.

This up-to-date resource guide captures and organizes the experience of selected staff training and user awareness programs, enabling other libraries to begin or improve programs. The first part of the guide provides a general discussion of program rationale, definition, lists of care and handling concepts to teach, and practical recommendations for implementing a phased approach, including continuing education over the long term. The second part provides examples from academic libraries of actual preservation promotional materials, training practice outlines, and policy manuals. A selected readings list is also included.

Brandon, Janice. "Menu-riven Library Fights Back." *American Libraries* 18, no. 4 (April 1987): 306.

Montana State University Libraries' campaign to fight food in the library included live "vermin" in a display case. Secured in a cage, Miss Bianca, a white mouse, rapidly transformed a withdrawn book into a nest (photo included in article). Additional education exhibits displayed careless damage and fragility of materials.

Brennan, Mary Alice. "A Practical Guide to Preservation in School and Public Libraries." *Eric Digest* (Syracuse, NY: Syracuse University, 1991), EDO-IR-91-4.

This two-page digest, based on Maxine Sitts's *A Practical Guide to Preservation in School and Public Libraries*, calls for a grassroots preservation movement, beginning with increasing awareness in school and public libraries. Starting points for a possible educational initiative are described, organized around a framework of three essential elements: awareness, judgment, and advocacy.

Buchanan, Sally A. "Preservation Perspectives: Saving the Other Stuff." *Wilson Library Bulletin* 68, no. 10 (June 1994): 69–70.

This article outlines five basic preservation planning steps to use with genealogical, historical, and legal records, as well as photographs. Once appropriate preservation action has been taken, educating staff and the public about care and handling of these types of material is of critical importance. All users should be introduced to basic techniques. One suggestion is to require new users to view an educational slide show before accessing certain materials.

Buchanan, Sally A., and Mia Esserman. "Preservation Perspectives: Staff and User Education." *Wilson Library Bulletin* 69, no. 2 (October 1994): 63–64.

For Buchanan, the answer to the paradox "Preserving collections makes them available for use, but using library materials destroys them" lies not in restricting use but in educating staff and users about preservation issues. All staff should understand why policies (such as no food and drink) are critical, and all should be encouraged to be observant to preservation needs as part of their daily work. She notes that most users have never been taught how to care for library materials. Effective user education offers opportunities to bring "new people into the preservation fold."

Casteleyn, Mary. "Evaluating Training." In *Handbook of Library Training Practice*, ed. Ray Prytherch. Aldershot, England: Gower Publishing Co. 1986, pp. 90–125.

Casteleyn examines the assessment and evaluation of training courses, focusing on staff training. The author aims to (1) show the trainer different ways of interpreting evaluation feedback provided by training participants, (2) demonstrate that there are many levels of evaluation, and (3) teach the trainer to assess the effectiveness of current evaluation methods.

Clareson, Tom. "ALA Preservation Education and Outreach Discussion Group." *Conservation Administration News* no. 55 (October 1993): 14–15.

Clareson reports that the Preservation of Library Materials Section's Preservation Education and Outreach Discussion Group meeting was a major highlight of the 1993 American Library Association (ALA) annual conference. During the discussion, Cheryl Holland, preservation librarian at Washington University, described using videotapes, library and classroom instruction on care and handling of materials, and career fair demonstrations on preservation to reach students. Sharlane Grant, head of the Preservation Department at Arizona State University, pointed out that preservation education for children and young adults might begin to turn the tide of vandalism and lack of concern for materials in academic libraries.

Clement, Elaine, and Patricia A. Scott. "No Food, No Drink, No Noise." *College & Research Libraries News* 55, no. 2 (February 1994): 81–83.

Successful poster and bookmark design project utilizing help from graphic arts class is the focus of this article. Recommendations for what is needed for a successful campaign to keep food and drink out of the library are given.

Clements, D. W. G. "The Current Work of the British Library and Its Possible Future Contribution." *Journal of Librarianship* 17, no. 2 (April 1985): 91–94.

Each individual institution must ensure that staff and patrons have an awareness of preservation problems and the part they can play in slowing down the rate of deterioration. This article points out that training needs to incorporate all staff and notes the particular necessity of including junior-level staff in educational programs.

Conservation DistList. An interdisciplinary moderated listserv, the DistList is open to conservators, conservation scientists, curators, librarians, archivists, administrators, and others whose work/life touches on the preservation of cultural property. Participants are asked to fill out a brief questionnaire in order to be included in the ConsDir (directory). To receive the questionnaire and sign on to the DistList, send a one-line note: (subscribe consdist YourFirstName YourLastName to consdist-request@lindy.stanford. edu).

CoOL (Conservation OnLine), a project of the Preservation Department of Stanford University Libraries, is a full-text database of conservation information covering conservation of library, archives, and museum materials. Available at Web address (http:// palimpsest.stanford.edu/).

DeCandido, Robert. "Out of the Question: R-E-S-P-E-C-T." *Conservation Administration News* no. 57 (April 1994): 13–14.
DeCandido describes the highly successful features of a series of educational workshops on shelving and handling for groups of pages working at the Research Libraries of the New York Public Library. Sessions were held in the stacks among the books, which encouraged dialogue and exchange of views. This approach enhanced opportunities to share experiences as colleagues, to convince shelvers that they are critical to the preservation process, and to highlight the value of collections.

Dowell, Connie Vinita. "An Award Winner Brings Preservation Out of the Lab." *College & Research Libraries News* 54, no. 9 (October 1993): 524–526.
Dowell, who was a John Cotton Dana judge, describes this award-winning public relations campaign to inform patrons of preservation issues. The use of a graduate graphic design class to design a series of posters, table tents, and bookmarks were highlights in the academic category of the John Cotton Dana award. The Indiana University Libraries Preservation Awareness Week activities are described as well as the graphic materials.

Drewes, Jeanne. "ALA LIRT Midwinter Forum." *Conservation Administration News* no. 50 (July 1992): 13–14.
Drewes reports that the ALA (American Library Association) Library Instruction Round Table held a midwinter discussion forum titled "Library Instruction and Preservation Education: Converging Concepts" and that a variety of ideas for capitalizing on a "teachable moment"—whether inside or outside the classroom—were discussed. In addition to traditional methods such as displays and handouts, or "Preservation Bites" within 50-minute lectures, menu selections describing the care of materials might be added to online catalogs with message systems. The speakers included: Miriam Kahn, Munters Moisture Control Services; Carla Montori, University of Michigan; Julie Page, University of California–San Diego; and Katherine Walter, University of Nebraska.

Eberhart, George M. *The Whole Library Handbook.* Chicago: American Library Association, 1991.
The chapter on operations includes a short but insightful section on preservation including training of special collections staff and patrons. Ways to address the education

of patrons about the brittle books problem is also mentioned. A preservation quiz is included from the University of British Columbia Library.

Evans, G. Edwards, Anthony J. Amodeo, and Thomas L. Carter. *Introduction to Library Public Services*. 5th ed. Englewood, CO: Libraries Unlimited, 1992.
This textbook integrates appropriate preservation information into each chapter, paralleling the way preservation should be integrated into each library function. This was consciously done to avoid the all-too-common perception of preservation as a "separate" activity, of concern only to rare book librarians and archivists. Chapters on circulation, reference services, and library instruction address patron education directly. This book, which addresses all types of libraries, is appropriate for both graduate and library and media technical assistants' programs and has been used by libraries for staff training in the various public services.

Feather, John. "Staff Training for Preservation." *Library Management* 11, no. 4 (1990): 10–14.
The need for focused preservation education for the various levels of staff is emphasized and well articulated. Feather sees three levels within the library structure that warrant special attention for training: general staff training, professional staff, and technical staff. Includes extensive reference to British and European publications on preservation and conservation training.

Ford, Helen. *The Education of Staff and Users for the Proper Handling of Archival Materials*. RAMP Study PGI-91/WS/17. Paris: UNESCO, 1991. RAMP documents can be ordered by U.S. residents from the West Virginia Library Commission. Send request to Karen Goff: fax: 1-304-558-2044.
This work provides valuable guidance on the use of physical aids for items during reference use, mechanical handling devices, and the production of reference copies or surrogates. The volume also provides instructions for the care and safe handling of records by staff and researchers.

Forde, Helen. "Conservation Training at the Public Record Office." *Journal of Librarianship* 17, no. 2 (April 1985): 95–100.
The policy of the United Kingdom's Public Record Office is "to extend preservation practices throughout staff training courses and to do as much as possible to make readers aware of ways they can also contribute." There are, for example, notices on every desk in research rooms with "do's" and "don'ts," and visits to the Conservation Department are part of the standard tour of the office. Staff at all levels are initially trained, continuing education is ongoing, and internal training techniques and content are reviewed regularly.

Foster, Jocelyn. "Are You a Book Batterer?" *College & Research Library News* 44, no. 4 (April 1983): 117.
This short quiz, although lighthearted, points out the serious and frequent ways books are often mistreated. It is an effective handout for training sessions and particularly useful for sparking discussion about the care and handling of books.

Fox, Lisa L. "A Two-Year Perspective on Library Preservation: An Annotated Bibliography.'' *Library Resources & Technical Services* 30, no. 3 (July–September 1986): 290–318.

Compiled for the years 1984 and 1985, this annotated bibliography provides a thorough perspective on library preservation at the time and is still a useful guide. Section V is titled: ''Education and Training: Reports and Resources.''

Garlow, Doris, and Sally Snyder. ''Kids Don't Go for Dirty Books.'' *Nebraska Library Association Quarterly* 20, no. 1 (Spring 1989): 27.

One way for librarians to demonstrate to children that books are valued and important is to display them in appealing ways and to keep them in good repair. Children respond to presentation, and if a book is worth adding or retaining in a collection, that value should be reflected both in the way the book is presented and in its physical condition. This article makes these points clear from the perspectives of a concerned parent and her child. (For an expanded version of this article, see pages 153–155 of this book.)

Gyeszly, Suzanne D., Deborah Brown, and Mary Kaye Donahue. ''Preservation at Texas A&M University.'' *Conservation Administration News* no. 15 (October 1983): 5–6, 8.

The authors relate that the rate of growth of the library's collection, coupled with Texas A&M University's commitment to building research-level depth for its faculty and graduate students, triggered a joint commitment within the library to link preservation and resource development activities. They also note that one of the five other programs implemented to support collection stability is a program on faculty, staff, and student awareness and education and that ultimately the success of the overall preservation program is in the education of library and academic faculty, staff, and students.

Harvey, Ross. *Preservation in Libraries: Principles, Strategies and Practices for Librarians*. New York: Bowker, 1993.

Harvey devotes a complete, comprehensive chapter toward educating users and staff in this preservation manual. ''An Attitude of Respect'' is based on the premise that careful handling does not come naturally to either users of libraries or those employed in them and must be taught. The first section addresses various means of user education in preservation, and the second examines the place and significance of preservation education and training for librarians. The chapter includes numerous references to useful educational resources.

Hood, Marilyn. ''Getting Started in Audience Research.'' *Museum News* 64, no. 3 (February 1986): 25–31.

Marilyn Hood presents the steps for preparing to do audience research, including self-evaluation, planning, identifying resources, and knowing when audience research is *not* necessary. Hood also presents and evaluates some of the most common techniques of audience research, such as questionnaires and interviews.

Howard, J. ''Preservation Awareness in Public Libraries.'' *Australasian Public Libraries and Information Services* 5 (June 1992): 78–83.

A convincing argument for preservation concerns in public libraries and an argument against the idea that public library service is at odds with the need to conserve library materials.

Intner, Sheila S. "Preservation Training for Library Users."*Technicalities* 14, no. 9 (September 1994): 7–10.

Offers approaches for reaching library users with positive messages about the cumulative effects of usage and handling. Included are examples to illustrate methods of transporting to reduce potential hazards; handling materials during use to minimize wear and tear; and storing materials while in a person's care to reduce physical risks to the materials. All types and formats of library collections are addressed.

Kaufman, Diane. "Building Preservation Awareness." *College & Research Libraries News* 54, no. 10 (November 1995): 707–708.

This article details the strategies for a public awareness campaign about preservation issues at Virginia Tech. The focus of the campaign was on the cost of mutilation of library materials. (For additional information on this campaign, see pages 123–127 of this book.)

Kivia, Ivarature. "Preserving Library Materials in the South Pacific." *Information Development* 10, no. 4 (December 1994): 256–262.

Environmental factors, insect and animal pests, and planning factors make preservation in the South Pacific particularly problematic. In addition to these, Kivia places equal weight on the ways humans (often including librarians) cause damage to books through careless handling and storage of materials, shelving, photocopying, and defacement.

"Librarian Superhero Debuts in Preservation Comics." *Library Journal* 113, no. 6 (October 1, 1988): 21.

A librarian at Arizona State University Libraries created an outreach product geared toward educating users about preservation issues. The comic book, titled *The Librarian*, features a female superhero who "fights the never-ending battle against acidic paper, book vandalism, and the destruction of books."

LOEX Clearinghouse for Library Instruction, National Library Orientation Exchange. Publishes *LOEX News* and provides library instruction information and materials. Cost for institutional membership is $60.00 per calendar year. All sample instruction materials, including videos and computer-assisted instruction (CAI), are available for loan. LOEX Clearinghouse, 217-D University Library, Eastern Michigan University, Ypsilanti, MI 48197; 1-313-487-0168; E-mail (lib_shirato@emunix.emich.edu).

Loomis, Ross J. "Please, Not Another Visitor Survey." *Museum News* 52, no. 2 (October 1973): 20–26.

Loomis discusses the reasons why staff do not appreciate or value user surveys and points out that some of these reasons—lack of planning, hostile responses from users, increased workload—have validity. Loomis counters that a well-planned and -executed survey should eliminate these problems as well as provide essential data for the institution.

Lubans, John L. "Evaluating Library-User Education Programs." In *Educating the Library User*. New York: R. R. Bowker, 1974, pp. 233–253.

Published in 1974, Lubans's article analyzes the problems frequently encountered in library user education evaluation and presents examples of evaluation methods found to be successful in the past, including sample evaluation forms.

Mackeracher, Dorothy. "The Learner and the Library: There's More to Learning Than Meets the Eye." *Library Trends* 31, no. 4 (Spring 1983): 599–619.

In "The Learner and the Library," Mackeracher presents the concept of learning as an active, natural process that includes sense making, information seeking, planning, deciding, acting, and getting feedback. According to Mackeracher, this process can be negatively affected by a variety of internal and external conditions. In order to effectively educate users, then, libraries must both take the users' learning styles into account and develop enabling, collaborative facilitation strategies to help users learn.

Marcum, Deanna B. *Final Report of the Preservation Education Institute*. Washington, DC: Commission on Preservation and Access, September 1990.

The Preservation Education Task Force was charged with exploring the current state of preservation education and with projecting needs for future decades. The Preservation Education Institute's *Final Report* begins with a nine-element definition of *preservation*, noting that the concept of preservation has changed and that new strategies for education must emphasize stewardship of the accumulated human record. Its recommendations include not only developing new academic offerings for schools of library and information science but also identifying all potential audiences for preservation education.

Marcum, Deanna B. "Preservation Education." In *Advances in Preservation and Access*, vol. 1, ed. Barbra Buckner Higginbotham and Mary E. Jackson. Westport, CT: Meckler Publishing, 1992, pp. 115–123.

Marcum's article in this volume briefly summarizes the emergence, in the mid-1980s, of preservation as a highly visible area within librarianship. After highlighting the importance of the formation of the Commission on Preservation and Access (CPA) and the Office of Preservation within the National Endowment for the Humanities, the article describes the establishment of the Task Force on Preservation Education within CPA and its findings: There is an unprecedented need for an understanding of preservation as both an attitude and a set of activities; preservation, an integral part of making recorded knowledge accessible for as far into the future as possible, cannot be separated from other fundamental functions of the library.

Olley, Lorraine. "Indiana University Libraries Presents Preservation Awareness Week." *Conservation Administration News* no. 53 (April 1993): 10–11.

To bring the 1992 National Library Week commemoration into focus at Indiana University (IU), the IU Libraries presented a preservation campaign that was directed at library users and emphasized that vandalism and careless handling can be as damaging to library materials as floods and other disasters. This article describes the planning process, design and creation of materials, funding sources, speakers, exhibits, and other events associated with the weeklong presentation. Contact information, for obtaining more details or samples of public awareness materials, appears at the end of the article.

Page, Julie A., and George J. Soete. "Preservation Orientation for Library Staff." *College & Research Libraries News* 55, no. 6 (June 1994): 358–360.

Page and Soete provide an outline, based on the University of California at San Diego approach, for other libraries developing staff education programs. Their article highlights the importance of staff education, then presents considerations for designing a training session, the basic conceptual points to be conveyed to all participants, practical training objectives, and a more detailed outline of a training session. Finally, the article suggests distributing preservation guidelines to all new staff as they complete Library Personnel Office requirements, then reinforcing the importance of preservation through statements of responsibility in all staff job descriptions. (A reprint of this article with an addendum appears on pages 49–55 of this book.)

Paietta, Ann. "Access Services: The Human Factor." In *Advances in Preservation and Access*, vol. 2, ed. Barbra Buckner Higginbotham. Medford, NJ: Learned Information, 1996, pp. 391–399.

Paietta states that the impact readers have on library materials is rarely addressed in the library literature. She suggests approaches for both staff and reader education through good stack maintenance habits and raising user awareness to proper handling of materials. Highlighted is the role that access services staff can take in preservation education and the "win-win" situation that results from integrating and involving both staff and users in the education process. Several other essays in Part 7, "Education and Training for Libraries, Archivists, and Readers," of this volume address library and archival education of staff and administrators.

Palmer, Joseph W. "Audiovisual Programs Related to Preservation: A Mediagraphy." *Collection Building* 13, no. 1 (1993): 7–20.

Most complete listing of preservation-related audiovisual materials organized by subject categories. Includes annotations, citations to articles for further description, and ordering and interlibrary loan information.

Phillips, Jack J. "Evaluation Instrument Design." In *Handbook of Training Evaluation and Measurement Methods*. 2nd ed. Houston: Gulf Publishing Company, 1991, pp. 80–117.

In this chapter, Phillips provides an analysis of important issues that must be addressed in the design of evaluation instruments. According to Phillips, the characteristics of effective evaluation instruments are: (1) validity, (2) reliability, (3) ease of administration, (4) brevity and simplicity, and (4) economy. Phillips discusses how to design common evaluation instruments such as questionnaires, surveys, tests, interviews, and focus groups and evaluates the positive and negative aspects of each.

PRESED-L was created by the Association for Library Collections & Technical Services (ALCTS) of the American Library Association (ALA) to supplement the Preservation Course and Workshop Instructors Discussion Group of the Preservation and Reformatting Section (PARS). Subscribe at: LISTERV@UICVM.UIC.EDU (in message say: subscribe PRESED-L Your Name).

PRESED-X (Preservation Educators' Exchange) is a Web site of syllabi for semester courses on preservation given in library and information schools, announcements of upcoming institutes and conferences, and other resources on preservation education (http://www.well.com/user/bronxbob/presed-x/presed-x.html).

Preservation Education in ARL Libraries. SPEC Kit 113. Washington, DC: Association of Research Libraries, Office of Management Studies, 1985.

This publication describes ways to increase preservation awareness of staff members, patrons, and other constituents and is full of sample materials used in ARL (Association of Research Libraries) libraries, such as copies of policy statements, bookmarks, brochures, outlines for staff orientation programs, and articles and newsletters to help garner financial support for local preservation programs.

Ratcliffe, F. W. "The Current Situation in the United Kingdom." *Journal of Librarianship* 17, no. 2 (April 1985): 85–91.

"Conservation, like charity, begins at home." Ratcliffe calls for reeducation directed to all existing staff, governing bodies, and users. Conservation education, for example, should be included in introductory talks and guided tours of libraries. Preservation efforts that cost money will "profit the library little if staff and readers still mishandle materials." Ratcliffe writes that the educational gap must be bridged, whether in library schools, in-house, or in daily practice, before preservation "will be seen in its true perspective."

Reynolds, Anne L., Nancy C. Schrock, and Joanna Walsh. "Preservation: The Public Library Response." *Library Journal* 114, no. 3 (February 15, 1989): 128–132.

A report on a survey conducted by the Wellesley (MA) Free Library to determine the types of damage in its collection. The survey was used to support programmatic and financial planning, showing that a small-scale survey can have an effect in planning.

Ritzenthaler, Mary Lynn. *Preserving Archives and Manuscripts.* Chicago: Society of American Archivists, 1993.

Ritzenthaler begins Chapter 6, "Handling Archival Materials" (pp. 67–75) by noting that it is at the point of human contact that materials are most endangered and that all persons coming into contact with library and archival materials must be trained, oriented, and periodically reminded regarding safe and appropriate handling practices. The remainder of the chapter provides a number of basic rules to help protect all materials plus a thorough description of proper handling techniques for paper records, bound volumes, photographic materials, and various types of machine-dependent materials.

Ryckman, Pat. "Taming the Chimera: Preservation in a Public Library." *North Carolina Libraries* 52, no. 1 (Spring 1994): 8–9.

Ryckman gives a general overview of preservation issues and solutions for small public libraries including tips on educating the staff and public. She sees this as the most cost-effective means of prolonging the life of both rare and circulating materials. (Reprint of this article is in Chapter 2 of this book.)

Salinger, Ruth D., and Basil S. Deming. "Practical Strategies for Evaluating Training." *Training and Development Journal* 36 (August 1982): 20–26.

Salinger and Deming maintain that training evaluation must address four basic questions: Does the training produce appropriate learning? Does the training transfer to the job? Is knowledge or skill maintained over time? Does the value of improved performance meet or exceed the cost of training? To help trainers answer these questions, Salinger and Deming present six evaluation strategies and discuss the appropriateness of each in a variety of settings.

Schoonmaker, Dina. "Staff Training and User Awareness." In *Managing Preservation: A Guidebook*. Columbus, OH: State Library of Ohio & Ohio Preservation Council, 1995. Chapter 5, pp. 63–74. Chapter 5 of this publication includes the rationale for teaching proper handling methods, approaches for both staff and user education, and how to include staff in supporting a preservation program. "The education of staff and users in proper materials handling techniques can be done on a shoestring but yields great dividends. Institutions should be creative and personalized in their approach to the challenge while ensuring that the message conveyed is clear."

Screven, Chandler. G. "A Bibliography on Visitor Education Research." *Museum News* 57, no. 4 (March/April 1979): 56–59, 86–89.
Screven's 1979 bibliography on user education provides an extensive, nonannotated list of resources in the areas of audience research, behavior studies, and experimental research.

Sedinger, Theresa. "Preservation and Conservation in the School Library." *Book Report* 10, no. 4 (January–February 1992): 34.
School librarians traditionally think of themselves as teachers as well as librarians, promoting reading, learning, and the love of books. Sedinger suggests that another role be added—that of conservator. Librarians working in schools are uniquely qualified to educate students, teachers, alumni, school board members, and citizen groups about the value of preservation programs.

Sitts, Maxine K. *A Practical Guide to Preservation in School and Public Libraries*. ERIC Document 340391. Syracuse, NY: Syracuse University, 1990. (See Brennan entry for ERIC Digest citation.)
Sitts describes some of the ways preservation and conservation programs in school and public libraries can improve nearly every phase of operations while supporting education. Librarians in these settings play a pivotal role, particularly in setting examples for patrons regarding proper care and influencing future generations. Highlighted in the third section are ways librarians can communicate with financial supporters, vendors, and users through educational programs.

Sullivan, Peggy. "Preservation & Judgment." *School Library Journal* 36, no. 7 (July 1990): 16–19.
Sullivan points out that preservation is a concern of a broad cross section of the library field—problems affect all areas of the library, and preservation must be the concern of everyone. The history of children's books, for example, is a part of the story of preservation that is still being written. This is a strong motivational piece for public and school library preservation education programs.

Swartzburg, Susan G. "Audiovisual Aids on the Preservation and Conservation of Library and Archival Materials." *Conservation and Administration News* 49, no. 2 (April 1992): 8–13.
Swartzburg has put together a selective bibliography of audiovisual aids, including slides, films, and videotapes, useful for classroom and workshop instruction. Most of the resources are available through state and regional agencies, from library schools, or from

the Library of Congress Preservation Office. Annotations include full bibliographic information and summaries.

Swartzburg, Susan G. *Preserving Library Materials: A Manual*. Metuchen, NJ: Scarecrow Press, 1980.
The second chapter in Swartzburg's book focuses on preventive preservation as the most important aspect of a preservation librarian's job. Key to the preservation of collections is a staff training program in which all staff members are taught to respect materials in their care and are made aware of practices that could be harmful to their collections. Daily routines, such as housekeeping and shelving, require specialized knowledge. Maintenance staff in a library, for example, may need to be taught skills that include gentleness and dexterity.

Thompson, John M. A., "Visitor Services." In *Manual of Curatorship*. London: Butterworths, 1984, pp. 377–488.
The articles in "Visitor Services" present research on the behavior and psychology of the museum visitor and on the instructional function of museum exhibits. The articles address a range of issues related to exhibition planning, design, and evaluation.

Tiefel, Virginia. "Evaluating a Library User Education Program: A Decade of Experience." *College & Research Libraries News* 50, no. 2 (March 1989): 249–259.
Tiefel presents the user education evaluation methods used at Ohio State University. Those methods include pre- and posttests and stress the importance of planning reliable and valid evaluations. Tiefel also makes recommendations for how to implement an evaluation.

Turner, John R. "Teaching Conservation." *Education for Information* 6, no. 2 (June 1988): 145–151.
Turner analyzes the potential components of conservation education that he believes should be taught in all library schools and to every librarian. Acknowledging that the subject can be complex and technical, he suggests two realistic syllabuses—one for all students and one for specialists. The article provides background for creating possible components of training programs.

Twomey, James E. "Descriptive Analysis of a Conservation Awareness Program." *Journal of Education for Library and Information Science* 29 (Winter 1989): 197–208.
This article describes the results of a study designed to evaluate a series of seminars and workshops on conservation awareness. While pretests indicated that awareness of conservation problems was high, knowledge of history and solutions was low. Library science students who participated showed heightened sensitivity to, and knowledge of, conservation decision making and technique. The article discusses the formulation, implementation, and evaluation of the program in detail. The importance of removing psychological barriers between conservators and librarians is also emphasized.

Varlejs, Jana. "Preservation Education: A Call for Cooperation." *Art Documentation* 9, no. 4 (Winter 1990): 193–194.
Since preservation is an issue of concern not only to librarians but also to archivists, records managers, historical society administrators, and others charged with the protec-

tion of collections, the author calls for cooperation. She notes that there are many players in the preservation education field and that there is considerable duplication as well as some gaping holes but adds that everyone seems to agree on the key point that preservation education must be largely *continuing* education.

Watson, Duane A. "The Divine Library Function: Preservation." *School Library Journal* 33, no. 3 (November 1986): 41–45.
Education, the essence of the school librarian's role, is also the basis of preservation—librarians who serve children "start the cycle of knowledge and concern for books." Even those managing the smallest libraries reduce problems by modeling attention to shelving, bookends, and handling. Preservation education programs create new partnerships, particularly when geared toward teachers, administrators, custodial staff, boards of education, and parents, as well as toward children.

Williams, Karen. "Preservation and Conservation in the Elementary Schools." *Conservation Administration News* no. 52 (January 1993): 4–5, 7, 13.
Goals, objectives, and activities structure a sample preservation policy statement written for Westwood Elementary School in Stillwater, Oklahoma. Williams's objectives include specific educational activities designed to promote awareness of preservation needs among students, faculty, administrators, and media center staff.

Williamson, Michael G. "The Evaluation of Training." In *Handbook of Library Training Practice, Vol. 2*, ed. Ray Prytherch. Aldershot, England: Gower Publishing Company, 1990, pp. 90–125.
Williamson provides a basic introduction to the concept of training evaluation including the terminology of evaluation, the reasons why evaluation is necessary, and strategies for evaluation.

Wooley, James. "Special Collections Lending: A Reader's View." *Rare Books and Manuscripts Librarianship* 3, no. 2 (Fall 1988): 121–125.
For special collections, preservation concerns often overshadow librarians' concerns for advancing learning by making materials available, especially on interlibrary loan. Speaking from experience as a borrower of rare books on interlibrary loan, and as an advocate of preservation education, this author observes that the primary barrier to special lending is a distrust of the librarian on the other end. He then suggests that a combination of more knowledge concerning the borrowing library and agreed-upon structure and procedures could enable special lending to function satisfactorily.

Index

About the Editors and Contributors

JEANNE M. DREWES is Head of the Preservation Department at Johns Hopkins University, Milton S. Eisenhower Library. Previously she was Assistant Preservation Libarian at Michigan State University. She received her M.A.L.S. from the University of Missouri–Columbia and was a Mellon Intern for Preservation Administration at the University of Michigan. She is a member of the American Library Association and is active in the Preservation and Reformatting Section. She has participated in preservation education programs for the American Library Association as well as teaching workshops for a number of organizations, and has published on the topic of preservation education and in other areas of preservation.

JULIE A. PAGE is Preservation Librarian at the University of California at San Diego (UCSD) and has actively promoted preservation education since establishing an ongoing preservation program there, with staff education as a major component. She has co-chaired preservation education programs for the American Library Association and has published in preservation education and disaster preparedness and recovery. She is a member of the Education Committee of ALA/ALCTS (American Library Association/Association for Library Collections and Technical Services) Preservation and Reformatting Section. Graduating with an M.L.S. from UCLA, she was Art Librarian at the Rochester (NY) Public Library. She returned to California in 1978 as a Reference Librarian in the UCSD Undergraduate Library, then spent 10 years as a Serials Cataloger before becoming Preservation Librarian.

ANTHONY J. AMODEO received his M.A.L.S. at Rosary College while working as Reference Assistant and Conservation Liaison in Special Collections at the Newberry Library. After working as Illinois Cooperative Conservation Librarian, he took a position at Loyola Marymount University, Los Angeles, where he is currently Associate Reference Librarian and Coordinator of Instruction. He has served on the boards of the Los Angeles Preservation Network and the California Clearinghouse on Library Instruction. He is a member of the American Library Association and the Catholic Library Association.

ANNITA ANDRICK received her M.A.L.S. from the University of Denver in 1985 while Assistant to the Curator, Archives and Special Collections at the University. She is Librarian and Archivist at Erie County Historical Society, Erie History Center; Chief Executive Officer/President of the AAM Media & Technology Standing Professional Committee; and a member of the Steering Committee of the Pennsylvania Statewide Preservation Plan.

SUSAN E. ANNETT is Principal Librarian for Public Services at the Santa Monica Public Library. She received her M.L.S. from the University of Iowa and has been an art and audiovisual librarian in public and museum libraries. She is a member of the American Library Association and the Art Libraries Society of North America.

SHARON BENNETT received her M.L.S. from the University of South Carolina. She has worked for the last four years as the Preservation Education Coordinator for the South Carolina State Library Preservation Education Program and has been Archivist for the Charleston Museum for the past 15 years.

ELAYNE BOND began her career at Northwestern University Library in 1980 in the Collection Management division. She has been a member of the Preservation Department for 12 years and is currently Head of Materials Processing.

CHARLOTTE B. BROWN received her M.L.S. from the University of Rhode Island, specializing in archival theory and practice. She has held positions at Harvard University, the University of Maryland, and Franklin & Marshall College and is currently the Assistant Head for Special Collections at the University of California at Los Angeles. Brown received her preservation training from Yale University and has been involved with the preservation practices for special collections materials for over 20 years.

BRENDA CLARK has worked for five years as assistant professor of graphic design at the Michigan State University Department of Art. Previously she taught illustration at Kent State University, where she earned her Master of Fine Arts degree. During the mid-1980s she was a graphic designer at Kansas State University.

CAROLYN K. COLLINGS received an M.A.L.S. and a Master in Education from the University of Missouri–Columbia (UMC). While employed at Elmer Ellis Library on the UMC campus, she served as chair of an ARL/OMS (Association of Research Libraries/Office of Management Services) task force on preservation. She was a Reference Specialist for the State Historical Society of Missouri prior to her current position as Archivist for the Local Records Program, Office of the Secretary of State of Missouri.

CYNTHIA FRAME is Head of Preservation and Archives at the Union Theological Seminary in New York City. After completing her M.L.S. at Columbia University, she served as Mellon Intern for Preservation Administration at the Research Libraries of the New York Public Library.

DORIS GARLOW was formerly at the Nebraska Library Commission for 18 years. She received her B.A. from Nebraska Wesleyan University and M.L.S. from Emporia State University in Kansas. She worked at the Lincoln City Libraries, the public library in Lincoln, Nebraska, and has volunteered in school libraries.

HARLAN GREENE is Director of the North Carolina Preservation Consortium, a statewide educational nonprofit affiliated with the School of Library and Information Sciences at North Carolina Central University in Durham. In that capacity, he has developed programs and publications for the general public; public, academic, and special libraries; and various archives and repositories. He also teaches a library and archival preservation course at the School of Information and Library Science at the University of North Carolina–Chapel Hill.

SHARLANE GUBKIN worked part-time in Cataloging while pursuing a formal apprenticeship in book and paper conservation. She is presently Head of the Preservation Department of University Library, Case Western Reserve University, in Cleveland, Ohio.

FREIDA HAMMETT received both her undergraduate and graduate degrees from the University of North Carolina–Chapel Hill. She has taught all levels from preschool through college. She is a trained Montessori teacher and attributes her ability to develop interesting and age-appropriate lessons to that training. She was Head Librarian at Centerville Elementary in Anderson, South Carolina, for four years before going back into the classroom to teach three- to six-year-olds at the Waseca Learning Environment in Athens, Georgia.

NORMANDY SIMONS HELMER is Head of the Preservation & Binding Department at the University of Oregon Library. She is a member of the American Institute for Conservation of Historic and Artistic Works, the Guild of Book Workers, the Preservation and Reformatting Section, the Association for Library Collections and Technical Services, and the Library and Information Technology Association, and is a founding member of the Oregon Library Association's Preservation Committee. A Bryn Mawr College graduate, she is pursuing an M.L.S. at Syracuse University.

EDWARD H. HUTCHINS is the proprietor of Editions, a workshop for designing and producing artist book multiples. His work is found in most contemporary book arts collections. He frequently gives workshops and lectures on the book arts in libraries and educational institutions.

KAREN JONES is Collections Conservator at the Jefferson County Public Library in Lakewood, Colorado, and currently serves as President of the Colorado Preservation Alliance. She has a B.F.A. from the University of Connecticut. In 1994, she received the first Gaylord Brothers Collections Conservation Award.

DIANE KAUFMAN has worked in both public and academic libraries for the past 11 years. She has worked in the Preservation Department for the past six years and, in 1995, became the Head of Preservation at Virginia Polytechnic Institute and State University. She taught school for 18 years and holds an M.S. from Kansas State University.

DANIELLE KEABLE is the Head Librarian at the Bibliothèque Côte-des-Neiges in Montréal, Québec.

KENNETH LAVENDER is Curator of the Rare Book and Texana Collections at the University of North Texas (UNT). In addition, he teaches courses in preservation and rare book librarianship for the UNT School of Library and Information Science. He is coauthor of *Book Repair: A Manual for Librarians* (Neal-Schuman, 1992).

SUSAN MIDDLETON received her M.L.S. from Indiana University in 1977. She worked in academic, business, and public libraries before joining the faculty at La Jolla Country Day School in 1985. As lower school librarian, she works primarily with students in nursery through fourth grade and also serves as Head Librarian. She is active in local reading association councils and has presented at local and state conferences.

JANICE MOHLHENRICH is Preservation Librarian at Marquette University in Milwaukee, Wisconsin. Since 1989 she has been active in WISPPR, the Wisconsin Preservation Program, and has presented many workshops on preservation topics. She graduated from library school at Simmons College, Boston, Massachusetts, and is currently pursuing a Ph.D. in Educational Administration at Marquette University.

MICHAEL G. MOORE was Associate Director for Technology Services at the University of Michigan Health Systems. He has been working with computers since 1982 and has had responsibilty for Web development in his positions. Currently he is at the Applied Physics Laboratory, Johns Hopkins University.

JANE MUELLER received her M.L.S. from California State University, Fullerton, and began a career as staff aide for the Orange County Historical Commission. In 1979, she served as Director for a National Endowment for the Humanities–funded project for the Santiago Library System in Orange County, identifying local history collections in southern California for database retrieval. In 1984, she became Librarian for the Fullerton Public Library, serving in local history and reference, and conducted hands-on paper preservation workshops for library patrons.

LORRAINE OLLEY received her M.A.L.S. from the University of Chicago in 1982 and the Advanced Certificate in Preservation Administration from Columbia University in 1992. She is currently Head of the Preservation Department at Indiana University Libraries–Bloomington. In 1992, she chaired the Preservation of Library Materials Section of the American Library Association/Library Collections and Technical Services.

PATRICIA E. PALMER has been involved in developing preservation programs since 1981 and has been the Head of Preservation Services at Virginia Commonwealth University since 1990. She has been active in preservation education efforts by serving on the Association for Library Collections and Technical Services Education Committee and the Preservation and Reformatting Section Education Committee and participating in numerous outreach activities.

ANNE L. REYNOLDS has been active in libraries since 1961 and has been Director of the Wellesley Free Library in Wellesley, Massachusetts, from 1981 to 1996. It provides reference and interlibrary loan services to 26 neighboring libraries in its capacity as a contracting library for the Eastern Regional Library System. Preservation has been an issue of major concern to her. A comprehensive analysis of the Wellesley collections designed to address public library preservation problems was completed and an action plan developed to address the preservation needs of this busy public library.

ANN RIDOUT began working in the Book Repair Unit of the University of Michigan Library in 1970. Currently a Senior Bookbinder for the University of Michigan Library's Conservation and Book Repair Unit, she regularly conducts workshops in basic book repair for staff at the university and other libraries around the state.

LYNN E. ROHRS received her master's degree in English curriculum and reading from the University of Nebraska. After teaching language arts for several years, she became certified as a Library Media Specialist. She currently holds that position at Westwood Elementary School in Stillwater, Oklahoma, and is a member of the Oklahoma Library Association.

ANDREA ROLICH is Preservation Librarian at the University of Wisconsin–Madison and serves on the Steering Committee of the Wisconsin Preservation Program (WISPPR). Her duties include planning and presenting workshops and education sessions for library staff and users at the university and at libraries of many types and sizes throughout the state.

PAT RYCKMAN received her M.L.S. from the University of North Carolina–Chapel Hill. Her interest in preservation developed as Manager of the Carolina Room at the Public Library of Charlotte & Mecklenburg County and continues in her position as New Technologies Manager, where she worked to produce a local history multimedia CD-ROM.

BECKY RYDER has served as Head of the University of Kentucky Libraries Preservation Department since 1992. She teaches a course in preservation management in the School of Library and Information Science, and she is active with preservation outreach activities throughout the state. Her prior experience includes binding and book repair positions in the libraries at Virginia Tech and the University of Virginia.

NANCY CARLSON SCHROCK has been self-employed as a Book Conservator and Consultant on library preservation based in Winchester, Massachusetts, since 1978. Her work with public libraries has included a comparative survey of book condition in four Massachusetts libraries and preservation training/program development for public libraries in Wellesley, Concord, and Winchester. She currently serves as Conservation Consultant to the Harvard University Library and manages the Gaylord Preservation Help Line, a telephone service providing preservation information to librarians, archivists, museums, and the general public.

MERRILY SMITH has worked in the Preservation Directorate, Library of Congress, since 1978. She holds a B.A. degree in German and an M.S. degree in Human Resource Development and is a trained book and paper conservator. A specialist in adult learning, Smith is experienced in the design and evaluation of preservation education events and has lectured on preservation at many institutions of higher education.

SALLY H. SNYDER is the Library Services and Construction Act (LSCA) Coordinator at the Nebraska Library Commission, a state agency with the mission of statewide promotion, development, and coordination of library services. With a Master's in Public Administration from the University of Nebraska at Omaha, she has worked at the Commission for 11 years. She is a copresenter for the statewide children's book review program. Formerly, she taught children with physical handicaps at the J. P. Lord School in Omaha and worked 8 years at the Estes Park Public Library in Colorado, the last three years as Children's Librarian.

GEORGE J. SOETE is an Organizational Development Consultant with the Office of Management Services, Association of Research Libraries. He also has his own consulting practice. As a consultant and trainer, he assists libraries in areas such as strategic planning, team building, and resource sharing. He was formerly Associate University Librarian for Collections at the University of California at San Diego.

PEGGY SULLIVAN, Dean of the Graduate School of Library and Information Science at Rosary College in Illinois, has worked in public libraries, a school library system, academic libraries, and library education. She has also held several staff assignments at the American Library Association. Her interests in preservation are practical, with the emphasis on access through preservation.

CHARLOTTE A. TANCIN is Librarian at the Hunt Institute for Botanical Documentation at Carnegie Mellon University in Pittsburgh. She earned her M.L.S. at the University of Pittsburgh in 1983 and is a member of the Council on Botanical and Horticultural Libraries, the American Library Association, and several other professional organizations.

SARA WILLIAMS TRAPOLIN received her M.L.S. from Louisiana State University in 1982. She spent the next six years at the University of Georgia, where she taught freshmen in the University 101 program and began an active career in bibliographic instruction and library orientation. She currently coordinates the introductory library skills program for students of freshman writing at Tulane University.

DUFFY TWEEDY received his M.L.S. and an M.A. in History from Indiana University in 1988. His first professional position was at Ball State University, and he has been Instruction/Outreach Coordinator at both the Undergraduate and Social Sciences & Humanities Libraries at the University of California at San Diego. He has been active, holding various offices, in the California Clearinghouse for Library Instruction.

ESTEBAN VALDEZ received his M.L.S. in 1992 from the University of Arizona Graduate Library School. He began his career as a University of California Minority Resident Librarian and is currently the Coordinator of Reference Services at the University of California at San Diego Undergraduate Library.

RICHARD VAUGHAN is the Acquisitions and Serials Control Librarian at the Indiana University (IU) School of Law Library–Bloomington. As a member of the IU Library faculty, he served as a member of the Libraries Preservation Committee in 1994–1995 and 1995–1996.

EVELYN BURKE WEIBLE received her M.L.S. from the University of Washington–Seattle. She began her career as Children's Librarian with the New York Public Library. She explored several other library career avenues but with a second Master's in Curriculum and Instruction from the University of Wisconsin has been an elementary school librarian since 1971 in Middleton, Wisconsin.

KENNETH WHITE is the Director of the Archives and Records Center of the Catholic Diocese of Pittsburgh. Prior to this, he worked as an Archivist/Records Manager for the Texas State Library, Utah State Archives, and New York State Archives.